Moving Music

Dialogues with Music
in Twentieth-Century Ballet

Stephanie Jordan

DANCE BOOKS
Cecil Court London

Music Credits

Elgar, *Enigma Variations*: © Copyright by Novello & Company Ltd. Reproduced by permission.
Schoenberg, *Verklärte Nacht*: © Copyright by Universal Edition AG, Vienna. Reproduced by permission.
Stravinsky, *Agon*: © Copyright 1957 by Hawkes & Son (London) Ltd. Reproduced by permission of Boosey & Hawkes Music Publishers Ltd.
Stravinsky, *Capriccio* for Piano and Orchestra: © Copyright 1930 by Hawkes & Son (London) Ltd. Revised edition © Copyright 1952 by Hawkes & Son (London) Ltd. US Copyright renewed Reproduced by permission of Boosey & Hawkes Music Publishers Ltd.
Stravinsky, *Le Sacre du printemps*: © Copyright 1912, 1921 by Hawkes & Son (London) Ltd. Reproduced by permission of Boosey & Hawkes Music Publishers Ltd.
Stravinsky, *Scènes de ballet*: © Copyright by B. Schott's Soehne, Mainz. Reproduced by permission. Reproduced by permission of Chester Music Ltd for British Commonwealth, Republic of Ireland and South Africa.
Webern, Symphony Op. 21: © Copyright 1929 by Universal Edition. Copyright renewed by Anton Weberns Erben. Reproduced by permission. Balanchine's piano transcription by permission of The George Balanchine Trust.

Choreography/Labanotation Credits

Balanchine, *Serenade*: © The George Balanchine Trust. Notated by Virginia Doris, 1984.
Balanchine, *Agon*: © The George Balanchine Trust. Notated by Virginia Doris, 1987.
Balanchine, *Rubies*: © The George Balanchine Trust. Notated by Judy Coopersmith, 1985.
Balanchine, *Symphonie Concertante*: © The George Balanchine Trust. Notated by Ann Hutchinson Guest, assisted by Els Grelinger, 1948.
Balanchine, *Tchaikovsky Pas de Deux*: © The George Balanchine Trust. Notated by Natalie Gordon, 1997.
Balanchine, *Valse fantaisie*: © The George Balanchine Trust. Notated by Suzanne Briod, 1984–85.
Tudor, *Jardin aux lilas*: © The Antony Tudor Ballet Trust. Notated by Airi Hynninen, 1981, corrected and revised by Muriel Topaz, 1992.
Tudor, *Dark Elegies*: © The Antony Tudor Ballet Trust. Notated by Airi Hynninen, 1980.
Tudor, *The Leaves are Fading*: © The Antony Tudor Ballet Trust. Notated by Airi Hynninen, 1975.
All other Labanotation by Natalie Gordon, 1997.
The Labanotation scores of *Serenade*, *Agon*, *Rubies*, *Symphonie Concertante*, *Valse fantaisie*, *Jardin aux lilas*, *Dark Elegies* and *The Leaves are Fading*, and the table of *Undertow* metronome markings (Table 5.1), are used with permission of the Dance Notation Bureau.
Ashton choreography examples are used with permission of Anthony Russell Roberts.

Other Credits

Illustrations 1, 3: © The George Balanchine Trust. Photographs by Paul Kolnik.
Illustration 2, Examples 5.1 and 5.15: Dance Collection, The New York Public Library for the Performing Arts. Astor, Lenox and Tilden Foundations.
Illustrations 4, 5, 7: Photographs by Leslie E. Spatt.
Illustration 6: Photograph by Malcolm Dunbar.

Moving Music

To Howard

Contents

Illustrations

Acknowledgements

So many in the dance profession – dancers, conductors, pianists as well as those who notate and stage ballets – have assisted me in the research for this book. To them, first, my thanks for being so generous with their time and, importantly, although they did not necessarily see things my way, for their pragmatism and good sense, which usefully disrupted my academic prejudices.

Special thanks too to my readers, all specialists who were quickly able to spot errors as well as to add invaluable points for consideration: Geraldine Morris, Ashley Page, Giannandrea Poesio, Jane Pritchard, Nancy Reynolds, Marian Smith, Muriel Topaz and David Vaughan.

If my readers regularly made me think again, so too did my doctoral students at Roehampton and the Master's degree students on whom I tried out my new course on Ballet and its Music. Students argue and make their tutors clear about concepts that have not yet reached the point of clarity. I am so glad that I taught these students before finishing the book!

I am grateful to a number of people and organisations for their help with materials that I needed for research and publication, especially to Monica Moseley at the New York Public Library Dance Collection, Ilene Fox at the Dance Notation Bureau, Jean Johnson Jones at the Labanotation Institute, Barbara Horgan at the George Balanchine Trust, Sally Brayley Bliss at the Antony Tudor Ballet Trust, Anthony Russell Roberts at the Royal Ballet, also Judith Chazin-Bennahum, Julie Kavanagh, Lars Payne and Victoria Simon.

Without the sponsorship of the following organisations, this project would not have come to fruition: the Radcliffe Trust (and my special thanks here to Ivor Guest, now trustee, for his advice), the British Academy and Roehampton Institute London. It was their support that enabled me to take study leave, to research in New York and to include notation examples in this book.

In respect of the latter, I owe a great debt to Natalie Gordon for her notation of some of the dance examples and transcription of others already in score to Labanwriter; I learnt much from working with her on a task much more considerable than either of us originally envisaged. Jonathan Thrift and Terry Butcher are thanked for the preparation of the example from Balanchine's *Agon*, also

Paul Terry of Musonix and Jacqui Finnis for their meticulous preparation of my music examples.

I am of course greatly indebted to Sanjoy Roy, my editor at Dance Books. I could not have wished for a finer one, or a more patient supporter in the final stages of a book. And I thank David Leonard, my publisher, for his wisdom, knowledge and encouragement, and above all for his continuing dedication to a scholarship which keeps dance at its centre.

Finally, as always, my thanks to my husband Howard Friend, on whose musicianly (and friendly) advice and inspiration, as well as firmness with the editorial pencil, I constantly rely.

Stephanie Jordan

Foreword

The Hollywood composer David Raksin once remarked on the crucial contribution of music to film, 'All you have to do to get the point of film music across to the skeptical is to make them sit through the picture *without the music.*'[1] There is no reason to suggest that dance watchers are quite so sceptical as Raksin's filmgoers about the importance of music to dance. Indeed, we talk about music being indispensable to dance. The few silent pieces help to prove the point. The partnership is somehow sanctified, supposedly extending back to the beginnings of human existence. We rate musicality as one of the supreme attributes of the dancer and choreographer. Some music urges us, the audience, too, to move when we hear it.

Yet Raksin's observation is relevant to a discussion of music and dance. We only have to consider the misuse and misunderstandings of music within the dance community, the inadequate language of communication between many musicians and dancers, the inconsiderable and often superficial discussion of what goes on between music and dance, to realise that the real importance of the musical contribution to dance is only sketchily understood. So far, training methods for dancers and choreographers and curricula for degree students have done little to change this. We might ask, for example: if nearly all dance happens to music, what does the music do for the dance? And what does dance do for the music? Do we hear as much as we see? What is this property called musicality? Can music be subversive: are there issues of power to consider?

In this book, I set out to develop the debate, in the belief that, when we go to the theatre, whether we realise it or not, music can be just as important to our experience as dance, if not more so. Music and dance are seen as interactive, interdependent components or voices, each working upon the other, so that the whole experience becomes more than the sum of its parts. The result is that it becomes possible to talk about distinctive musical-choreographic styles, for instance, the particular style of a work or a choreographer.

An immediate problem that we face is of language, the means through which to talk about relationships between music and dance. Such language rapidly becomes technical, embracing two disciplines, not just one, and certain terminology and formal concepts have to be grasped. Whereas this book attempts to provide an accessible route to understanding such technicalities, and allows readers to approach the topic of structure at a variety of levels, it does not apolo gise for or skirt around technical discussion. Indeed, we have to address techni cal issues in order to reveal the complexities of musical-choreographic relation ships, to uncover the links, for instance, between formal device and meaning accurately applied technical terms mean precision in communication. For all this, analysis can still contain poetic vision, and, with a renewed acuteness of listening and observation, perhaps a new kind of poetic vision.

Seeing this 'technical' issue as a problem at all could be a comment on the current state of dance scholarship. Now, for excellent reasons, dance scholars today are eager to situate dance within an interdisciplinary framework, to raise the level of dance scholarship by drawing from academic traditions of longer standing, and to respond to the key academic debates of our times. The major thrust of this interdisciplinarity has been towards contextual studies of dance using models from feminist theory, literary criticism and the social sciences. Im portant work is being done that relates dance to a broad cultural context. But, believe, it is now time to use ideas from that expanded vision, and to turn them back on to the dance texts in all their complexity, and particularly their move ment and musical aspects.

A point in question is the continuing remoteness of dance scores (Benesh or Laban) to most scholars. Perhaps 'dance notation' seems distant from the sexiest concerns of today and is now even perhaps a sign of older-generation scholar ship. But, as musicologists well know, scores offer another kind of looking side ways: structural issues relate to the broader issues of context in remarkable ways. I would like to suggest that it is possible to combine these apparently op posing perspectives, dance theory and broad cultural theory, and to open a dia logue between them, which is just what has already happened in the other arts.

In terms of my own work, the discipline of musicology has been extremely useful for its methodological models, though I am not advocating that one can apply every musical idea unreservedly to dance. It is useful to consider the recent upheavals within the discipline of Western musicology itself, since the 1970s when musical works were regarded as autonomous, unified entities, aching for strictly abstract, non-contextualised formal analysis. There have been major changes in musicology during the 1980s, and ethnomusicological thinking was by this time proving highly influential. 'Emotion and meaning are coming out of the musicological closet,' wrote Rose Subotnik.[2] Susan McClary exploded into the dusty museums of musicology with her *Feminine Endings* (1991),[3] shook up a good number of colleagues, who then worked with, or rather reworked and critiqued, her theory in a variety of in-depth historical and analytical projects They borrowed, as appropriate, from earlier tradition, not ignoring forma analysis of harmony, counterpoint, melodic structure and so on. Indeed, they drew on the means of formal analysis to unmask the claims of formal analysis. Similarly, in this book, I am trying to face the new challenges of bringing together methodologies and perspectives.

My earliest method for examining interrelationships between music and dance was devised as part of doctoral research into the work of the American modern dance pioneer Doris Humphrey (her series of 'music dances', from the early music visualisations to her final work, *Brandenburg Concerto* – first movement, 1959).[4] My departure points here were the established theory of music visualisation, developed by Humphrey's teachers, the choreographers Ruth St Denis and Ted Shawn (a theory for creating dance material in imitation of the elements of music, see Ch. 2, p. 74), Humphrey's own theories and other dance rhythmic theory. However, in order to reveal the complexity of the works analysed, it was necessary to reorganise and expand from these theoretical beginnings. The augmentation of rhythmic concepts was crucial, and it is here that I was especially indebted to music theory. This method immediately proved relevant beyond Humphrey's work to ballet, appropriate to the strong rhythmic step component and particular emphasis on musicality in ballet, and it was clearly able to demonstrate subtle distinctions between choreographers' musical styles.

The method has continued to develop, but developing and applying it has always been a two-way process. In other words, while use of the method can be revealing about a work, application of it can also lead to its own refinement. Seeing and hearing have generated methodological concepts, which in turn have generated seeing and hearing ever more distinctively and differently. I still consider rhythm a logical basis for examining structural relationships between music and dance alongside the principles of visualisation. However, I accept that there are further areas to explore in more detail, such as the reflection of tonal tension in the structuring of dance material.

After undertaking initial research for my chapter on Balanchine, I felt the need to situate my structural analyses within the broader framework suggested earlier. I have become increasingly interested in the meaning or narrative aspects of musical-choreographic analysis, incorporating ideas from the new musicology and from film music theory, which so often have taken their models from literary theory. I have also adopted a more dialectical mode, referring out from my musical focus and back again to relate musical concerns to the other aspects of a ballet. While I believe that there are occasions for a specialised analytical approach, such an approach loses its force if operated in isolation.

My book does not stress the working process and collaboration of choreographer and composer, only as much as these affect performance interpretation, or as general background to a ballet. Besides, examples of the collaborative process are already well documented and a commission or style of collaboration does not necessarily produce a particular kind of work. Given, too, the current intellectual shift from author (process and intentions) to reader and the fact that twentieth-century ballets to existing music far outnumber those to commissioned scores, it seemed valid to concentrate on the dance texts. Focusing on dance texts has led me to limit my parameters further. I have selected three choreographers for special examination and chosen examples of their works for detailed analysis. Such a strategy has enabled me to reveal distinctive musical-choreographic styles as well as show musical-choreographic dialogue as a force throughout a single work, with illustrative moments in that dialogue integrated back into the work as a whole. I have chosen the choreographers Balanchine, Ashton and Tudor, because they demonstrate a range of musical-choreographic styles and because I was unashamedly guided by my passion for their work. I am hardly alone in esteeming their work so highly.

The book is in two parts, the first a general introduction to musical-choreographic styles, issues and methods, the second containing chapters devoted to each of the three choreographers. The first chapter (in Part 1) is a survey of musical-choreographic practice and associated ideas from a historical perspective. It provides a context for the work of Balanchine, Ashton and Tudor, covering work made and principles formulated from immediately prior to the start of their careers up until the period of their artistic maturity. Thus I have concentrated upon the first half of the twentieth century and the cultural traditions with which these three choreographers were most closely associated, American, British, French and Russian traditions. Writing such a survey was in some respects exasperating; literature relevant to the task is scarce. There is a body of documentation on the choreographers and artistic movements that I refer to, but musical aspects have often been given scant attention or the examination of interaction between music and dance has been too imprecise for my needs. Piecing together information, wherever possible, I have conducted my own investigation of ballets that are still with us or available on film.

Chapter 2 (in Part 1) addresses theoretical issues directly, drawing from the ideas introduced in Chapter 1, but linking in current theory to provide a model for examining music and dance as interdependent components. The chapter also examines issues of textual identity, introducing the dancer as protagonist in shaping both the creation and performance of a ballet text and summarising the problems raised by the analytical resources of films and scores. This chapter defines the methodology and terminology that inform the rest of the book.

In Part 2, the chapters on Balanchine, Ashton and Tudor give an outline of their musical-choreographic practice in general terms, surveying their full output, and then analysing sample works in their entirety. The samples were chosen to demonstrate a choreographer's range of style, also as early and late works in his career, ballets with and without plots, ballets to existing scores, to arranged scores, and just one to a commission. But dance being dance, resource availability was a deciding factor. For each work, I needed a range of video/film material and scores to examine and compare, and, with a view to my readers' access to these ballets, I was on the look-out for work on commercial video or that had been broadcast on television. All the works chosen for analysis have been critically acclaimed and, as ballets go, are a regular part of the repertoire. Even so, none of the work is as readily accessible as I would wish. In recognition of Balanchine's larger output and range, I have analysed three of his ballets, but two each by Ashton and Tudor.

The book is open-ended. I make no attempt at this stage to pull threads together, to draw conclusions from across the different musicalities of choreographers and their ballets, nor indeed conclusions on what is musicality. The last question seems even trickier now than when I started research for the book. I do not apologise. I can only reiterate the point about how much more work needs to be done.

I acknowledge the work already undertaken by those music specialists who have written about ballet music and other musical aspects of ballet: scholars, critics, dance accompanists such as Edwin Evans, Richard Fiske, Noël Goodwin, Elizabeth Sawyer, Humphrey Searle, Katherine Teck and Roland John Wiley. Their work has provided an invaluable background to my own. In terms of a scholarly analytical approach to musical-choreographic relationships, it is comforting and inspiring to note the developing field, a spate of fine work recently carried out, for example, by Paul Hodgins, Sophia Preston, Rachel Richardson, Marian Smith, and Robynn Stilwell.[5] A number of these scholars have had the benefit of a training in both music and dance. I learn from them all. I still return to the ideas of Doris Humphrey, whose comments on music in *The Art of Making Dances* are some of the most potent and best expressed anywhere.[6] Amongst dance critics, a major inspiration is Edwin Denby, the most sensitive of all to rhythm, phrasing and musicality.[7] His indeed was a listening eye, and he expressed what he saw and heard with a rare mixture of poetry and precision.

My book aims to be useful both to the general audience of dance enthusiasts and to those working within dance, choreographers, dancers, rehearsal directors wrestling with issues of revival and reconstruction, scholars and students of dance theory. It would be particularly gratifying to think that the stylistic information and argument here could be of use to the profession as well as to the academic world. Music being so central a part of dance, it is my conviction that this book falls within the broadest discipline frameworks of dance analysis and history, and it gives me pleasure to think that my analyses could be referred to and critiqued in later ones that do not necessarily make so much of musical considerations as I do.

The chapters are self-standing and do not have to be read in the order given. There are technical sections, including notation examples. However, this book is accessible to those readers who do not wish to follow every detail of structural analysis. The analyses are written so that the line through is clear for those who neither read dance nor musical notation. The most technical methodology chapter could be skipped entirely, or read at the end once a general understanding of my topic has been attained, or simply used as a reference point for definitions of terminology. The notation examples are in the Laban system, for consistency and because it is the one with which I am most familiar. For the sake of ease of comparison, I have sometimes used musical rhythmic notation for dance movement as well as for music.

Whichever route the reader chooses to take, my ultimate aim is to help her/him to see and hear more and to understand how seeing can be informed by hearing, and hearing by seeing. In the dance world, music often means misunderstanding and missed opportunities. But I take my cue from Balanchine's passionate utterance: 'I must show them the music. Music must be seen!'[8]

Part 1

1

Liberation Movements

Musical Theory and Practice in Twentieth-Century Ballet

The designer Alexandre Benois describes the aesthetic aims of the early Diaghilev Ballets Russes: 'For us it was the music which provided ballet with its centre of gravity. The moment had arrived when one listened to the music and, in listening to it, derived an additional pleasure from seeing it. I think this is the mission of ballet.'[1] Later, George Balanchine again claims the primacy of music, for choreographer and dancer: 'I cannot move, I don't even want to move, unless I hear the music first. I couldn't move without a reason, and the reason is music.'[2] A statement by the critic Edwin Denby suggests an equal partnership between music and dance within a ballet: 'The excitement of watching ballet is that two very different things – dancing and music – fit together, not mechanically but in spirit. The audience feels the pleasure of a happy marriage.'[3]

But the marriage is not always one of equal partnership. Wanting more for the dance, Antony Tudor once remarked rather cheekily that, although he was not against music being the propelling force in a ballet, 'The general audience sitting out in front doesn't realize that it's the music that's sending them most of the time and not the choreography . . . With me, music must become a *partner*, and not the sole source of inspiration.'[4]

Benois, Balanchine, Denby and Tudor were all active during times when the theory and practice of relating music and dance were being questioned and revised: from the early twentieth century onwards, we see a body of literature, including numerous series of articles in the dance journals, devoted to the subject. This took place alongside the other debates about dance, which was now 'growing up' into a serious art form. As dance exploded into new prominence and diversity in the twentieth century, with a new, radical strand of modern or contemporary dance added to ballet and nudging the older tradition to inspect its own terms, it is hardly surprising that this fundamental and apparently natural alliance or 'marriage' should also come under discussion. In fact, even the matter of natural alliance came under scrutiny. Were music and dance so inseparable after all? Was it not possible to create silent dance? Questions of power relationships and the autonomy of dance became more urgent, between music and dance, between musician and dancer. With the rarest exceptions, ballet choreographers have continued throughout the century to admit the power of music, so often to start off their own creative impulses, as well as to encourage our involvement as spectators. However, the possibilities for different ways of relating music and dance have broadened considerably during the twentieth century.

Musical developments in dance have also been affected by the stabilisation of the dance work as an independent conceptual entity during our century, with a relatively fixed form, devised by one acknowledged choreographer and usually one composer. We can compare this with earlier practice where ballets were highly flexible conceptions that could be edited, added to, or remoulded for different occasions and casts. Before the mid-nineteenth century particularly, ballet scores regularly incorporated borrowings from existing, often well-known music.[5] Now, a ballet could have a narrative but it could also be plotless and therefore, in a fundamental sense, 'about' its music. The one-act structure, already well-established, became the dominant framework for ballet.

In the early decades of the twentieth century, it was the predominant view amongst forward-thinking artists that music was a vital quality ingredient in dance, in some cases the most important means for raising standards and for inspiring choreographers to move beyond the established dance rhythms and movement clichés of ballet. Good music could offer seriousness and depth to dance. In 1914, Fokine, the first Ballets Russes choreographer, outlined in a letter to *The Times* (London) his five principles for choreography.[6] In the fifth, he advocated a new open musical repertoire for ballet, every kind of music potentially suitable, with the crucial proviso that it was expressive and appropriate to the subject matter of the ballet.

Music was also a liberating force. Its forms, such as repetition and theme/variation structures and contrapuntal textures, could play an important part in the development of new choreographic forms, particularly more expansive 'symphonic' forms without the restraints of plot. They could also operate as a sophisticated complement to the new symphonic dance structures. The late nineteenth century had witnessed the potential of scenes of symphonic proportions using specially written ballet music, for instance, by Tchaikovsky, Delibes and Glazunov, but the structural potential for dance, guided by musical principles, was interrogated much more deeply during the twentieth century.

Giving the lead to music was important to the new 'barefoot' or 'free' forms of dance, precursors to modern dance in both Europe and the US. Isadora Duncan (see pp. 22–5) was a leader of the interpretive movement promoting music as a basis for dance, and her influence carried over into ballet. Other artists led by music included the Canadian Maud Allan; a number of Americans, Loie Fuller, who began to choose more sophisticated music after Duncan had danced with her group in 1902, Ruth St Denis and Ted Shawn (Denishawn), who coined the term 'music visualisation' (c. 1917) for their music-based dances, Irene Lewisohn, who staged a celebrated series of 'orchestral dramas' in the late 1920s, and Michio Ito, a Japanese dancer who worked in Europe and the US. The eurhythmics school of the Swiss music pedagogue Emile Jaques-Dalcroze (see pp. 26–35) was also highly influential. Later, there were reactions against this principle of music guiding dance, even to the point of considering music a tyrannical presence, and then, afterwards, a liberalisation of views once more. Yet, it is significant that, even as he rejected the domination of music, Louis Horst, composer-accompanist for Martha Graham, still based his course in choreography on musical forms, justifying this in the absence of developed dance theory.[7]

The use of strong existing scores that had not been composed for ballet provided the new dance with depth and alternatives to the cliché rhythms and short dance and mime numbers of traditional ballet music. This approach was not unknown in ballet, but, from the late nineteenth century, Duncan and other artists from outside ballet were instrumental in bringing it into new prominence. Ballet choreographers since have continued to use nineteenth-century ballet music, to be sure (like Ashton, on a number of occasions), but there have been any number of other options: continuous symphonic scores of large proportions, as well as piano miniatures and songs, or the non-ballet scores by ballet composers like Tchaikovsky and Stravinsky (Balanchine's favourites). New musical choices brought new challenges to dancers, who now might be required to analyse and count their music after years of simply moving to easy melodies and rhythms.

However, during the early years of the century, ballet also became an important commissioning platform for composers of the highest order. Composing for the ballet was now seen less as a job for opera house hacks than an undertaking for serious composers. One of the most important achievements of the impresario Diaghilev was the establishment of this new platform, a flurry of musical commissions, raising the status of dance by putting it alongside the most interesting and complex contemporary music and in the company of fine composers and performing musicians.

Diaghilev and his Legacy

Diaghilev, though not an artist himself, was remarkable for imbuing the policy and repertoire of the Ballets Russes with his own artistic stamp, and his musical ideas were central to this. Perhaps this is hardly surprising when we learn that he was a competent pianist who had also studied singing and music theory, at one point had the ambition of becoming a professional musician, tried his hand at composition and approached Rimsky-Korsakov for tuition. Even as an impresario (organising concerts first before ballet), he was still to use his musical knowledge as an editor of a number of opera and ballet scores, and he readily made recommendations to his composers.[8] Consider this statement by Vittorio Rieti, a warm tribute to Diaghilev's musical passions: 'He was very meticulous. He checked everything bar by bar . . . He was a real musician. For him the music was the basis of the ballet.'[9] Perhaps too it was Diaghilev's musical background that prompted him to look to musical models for choreographic development: this could well be the root of his interest in Dalcroze eurhythmics (see p. 28).

Music was part of Diaghilev's theatrical model of a synthesis or fusion of the arts (see pp. 17–18), borrowing from the Wagnerian theory of *Gesamtkunstwerk*. This model governed the early Ballets Russes, stemming as it did from a very powerful late nineteenth-century aesthetic. It also prompted an important notion of collaborative working process. The reality was more often than not the direction of Diaghilev and his inner court rather than genuinely joint creation: Lynn Garafola suggests that Diaghilev's best works were rather held together 'by the community of values to which their contributing artists subscribed'.[10] Diaghilev produced an unparalleled array of contributions from composers, choreographers and visual artists. Stravinsky was outstanding amongst the Ballets Russes composers, writing a series of scores for Diaghilev. Noteworthy too are a number of French composers, including Debussy, Ravel and Satie, then the younger generation of Auric, Milhaud, Poulenc and Sauguet, also de Falla, Richard Strauss and Prokofiev.

Under Diaghilev too, commissioned music for dance was to escape the clichés of nineteenth-century ballet. Interestingly, the playwright and opera librettist Hugo von Hofmannsthal had written in 1912 to Richard Strauss encouraging him not to think that he had to write in the rhythms of 'ballet music'. Nijinsky was the first choice choreographer for Strauss's *Legend of Joseph* (1914, in the event set by Fokine): 'I fear it is the idea of ballet, of the need for accentuated rhythms which has misled and confused you. Therefore I must make myself the spokesman of Nijinsky who implores you to write the most unrestrained, the least dance-like music in the world . . .'[11] Now, too, at least in the early Ballets Russes, the structuring of ballet scores was altogether different, more continuous and more symphonic. It is significant that a different kind of concert score arose from these ballets, no longer the suite of short dances, but, as in the case of *Daphnis and Chloe* (Ravel, 1912), simply scenes lifted bodily from the ballet.

If Diaghilev's heart lay in the novelty and excitement of commissions, he also took existing music into the repertory. There again, his stamp was felt: in helping to choose Debussy's *Prélude à l'après-midi d'un faune* (1912) for Nijinsky; in his own rearrangement of Arensky's score for *Une Nuit d'Egypte* (now renamed *Cléo-*

pâtre, 1909), into which he inserted existing music by a number of composers;[12] and in his decision to commission a re-orchestration of Chopin for *Les Sylphides* (1909, abandoning the original Maurice Keller for an orchestration by several composers, among them Liadov, Glazunov and Stravinsky). But there is always a difficulty in applying a narrative to an intact, existing musical score. Usually, choreographers find it hard to fit their narrative timing to that of the score, and there are few successful works of this kind.[13] Perhaps partly for this reason, but almost certainly because Diaghilev enjoyed the personal artistic involvement, he promoted a compromise tradition of arrangement, a twentieth-century version of the long-standing tradition of inserting existing musical material into ballet scores. Thus, there were the scores for *The Good-Humoured Ladies* (Scarlatti, arranged by Tommasini, 1917) *La Boutique fantasque* (Rossini, arranged by Respighi, 1919), *Le astuzie femminili* (an opera-ballet by Cimarosa, arranged by Respighi, 1920). Diaghilev had a hand in choosing the original music and directing the orchestrators for all of these ballets, and in the case of *La Boutique fantasque*, we might well question who was the real musical author. Garafola asks:

> Gioacchino Rossini, who wrote the early nineteenth-century piano pieces on which the score was based? Respighi, the orchestrator, who added a handful of connectives? Or Diaghilev, who assembled the music for the ballet from numerous compositions, pruned bars and passages, changed chords, keys, and tempi, corrected Respighi's additions, and wrote notes to himself like, 'Don't forget that all the chords must approximate stylistically the *old* Rossini of *Barber* [*of Seville*]'?[14]

In the case of *Pulcinella* (1920), Diaghilev chose the original Pergolesi works, but Stravinsky pressed beyond the normal terms of arrangement by recreating the baroque music with twentieth-century rhythms and harmonies. These arrangements were not simply demonstrations of Diaghilev's own musical tastes, but also of his developing aesthetic point of view, after *Gesamtkunstwerk*: 'period modernism' to Garafola, 'time travelling' to the British composer-conductor Constant Lambert, as he wrote his classic 1934 manifesto *Music Ho!*[15] This is modernism (see p. 20) according to the terms of neo-classicism. *Pulcinella* introduces the past (the classical element) in duality with the present. Baroque Pergolesi and *commedia* are juxtaposed with the twentieth-century styles of Stravinsky and Massine, history drawn attention to ironically through reiterated disruption. We will see later (p. 19) that this sort of disjunction lies at the very heart of modernist practice.

A less celebrated but influential outcome of Diaghilev's work was the major attention that he brought to music outside the musical mainstream of western Europe. Much of the music that he introduced in the early seasons of the Ballets

Russes was new and exotic in style to Europe: that of the Russian nationalists like Balakirev, Borodin, Mussorgsky and Rimsky-Korsakov, for example. According to Charles Ricketts, by 1917, in the midst of World War I, Diaghilev had developed a policy not to use German music, 'which he wants to persecute and suppress; he means to scrap *Carnaval* [1910], *Papillons* [1914] and the *Spectre of the Rose* [1911].'[16] But it was not only Russian music for the ballet that made some people reconsider their values inherited from the nineteenth century and question the supremacy of the Austro-German tradition (see pp. 13–14). Diaghilev provided interval music within his London programmes, bringing to a pre-radio public little-known concert music by French, English as well as Russian composers. Lambert, for one, was liberated by the experience.[17] Diaghilev kept up his musical standards by employing a number of conductors of outstanding talent: Pierre Monteux, Ernest Ansermet, Eugene Goossens, Roger Desormière, to mention but a few.

We have seen how central Diaghilev was to the musical practice of the Ballets Russes, but he was also hugely influential upon future developments, at least for a while. The collaborative model was taken up by a number of companies and directors, by, for instance, the short-lived Ballets Suédois (although this company weighted the design rather than musical component), by Ida Rubinstein, by the Camargo Society, which boosted the Vic-Wells Ballet, forerunner of the Royal Ballet. In Britain, for many years, critics writing on the subject of music and ballet would cite Diaghilev's model as the ideal for creating ballet. The practice of setting ballets to arranged scores was also readily adopted in Britain by, for instance, Ashton and MacMillan (with their colleague musicians Lambert and John Lanchbery).

Nevertheless, specially commissioned ballet scores were to become a relatively rare phenomenon, particularly after World War II. Denby was already lamenting this in 1943, as he surveyed the American ballet scene:

> Such a lack of interest by the big companies in living musicians of some originality is very sad. They seem to have no curiosity about the intellectual life around them. It is perfectly proper for a ballet company to choose old music of contemporary interest for some new ballets. But there is something fossilized about a company that cannot go out and buy itself a brand-new score or two every spring . . .
>
> The spirit of a company, the vitality of the dancers, begins to sag without an occasional contact with what is liveliest and boldest in the artistic activity around.[18]

Horst Koegler cites a few recent examples of functional music being tailored specifically for a ballet choreographer and without any separate concert existence intended, William Forsythe's regular collaboration with Thom Willems being the most well-known instance of this.[19]

There are a number of reasons for this tailing-off in the number of commissions. Possibly the most important is the increased accessibility of musical recordings during the course of the century and, with this, the choreographer's power to develop an extensive repertoire of possibilities, even to compile his/her own scores. There is also the expense involved, much more than with existing scores, even those still in copyright. But artistic directors may be more or less conservative too in their tastes: they may be more or less ready to run risks with their audiences in terms of new music, and they may have music more or less high on a company agenda. Time is another costly factor, as collaborators procrastinate or change their minds. Commissions can push collaborators usefully into new, unexpected directions, but they also involve risk, compromise and trust. One of the greatest difficulties with commissions is hearing the final orchestral sound. A famous example of this is Ashton setting to work on Henze's *Ondine* (1958) from a piano reduction: he asked for a recording to be made of the full score and ended up rechoreographing most of what he had already made when he heard the recording.[20] Certainly within British ballet, occasions when orchestral tapes are made during the rehearsal period have been rare. This happened again with Brian Elias's score for MacMillan's *The Judas Tree* (1992).

However, it is salutary to consider that, before recordings became available, choreographers regularly faced the challenge of imagining orchestral sound, whether the score was a commission or an existing piece. Nijinsky rehearsed Debussy's *Prélude à l'après-midi d'un faune* to a piano reduction; the piano sound is more percussive than that of the orchestra and may well have influenced Nijinsky even if he had already heard the music in concert. Similarly, it has been suggested that the creation of *Jeux* (1913) to a piano score was of vital significance to the resulting choreography, noted for its motoric, stressed rhythmic style. Nijinsky had no way of hearing the brilliant shimmering of what Debussy called his orchestra 'without feet' until just before the premiere.[21] On the other hand, Stravinsky's two-piano reduction of *Le Sacre du printemps* (1913) retained much more of the orchestral character, and Nijinsky's choreography matches much more closely the sensibility of the orchestral version.

As well as commissions, other musical practices and attitudes seem not to have continued as Diaghilev once promised. The tradition of celebrated concert conductors playing a major role in ballet continued for a while with the follow-up Ballet Russe de Monte Carlo and Original Ballet Russe, and with Ballet Theatre in America, but since then it has largely died out, beyond occasional guest appearances. There have been examples of excellent musical leadership in ballet along the way, Lambert profoundly influential upon the whole artistic ethos of the fledgling Royal Ballet, Robert Irving at New York City Ballet, where Balanchine put an unusual degree of energy into ensuring high musical standards.

Despite Diaghilev's enterprise, the music world continued to look down upon ballet. Music critics for many years went on covering ballet as a lesser, more frivolous art than their own. There is now the suggestion that the most cited collaboration of the century, that of Stravinsky and Balanchine, originated in an uneasy power relationship.[22] It was only in the 1960s that the mere craftsman ballet-master was fully recognised as an equal, and, in fact, they only collaborated from scratch on four pieces. Yet, Stravinsky is a composer who professed to love the ballet. His lack of respect for Nijinsky and shifting evaluations of his choreography are well known (see p. 37).

Existing Scores: From Concert to Ballet

With the advent of radio and burgeoning of musical recordings, turning to existing music became the most popular approach in ballet. This was not Diaghilev's favoured model, rather that of Duncan and Fokine, but now, whether or not they read music or played the piano, choreographers had immediate access to a vast musical repertory in its full orchestral colours.

Using existing scores from preference might sound like an easy, comfortable route to take. Yet, whereas people are inclined to lament the lack of exciting collaborations of composers and choreographers, the special opportunities for close analysis from existing scores and recordings are not fully recognised. Existing music offers its own important challenges, avenues for particularly thoughtful, detailed response from a choreographer. A choreographer has more time to get to know the structural details of a piece of music as well as its large structure, to compare different musical interpretations, and, perhaps most important of all, to hear the final orchestral sound. Composers have found the result revealing, witness Stravinsky on Balanchine's 1963 setting of his *Movements for Piano and Orchestra*: 'The choreography emphasises relationships of which I had hardly been aware . . . and the performance was like a tour of a building for which I had drawn the plans but never explored the result.'[23]

Searching the musical repertoire opened up a vast historical opportunity: suddenly a more 'authentic' picture of various different pasts as choreographers matched theme, design and musical period. Thus, there is Fokine's *Carnaval*, with its Biedermeier setting and characters taken from Schumann's musical programme (a mix of autobiographical and *commedia* sources), and his *Les Sylphides* to orchestrated Chopin piano pieces, commenting on the *ballet blanc* of the romantic period. The 'time travelling' ballets were like windows on two worlds simultaneously.

There is too the consideration that a good proportion of twentieth-century music has lost its contact with a large public, quite apart from being less 'dancey', pulse-based, in its rhythms. Neo-classical music, with its one foot safe in the past, is an exception. Other music that sprang from the crisis in tonality (atonal, twelve-note, electronic and aleatoric music) distanced itself from its contemporary public, who preferred older tonal styles, especially those of the eighteenth and nineteenth centuries, music that seemed more 'legible' to the ears. More recent music that has pastiched previous styles or the relatively consonant styles of minimalist/systems music have been more popular with choreographers and audiences alike. It is no surprise that Ashley Page's *Fearful Symmetries* (1994), set to John Adams' motoric, minimalist-derived eponymous score, became Page's most acclaimed work for the Royal Ballet to date, and it was given far more performances than initially expected.

During the first few decades of the century, the new movements in music appreciation were important to choreographers, an education in the classics promoted by such men as Stuart Macpherson and Percy Scholes in Britain and Walter Damrosch in the US. These movements expanded rapidly with the advent of broadcasting and recording. As well as the promotion of community and young people's concerts, there were radio programmes in music appreciation, record guides, lectures for laymen, and in 1928, Walter Damrosch inaugurated the NBC Music Appreciation Hour. In the US certainly, there was a move to build a new, democratised arts constituency, to enlighten the new white-collar masses. As Joseph Horowitz put it in his book *Understanding Toscanini*, 'To partake in great music's exclusivity was made a democratic privilege.'[24] Duncan and later Massine both capitalised upon this new popularity of the 'great' music of the past, whilst they used it to demonstrate that dance was now of equal stature to music. But they were also using 'absolute music', the very term suggesting music not intended to be danced. Not surprisingly, their work to the 'great' symphonies caused considerable controversy.

Absolute music is a concept that, in our own century, grew to dominate musical thinking in a manner that it had never done before. It was centred within the formalist notion of equating form and content, music expressing nothing but itself, and it referred to music without text, function or programme. This indeed was the thinking behind the esoteric, context-removed, structural analysis of twentieth-century musicological tradition. But this thinking was given extra impetus by the complementary aesthetic of Stravinsky (see p. 66) and reflected in the more streamlined, bright and emotionally restrained styles of performance promoted by, for instance, Stravinsky himself and the conductor Toscanini.

Nineteenth-century precedents to this extreme view of musical absolutism do not blend content and form so straightforwardly. Instrumental music represented to many the pinnacle of musical experience, and the symphony itself had a key role to play here, seen, for instance, by E.T.A. Hoffmann as the 'opera of the instruments'.[25] For some, the symphony took over from opera and vocal music in status, endowed with a hallowed first movement form, sonata form. The possibility of textless music and a concomitant weighting towards abstraction were seen to make music stand supreme above other arts. However, theorists admitted that such music could have a poetic and spiritual content, it could initiate a quasi-religious experience, a glimpse of the infinite or beyond, and, midway before the extremes of abstraction in twentieth-century thinking, musical form itself was still equated with the spirit.[26] Although celebrated for developing the notion of form perfected and complete in itself, and in the opposite camp to Wagner, the critic Eduard Hanslick allowed for the interpretation of music as metaphor for the movement of the universe, enabling a glimpse of the infinite sublime experience.[27]

There is a good deal of evidence too that nineteenth-century listeners heard music concretely rather than abstractly, attaching all sorts of poetic and visual associations to music. Indeed, the nineteenth-century view of the symphony was predominantly narrative, the work conceived as a sort of 'composed novel' Not that the symphony chronicled particular events; rather, it embodied a series of emotions, a story of feelings, and a number of plot archetypes were readily understood, such as suffering followed by redemption, or struggle followed by victory. Anthony Newcomb explains this in his study of Schumann's Second Symphony Op. 61, which he relates to the suffering-redemption plot. He claims that such narratives could negotiate a relationship with formal types; in other words, to evaluate a work purely on the grounds of its abstract structuring principles is invalid, at least according to the terms of the nineteenth century.[28] It is interesting then to read that, early in the nineteenth century, the French composer Jerome-Joseph de Momigny attached his own text to Mozart's String Quartet in D minor, K.421, believing, Roger Parker says, that 'Wherever there is music . . . words will lurk beneath the surface, ready to voice specific dramas when invoked for the purpose of critical understanding.' Mozart's Quartet contained 'a specific expressive sentiment' that could be clarified through words.[29]

Such narrative conventions are the reason why, perhaps, a Dutch writer commenting on Duncan's performance of Beethoven's Seventh Symphony, felt so certain that Duncan did not understand what the symphony was really about (see p. 23).[30] As the twentieth century progressed, musical criticism tended to move more and more towards discussion of purely formal issues. But there are overlapping traditions. As late as 1935, two years after the premiere of Massine's *Choreartium* (to Brahms' Fourth Symphony in E minor, see p. 50), Donald Tovey's programme notes on symphonies were published as a collection, including one on this Brahms symphony. These are very much in the vein of nineteenth-century narrative writing.[31]

On the other hand, there were no doubts at this time about the absence of earthly sensuality or of ephemeral bodily presence from music of this stature. R. Ansell Wells wrote in *The Musical Opinion* in 1939:

Movement is essentially transient, a thing of the moment which is, at its best, the outward, visible and spontaneous manifestation of momentary impulse; but the great symphonies, on the other hand, are the expressions of Eternal Truth which is the unaltering and unalterable foundation upon which rests the whole order of things. The great music which expresses this Truth is, for those who appreciate it, as fundamental and unalterable as the Truth itself. The greatest symphonies of Beethoven, Brahms and Bruckner are colossal, staggering in their impressiveness, and leave one with that feeling of awe in the presence of an immensity which is evoked by the sight of a great mountain rising in all its rugged grandeur from the plain, towering upwards, to be lost in the whiteness of cloud and eternal snows.

The symphonies stand rock-like and immovable, eloquent of the age-old truths which they express, and they can have no relation to the whirling and jigging of puppet figures upon a stage.[32]

Such music critics did not always speak so disparagingly of ballet, provided that they approved the musical choice. They were also clearly oblivious to the contingent background to the canon of music that they inherited and promoted. The meaning of a piece of music comprises what it generates through history as well as those meanings from the time in which the work was composed. Aura is part of a work's meaning too. Lydia Goehr, in her book *The Imaginary Museum of Musical Works*, has examined the history and implications of the nineteenth-century *Werktreue* concept, which divorced musical works from social function and made them autonomous entities. It also legitimised the present by recourse to the past, making that past timeless by stripping it of extra-musical associations: 'The canonization of dead composers and the formation of a musical repertoire of transcendent masterpieces was the result both sought and achieved.'[33] It is quite clear from this that some music acquired transcendental meaning over time.

One further point here: the historic, musical canon was dominated by the Austro-German musical tradition, with Bach and Beethoven seen mid-century, by composers too, as the prime marker points in historical tradition.[34] Some time later there were three Bs: Bach, Beethoven and Brahms. Well before the end of the nineteenth century, the canon was firmly in place, powerful internationally, and the heroes without exception German. In 1871, a British clergyman and amateur musician H.R. Haweis compared and evaluated Italian music as voluptuous, French as frivolous and sentimental, German, 'moral, many-sided, and philosophical',[35] the last to do with the mind, and therefore most important and of the highest value. The international hierarchy for music remained intact into the twentieth century.

Is it surprising then that choreography to the symphonies, or absolute music or Austro-German absolute symphonies, should cause such a furore? By mid-century, the controversy had died down and there was general acknowledgement that musical choice in ballet should be more open. But by this time, dance had argued its own case for this, and the modernist style of ballet that could answer the purists' complaints was becoming steadily more convincing. Such ballet was not structured by narrative timing – narrative here referring to linear plot or storyline. It did not ask for programme music, but rather for the form-led or supposedly form-led, music (see Ch. 2, p. 67) from which it took ideas. In the 1930s, the disparity between the timings of the dominant narrative ballet and absolute music had been the root of another criticism. In his 1936 article 'Music and Action', Lambert clearly saw dance primarily in narrative terms, even the Massine symphonic ballets that moved towards abstraction (see p. 55). Dance needed a particular kind of music, either specially written or an existing score expressing 'direct or present action' as opposed to 'recollected or imaginary action'. He outlines two different kinds of musical timing, to correspond with these two different 'action' metaphors. Sometimes a composer's themes

> succeed each other in dramatic sequence like the acts of a play, sometimes their sequence and their position in time is dictated by purely formal reasons. In a symphonic poem by Liszt or Strauss the former is the case . . . But this is not so in the case of a Mozart symphony. We have it on his own authority that Mozart conceived a symphony in its full form in one moment of time. It stands to reason, then, that the return of a theme in his works can have no narrative or dramatic significance.[36]

But the point makes little sense when we consider that Balanchine's series of music ballets do not try to press narrative upon the formal structures of Mozart and Bach. This choreography was rather dictated, much like its music was read by formal concerns. It is no coincidence that the furore over using symphonic and absolute music died down by the 1950s, by which time Balanchine, a leader in this movement, had his own established company, and had gained fuller critical recognition. Now, John Martin, the powerful critic of the *New York Times* had turned in his favour just as he had come round to the modern dance choreographer Doris Humphrey's use of Bach.[37] Soon, Balanchine was to have a developing 'school' of like-minded choreographers around him. The plotless ballet suited concert music; setting plots to existing music is fraught with difficulties.

We now pass to a discussion of the changing twentieth-century theoretical frameworks underpinning relationships between music and ballet, and then to a survey of the specific work that has pinpointed musical issues. The choreographers and traditions covered provide the context in which Balanchine, Ashton and Tudor developed their own approaches.

Theories of Relationship between Music and Dance

Early this century, a theory existed of equivalence between one art medium and another, a belief in the possibility of translation between media. This went hand in hand with ideas that music could liberate dance and could act as a starting point for dance inspiration. The philosopher Suzanne Langer refers to a theory of 'dance as a gestural rendering of musical forms', citing the dancer Alexander Sakharoff's *Réflexions sur la musique et sur la danse* (1943): 'We – Clothilde Sakharoff and I – do not dance *to* music, or *with* music, we dance *the* music.' This is a point that Sakharoff makes several times, acknowledging Isadora Duncan as the person who taught him this distinction, not to dance *with* music, 'but to dance *the music itself'*.[38]

A survey of statements from the early years of the century indicates that equivalence operated according to different terms, either structural or emotional. Emile Jaques-Dalcroze developed a list of structural equivalents, what he called common elements between music and his 'moving plastic':

Pitch	Position and direction of gestures in space
Intensity of sound	Muscular dynamics
Timbre	Diversity in corporal forms (the sexes)
Duration	Duration
Time	Time
Rhythm	Rhythm
Rests	Pauses
Melody	Continuous succession of isolated movements
Counterpoint	Opposition of movements
Chords	Arresting of associated gestures (or gestures in groups)
Harmonic successions	Succession of associated movements (or of gestures in groups)
Phrasing	Phrasing
Construction (form)	Distribution of movements in space and time
Orchestration (*vide* timbre)	Opposition and combination of divers corporal forms (the sexes)[39]

When speaking of equivalence between music and dance, Duncan preferred to stress feeling and emotion, expressing the *Geist* or spirit of the music.[40] She described her performances under the baton of Walter Damrosch in the US (see p. 23):

> Often I thought to myself, what a mistake to call me a dancer – I am the magnetic centre to convey the emotional expression of the Orchestra. From my soul sprang fiery rays to connect me with my trembling vibrating Orchestra . . . For each musical phrase translated into a musical movement, my whole being vibrated in harmony with his.[41]

The concept of equivalence was also about a deep relationship stemming from the gestural basis of music itself, and indeed of all the arts. This was the view of Jean d'Udine (pseudonym for Albert Cozanet, a one-time student of Dalcroze), writing in 1910, 'Every artist genius is a specialist in mime.' According to d'Udine, if the motor image behind the dance was the same as that behind the music, then equivalence could still hold: the image could be realised in different ways. A musical chord, for instance, could be represented in a variety of movement provided that the basic motor image was shared, that there was common ground 'between the image that I perceive from this harmony and the image that I sense physically from the gesture that I make'.[43]

Sakharoff said much the same thing, stressing deep, spiritual correspondences perceived by the inner ear and eye rather than surface relationships. He believed that Duncan understood the point well: 'Isadora understood the interior meaning of the music and she took care not to fall into the trap of musical illustration; she took inspiration from the music rather than faithfully observing its detail.'[44] Ideas such as these sprang from outside ballet tradition, fuelling the widespread music interpretation and visualisation movements of the early decades of the century. But these ideas resonated strongly with what happened within ballet.

The root of these ideas about equivalence is the essentially romantic theory of organicism, wholeness, a long-standing tradition in the arts of transcending dualities. Indeed, art was seen as having the potential to mend what T.S. Eliot called the 'dissociation of sensibility', a notion of divided or lost self that was far from new (and Eliot himself traces the roots of the concept back to the mid-seventeenth century.)[45] It seems that dance held on to this ideal rather longer than the other arts. In his articles 'Postmodern Dance and the Repudiation of Primitivism' and 'Merce Cunningham and the Politics of Perception', Roger Copeland refers to the 'quest for wholeness' in dance tradition prior to Cunningham and post-modern choreographers, in both ballet and modern dance. Copeland allies this notion to primitivist thinking, 'the idea that dance can somehow help restore a sense of unity or connection otherwise alien to the modern world.'[46] Martha Graham, in her *Notebooks*, writes: 'What is the beginning? Perhaps when we seek wholeness – when we embark on the journey toward wholeness.'[47]

Such unity or wholeness arises from the identity of spectator and dance, dancer and dance. There is the suspicion that language introduces the principle of duality, words arbitrarily related to what they want to convey. Through dance, history can be at one with the present, the body at one with nature. Duncan appropriated music of the past, not as an opportunity for commentary upon difference, but so that she could be in harmony with the people of a former age and follow the route to nature afforded by great composers:

> The great composers – Bach, Beethoven, Wagner – have in their works combined with absolute perfection terrestrial and human rhythm. And that is why I have taken as a guide the rhythms of the great Masters; not because I thought I could express the beauty of their works, but because, in surrendering my body unresistingly to their rhythms I have hoped to recover the natural cadences of human movements which have been lost for centuries.[48]

The drive for wholeness is also manifest within the tradition of synthesis of the arts, which could embrace poetry and visual arts as well as music and dance. This is a long tradition, beginning with the Greeks, revived in the Renaissance with the emergence of opera and in the work of the choreographer Beaujoyeulx, and again with Gluck and Noverre in opera and ballet in the mid-eighteenth century. Joan Acocella has identified three sources of synthesis in the late nineteenth century. First, there is the mystical Platonism of the symbolist aesthetic, based on the notion that all the arts had their source in a single divine truth, as 'different refractions of the same celestial beam'. Uniting the arts gave the best chance of reproducing that beam. There are also sources in the doctrine of correspondences that stemmed from poetry, and the theatrical *Gesamtkunstwerk* principle of Wagner.[49] The latter model was questioned by many at the time.[50] Was it theoretically possible to have true synthesis and equality between the arts? Did the choreography sometimes suffer as music became, in Benois' terms, the centre of gravity (see p. 3), or did music usefully cover up lack-lustre choreography? Was it perhaps the case that the more sophisticated the individual art forms became, the less suited they were to fusion and equal weighting with each other?

The Diaghilev Ballets Russes were seen as a late flowering of symbolism, with the *Gesamtkunstwerk* principle clearly in operation, the arts fused into a hedonistic whole. The critic Camille Mauclair wrote of

This dream-like spectacle beside which the Wagnerian synthesis is but a clumsy barbarism, this spectacle where all sensations correspond, and weave together by their continual interlacing . . . the collaboration of decor lighting, costumes, and mime, established unknown relationships in the mind.[51]

Another critic, Henri Ghéon, sensed the merging of elements in *Firebird* (1910) as if there were no distinction between artistic contributions: 'Stravinsky, Fokine, Golovine, I only see one author.'[52] Jann Pasler has argued that the synthesis initiated by *Firebird* and *Petrushka* (1911) deepened further with *Le Sacre* and *Jeux*, where the focus on story had diminished:

The synchronization in the construction of the arts brought the public's perception of the whole to its completest. Because of the intimate bond in the visual, aural, and kinesthetic aspects of the ballet, the public's modes of perception became blurred.[53]

This Ballets Russes model of unity continued as an ideal for many artists and critics. Edwin Evans, the music and ballet critic who became one of the founders of the Camargo Society, insisted on unity of structural detail, praising the 'Cat's Fugue' in Massine's *The Good-Humoured Ladies*:

See how much both music and the dance gain by such interpenetration, the music in being visualised, and the dance in availing itself of the devices which form the texture of the music. The result is an organic whole.[54]

However, of greatest importance was Diaghilev's collaborative process, which was rated more highly than the practice of using existing scores in their entirety or specially arranged. There is another point to be made here, about exclusivity the artwork seen as watertight object, a notion existing that the separate media elements fused together should at best have no life of their own outside the ballet. Thus, we find extreme statements such as this one by Arthur Bliss, composer of de Valois' *Checkmate* (1937) and Helpmann's *Miracle in the Gorbals* (1944) and *Adam Zero* (1946): 'The most desirable music for ballet is music which can have no complete or logical life apart from its association with dancing'.[55]

Attitudes to absolute music evolved from the same exclusive aesthetic, the great symphonies, for instance, seen as not only internally organic, but closed off, hermetically-sealed entities, next to which dance was an intrusive, messy accretion. Thus, Bliss went on to say, 'All great symphonies and concertos live by their own self-imposed laws and are complete, vital, satisfying entities. Why superimpose another art? Would you add the tail of a peacock to the body of a lion?'[56]

Artistic movements overlap, and no more so than in the first half of the twentieth century. It is important to develop this point here. This was a time of critical change in the arts, a crisis period of displacement and lost harmony. The new modernism is seen here, according to the terms of Roger Shattuck, as embracing a number of 'isms' that sprang up after symbolism, like futurism, cubism and simultanism. All of these represented arts of juxtaposition rather than transition, revealing the jerky reality of subconscious thought processes and seizing upon a new kind of experience through divergence and collage.[57] This was a period of fracture in the arts (see, for instance, Picasso's work, from *Les Demoiselles d'Avignon* [1907] onwards), a sensibility that the new art form of cinema could only celebrate with its early stop-start surfaces and its fragmented patterns of editing. It was also the beginning of theories of separation and disjunction between the combined arts, as in theatre. The broken object distances the viewer: it encourages a more analytical attention. The *Gesamtkunstwerk* principle now came in for criticism. For instance, Brecht wrote:

> The process of fusion extends to the spectator, who gets thrown into the melting pot too and becomes a passive (suffering) part of the total work of art. Witchcraft of this sort must of course by fought against. Whatever is intended to produce hypnosis, is likely to induce sordid intoxication, or creates fog, has got to be given up.
> *Words, music, and setting must become more independent of one another.*[58]

Meanwhile, in dance, it was those outside ballet who expressed theoretical developments most strongly.[59] Equivalence between the arts became an irrelevance, the modern dance pioneers after Duncan and Denishawn considering it reactionary to hold on to the principle of music leading dance. Whereas music was once considered a liberating mechanism, it was later viewed with suspicion: it could limit the development of a choreography. Autonomy for dance was sought, alongside new structural relationships between music and dance. Indeed, in 1936, John Martin announced the emergence of dance in America from what might be called its musical state . . . Nobody in any part of the world is any longer justified in dancing music interpretations under the impression that he is being modern'.[60]

Influenced by parallel contemporary developments in Central Europe, American modern dance produced a spate of silent dances from the late 1920s into the early 1930s, and in the 1930s and 1940s a new radical theory of music and dance prevailed. Music was now to serve dance, composed for dance, sometimes even after the dance, and, if not a commission, then the music had to be contemporary or traditional American. The new theory overlapped with older theory, as older schools of music interpretation and visualisation continued to operate. It itself became toned down by the 1950s, when musical practices and criticism became more liberal in ballet (see p. 14) as well as in modern dance. But by then, Merce Cunningham had sprung upon the scene.

From mid-century onwards, Cunningham promoted extreme independence between music and dance, both conceived entirely (or virtually entirely) separately. Cunningham advocated the opposite to wholeness and connectedness. If music coloured the look of the dance (see Ch. 2, p. 65), this was most apparent to those who had seen the dance in silence, and observed the effect of music in late rehearsal or performance. It is more important that Cunningham's method pointed up disjunction to audiences. Copeland is committed to the moral principle of encouraging clarity of perception behind this approach, as he imagines Cunningham's explanation: 'It's more important – at this point in time – that we dis-connect, at least as long as we live in a society whose perceptual habits have been conditioned by commercial television where the boundaries between the most diverse phenomena begin to break down and become blurred.'[61]

The effect of juxtaposition of independent elements is also pointed up when meaning is a major issue, when there is incongruity between the connotational values of music and dance. The American postmodern choreographer Yvonne Rainer, for instance, made her pedestrian dances of the 1960s appear more pedestrian, more prosaic, even humorous, by contrast with high romantic or popular music.

These are extreme cases. In ballet, we find plenty of other examples that demonstrate a shift in thinking away from wholeness, even though they are less radical in kind. Diaghilev himself was ready for the shift. It is demonstrated in his 'time travelling' work, like *Pulcinella*. Lambert was quick to note this. Observing Diaghilev's rejection of the Wagnerian model, his tone is disparaging:

> Once the music of a ballet is allowed to be in two periods at once, there is no logical reason why the decor and choreography should share that particular type of pastiche or time travelling. Congruity between the various elements in a stage presentation is an essentially Wagnerian ideal . . .
>
> By realizing that his [Diaghilev's] earlier preoccupation with a sense of style and congruity was in essence Wagnerian he was able to invest with a revolutionary glamour the scrapbook mentality which in his later years he exploited with so marked a success.[62]

Gradually over the years, the fixation with notions of translation and equivalence of music and dance lessened. Ernest Newman, for instance, chief supporter of Massine's symphonic ballets among the music critics, preferred the gentler terms of 'parallelism' and 'correspondence'.[63] Meanwhile, with the developing modernist ballet, new ideas about conversation and counterpoint between the two strands of music and dance began to emerge. Listen to Lincoln Kirstein pointing out how the relationship between music and dance in the *Agon* (1957) *pas de deux* helps us to see and hear more clearly. It is as if he has learnt Cunningham theory. Here, the dance impulse establishes itself independently over an interrupted style of musical canvas:

> Concentrated semi-silences permit no rest or relaxation; indeed, dancers often move on silence, as sometimes they stay quiet on focuses of sound. Motivation from aural discontinuity in a metrical structure pinpoints movement, clearing our often blurred or inattentive eyes from familiar or expected combinations. Miniature shocks, like small short circuits, clear the eye and ear, demanding closer viewing.[64]

Doris Humphrey is interesting as a choreographer who promoted and responded to the 'independent' thinking within modern dance, but who continued to make music-based dances, and was criticised for doing so, through the radical 1930s and 1940s. Having made music visualisations in the 1920s, she then insisted that her next music-based pieces were not in this strict genre. It was, she declared, important to maintain the integrity and independence of dance. Co-operation she approved of, and the 'happy marriage', but her new technique included counterpoint:

> The dance should be related to, but not identical with, the music, because this is redundant – why say in dance exactly what the composer has already stated in music? – and because the dance is an entirely different art, subject to physical and psychological laws of its own.[65]

Within the world of ballet, we find Stravinsky saying much the same kind of thing:

> Choreography, as I conceive it, must realize its own form, one independent of the musical form though measured to the musical unit. Its construction will be based on whatever correspondences the choreographer may invent, but it must not seek merely to duplicate the line and beat of the music.[66]

We now come to an assessment of individual contributions and of specific work that has been particularly important to twentieth-century traditions of musicality in ballet.

Isadora Duncan

The influence of Isadora Duncan (1877–1927) upon ballet was considerable, and her ideas spread widely as she travelled through Europe and the US. At her first appearance in Russia in 1904, Fokine saw her perform, and, although he himself attempted to play it down, her seminal influence upon his development as a choreographer is now generally agreed. Duncan received the support too of some eminent musicians and fine orchestras: the London Symphony and Lamoureux Orchestra, the Colonne Orchestra under Edouard Colonne and Gabriel Pierné, and, in America, the New York Symphony Orchestra under Walter Damrosch. And yet it was her approach to music that often created deepest controversy.

Duncan's musical selections developed with the early support of the music critic John Fuller-Maitland, who urged her to improve her choices and to choreograph Chopin piano miniatures for one of her appearances in London in 1900. This programme, billed as 'The Illustration of Music by the Dance', was introduced by the composer Sir Hubert Parry. When Duncan gave her all-Chopin recital in Russia in 1904, she danced two of the pieces which were later used by Fokine in *Les Sylphides*, the Prelude (Op. 28, No. 7) and Mazurka (Op. 33, No. 2). Duncan was soon dancing to a wide range of music, from Baroque to contemporary, and using the musical titles: piano pieces including miniatures and sonatas (such as Beethoven's *Moonlight*, c.1904, and *Pathétique*, 1916); symphonies (Schubert's *Unfinished Symphony*, 1914; Tchaikovsky's *Pathétique Symphony*, 1916; three by Beethoven, his Seventh, 1904, parts of his Fifth, 1915, and Ninth, performed by the Moscow Duncan dancers, 1928–32); and selections from operas by Gluck and Wagner.[67] Most of her dances were solos, although some pieces were choreographed for her pupils. Most frequently, Duncan used nineteenth-century music and, for nationalist or political statements, music from the countries where she was resident, for instance, pieces by the Russian composer Scriabin and *Le Marseillaise*. Contemporary choices were relatively few: generally, Duncan did not feel comfortable with the more radical musical developments of her time. Instead, she worked on achieving a harmonious relationship with the past through the great music of the past (see p. 17).

Duncan's writings on the subject of music reveal changing views. In *My Life*, she wrote of her experiments in silence to reach new movement, from which her early dances to Chopin and Gluck evolved.[68] But in 1906, she was speaking of a silent dance as an end in itself, self-sufficient dance as an ideal. The same year, in a letter to Gordon Craig, she expressed her uncertainties on the entire subject, her concern to know more about music and how it might relate to dance:

I would like someone to help me *learn* more about music, and study more exactly its different relations to dancing. . . . Does the dance spring from the music, as I think it does, or should the music accompany the dance – or should they be born together?[69]

Occasionally, Duncan suggested that she 'translated' music into dance or presented the spirit of the music (see p. 16), but more often her point was that she simply used music as a starting point for dance ideas. Some dances were a kind of dramatisation of musical programmes or of songs, with mimetic gesture. For instance, in her *Orpheus*, the full version of which was premiered in 1911 (the piece had developed since 1900), she made clear reference to the narrative, assuming the role of Orpheus, the Shades, most often acting like a member of a Greek chorus.[70] Or, in her dances to the *Pathétique Symphony*, she responded to the music as a young, carefree woman, then as a leader rousing the crowd to challenge and battle, and finally a grieving earth-mother.[71]

Reflecting the common view of the era that there was such a thing as equivalence between music and dance, critics (in those days music or theatre critics) questioned whether these 'interpretations' were harmful to music and whether Duncan interpreted her music correctly. Ernest Newman, the music critic who later championed the symphonic ballets of Massine, was concerned about her interference with his own interpretation of Chopin.[72] The piece which created the most controversy of all was her setting of Beethoven's *Seventh Symphony* (1904): the orchestra played the first movement alone, after which she danced the last three movements. Beethoven was considered sacrosanct: 'One cannot touch Beethoven. Leave him to his world which encompasses all.'[73] Sibmacher Zynen was surprisingly secure about the meanings of this symphony, and equally certain that Duncan did not understand or visualise them:

> She revealed a complete lack of understanding of the rhythm . . . missed even the slightest feeling for the distressful, sorrowing voice of the melody, wrapping itself around the rhythm 'as the ivy vein around the oak,' as Wagner once said . . . she did not feel the music. An eminent authority had described how the opening chords of the Allegretto reminds [*sic*] us by their solemn procession of the tragic gravity of life. Are they some heroes and martyrs who march before us as a captive troop in mute resignation? You see, the theme has been made clear and she did not use it! . . .[74]

In defence of Duncan, Frits Lapidoth suggested that she simply took what interested her, what she found in the music, her own interpretation, to suit her purposes. Twenty years after her death, he recalled the controversy:

> It was *not* at all her idea to complete an orchestral number or just to illustrate

it, but to express her feelings and her visions, that she felt in herself and saw come up before her spiritual eye, when hearing certain works of music. It was *not* plastic transposition of the musical idea, that she pretended to give; but expression of her own sensations and imaginations, awakened by the music.[75]

Accounts of Duncan's relationship to musical structure differ considerably. The Dutch critic Leo noticed some clear, frequent structural relationships, although his tone is disparaging:

A high squealing note made her stand on tiptoe, a glissando of the violins caused her to glide over the stage like a lump of butter in a hot pan, a grace note caused her to blink her eyes, a chromatic run made her trip as a scared sparrow along the foot-lights, and an arpeggio undulated her fair, bare arms.[76]

However, reviewing Duncan's return visit to London in 1908, Fuller-Maitland considered that she misinterpreted some of her music (dances from Gluck's *Iphigenia in Aulis*, 1904–05) precisely because structural relationships were lacking:

Here is the art of posing as an accompanist to the music, rather than an inevitable series of movements for the sake of which the music seems to have been composed. Rhythmical as her performance was, it seldom follows with minute fidelity the notes of the music translating them into steps.[77]

Dalcroze (see pp. 26–30) criticised her musical approach for similar reasons: 'She rarely walks in time to an *adagio*, almost invariably adding involuntarily one or more steps to the number prescribed by the musical phrase'.[78] Levinson noted how impossible it was for a single artist to respond to the complexities of musical part-writing:

The Bacchanale in the Grotto of Venus from *Tannhäuser* is a complete failure. The performer does not have the ability to communicate the *multileveled* musical image in which melodic figures at times stand out distinctly and then slip back into the sea of orchestral polyphony. The Bacchanale cannot be realized without the contrapuntal opposition of separate groups within the dancing mass.[79]

It seems that Duncan's later settings of large romantic works adhered to musical structure generally less closely than early works. Observers often testify that the later works included frequent stillnesses and a preponderance of slow legato movements, which must have meant independence between music and dance structures. The Boston critic Henry T. Parker, who saw Duncan dance in 1922, reflects on this: 'Isadora is ceasing, inevitably, to be a dancer in the sense of vivid motion. Instead, she is becoming sculptress . . . Becoming sculptural, she becomes also more independent of the music.'[80] St Denis greatly admired Duncan when she saw her perform in California in 1917. She too noticed Duncan's tendency to stand still, and how this was completely at odds with musical passages of high energy: 'She stopped when the music became too complicated and compromised by making one of her unforgettably noble gestures in complete disregard of the music.'[81]

However, aside from the relationship of her choreography to musical structure, we need also to consider the nuances of rubato in performance, the play with music which differed from one performance to the next and gave the impression of improvisation. 'She went moving on, before or after it [the music],' wrote Gordon Craig, referring, presumably, to this play.[82] Most interestingly, Duncan introduced the effect of active listening and response to her music, drawing attention to this process as part of the content of her dance. This is perhaps what is at the root of Denby's observation of Maria Theresa, one of the original Duncan dancers, as he describes the Duncan technique: 'the way the body seems to yield to the music and still is not passively "carried" by it, but carries itself even while it yields.'[83] In other words, there is a self-consciousness about the act of yielding, which brings to the foreground response to music as content.

The whole look of the Duncan dancer suggests an openness to receive inspiration, infusion, from the Beyond, in other words, from the external force or spirit emanating from the music. In our own time, this is evident in the performances of Julia Levien and Annabelle Gamson, both of whom have revived Duncan dances. Duncan was often perceived to be actively listening, indeed, sometimes waiting and listening before starting to dance. Several writers remember Duncan making a gesture of listening to the music and miming the playing of the flute at various points in Beethoven's *Seventh Symphony*.[84] Although he probably would have denied the source, this Duncan rubato and listening is also an important part of Fokine's work. After Duncan, his sylphides also 'run, hesitate, turn, and yield to Chopin music' (see p. 35).[85] There are a number of gestures of hand to the ear in *Les Sylphides*, listening to the messages from other sylphides perhaps, but also to those from the music. There are others too who absorbed something of Duncan's musicality: like Ashton, who was inspired to choreograph a dance for Lynn Seymour from his memories of Duncan, *Five Brahms Waltzes* (1976), but whose own style incorporated this same sense of freedom, anticipation and lag.

Emile Jaques-Dalcroze

The Swiss music pedagogue Emile Jaques-Dalcroze (1865–1950) both derived ideas from and contributed to the music-based, free style of dance of the early twentieth century. His career developed in directions close to dance culture. Originally establishing a movement technique to develop rhythmic sensitivity in musicians, his method, formulated in Geneva during the 1890s, became a physical as well as musical training. Indeed, it was eventually seen as a training of the whole person. Dalcroze's method was known as eurhythmics or rhythmic gymnastics, although when it generated more dance-like work, he would introduce the term 'plastique'. Learning from his pupils, he integrated ideas from the new, 'free' dance (in his own practice, he would have nothing to do with ballet) so that the movement invention within eurhythmics became more subtle and varied. At the same time, his school, established in Hellerau near Dresden in 1911, became a training ground for a number of important later dancers, such as Hanya Holm, Michio Ito, Kurt Jooss, Marie Rambert, Uday Shankar and Mary Wigman. Thus, while Dalcroze came from a musical background, in a new climate of musical prominence in dance, he demonstrated that he could have a highly constructive dialogue with dance. The Dalcroze method enjoyed considerable international renown, through lecture-demonstration tours from the first decade of the century onwards. Branch schools sprang up rapidly in a number of cities round the world, for instance, in Paris, London, Vienna, Stockholm, St Petersburg and New York. The Denishawn music visualisations owed a great deal to his method (see Ch. 2, p. 74).

Dalcroze offered a precise structural approach to making movement to music, a precise means of negotiating with musical structure and a clear analysis of metre and beat in relation to phrase. This analytical attention to structure became a modernist feature in itself, in the hands of those choreographers who borrowed from Dalcroze. Primarily, he developed techniques for visualising beat, metre, and details of rhythmic pattern, but he also encouraged response to pitch and dynamics, as his chart of structural equivalents demonstrates (see p. 15).

There were exercises in counterpoint within the body, arms beating different rhythms, for instance, from the feet, but also in counterpoint between movement and music. Selma Odom describes typical class exercises:

Students might begin by walking around the room, following the teacher's playing [improvisations on the piano], responding directly to the beat and to changes in speed and dynamics . . . They might also be asked to react quickly, starting and stopping, or responding to changes in tempo, moving perhaps twice as fast or twice as slow, following the musical cues. Another fundamental practice was the 'stepping' of rhythmic patterns . . . [Dalcroze] would play, and after listening carefully, the students would immediately repeat what they heard in movement, matching their steps to the duration and sequence of notes they perceived. Sometimes they would 'echo' the patterns, moving in silence, immediately following the example played, or they would move in canon, making one pattern while listening to the music for the next one . . .

The work to develop the sense of measure, or bar time, was formed by enlarging the basic arm motions of conducting . . . Experienced students could beat regular bar time with their arms while simultaneously stepping rhythms of great complexity . . .

[Dalcroze] developed literally hundreds of exercises to help students feel the infinite variety of what could be achieved through shaping the flow and energy of breathing. Other concepts were also used to encourage the sense of phrasing, such as contrasting muscular force (light or heavy movements), using a real or imaginary weight or resistance (stretching an elastic), or simply taking turns moving with a partner or in groups (alternating voices, movements versus stillness).

Exercises such as stepping rhythms, beating bar time, or abdominal breathing with sudden contraction could all be done in a more or less straightforward, neutral manner ('realizations'), or with stylized or emotional variations ('expressive realizations'). The work with expression led to 'plastique animée' – choreography, really – of more complex forms such as inventions, fugues, and rondos. Here the movement would fuse stepped rhythms with almost any sort of expressive body attitude and gesture appropriate to the music. Sometimes students even created what was called 'plastic counterpoint,' or realizations independent of, but related to, the music.[86]

In some writings Dalcroze suggested that a freer approach to music might be adopted after a strict training in his method, and his earlier writings suggest tighter relationships between music and dance than later essays. In 1912, he wrote:

The art of plastic rhythm is to designate movement in space, to interpret long time-values by slow movements, and short ones by quick movements, regulate pauses in their divers successions, and express sound accentuations in their multiple nuances by additions or diminutions of bodily weight, by means of muscular innervations.[87]

By 1918, he had changed his tone:

To dance in time is not everything. The essential is to penetrate the musical thought to its depths, while following the melodic lines and the rhythmic pattern, not necessarily 'to the letter' – which would be pedantic – but in such a way that the visual sensations of the spectator may not be out of harmony with those of his auditive apparatus.[88]

In his *Eurhythmics, Art and Education* (1930), he drew the firm conclusion that, with the maturation of dance into a self-sufficient art form, the domination of music should lessen. Dance 'will no longer melt away into music, but will become its ally . . . No longer will there be identification, but rather super-position and collaboration.'[89]

Presumably, Dalcroze envisaged several stages in the development of independence between dance and music. Yet it is important that he retained his belief in collaboration and the harmonious whole, and that the emotional impulse behind the music should find itself embodied again within the dance: 'The main thing is that the emotions, which have inspired the sound rhythms and the form in which they have taken shape . . . should be reproduced in their plastic representation, and that the same life force should animate sound music and the music of gesture alike.'[90] It is important too that Dalcroze, while admitting dance as an independent art, and even on occasions a silent presentation, still saw music as the salvation for dance, its way forward as an art.

The Dalcroze method spread into the ballet world, despite his own reservations about ballet. Most well known, Diaghilev visited Hellerau twice in 1912, with Nijinsky. He then engaged Marie Rambert to teach his Ballets Russes and to work with Nijinsky on *Le Sacre*, although only three classes actually took place, because the dancers boycotted classes. Prince Volkonsky, the former Director of the Imperial Theatres, who powerfully promoted the method in Russia for some years, advised Diaghilev to visit Hellerau.[91] For Diaghilev, the method was exciting, possibly because it was new and seen as part of the experimental arts world, partly too because it offered a way in which to work closely with musical structure, at a time when dancers were using new kinds of music, including complex contemporary music. Jacques Rouché, the forward-looking director of the Paris Opéra, was so impressed with the method that he set up a eurhythmics department there in 1917, aiming to improve standards, and inviting 'free', Dalcroze-trained dancers to appear alongside the classically-trained dancers.[92] There were tensions between the factions, and the department closed in 1925, but it is an interesting development within a highly traditional ballet institution.

The Dalcroze name became something of a catchword for rhythmic exercises and counterpoint in dance. Most comments from the ballet world on Dalcroze emphasise the drill aspects of his work, a dry approach that used counts, with clear articulation of pulse. Originally worried by Nijinsky's dislocated approach in *Faune* (see p. 37) and Fokine's inexact response to music in the procession in

Cléopâtre (see pp. 31–32), Rambert later favoured a freer approach than that with which she associated Dalcroze.[93] Derogatory comments came from Fokine, about 'rhythmomania',[94] and from the critic André Levinson, who referred to 'gymnasiarchs'.[95] The counting and visualisation of rhythms in Nijinsky's *Jeux* led Debussy naturally to think of Dalcroze:

> This man [Nijinsky] adds up demi-semiquavers with his feet and proves the result with his arms. Then, as if suddenly paralysed on one side, he watches the music go past with a disapproving eye. It seems that this is called 'stylisation of gesture.' It is ugly! It is in fact *Dalcrozian*, and I consider M. Dalcroze one of the worst enemies of music! And you can imagine what havoc this method has caused in the soul of this young savage, Nijinsky![96]

In fact, it is odd that the majority of choreographers discussed later in this chapter made a point of dissociating themselves from eurhythmics, but did this despite connections with Dalcroze having been identified in their work. Nijinska provides perhaps the strangest example of this. Her school in post-revolutionary Kiev was widely considered to have had links with the Dalcroze method.[97] Yet, in her memoirs, in which she recollects visiting Hellerau in 1912 with Diaghilev, she is entirely disparaging:

> A group of young girls came onstage. They followed each other in a long chain led by an older student. The girls walked to the 2/4 beat of the music; at the same time one arm was gesticulating to a 3/4 time and the other was marking a 4/4 time . . . I was not impressed by what seemed to me to be a pseudomusicality, acquired by long training. It reminded me of the skill acquired by jugglers who practice for hour after hour to be able to juggle bottles, plates, or balls, to perfect their circus acts.[98]

Is this really how she felt in 1912? By the 1920s, her attitude is not surprising. By then, she had embraced neo-classicism. She insisted to Rouché that, if asked to teach at the Opéra, she would not wish to have anything to do with its eurhythmic dancers.[99]

These confusing evaluations of Dalcroze raise a number of questions. Was the connection between all these ballet choreographers and Dalcroze a real, direct one, or indirect, as if by osmosis? Were the contemporary critics on the look-out for Dalcroze as a contemporary style of some notoriety? Did critics spot the style for a moment or two in a ballet, and then note the moment out of context, giving it an exaggerated importance? It is not unlikely that choreographers would have wanted to remove themselves from the more schematic, mechanical applications and amateur free-style physical demonstrations associated with eurhythmics. But perhaps too they felt the need to disassociate themselves from something that had once (in the 1910s) been very fashionable, a craze that had passed.

Nevertheless, the eurhythmics method did offer a way forward to choreographers, with its rhythmic and contrapuntal intricacies. Perhaps its use appeared fussy and mechanical in the early decades of the century because choreographic structures tended to be relatively simple at that time. We will consider this later in a discussion of *Le Sacre* (see pp. 39–42). Certainly, there is plenty of evidence to suggest that the Dalcroze influence was far greater than is generally thought, offering as it did a way of working closely with a highly complex score, not just skirting around its structural detail. In the right hands, the method could be used imaginatively; choreographers demonstrated its range in a rich variety of styles.

The tradition of an analytical approach to structure has remained in ballet, even if the Dalcroze method is no longer the reference point. It is fascinating that Stravinsky once approved 'a form of rhythmic gymnastics', though with the proviso 'more artistic than those of Dalcroze'.[100] The date of his statement is 1914. Here, he indicates his own aesthetic bias very clearly and unwittingly points towards the strong rhythmic link with his music that Balanchine was to celebrate years later.

Michel Fokine

Michel Fokine (1880–1942) must surely have been thinking of Dalcroze when he wrote in support of Nijinsky's *L'Après-midi d'un faune*. In this work, he says, though not in later ones, Nijinsky escaped the trap of 'rhythmomania':

I especially approve of his resisting any movement despite the apparent demands of the agitated measures of the music. At that time Nijinsky was still free from the rhythmic gymnastics to the influence of which he regrettably succumbed in his compositions which followed 'Faune'.[101]

Yet some linked Fokine himself with the Dalcroze culture. André Levinson spotted the connection in *Les Préludes* (Liszt, 1913) when he saw it at the Maryinsky Theatre. Described by Cyril Beaumont as 'symbolical of man's eternal struggle between life and death',[102] the ballet tended towards abstraction. Levinson dismissed it as a 'vain wish to rival Dalcroze':

In sections dance has been replaced by the beating out of the rhythm with the hands and feet. Energetic stamping corresponds to accented notes and pauses correspond to extended notes. There are even attempts to convey the tempo's acceleration and slowing by an unwitting parody of the 'system' so studiously created.[103]

The British critic Ernest Newman notices similar mimicry in other, later ballets:

Fokine is constantly 'pointing' this or that feature of the music in his choreography; the trouble, so far as I am concerned, is that too often the pointing is almost unbelievably naive. I do not mind so much when, in *L'Epreuve d'Amour* [1936], he adopts the very obvious device of making his dancers stamp when Mozart's 'cellos and basses seem to stamp: it is not very brilliant invention, but it may pass. But when, in those long wood wind chords in the 'Midsummer Night's Dream' Overture [in the plotless ballet *Les Elfes*, Mendelssohn, 1924], he makes his elves do a jerk of now head, now body, on each chord in turn, I feel that the limit has been reached of my tolerance of naivete.[104]

Newman compares Fokine's approach unfavourably here with Massine's symphonic ballets (see pp. 50–6) where the movements formed a more 'organic part of a large design'. Fernau Hall's comments yet again suggest a mechanical Dalcrozian approach: he describes how, in *Les Eléments* (Bach, 1937), Fokine twice attempted to duplicate a fugal structure:

His solution of this problem is obvious almost to the point of banality. The entrance of each voice in the fugue is personified by the appearance of a dancer, who leaps from a hidden platform in the wings on to the stage, runs down stage, leaps again down a flight of steps, and begins to do pirouettes alongside the other 'voices'. In this case the choreography corresponds to the music only too well.[105]

All the critics make mockery of these moments of close relationship between music and dance. But were these mere isolated moments that stood out and were exaggerated in reviews, or did they represent the regular style of a piece? We recall that Rambert presented the opposite view, observing just how much Fokine's approach was unlike Dalcroze's, and at this time, she herself was still thoroughly committed to the Dalcroze method. When she first arrived direct from Hellerau to join the Ballets Russes, she voiced her opinions to Diaghilev:

I said I thought that the procession in *Cléopâtre* should have corresponded more exactly to the rhythm of the music, which was how Dalcroze would have done it. I know now that the great Fokine was absolutely right in his looser treatment of that passage.[106]

Fokine had a background in music. He had studied the violin and piano and played in a balalaika orchestra, an experience that involved copying out musical parts for the different players and thus developing his knowledge of rhythm and musical scoring.[107] His autobiography reveals both knowledge of, and a sensitivity to, musical matters, as a general approach and in response to the details of phrasing and structure. Fokine's ideas about music form a part of his principles for the reform of ballet: he was concerned for unity of conception across all the arts contributing to a ballet and for expressive music (see p. 4). Establishing a new musical practice in ballet, his ideas fitted the Diaghilev model of collaboration between creative artists and, in the early years of the Ballets Russes, a symbolist-derived model of wholeness and unity. He also promoted existing music, much of it far removed from traditional ballet music. It was Fokine's ballets that did the most for Russian music in the West, using music by composers such as Tcherepnin, Rimsky-Korsakov, Borodin, Balakirev and Mussorgsky.

Fokine's collaborations were the first to bring Stravinsky to the forefront of ballet composition. Already in his *Firebird* and *Petrushka* scores, there was a new, exotic orchestral sound world, descriptive landscapes in music from which 'dances' would emerge and merge back again, sometimes seamlessly, sometimes more abruptly, always differently. These ballets began in different ways, the first having a scenario already completed by Fokine, the second written and planned by the composer and designer Benois before Fokine stepped in. It would be fair to say that the music is central to the success and survival of both these ballets, carrying as it does the narrative action, depicting character and emotion, underlining gesture, and sometimes leading us through somewhat static passages on stage. Often there is a collage of simultaneous or successive components of material. A wonderful example is the appearance and disappearance of characters and situations out of the crowd music in the first and last scenes of *Petrushka* – the two street dancers, the bear, the coachmen, the masqueraders, and so on. Stravinsky later voiced some reservations about Fokine's work,[108] and, as a neoclassicist, he also stopped writing such descriptive music (later, he preferred to see *Le Sacre* too in architectural rather than narrative terms),[109] but this does not deny the important historical position of the two ballets on which they collaborated. Here was a new style of contemporary ballet music, revolutionary in dissonance and rhythmic asymmetry and answering Fokine's wishes to escape from the conventions of set numbers and nineteenth-century ballet rhythms. Fokine explored further in these directions as he set commissioned scores by Ravel, *Daphnis and Chloe* (1912), and by Richard Strauss, *Legend of Joseph* (1914).

However, it is likely that Fokine's preference was to use existing symphonic scores, problematic as this might sometimes turn out to be. *Schéhérazade* (1910) aroused considerable controversy for altering the original Rimsky-Korsakov programme, which was based on tales from *The Thousand and One Nights*. But it was probably Bakst who came up with the idea of using another of the tales from this source.[110] The conservative Levinson was critical of Fokine's other early ballets made outside the Diaghilev repertory to existing music, arguing that they were 'a parasite of others' musical glories' and burdened with the problems of fitting dramatic action to set music. In the case of *Les Préludes*, he felt that Liszt's music had no dance flavour. *Eros* (1915) was set to Tchaikovsky's *Serenade for Strings*, the music that Balanchine later used for his celebrated ballet *Serenade*. Fokine introduced the theme of two statues coming to life in front of a young girl. Levinson considered the music primarily a 'backdrop for the mood', a negative assertion about a musical approach that became common in later years.[111] In *Francesca da Rimini* (1915), he found a lack of dramatic compatibility between music and dance, with the jarring of their respective narratives:

> How is it the ballet master's hand didn't tremble when he willfully allowed Tchaikovsky's lyrical second theme, in which all the heavenly sweetness of Francesca's confession sounds forth, to become a series of separate episodes and pauses culminating in the scene of the double murder of Paolo and Francesca?[112]

By far the most influential of Fokine's works is *Les Sylphides* (1909). This is the ballet that both Balanchine and Nijinska have referred back to as a seminal experience,[113] and it is also a ballet that Ashton took special care over when he was director of the Royal Ballet. It was not only the movement style that interested choreographers, but also its statement that ballet could be about music, just steps to music. The first version of this ballet (1907), then called *Chopiniana*, was much more heavily based in narrative, a series of pictures depicting aspects of Chopin's musical world. Framed by national dances, there were a number of scenes: one that introduced the composer – to a Nocturne, Chopin suffering hallucinations of dead monks rising from their graves and then finding solace in his Muse at the piano; a wedding story (a young woman leaving an elderly man to whom she is betrothed for her young lover); a romantic-style duet that was kept for the second, now familiar version of the ballet. The music was Glazunov's existing arrangement of Chopin piano pieces (called *Chopiniana*), with one additional number, the Waltz in C-sharp minor for the duet, which Glazunov orchestrated specially for the ballet. With the exception of this waltz, the second version of the ballet used new Chopin pieces, and it has been orchestrated over the years by a number of different composers (see p. 7).

Structural relationships between music and dance in *Les Sylphides* are close.

The framework of the steps suggests visualisation of music, and Fokine's own analysis of a sample of the work makes this point strongly. Thus, he describes the relationship between soloists to melody and corps to accompaniment in the second half of the opening Nocturne Op. 32, No. 2: '[The corps] mark the rhythmic beat whilst the principals are drawing their line of dance to the melody and harmonizing its rise and fall with the rise and fall of their movements.' He analyses the whole of the solo Waltz Op. 70, No. 1 as a visualisation of musical structure:

Valse (Op. 70, No. 1)

I set my soloist four tasks. Firstly she has to mark the rhythmic beat of a valse. This means that in roughly every other bar she dances either some valse step, or steps with three changes of weight; or else marks the three beats by gradually lowering her hand (in the third phrase); or beats one foot on the other (at the end of the fourth phrase). This marking of the beat (or pulse) otherwise than by the feet is a particular feature of some Russian folk dances which I utilized in order to make my classical dance seem more rhythmically sensitive.

Secondly, the dancer's movements follow the pattern of the melody. As the music soars up and down in an arpeggio and is then held on a high note during the first phrase, so the soloist soars upwards in a *grand jeté en avant*, momentarily holds herself in the air, falls into a valse step then, as the note is held, poses in an *arabesque*. Something similar happens in the second phrase where, instead of marking the beat with a valse step, she springs three times, each time lowering the leg very slightly to match the descending notes to which these *jetés* are danced. In the third phrase, the soloist not only marks the beats but also the descending notes with the lowering of her hand. During the fifth phrase she swings up and down with the lilt of the melody, turns in *attitude* as a high note is held, then she 'embroiders' round her high note by making a circle round that same spot *sur les pointes* before crossing the stage to the opposite side with a long held *arabesque*.

Thirdly I allow the formal musical structure to dictate the choreographic pattern. The first musical phrase of sixteen bars is repeated, so the second four short dance phrases are also a repeat of the first four movements. But because Glazunov made some slight changes in his orchestration of the repeat, I make slight changes in my choreography. For example, the *grand jeté en avant* of the first passage becomes a *grand jeté entrelacé*. The third, and first eight bars of the fourth musical phrase state new ideas, so does the dancer, but the last eight bars of the latter restate the third phrase and the dancer similarly repeats her long *arabesque*. But instead of dropping her front hand gradually to the descending notes, she presses both hands softly outwards, as if she were calling her fellow sylphs to the dance. The final phrase is a repeat of the last two bars during which the dancer turns and disappears from sight. This slight variation in the last two bars of a phrase I have noted throughout. The valse is made up of short four-bar phrases merging into each other, with an imperfect cadence at the end of each sixteen bars. The dancer is guided by these links in the musical continuity and usually repeats her *enchaînements* three times, but the fourth time she does not make a perfect repeat because she has to draw her line into a preparation for the next phrase and in the last *enchaînement* prepare the way for the next dancer.

Fourthly, I allow the musical structure to determine the floor pattern so that the circling of a valse is continually being made visible as the dancer circles the stage, or turns in her *grands jetés entrelacés, pirouettes* and other steps.[114]

Fokine's musical analysis is casual in a couple of instances. He refers to a repeat of the first sixteen bars of music with varied orchestration, but the music does not repeat at this point. He also refers inaccurately to the imperfect cadences at the end of each sixteen bars, at points when there are perfect, more complete, cadences.

It is interesting that Denby singles out *Les Sylphides* and *Carnaval* as examples where 'the relation of dance steps to music . . . is blunt but bold'.[115] But the slight give and take in performance which is a matter of personal style and is not recorded in structural dance notation brings great life to such a plain framework. Fokine himself taught continuity across dance phrases and through musical cadences, and it is significant that when he was not around to direct, a dull adherence to beat would often return.[116] Irina Baronova, rehearsing the Prelude for a lecture-demonstration, pointed out moments where the movement should be slightly delayed after its related beat: she asked her dancer to land an *assemblé* just after the moment of beat, to step onto pointe just after the note in order to give the impression of sustaining the suspension longer.[117] Fokine said about this dance: 'Please listen to the music, let it tell you what to do. Let it carry you in its arms.'[118] As Alicia Markova points out, Fokine wanted the effect to be spontaneous.[119] Duncan, 'the first to run, hesitate, turn, and yield to Chopin,' must surely have touched him (see p. 25). The style of *Les Sylphides* is a style of listening and responding to, or echoing, the music, dancing to 'the call of the note',[120] the effect improvisatory. Thus, the dancer lets the audience know that the music prompts performance of the dance, an interpretative stage beyond the actual steps. With this effect, despite fairly predictable structural relationships between music and dance, *Les Sylphides* comes alive and looks unpredictable.

This kind of performance style also removes the danger of what was perceived by some as mechanical Dalcrozism in Fokine's work. In fact, Fokine speaks out in his autobiography against mechanical approaches to music. He refers specifically to the problem posed by complex musical rhythms that had to be counted in order to be accurately danced. He sounds conservative as he questions the need for such rhythms and asks for a more repetitious, authentic musical style for national dances; he criticises the *Petrushka* Finale, which had presented major hurdles to the Ballets Russes dancers, totally unused to this level of musical difficulty. But Fokine has a point: he wants his dancers to be bonded with their music, through intense listening, as in *Les Sylphides*, to be completely immersed in its spirit and drive:

> One of the elementary characteristics of the dance is the pleasure derived from the repetition of the movements, and a typical characteristic of any national dance is the repetitious order of its rhythm . . . Heaven forbid that I should set a rule once and for all! What I should like to suggest is this: changing of rhythms without plausible necessity amounts to thrusting a spoke in the dancers' wheel.[121]

Fokine is most well known for his Diaghilev ballets, a number of them to commissioned scores, some of them taken into the Ballets Russes repertory after earlier performance in Russia. His later works were set mostly to existing music, some with an additional element of narrative or character, as their titles suggest. Bold in using large-scale, symphonic scores, he created, for instance, *Les Elfes* (1924), a plotless ballet using not only Mendelssohn's *Midsummer Night's Dream* Overture (see p. 31), but also the second and third movement of his Violin Concerto – he had used Mendelssohn's *Dream* music once before, in 1906; *Medusa* (1924) to Tchaikovsky's *Pathétique* Symphony; *Fra Mino* (1925) set to Schumann's Symphonic Études and based on 'The Saintly Satyr' by Anatole France; *Les Eléments* (1937), to Bach's B-minor Overture, a plotless ballet, but with characters from Greek mythology and figures representing the elements. It is also noteworthy that Fokine collaborated with Rachmaninov on a late ballet, *Paganini* (1939). He consulted the composer about the plot and used the recently composed *Rhapsody* with musical modifications made specially for the ballet: two Variations repeated, one of these, the eighteenth, brought back at the end of the score, half a tone higher than at its first appearance.[122]

Vaslav Nijinsky

Following Fokine in the Ballets Russes, Nijinsky (1890–1950) has long been dogged by his image as an inspired but undisciplined choreographer, unable to communicate his thoughts in rehearsal, a genius of a dancer, later to suffer mental breakdown. His reputation as a choreographer rests on his four Diaghilev ballets *L'Après-midi d'un faune* (Debussy, 1912), *Le Sacre du printemps* (Stravinsky, 1913), *Jeux* (Debussy, 1913) and *Till Eulenspiegel* (Richard Strauss, 1916), a highly controversial quartet. But it is probably Stravinsky's comments about his choreography for *Le Sacre* and his musical incompetence that assured the subsequent negative view of Nijinsky's creativity, supported by Debussy's contempt when he used his music.[123] Stravinsky later recanted, but by then Nijinsky's poor reputation had become received opinion, at any rate within the music world.

Recent reconstructions of the four Nijinsky ballets for the Ballet Russes have led to a radical reassessment of his contribution, not least revealing a very distinctive musicality, way ahead of its time. Of special importance to this reassessment are the two reconstructions by Ann Hutchinson Guest and Claudia Jeschke in 1989 of his *L'Après-midi d'un faune* and by Millicent Hodson and Kenneth Archer in 1987 of his *Le Sacre du printemps*.[124] The former was based on a decoding of Nijinsky's own notation of the work, which reveals immediately an analytical and rhythmically acute mind. Nijinska, his sister, indicates in her memoirs that Nijinsky was musically educated, indeed remarkably able musically. She recounts how they both studied the piano at the Imperial Ballet School in Russia, but that as a child 'he could play any musical instrument that he came across. Without any lessons he had been able to play his brother's accordion, clarinet, and flute.'[125] She also recalls his 'unusual talent of being able to hold perfectly in his memory a piece of music he had heard only a few times.'[126]

Faune, Nijinsky's first choreography, was already a breakthrough in musical terms, quite apart from its new two-dimensional movement style, with the Faun and nymphs moving as if in grooves across the stage, feet parallel, hips and faces towards the wings, upper bodies twisted towards the audience.[127] Frequently alluded to both at the time of the premiere and later are the disjunctive relationships between music and dance. Nijinsky had already noted in an interview prior to the premiere that his choreography would not adhere 'very tightly to the music'.[128] Just arrived from the Dalcroze school, Rambert was, not surprisingly, shocked by 'the discrepancy between the impressionistic music of Debussy and Nijinsky's absolute austerity of style',[129] while Fokine on the other hand praised Nijinsky precisely for the moments of 'resisting any movement despite the apparent demands of the agitated measures of the music'.[130] Hugo von Hoffmannsthal points out the crucial difference between Fokine's approach in *Carnaval* and Nijinsky's in this

severe, earnest, rhythmically restrained pantomime to a piece of music by Debussy, which is well known to all. But this music is by no means the key to this ballet, as perhaps Schumann's *Carnaval* is the key – and a sure-fitting key – to the ballet *Carnaval*. *Carnaval* always seems to flow on as an improvisation on the music. But with the severe inward strength of Nijinsky's short scene, Debussy's music seems to fade away gradually till it becomes merely the accompanying element – a something in the atmosphere, but not the atmosphere itself.[131]

Many years later, Richard Buckle was able to assess the work within the historical tradition of musical-choreographic practice, observing a brand new freedom of relationship and that 'a step had been taken which might lead to dancing without any musical accompaniment at all'.[132]

In fact, the freedom of relationship is not at all casual, as the precise timing in Nijinsky's notation demonstrates. Walking nearly always fits the pulse. Yet the effect is free, and it is revealing that the dancer Lydia Sokolova remembers the feeling of walking across the music.[133] Then, there are the nervous, jerky starts of the Faun, a quick turn of the neck as if listening, a sudden stretch of the neck indicating alertness, or more pronounced physical accents as he laughs or abruptly confronts one of the nymphs. None of these 'moments' relates to a stressed moment in the music. Nor does the single jump in the ballet, which occurs in the duet with the chief nymph, suddenly out of nowhere. Yet, at other times, there are scurries to musical scurries, repetitions to musical repetitions. The work mixes harmonious relationships with disjunction.

More important than this, *Faune* was seen to stretch the boundaries of artistic coherence, as Rambert observed, 'an absolute austerity of style' opposing 'impressionistic music'. Debussy himself was most unhappy with this disparity, provoked by Nijinsky's

marionettes . . . figures cut from pasteboard . . . Imagine if you can the discrepancy between a sinuous, soothing, flexible musical line on the one hand, and on the other a performance whose characters move like those on Greek or Etruscan vases, ungracefully, rigidly, as though their every gestures were constricted by the laws of plane geometry. So profound a dissonance can know no resolution.[134]

We are referring here to two different aesthetics. Debussy's work was bound up with artistic movements of the nineteenth century, particularly symbolism, and to some extent the related pre-Raphaelite and art nouveau movements. The much younger Nijinsky developed his artistic sensibility at a time of critical change in the arts, and a number of writers have now situated him securely within twentieth-century tradition. He was already acquainted with the latest advances in the visual arts, the shift towards a new objectivity and distancing of the viewer to encourage a more analytical attention (see p. 19). Interviewed before the premiere, Nijinsky and Diaghilev came straight out with the explanation that *Faune* was cubist theory applied to choreography.[135]

However, *Faune*'s disjunctions between music and dance are another means of defining this new modernist objectivity, perhaps the most important means. It is as if Nijinsky pre-empts Brecht's repudiation of the Wagnerian principle, his railing against the 'witchcraft' of artistic fusion (see p. 19). The climactic moment of stillness between Faun and chief nymph is a shock moment that draws attention to device, the switch from the visual to the aural; as much as the music swells from pianissimo and envelops us with its 'witchcraft', the angularity, the stillness and then very slow bowing and rising of the nymph dissociates us from it, pulls against its emotional power. *Faune* is a dual experience, seductive, certainly to many viewers at the time, but also distancing, and even looking forward to the aesthetic of Merce Cunningham (see p. 20).

Debussy and many critics observed artistic disjunction again in *Jeux* (1913),[136] although, by this time, the disjunction was of a different kind. Nijinsky had been influenced by Dalcroze (see p. 28), and he used the rhythm and pulse of the commissioned score as a basis for movement, which included the stressed movements of sport. The ballet suggested amorous encounters between three tennis players searching for a lost ball at twilight. It is likely here that the dynamic weightings of music and dance conflicted, Nijinsky having rehearsed to piano, not comprehending Debussy's shimmering 'orchestra without feet' until the orchestral rehearsals (see p. 9).

Meanwhile, Nijinsky had embarked on the choreography for *Le Sacre*, in which the variety and sophistication of musical-choreographic relationships is astonishing. The relationship with the Dalcroze method here is worth teasing out. Even before Rambert's appointment to the Ballets Russes to help him with this piece, Nijinsky had begun working on the Sacrificial Dance. According to Nijinska, who danced for him, he followed the 'breath' of the music, in precise co-ordination with the music. He 'did not "graphically" render each musical note by a physical movement', nor did he count the beats aloud as he did later when heavily influenced by the Dalcroze system.[137]

The rest of *Le Sacre* shows both regular, strict visualisation of musical structure and rhythmic counterpoint (see Ch. 2, pp. 87–8), another aspect of the Dalcroze method. I am basing my analysis on the meticulous reconstruction of the choreography by Millicent Hodson. A clear example of Dalcroze visualisation within the human body occurs near the beginning, in The Augurs of Spring (from [13] in the musical score). The men jump, making an accent on every four beats, the first metrical accent of each bar (which Stravinsky calls the 'tonic' accent[138]), while their arms and upper body move in dislocated opposition to the legs with the irregular, marked, dynamic accents in the music. The rhythmic structure of the music is thus visualised within the body here, the look of the score with its bar-lines as well as what is most readily heard (see Ex. 1.1).

There is no other example of such detailed mimicry within the body in *Le Sacre*, although there are a number of occasions when a multi-stranded musical texture is demonstrated by different groups of dancers. Hodson suggests that Nijinsky worked in minute detail with the music early on in the process of creating the choreography, but realised the impossibility of filling the piece with such complication, for reasons of time, the capabilities of the dancers, and so on.[139] Visualisation of the music, she suggests, might also have been prompted by another source, the Slav tradition of ritual dance, in which details of sound and motion combine together to create a greater ritual force.[140]

Some critics noticed other links in *Le Sacre* between orchestration, costume colour and arrangement of dancers. Propert, for instance: 'The scarlet groups would instantly dominate the stage in some passage of horns and trumpets, while violins or flutes carried the sense of white or grey, of orderly ritual or wavering uncertainty.'[141] The *Times* critic commented on the transition passage between the Ritual of Abduction and Spring Rounds: 'the dancers thin out into a straggling line, while the orchestra dwindles to a trill on the flutes; then a little tune begins in the woodwind two octaves apart, and two groups of three people detach themselves from either end of the line to begin a little dance that exactly suits the music.'[142]

When introducing counterpoint against the music, Nijinsky maintained firm contact with the musical pulse. He arranged his choreography independently in terms of metre and phrases (see Ch. 2, pp. 87–8): dance counts operate differently from the counts suggested in the musical score. Stravinsky remarked on this disparity in his notes on the choreographic indications in his four-hand piano score.[143] It was the kind of disparity already embedded within his own

Ex 1.1. Stravinsky, *Le Sacre du printemps*.

polyrhythmic music (music with different rhythmic systems operating simultaneously). For instance, near the beginning of the Second Part, Mystic Circles
of the Young Girls, the women form circles, sometimes responding to the entry
of an instrumental group, but operating in independent rhythmic systems. They
dance in units of 5, 3 and 2 counts (from 5 bars after [93] to [97]). The initial
flute melody creates the impression of 5/4 or, in dance language, '5-count'
metre; the accompanying strings are organised in 3/4, '3-count' units. Nijinsky
might well have been prompted by this organisation, even through the barring
in the score does not reveal either of these musical strands. But after this, Nijinsky develops his choreography independently of both the sound and look of the
score. To complicate matters further, there are canons and several lines of dance
polyphony. Arms shoot up at different times in a criss-cross of accents that have
nothing to do with the musical legato. Another example, before the Sacrificial
Dance of the Chosen One (at [135]): the women form an outer circle moving in
3-count units across the music, which shifts after one bar of 3/4 into 2/4 (and
against the rhythm of the circle of men inside).

In a section within the Spring Rounds (at [53]), Nijinsky's tactic was not only
to introduce counterpoint between dancing groups, but also to split up the musical phrase into units of one bar. He allocated each dancing group to bars of a
particular time signature, and gives each group a particular rhythmic role
within these bars. Thus, the breakdown of the passage, derived from a diagram
by Hodson,[144] is as follows, the counts indicating when the dancers move:

The layout of the music:

1	2	3	4	5	6	7	8	9	10	11
4/4	4/4	4/4	5/4	4/4	3/4	4/4	4/4	3/4	4/4	4/4

First unit: Young women (blue)   Dropping the upper body to the floor and then
slowly unfolding
1, 2, 3, 4 for each bar of 4/4 (bars 1, 2, 3, 5, 7, 8, 10)

Second unit: Adolescents (red)   The same movement as the women in blue
–, 2, 3, 4/ 1 (following bar) of bars of 4/4 (bars 1, 2, 3, 5, 7, 8, 10) (leaving the
first beat as a rest, thus in syncopation with the women in blue)

Third unit: Women (purple, with tall hats)   Two high step forwards
–, 2,3 of each bar of 3/4 (bars 6,9)
(no one moves on the first beat of each bar of 3/4, creating a rest here)

Fourth unit: Young People and Young Men
–, –, –, –, (and) 5 (and) of the 5/4 bar (bar 4) and

–, –, –, (and) 4 (and) of two bars of 4/4 (bars 8 and 10)
(Rambert marked these bars (in her piano score) for the percussive syncopated plunge forwards of the men)

Fifth unit: Adolescents   Accents, pulling the arms alternately upwards and down towards the floor
1,–, –, – of each bar of 4/4 (bars 1, 2, 3, 5, 7, 8, 10)

Unison: All (bar 11)

Counterpoint in *Le Sacre* furthers the ritual expressiveness of the piece. Like cogs in a machine, the dancing groups work independently but in precise co-ordination. There is nothing haphazard here as they interlock with each other, pulse to pulse, drawing together in affirmative unison, their power all the greater from the parts assembling into a whole. The machine imagery is significant. Jacques Rivière noted it in his famous review of *Le Sacre*, and it also reflects the fact that Nijinsky saw *Le Sacre* as both deeply embedded in ancient ritual and as the expression of contemporary humanity.[145] The dichotomy of primitive and machine is the modernist dichotomy here, and, in musical terms, the ballet looks towards the motoric, pulse-driven work that Stravinsky was later to inspire from Balanchine.

Le Sacre is an extraordinary achievement musically: to work in so detailed and precise a manner with such a complex score, and without prior training of choreographer or dancers in this manner of working. Here was a new kind of music for dance and a new interaction between dance and music. Quite possibly, the piece looked fussy, too pernickety in musical response, to some contemporary viewers. Thus, the critic Edwin Evans saw 'evidence of industry rather than of musical feeling'.[146] Today, the choreography appears both powerful as ritual reference and extraordinarily rich in its musical treatment.

Faune was an important forerunner in terms of contrapuntal possibilities, but, as the *Times* critic noted, with its percussive violence of style in both music and dance, pulse joining pulse, *Le Sacre* produced a new fusion, 'a new compound result, expressible in terms of rhythm'.[147] That same critic too was unusual in his understanding of Nijinsky's choral polyphony, which, modelled on musical polyphony, set a powerful precedent to later textural developments in choreography. It was none too complex for him, even if it was for Evans, and he, at last, was positive about the Dalcroze connection: 'M. Nijinsky joins hands with M. Jacques Dalcroze; and it is in this direction that his theories on ballet are capable of indefinite expansion.'[148]

Bronislava Nijinska

Nijinsky's *Le Sacre* and *Jeux* were important to the choreographic career of his sister Nijinska (1891–1972). She played a key role in their creation, and in *Faune*, witnessing too the introduction of Dalcroze technique to the Ballets Russes, before embarking upon her own work as a choreographer. She left the Ballets Russes for a seven-year period in Russia from 1914 to 1921. In sympathy with the tendencies of her brother, Nijinska allied herself there to the constructivist movement, which focused on the expressive capabilities of geometrical forms, and she collaborated with the constructivist artist Alexandra Exter.

Between 1919 and 1921, Nijinska ran her own École de Mouvement in Kiev, and made a series of short works as experiments in abstract choreography, most of them to pieces by Liszt (*Études*, *Mephisto Valse* and *Twelfth Rhapsody)* and Chopin (*Nocturne*, *Prélude* and *Marche Funèbre*). One piece, *Fear*, was a solo in silence.[149] At the same time, she wrote a treatise that proclaimed the values of movement in its own right, and, indeed, this was the beginning of a number of statements in which she diminished the centrality of the ballet libretto.[150] In this respect, she considered herself different from Diaghilev in aesthetic, for, although she kept a narrative element in a number of ballets, Nijinska concentrated her attentions on movement development and its structuring in space, time and to music.[151] Not surprisingly, Fokine's *Les Sylphides* was an important precedent: 'the basis of my creative work, to influence all my artistic activity' (see pp. 33–5).

Nijinska was able to draw on a musical background, having studied piano, like Nijinsky, at the Imperial Ballet School in St Petersburg.[152] Ashton and de Valois both recalled her ability to analyse music in detail, and that she gave counts to the dancers. De Valois, who danced in *Les Noces* (1923), remembers with admiration that Nijinska took along the score 'with the ballet worked out on it'.[153] Greatly influenced by Nijinska (though not by her analytical approach to music), Ashton has mentioned her lively musical choices for ballet class, often an opportunity for trying out choreographic ideas: 'one day all Bach, then another day Chopin, or tangos'.[154]

Nijinska usually choreographed to existing musical scores, but she worked on new ballet scores on a number of occasions. Most notable were those of Stravinsky – *Le Baiser de la fée* (1928) for the Ida Rubinstein company, and the first ballet productions of *Le Renard* (1922) and *Les Noces* (1923) – and of Ravel – *Bolero* (1928) for the Rubinstein company, and she also choreographed an early ballet production of his *La Valse* (1929, rechoreographed 1931). One of her most famous works, *Les Biches* (1924), was created to a commissioned score by Poulenc. Chopin remained a favourite composer, inspiring her experiments in Kiev, later, her *Chopin Concerto*, a modernist evocation of *Les Sylphides* created for the Polish Ballet in 1937 (to the first concerto in E minor), and finally *In Memoriam* for the centenary of Chopin's death in 1949. A piece that she restaged on a number of occasions for different numbers of dancers was *Holy Études*, first set in 1925 to excerpts from Bach's Brandenburg Concertos and suites, later renamed simply *Étude*. Perhaps her frequent return to this work indicates its importance to her, despite the fact that, in the early days, the idea of choreographing to Bach was criticised. The dance evoked the style of ancient icons, the movement highly formalised, and dressed in Exter's silk tunics, capes and halo-like headpieces.

Some of these pieces use musical titles, but this does not necessarily mean absence of narrative content. *Variations* (1932) used selected Themes and Variations by Beethoven (orchestrated by Vladimir Pohl). There was no developed plot, but its three sections, Thème Pyrrhique, Thème Pastorale, and Thème Pathétique, evoked 'three historical epochs – classical Greece, Russia at the time of Alexander I, and France at the beginning of the Second Empire – linked together by a vague political thread that commented on the rise and fall of civilization.'[155] The *Brahms Variations* (1944, orchestrated by Ivan Boutnikov) was a lengthy construction using both the Handel and Paganini sets of Variations, but it was also billed as a ballet in two scenes, with a mythological theme (including characters such as Diana and Apollo).

The use of musical titles perhaps betrays Nijinska's belief that dance, like music, could function 'symphonically', meaning that movement could create its own forms and sustain these across broad canvases of time. Music provided a useful model, hence Nijinska used musical terminology. In an article in *The Dancing Times* in 1937, she wrote:

> *Noces* was the first work where the libretto was a hidden theme for a pure choregraphy: it was a choregraphic concerto.
>
> The work which I had done in Russia, together with *Noces* and *Biches* produced for Diaghileff, was as a foundation. These were the beginning of a long series of ballets in the form of a choregraphic symphony, sonata, étude, or concerto.[156]

She lists a number of works of this kind – *Étude*, *Les Rencontres* (Ibert, 1925), *Bolero*, *Nocturne* (Borodin, 1928), *La Valse*, *Capriccio Espagnol* (Rimsky-Korsakov, 1931), and *Variations*. Other statements are curious. Nijinska used large-scale musical forms, the concerto on two occasions, for plotless ballets, the Chopin and the *Schumann Concerto*, created for Ballet Theatre in 1951. Yet in the same 1937 article, the same year that she set the Chopin concerto, she speaks out against use of the musical symphony in a claim that dance should hold sway

n the organisation of large structures. Dance, in other words, should develop
symphonic structures of its own.

> In creating the choregraphic symphony, I did not choose a musical symphony
> for my music, for I did not care to bind myself to the already fixed ideas and
> form of the musician. That is why I took three themes and variations from
> Beethoven which answered to my concept for my choregraphic symphony
> *Variations* (1932). The choregraphic symphony and the musical symphony
> have each of them their independent formation of its idea. A musical sym-
> phony as a complete and independent composition does not demand, it seems
> to me, the supplement of any imagery. For that reason it is particularly dan-
> gerous to attempt to take advantage of a musical symphony for the interpre-
> tation of distinct choregraphic ideas.[157]

s Nijinska singling out the musical symphony as a special case, different from
he concerto? The question is raised, because when she talks about her selection
of Beethoven's themes and variations, she seems to be making a general statement about needing to mould her own structures.

In using musical structure, Nijinska was intent on negotiating a precise relationship, just as Nijinsky had done, whilst not attempting constant, detailed
matching in dance. Near the end of her life, looking back on her approach in *Les
Noces*, it sounds as if she is rejecting rigid Dalcroze technique for freer solutions:

> As to the question of choreographic interpretation of the music, the aca-
> demic idea of solely imitating the complicated and asymmetrical rhythms
> and measures in Stravinsky's music, by marking in the dance the strict time
> of the measure or the fractions, by adapting the pas to them, was not an issue
> for me, as it seemed not only inapplicable, but also a dancing absurdity.

nstead, she developed a broader conception of relationship:

> In bringing several musical measures together into a whole, I was creating a
> choreographic measure [in other words, she was choreographing to the mu-
> sical phrase] . . . The choreography appeared to me to have its own 'voice'.[158]

Yet, it seems that Nijinska was nevertheless committed to a concept of unity, the
'complementing' and 'blending' of parts: 'I listen to music through my eyes, so if
you would close your ears you could still hear the music – you could see the
music.'[159]

In *Les Noces*, the relationships between dance and music are unpredictable,
ranging between tight visualisation of percussive rhythm pattern and accent to

independent dance passages of adagio against this style of music, smooth movement into sustained sculptural groupings. When Nijinska does choreograph to the musical rhythms, there is always the same intense attachment to pulse and motor drive as in *Le Sacre*, but there is counterpoint as much as visualisation, patterns that cross the musical accentuation as well as reinforce it. In the opening section, for instance, 'At the Bride's House – Tresses', where the women form a line with the Bride in the centre, the irregular accents of *fondu-dégagé* between *bourrées* and steps on pointe sometimes match the brutal, percussive musical accents, sometimes force their way between these sounds. Furthermore, the dance accents do not correspond with the eccentric irregular barring of the music. The look of the score here does not relate to the musical accents that are actually heard. Nijinska must have been aware of this as she read the score.

Nijinska's other most celebrated ballet, *Les Biches*, also prints out pulse with clarity, and often plainly, ranging from the light stalking on pointe by the women to the plodding steps of the male athletes. Yet the dance material is again asymmetrical in phrasing, units shortened, lengthened or varied to shift emphases into unexpected places – and, besides this, Poulenc's score is already shot through with moments of rhythmic imbalance. One of the major ironies of this choreography stems from these subtle rhythmic twists.

Dancers and critics observed the visualisation of orchestration and phrase structures in early performances of *Chopin Concerto*.[160] Yet, given the likelihood that people remember and exaggerate the importance of moments of parallel relationship between music and dance, it could well be that this work contained at least something of the same play with and against music that we see in *Les Noces*.

Fyodor Lopukhov and Contemporary Soviet Developments

Of those choreographers who continued working in Russia, an interesting figure is Fyodor Lopukhov (1886–1973), as the avant-garde director of ballet at the Maryinsky from 1922 to 1930. To date in the West, we know about his work largely through Balanchine's comments (he danced in Lopukhov's work) and writings published in English by Russian authors. Across his career, most of his ballets are narrative in some respect, based on contemporary, *commedia* and folklore themes, and he is known for developing the acrobatic aspects of ballet style. However, of particular importance here are his experiments in dance abstraction and his reliance on music as primary force in his one-off experiment *The Dance Symphony: The Magnificence of the Universe* (1923) set to Beethoven's Fourth Symphony. This ballet has acquired enormous significance in dance history, especially surprising as it was performed only once.

Balanchine spoke highly of Lopukhov from his own experience in *The Dance Symphony*.[161]

As early as 1916, Lopukhov tried to create 'orchestral' choreography in *The Dream* (music by Nikolai Shcherbachev). Here were the seeds of later work. He tried to 'harmonize with the sounds of the various instruments of the orchestra and with the course of the theme – the leitmotif, sub-theme, counterpoint, harmonic changes, etc.'[162] According to Lopukhov, in the same year, 1916, he wrote his manifesto *A Choreographer's Paths* (published in 1925), with major sections on the relationships between music and dance, and an outline of his plans for the future *Dance Symphony*. Lopukhov is much more inclined towards formalism and abstraction than Fokine, although he pays special tribute to this choreographer. In *Sixty Years in Ballet*, he says that he had first been inspired by the example of Fokine's *Les Préludes* (1913) (see pp. 30–1). This work, with its generalised theme of man's struggle between life and death had persuaded him of the possibilities of plotless symphonic choreography.[163] The interest in formal aspects is also evident from Lopukhov's revivals and preservation of the Petipa legacy.

In his special chapter on symphonic dance, Lopukhov maintained that, next to the classics, there should be

> dance symphonies, with dance dominant, dance free of the close limitations of the story and accessories with which old ballets were encumbered. The art of dancing is great for the very reason that it is capable of conveying by itself, through the medium of choreography, a situation and surroundings that are in reality unseen, but felt. The art of dancing is capable of making the spectator experience such phenomena as wind or lightning far more strongly than scenic illusions of the same things.[164]

However, if the emphasis was on the essence of dance, music was still seen as the necessary complement to the development of this self-sufficient dance. Lopukhov wrote that the choreographer must begin his work by studying the orchestral parts and getting to know the intricacies of instrumentation. This, he believed, had not been a necessity for Petipa and those before him – in those days, most ballet music was sufficiently well treated by simply knowing the rehearsal *répétiteur* for piano and two violins. However, Tchaikovsky's more complex music called for a change in approach. Fokine, according to Lopukhov, was the first to make a special study of the details of the orchestral score;[165] we recall that he had had experience of writing out individual orchestral parts for his balalaika orchestra (see p. 32). Lopukhov himself was coached for a year in the art of score reading by the conductor Emile Cooper.[166]

Lopukhov's theory for relating music and dance includes the following:

1. Choreographic themes should be worked out like musical themes on the principle of antagonism, parallel development and contrast, not on the principle of stringing together casual steps. 2. Movements and music are linked together by the discipline of rhythm ... Dance should flow from the music and they should both speak of the same things. Music that depicts soaring can't be bound to a choreographic theme of *crawling*, even though the dance and the music passages are identical rhythmically.

The musical curve should coincide with the dance curve ...

It is possible to convey choreographically the change in musical tonality that the major key should correspond to *en dehors* movements, and the minor to *en dedans* ...

A ballet step properly used is capable, even when performed *sur place*, of conveying the quality of transient sonorities.[167]

This is what Lopukhov meant by 'dances in the image of music', rather than 'with music', 'to the accompaniment of music' or 'set to music',[168] reminding us of Sakharoff's similar distinctions in 1943 (see p. 15) and of early-century concepts of the wholeness of artistic experience (see pp. 15–19).

When it eventually materialised, Lopukhov's *Dance Symphony* pursued a broad cosmic and humanist theme, perhaps an outcome of the massive political upheavals of the time, perhaps too reflecting the mystical strand that was important in Russian developments towards abstraction.[169] However, the reality was formal statement rather than developed plot. There were the following sections.

First movement: Introduction: The Birth of Light – The Birth of the Sun
    Life in Death and Death in Life
Second slow movement: Thermal Energy
Third movement, scherzo: The Joy of Existence
Fourth movement: Eternal Motion

The choice of Beethoven for his *Dance Symphony* is not surprising, given Beethoven's popularity in post-revolutionary Russia, although musicologists disagreed that the theme of the choreography was a suitable one to match with this symphony.[170] Others objected to the abstruse programme theme in relation to the radical abstraction of the choreography, and the ballet suffered an extremely hostile reception. Lopukhov never ventured another ballet of this kind although Elizabeth Souritz tells us that he had plans to set other symphonies, Beethoven's Fifth, Tchaikovsky's Fourth, and Liszt's Faust Symphony. *The Dance Symphony* remains isolated in early twentieth-century Russian tradition, but a forerunner of the symphonic ballets of other choreographers such as Massine and Balanchine.

There is an interesting connection here again with the Dalcroze tradition, in the visualisation within the body of details of musical structure and especially part-writing. In *A Choreographer's Paths*, Lopukhov professes his reservations about the Dalcroze method, which he considered too mechanical.[171] Yet, he describes the choreography of the Infernal Dance in his version of *The Firebird* (1921): 'where the legs of the dancers did the *pas de basque* to a two-beat measure while the arms moved to three beats'. Danilova recalls a similar counterpoint in *The Dance Symphony*. Reviewers at the time criticised the choreographer's style for its reference to the inevitable 'rhythmic gymnastics' and oppressively strict parallelism with the music.[172] Lopukhov, like others, undoubtedly found the Dalcroze approach liberating at a time when new abstract dance forms needed to be created.

Other contemporary Soviet choreographers were more or less deeply engaged by the new ideas about use of music in dance. The Dalcroze method attracted wide interest: a school in St Petersburg was established soon after the first lecture-demonstrations there in 1912 (see p. 26). Others responded to the ideas of Duncan: numerous Duncan-based studios were in operation during the experimental 1920s in the Soviet Union. It is interesting too that the Imperial Ballet School introduced a wider arts curriculum in 1919, including the 'Listening to Music' course led by the composer Strelnikov; a number of celebrated artists and musicians were invited there to teach.[173] There was a particular interest in the music of Scriabin, in whose music an appropriate revolutionary fervour was detected. To his music were set pieces by Lev Lukin, Alexander Gorsky, representatives of various schools of free dance, as well as Kasian Goleizovsky (another influence on Balanchine), for instance, his *The Sonata of Death and Movement* (1918) to Scriabin's tenth Piano Sonata.[174]

Gorsky's choreographic style was more dramatically and realistically inclined than that of Lopukhov: he tended not to explore music in terms of structural correspondence.[175] However, in some respects, he pre-empted Lopukhov's symphonic practice. He created a much earlier work of this kind, the *Fifth Symphony* to Glazunov (1916), in which he introduced a plot about life in ancient Greece. His *En Blanc* (1918), to Tchaikovsky's Third Suite, was an abstract work, of special interest to the choreographer, who continued to work on it, including it in *An Evening of Symphonic Ballet* (1921), a studio performance that also comprised settings of Liszt's Second Rhapsody and Weber's *Invitation to the Dance*.[176] However, for whatever reason, these Gorsky ballets have never been considered significant to the same degree as Lopukhov's *The Dance Symphony*.

Like Lopukhov, Gorsky's more abstract, musically-led experiments were discouraged, and the later socialist realist philosophies prevented any reversal of original attitudes for some time. Igor Belsky's *Leningrad Symphony* (1961) to Shostakovich represents a return to the symphonic ballet in a later period, when political change admitted the return of ballets set to symphonies and other forms of instrumental music not written for dance.

Léonide Massine

Choreartium (1933), the symphonic ballet to Brahms' Fourth Symphony by Massine (1895–1979), provoked a massive musical controversy. It inspired the fury of the British music scholar and critic Jack Westrup, who considered it an outrage to 'the purity and integrity of a musical composition'.[177] A music-loving member of the public wrote in: 'Why put sensitive musicians to torture?'[178] Then, in his article, 'Massine's Little Miscalculation of the Eloquence of Legs', another critic, Richard Capell, considered that

> The acceptance of these symphony-ballets is a sign of a musically uncultivated community. . . Into the first movement of the E minor Massine reads the pursuit of a nymph by a pirate; into the second, a kind of eurhythmic class in a nunnery, with the abbess as drill-mistress! . . . Never to be forgiven is the absurdity of the succession of pirouettes performed by a row of young men on the sforzando E's in the ninth and following bars of the Passacaglia.[179]

It was left to Ernest Newman, the critic, and, significantly, a Wagner scholar (for he likened the symphonic ballet debate to that between Hanslick and Wagner in the nineteenth century), to indicate the hierarchy of composers here. No problem was envisaged with the *Symphonie fantastique* (1936), for instance:

> Berlioz has never been, among 'sensitive musicians,' the Sacred Person, the sort of Grand Lama of Music, that Brahms has always been to certain communities in this country.
> Even people who had looked indulgently on 'Presages,' because the music was only by a fellow called Tchaikovski [the Fifth Symphony, premiered earlier in 1933] demanded something with boiling oil in it for Massine when he dared to touch Brahms: it was like laying profane hands on the ark of the covenant. When it comes to Beethoven [*Seventh Symphony*, 1938], of course we are within measurable distance of the sin against the Holy Ghost.[180]

These quotations illustrate an extreme example of controversy over use of existing music in ballet, one that provoked not only individual articles and letters in the press by music and ballet critics, but substantial essays and books (one by Anatole Chujoy, the other a publication of collected writings by Newman[181]) devoted to symphonic ballet. It is these ballets that will be the focus here in a discussion of Massine's work, as they were in their time the most ground-breaking in terms of statement about music.

Massine produced these big ballets at the peak of his career after his formative years with Diaghilev, for the Ballet Russe de Monte Carlo and Original Ballet Russe, by which time he was an internationally renowned choreographer. In 1940, as his star was beginning to fade and opportunities to create more such ballets became less frequent, Massine admitted how important his series of symphonic ballets had been to him. They were, he said, 'what most of all interests me'.[182] The ballets are:

Les Présages, 1933 (Tchaikovsky No. 5)
Choreartium, 1933 (Brahms No. 4)
Symphonie Fantastique, 1936 (Berlioz)
Seventh Symphony, 1938 (Beethoven)
Rouge et Noir, 1939 (Shostakovich No. 1)
Labyrinth, 1941 (Schubert No. 9)
Antar, 1945 (Rimsky-Korsakov No. 2)
Leningrad Symphony, 1945 (Shostakovich No. 7, first movement only)
Clock Symphony, 1948 (Haydn, created for the Sadler's Wells Ballet)
Harold in Italy, 1954 (Berlioz)[183]

All these ballets except *Clock Symphony* use the theme of Man and Destiny, the drama between good and evil. For instance, *Les Présages* is about Man's fight to overcome adversity, temptations and warlike forces, with a Fate figure entering to Tchaikovsky's theme of Fate: the Hero triumphs over Fate and the spirit of war at the end. *Symphonie fantastique* borrows Berlioz's programme of the Poet in opium-induced dream, haunted by his Beloved, who turns from image of purity and love to witch, the final scene a Witches' Sabbath. In *Seventh Symphony*, Massine added a programme entirely of his own about the creation and destruction of the world.

Massine came from a musical background, both parents being professional musicians, while he himself learnt to play the violin and balalaika.[184] Under the auspices of Diaghilev's company, he was swept into the developing modernist movement that now placed design rather than music at the centre of a ballet and that warmly embraced both the chic and avant-garde of Paris. But the impetus for commissioning scores was still strong, and Massine worked with a string of notable composers, including Satie (*Parade*, 1917, *Mercure*, premiered at Les Soirées de Paris, 1924), Stravinsky (*Pulcinella*, *Le Chant du rossignol*, a remake of *Le Sacre du printemps*, all 1920), de Falla (*Le Tricorne*, 1919), and Prokofiev (*Le Pas d'acier*, 1927). There were also collaborations with a number of younger generation French composers, whom the choreographer continued to favour in later years. Massine was the choreographer of the time travelling, period-modernist ballets that used arrangements of music from the past, *Pulcinella* the most radical of these (see p. 20). Later, in 1938, he undertook an important collaboration with Hindemith, *Nobilissime visione*, a ballet about the life of St Francis of Assisi.

With the symphonic ballets, Massine rejected his folk interests, his brilliant characterisations and noisy futurist blasts for something more grand in scale and serious in tone. He capitalised upon the canonic hardening and aura of the great symphonies (see pp. 11–14). Ballets to symphonies would draw audiences and they would make ballet (and him as choreographer) look important. Aura was part of his content too. With a group of soloists and a dancing mass seen in both motion and huge sculptural configurations, the democratic deployment of dancers was a visual parallel to the democratic ideals that the symphony stood for: Theodore Thomas, conductor of the New York Philharmonic in the late nineteenth century, had preached that a symphony orchestra represented 'the culture of a community'.[185] Denby put it disparagingly: 'Like a cigarette company, he [Massine] is using famous names to advertise his wares'.[186] But it is over-simplistic to dismiss Massine as a showman. To some extent, the musical world went along with his cause. Bruno Walter tried to dissuade him from the approach,[187] but the symphonic ballets were performed with a number of major orchestras and under eminent conductors, like Thomas Beecham, Leopold Stokowski, Pierre Monteux, Eugene Goossens and Eugene Ormandy.

The main arguments against symphonic ballet can be summarised as follows: a piece of great music is self-sufficient, forming an organic whole; such music is too complex in its own internal workings for dance to match up to it; symphonic music is essentially a matter of the intellect and spirit, not the body; the composer never intended the music to be choreographed. Enthusiasts for symphonic ballet on the other hand argued that not only was it instrumental in bringing great music to a new public, but its large-scale organicism was an important advantage for ballet, helping to unify the form of the choreography, and providing a model for structuring plotless dance over a broad timespan.

Massine's second symphonic ballet, to Brahms' Fourth, was both the most controversial and the most radical, because of its particular shift towards abstraction, or rather, as we shall see, relative abstraction. It also poses interesting questions about the musical values of its period and its negotiation with these values.

It is possible to identify a number of ways in which Massine responded to Brahms' Fourth Symphony. It is very clear that the structural aspects of large-scale form, exposition, development and recapitulation, part-writing and counterpoint, contrasting themes and bridge passages, provided models for his own contribution. Massine was intensely analytical of musical structure through time, and of texture; his work is 'about' such things. Indeed, in these respects, he shared the formalist-modernist principles of many artists at the time, principles which were also paramount in musicological thinking, leading to a culture of abstract, formalist interpretations (see Foreword). The allusion by Capell to a 'eurhythmic class' is derogatory, but the architectural model of eurhythmics is embedded within *Choreartium*, and, as we shall see, it contributes to meaning. Form does not just express itself (see Ch. 2, pp. 66–8). The programme note for this ballet explains that 'it has neither theme nor story', and no characters are identified. Sometimes, there was no note at all. Many writers at the time emphasised that it was pure dance to music. However, from the outset, with its passionate gestures and facial expressions, *Choreartium* now seems thick with meaning, much more heavily laden with narrative than a good deal of Balanchine.

It is interesting that overlapping aesthetic forces existed in the 1930s. Modernism absorbed a number of different artistic impulses, and direct links with the nineteenth century remained. We recall that Tovey's programme notes still pursued the tradition of nineteenth-century narrative writing (see p. 12). There was a surge of neo-romanticism across the arts and a revival of interest in nineteenth-century romantic iconography and music; witness Massine's *Symphonie fantastique* and Ashton's *Apparitions* (Liszt, 1936).[188] As regards musical performance practice, there was still a group of conductors looking back to the nineteenth century in their emotional, brooding, 'sublime' performance styles, such as Furtwängler, Stokowski and Walter, alongside the drier modernist approaches of Stravinsky and Toscanini. It is fascinating to see which side Robert Sabin was on when he reviewed Massine's *Rouge et noir* in 1940. He was not against the principle of symphonic ballet, but he did have strong reservations about Massine's treatment of music. He described the slow movement:

> which takes on a sentimental and lugubrious character in the dance setting which it never had in its original guise . . . To one who has admired the elegiac melancholy and nobility of this music under Toscanini, the sight of a ballerina dripping emotion all over the stage of the Metropolitan induces savage thought.[189]

Massine clearly tended towards the romantic narrative view, according with the context of the later Ballet Russe companies, their mainly narrative repertory and emotional, 'vitalist' performing style; but he now realised this style in symphonic circumstances, in explorations of spirituality and associated messages. There are definite moods in *Choreartium*, suggestions of conflict and struggle, a will to strive and overcome, contrasting episodes of sorrowing and despair and brief light-heartedness. The hero who opens the ballet re-emerges during the last movement, alone and desperate during the final coda: he throws himself to the floor, his arm flung across his forehead (my evidence is from Tatiana Leskova's revival for Birmingham Royal Ballet, 1991).

Two critiques of the Brahms Symphony No. 4, one by a nineteenth-century writer Hermann Kretschmar (1887), the other by Tovey, emphasise the dark qualities of the symphony, a series of contrasting moods that point up the overridingly tragic, or sublimity-through-death statement. Kretschmar refers straightaway to an opening 'in a simple narrative tone' and, in true nineteenth-century spirit, to the 'natural sublimity' of the conclusion: 'The composition leads to the sphere where suffering and joy fall silent and that which is human bows before the eternal.'[190] Tovey is in no two minds about the tragic tone of the close: 'The hero is not fighting for his own happiness. He is to die fighting'.[191]

Massine's interpretation of the music also appears to stem from nineteenth-century-style narrative readings. His hero is held aloft at the very end beside two women soloists, one of several grand tableaux that feature in this ballet. A glance at the sublime? However, darkness is a major, stressed feature in the ballet. There is a group of men in black in the Passacaglia finale, sinister phalanxes making severe fighting gestures, not to mention the band of women and their leader in the second, slow movement, a bowed, lamenting chorus who occasionally burst into expressions of determination to overcome their grief. Massine does not go along with mainstream musical understanding of the narrative in this second movement, which tends to suggest lighter images of the pastoral, elegy and legend.

Massine's late romantic spirit is pressured, which is also revealed in his manner of negotiating with musical structure. He is heavily emphatic of the given. At the start, his 'panther-like'[192] hero visualises the question and answer and rise and fall of the melody, as he enters in passionate argument with a woman – 'the pursuit of a nymph by a pirate'. Soon, he is stamping, adding an insistent staccato edge to the musical notes, making them doubly emphatic. Thereafter, there is an overriding tendency to bring back dancers with associated musical themes, with the same or varied movement, to underline the reiteration of musical statement. Thus the leading pair of the first movement return regularly with their theme, alternating in leaps towards the chorus in the Coda, now as if in grim competition. The men who enter at the start of the last movement turn one by one in a line to the huge orchestral accents of brass and drums (we recall again the Capell review). Later, during a passage that sounds like a recapitulation built into this Passacaglia form, they appear multiplied in numbers, now turning in groups, one group after another.

By such emphasis on return and closure, Massine's statement seems to be bound rather than flowering organically in the romantic sense of Becoming. We might also consider that the recapitulation in nineteenth-century romantic music was already an ungainly, outmoded hangover from a classical past. It is as if Massine is desperately determined to make a point. Perhaps this is partly because he is so submissive to musical form in this work. However, as musical form itself speaks, Massine seems to use it to speak with an exaggerated insistence, which recalls the point that sonata first-movement form has been interpreted as a metaphor for authorial domination (see p. 67). Contrast the quiet solo flute variation in the last movement, which for Kretschmar 'creates the image of an unstable frame of mind'.[193] Massine makes it a solo for a woman (see p. 69), before the army of men returns with renewed force.

This tension within Massine's romanticism re-emerges in his programme note for *Labyrinth*, a symphonic ballet made in 1941 during the tumultuous events of World War II. Here, romanticism is seen in dialogue with classicism:

> In *Labyrinth* one revives the eternal myth of the aesthetic and ideologic confusion which characterizes romanticism, and especially, in the highest degree, that of our epoch. The 'thread of Ariadne', by which Theseus succeeds in finding the exit from the Labyrinth, symbolizes the thread of continuity of classicism – the saviour. All romanticism merely seeks more or less dramatically its 'thread of Ariadne', of classicism.

If Brahms' musical structures acted as a restraining device in *Choreartium*, provoking the formal impetus in the choreography and the meaning that that brings, Massine had already taken the liberty of making cuts in Tchaikovsky's music in the outer movements of *Les Présages* (according to Leskova's 1989 revival for the Paris Opéra Ballet). Perhaps here he wanted freedom for his dramatic impulse. *Symphonie fantastique* is a programmatic symphony with an *idée fixe* symbolising the appearances of the Beloved, so an evolving dramatic line already exists in the music here. It is not surprising then that Lambert welcomed this ballet, conforming as it did to his belief that music for ballet should express 'direct or present action' (see p. 14):

> This is undoubtedly the best of his 'symphonic ballets'. One of the reasons being that the music, apart from the first movement, is hardly symphonic at all; it is as programmatic as the music of *Thamar* [Balakirev] – if not more so – and thence lends itself to choreographic treatment far more successfully than the symphonies of Brahms or Tchaikovsky.[194]

Capell referred to a eurhythmic content in *Choreartium*: once again a critic is on the look-out for what he perceives as Dalcrozian connections with music. Yet we might consider here the differences between Massine's detailed approach to musical structure and that of other choreographers. Newman saw difference, preferring Massine's movement, more of an 'organic part of a large design', to Fokine's 'pointing' of the moment (see p. 31). In 1919, Massine had put himself on the line in a short published manifesto where he claimed that 'the correspondence between dancing and music must be created and found . . . and can be defined as a certain counterpoint to the musical design created by the composer.'[195] He speaks out against the principle shared by Nijinsky and Fokine of analogy between music and movement and is particularly critical of the extreme account of this principle in Nijinsky's *Le Sacre*. Later, during the time when Nijinsky was out of favour and condemned for his detailed imitation of musical structure, Stravinsky compares Massine's *Le Sacre* to that of Nijinsky. Massine's approach he saw as 'incomparably clearer'.[196] Comparing the two *Sacres* in 1922, although approving neither version, Levinson supports the notion of a difference in rhythmic density: 'Nijinsky's dancers were *hounded* by rhythm. Here [in Massine's ballet], they are relaxed in response to musical time, which, too often, simply eludes them.'[197] Later, Levinson is keen to communicate that Massine too can be guilty of fussy musicality, referring to his '*perpetuum mobile*, a movement falling on each note, a gesture on each semiquaver, a continual fidget to which we owe the breathless and spirited animation of *The Good-Humoured Ladies.*'[198]

Two long, striking passages of visualisation stand out in Massine's work. There is the third movement of *Symphonie fantastique*, In the Country, Lambert's favourite section in the ballet, where two shepherds play pipes matching the statement and answer of a lone English horn and oboe; to the *idée fixe*, the Beloved flies across the stage on wires; Wind creatures with wings run in as we hear a storm rise. Other characters on stage literally move to individual notes and musical gestures: the Musician, some picnickers, a deer. The tempo is slow enough for this step-for-note correspondence to be possible. It is too in the final section of *Nobilissime visione* where St Francis embraces a life of meditation and there is an affirmative fugue, the dancers *en masse* literally stepping out the emphatic melody line. This is extreme visualisation but highly effective in context.

My reading from revivals of *Les Présages* and *Choreartium* is that there are no passages that show the degree of rhythmic and textural intricacy of Nijinsky's *Le Sacre*. Massine absorbed the new ideas about choreographing musical structure into his personal style, and in the symphonic ballets this was both modernist in inclination and suffused with a late romantic emotionalism.

Escaping the Tyranny of Music

The initial drive to separate or free dance from music came from modern dance, not ballet (see pp. 19–20). For the moderns, there were passionate political imperatives to research a new kind of dance for a new freed body and a new freed woman, unencumbered by external restraining factors, whether formal or emotional in nature. Music, once read as liberating by Duncan, could now be read in quite the opposite way. The moderns were unwilling to submit to tyranny, including that of music.

Serge Lifar (1905–86) suggests an interesting link with modern dance, but the reasons for his theory of dance leading the creative process are less motivated by any politics beyond dance itself than they were for modern dance choreographers. Indeed, he is a conservative. Having studied at the Kiev Conservatory of Music and considered becoming a professional pianist,[199] Lifar turned to dance, joining the Diaghilev company in 1923 to become a star dancer and its last choreographer. Afterwards, he directed the ballet at the Paris Opéra for many years. Although he no longer enjoys a distinguished reputation as a choreographer, he nevertheless stands out for his strong, unusual theories of music and dance and for the controversy that they caused. Lifar's first major statement Le Manifeste du chorégraphe appeared in 1935, by which time Central European modern dance was well established, but he makes no reference to having learnt anything from the tradition.[200] An avid writer, Lifar continued on several later occasions to present his views on music and dance, and, for instance, a manifesto developed from his 1935 publication appeared in The Dancing Times in 1938.[201]

Lifar's thinking is as follows: that dance came first as an art, not music; the rhythms of much twentieth-century music are not only unsuited to dance, but are a destructive element; dance needs to develop along its own paths, away from the 'despotic yoke' of music, before the ideal synthesis of the arts can be attained; dance does not need musical accompaniment, and it must find its essential base, which is rhythmic, from dance, not music; the musician should create a score after the choreographer has composed the dance, just as a musician sets a piece of poetry after it has been written.[202] The last is one of the methods that modern dancers adopted, and Satie had apparently suggested the same to Massine in 1922.[203] In his 1955 book La Musique par la danse, Lifar argues that the music of Le Sacre, with its heavily pronounced rhythms, and particularly its shifting rhythmic structure, weighs down and enslaves the dance (he cites Levinson, who supports his argument here).[204] Likewise, Massine he considers enslaved by musical structure in Symphonie fantastique.

Lifar also believed that his method did not deny the musician's freedom: with the advent of film technology, the composer could work independently, provided that the general schema of the dance was adhered to. Indeed, Satie considered that this method gave power to the composer, who would no longer have to make changes or succumb to mutilation of his score after a choreographer stepped in. But here, Lifar's theory appears extraordinarily limiting, because he denies even the simplest, most innocent syncopation or counterpoint against the rhythmic structure of the dance. He indicates the variety possible to the musician working with a simple minim, minim rhythm in the dance:

But the following simple syncopation is not allowed:[205]

After his disappointment with Prokofiev's score for *Sur le Borysthène* (1932), Lifar made five works according to his new method. The first of these pieces, *Icare* (1935), achieved considerable popularity, its process of evolution sparking a lively debate between members of the dance and music worlds in the art magazine *Comoedia*. Lifar wrote down the dance rhythms in musical notation, hoping initially that Honegger would orchestrate the work for percussion; in the event, the task was fulfilled by the conductor J.E. Szyfer.[206]

Later works used a melodic element and fuller orchestration: *David triomphant* (1937, Rieti), Lifar's own solo variation in *Alexandre le Grand* (1937, Gaubert), *Le Cantique des cantiques* (1938, Honegger), the latter incorporating the extraordinary sound of the ondes Martinot. *Chota Roustaveli* (1946, Honegger, Tcherepnin and Tibor Harsanyi), which told a Georgian tale based on a poem by Roustaveli, contained additional brief passages of silence and, here again, there were some percussion-only sections.[207]

Ultimately, Lifar's theories do not appear to have had any lasting influence. They appear as an oddity, the project of an autocratic individual whose own work has not sustained interest, and we may well query his claim that his composers felt no constraint working with him. His theory too seems strait-jacketed, strictly limiting rhythmic possibilities, governed by a conservative nostalgia for the repetitive rhythmic structures that he believed were true and natural to the dance traditions of old. Although he does not advocate a return to the practice of the eighteenth and nineteenth centuries, with their limited repertoire of dance rhythms, he suggests that his new way forward might in fact be very old:

A dance, no matter what it is, whether it lasts two minutes or thirty, is built on a framework, on a unalterable rhythmic design, and on rhythmic figures which recur regularly and harmoniously (such has always been the nature of the dance, and such it still is, among all the peoples of the earth). The intrusion of an element, strange from the rhythmic point of view, destroys the dance.[208]

Lifar's ideal is for eventual synthesis and harmony between the arts, in effect, a return to the old ideal of wholeness. What is most interesting to us, perhaps, is the timing of his theory in relation to developments in modern dance, and his pinpointing the lack of parity between developments in music and choreography. Lifar draws attention to the major rhythmic complications of twentieth-century music which had no choreographic equivalent. He spots too the irony of Diaghilev's composers flocking enthusiastically to work with him just at the point when choreographers were tired of 'dance music' and non-'dance music' was de rigueur. Although he probably would not have admitted his own inadequacies, is he drawing attention to those of other choreographers and dancers at the time, their lack of rhythmic and musical training, their inability to engage structurally with the new musical developments, their imperative in these circumstances to use difficult new music largely as backdrop or soundscape? Lifar's eccentric manifesto highlights a major issue for the ballet world at the time.

Likewise, as Lifar's method leads nowhere, there is no tradition within ballet of silent dances. There is the example of David Lichine's La Création (1948), which showed a Dancer, a Choreographer and other characters representing concepts: His Ideal, His Uncertainty, His Temptation, His Idea. Quite possibly, the workmanly real-time theme of a choreographer creating a ballet persuaded Lichine to leave the work in silence. Perhaps in tune with developments in modern dance, Jerome Robbins was intent on clearing the mind for movement in his silent ballet Moves (1959):

> The score supports, conditions, predicts, and establishes the dynamics, tempo, and mood not only for the dance but also for the audience. Music guides the spectators' emotional responses to the happenings on the stage and creates a persuasive atmosphere for reaction. Moves severs that guidance . . . I wanted the audience to concentrate on movement.[209]

Also noteworthy is Roland Petit's Le Jeune homme et la mort (1946), a work about a Parisian painter taunted to death in his attic by his lover. Originally rehearsed to jazz, at the last minute Bach's Passacaglia and Fugue in C Minor was opted for, in orchestration by Respighi.[210] Obviously, such a process reduced the likelihood of close structural relationships between music and dance, but critics have mostly commented on the shock impact of hearing such noble music played in a harsh contemporary setting; in other words, the effect of such marked connotational separation of music and dance. Perhaps the music was meant to encourage us to see the noble dimension in the young man's personality or situation. It is the kind of device used since for purposes of humour and deconstructive politics by postmodern choreographers such as Yvonne Rainer, making an issue of the distance between plain, matter-of-fact movement state-ment and the conventionalised sentiment of high romantic or popular music (see p. 20).

Contemporary Practices: A Summary

No summary of contemporary practices in ballet can ignore the role of modern dance. Many of the younger modern dance choreographers today, especially those working within *Ausdruckstanz* and physical theatre, make no special issue of their dance relating to or even needing music. Of those modern dance choreographers who do work closely with music, some have made ballets, thereby influencing a tradition that has continued without break to make a point of musical values. If Merce Cunningham has made ballets or had works staged on ballet companies, like *Un Jour ou deux* (1973, for the Paris Opéra), *Summerspace* (1958, revived for New York City Ballet in 1966) and *Duets* (1980, revived for American Ballet Theatre in 1982), his extreme method of independ-ence has had no obvious impact on the ballet world. Other modern dance choreographers have infiltrated the musical workings of the ballet world more forcefully. The styles of modern dance mixed into ballet necessarily bring with them new styles of phrasing, sometimes less of the pulse emphasis that comes naturally from a step vocabulary, instead more of an emphasis on breath-style rhythm, and sometimes a different placement of accents. All this affects rela-tionship with music. Joan Acocella writes of Mark Morris working with ballet dancers: 'Where he will often place the accent in the middle of the phrase, to highlight that part, they will shift the accent to the end of the phrase. In a sense, this is just an extension of an old argument about gravity.'[211]

A new freedom of musical choice in ballet developed by mid-century, by which time, of course, Balanchine, Ashton and Tudor had established their mature respective styles and working methods. Choreographers could now choose any styles of music, from the newest aleatoric and electro-acoustic to the major composers from the past, and critics no longer objected. So too, some choreographers enjoyed radical mixes of different musical styles and composers within one work: like Maurice Béjart, *Nijinsky, Clown of God* (1971) to Tchai-kovsky and Pierre Henry and *Our Faust* (1975) to Bach and Argentine tangos; John Neumeier, *Don Juan* (1972) to Gluck and Victoria, *Meyerbeer/Schumann* (1974), and *A Midsummer Night's Dream* (1977) to Mendelssohn and Ligeti; Kenneth MacMillan, *Anastasia* (1971) to Tchaikovsky and Martinů; and Twyla Tharp, *Push Comes to Shove* (1976) to Haydn and Joseph Lamb. This mixing could be seen as an extension of the principle behind the 'time travelling' scores of Diaghilev's Ballets Russes.

In some hands, simply putting dance to music stresses ambiguity and difference, with irony, even jokes, as the dance slips between one style and another, meeting our expectations in its relationship with the music and then slipping into another gear, perhaps from grand ballet to vernacular or modern, or from formal response to the music to just listening and doodling. Such are the jagged balletic manners of Tharp and Mats Ek.

Tharp, more than any other contemporary choreographer, infuses her musical practice in ballet with today's vernacular, incorporating popular music and recorded sound. She does this, for instance, in her series of work to Frank Sinatra and in her *Grand Pas: Rhythm of the Saints* (1992) gala *pas de deux* for two Paris Opéra dancers, here using excerpts from Paul Simon music specially selected by Simon and Tharp. She is also unusually committed to commissions, new music for her own as well as for other companies, most celebrated perhaps her setting of Philip Glass in *In the Upper Room* (1986, Twyla Tharp Dance; 1988, American Ballet Theatre). Morris's commission of Virgil Thomson for *Drink to Me Only with Thine Eyes* (1988, American Ballet Theatre) was also highly successful. But commissions in ballet today are rare: William Forsythe, who has regularly collaborated with his house composer Thom Willems, is an exception.

Tharp and Morris belong to a group of choreographers for ballet who have taken more or less from the Balanchine example, still believing in the potential of dances that are primarily about dancing and music: like Jerome Robbins (his later work), Peter Martins, Choo San Goh and Ashley Page, to mention but a few. The most interesting of these choreographers continue to build from the structural experiments that began, as we have seen in this chapter, in the early decades of this century. Some of them too continue the tradition of looking to music for their structural models.

For none of this work is it useful to generalise about dance visualising or identifying with music. We are still inclined to want and talk about a feel-good harmony between what we hear and see, yet there is a theoretical inclination today to disconnect strands of experience and enjoy their differences and discontinuities as well as their similarities. Whereas it is useful and telling to consider why, at various times, artists and their audiences have believed in and made so much of wholeness and unity, it is part of current theoretical practice to be open to disjunction even within work made at a time when this was not an issue. There is no reason why relationships between music and dance should escape that practice. It is only when we disconnect that we understand the full continuum from work that is extremely disjunctive to work that seduces us with its harmonious relationships; in other words, to understand the full richness of possibilities between these two extremes. To do this, we have to look at individual works and consider how we look at them.

2

Hearing the Dance, Watching the Music

Issues of Analysis, Identity and Working Process

This chapter constitutes the framework for seeing and hearing that I use in the following chapters. I introduce relevant issues of meaning, and the concepts and structural categories that help us to understand the complexity of musical-choreographic style and of how that style contributes to the identity and meaning of a particular ballet. However, any analysis of dance has to address the particularly slippery nature of dance identity. Thus, I consider the problems of identity of ballets as performed texts, particularly those issues involving music, such as a dancer's musical style and understanding of musical-choreographic style, and then, finally, the range of documentation, often conflicting, from which we develop the sense of a text and its performance potential.

My proposed framework for analysing relationships between music and dance draws upon ideas introduced in Chapter 1, in conjunction with other current theoretical developments. I recognise that it has limitations and prejudices behind it, like all frameworks. Our frameworks for seeing, as Stanley Fish, the literary theorist would say, 'give texts [read dances] their shape, making them rather than, as is usually assumed, arising from them . . . linguistic and textual facts [the facts of the dance], rather than being the objects of interpretation, are its products.'[1] Yet, as he too says, these strategies are not entirely personal; they have relevance because they come into being and their application makes sense insomuch as we belong to 'interpretive communities'[2] bonded by common cultural considerations. In the light of this, I hope to explain the rationale behind my framework for seeing.

I am proposing a theory of interdependence and interaction between music and dance, but as a starting point we might consider power relationships, how the relative strengths of visual and aural perception have been viewed. Should we be talking of relationships between music and dance in terms of one main force and a supporting one, dance and accompaniment, or a more complex dual process? Or, as Gertrude Stein once put it, 'Does the thing heard replace the thing seen. Does it help or does it interfere with it . . . Does the seeing replace the hearing or does it not. Or do they both go on together.'[3]

Certainly, until recently, Western culture has tended to consider the eye superior to the ear as a perceptual mechanism. Doris Humphrey said as much: 'Not only is the eye faster, but, in a contest with the ear, will invariably take precedence.'[4] The theory extends back to the Greeks, who related the eye to the ordering structures of consciousness, whereas the ear was perceived as unmediated and having direct access to the soul, from which emotions spring. This model was accepted for centuries and sustained as scientific thinking of the nineteenth-century valued objectivity (which the eye promised) over subjectivity (connected with hearing). Thus, for instance, until only recently, 'visualism' has dominated anthropological research.[5] Likewise, until only recently, film theory has prioritised the visual over the aural too so that, as Christian Metz has pointed out, the very term 'voice-off' is telling, meaning absence or lack rather than presence.[6]

Music's relationship to the screen has been for years discussed as a one-way relationship, in terms of its parallelism and counterpoint to the primary visual image: does the music support the visual image or does it not? However, this view has been challenged on a number of occasions, and increasingly so recently, through ideological and psychoanalytic criticism. Theodor W. Adorno and Hanns Eisler, and later Jacques Attali, have proposed the power of music to deceive and manipulate, indeed precisely because it seems less mediated and more direct in its impact, and thus they recognise the subversive potential of music.[7] Using psychoanalytic theory, Claudia Gorbman has pointed out how music, because of its ability to connect the individual with the pre-oedipal imaginary (a state of integration or wholeness), facilitates the process by which the spectator slips into the world of the film.[8]

Gorbman, like others, rejects the parallelism/counterpoint dualism. She queries whether

> The music 'resembles' or . . . 'contradicts' the action or mood of what happens on the screen . . . Is there no other way to qualify film music which does not lie between these opposites but outside them? . . . It is debatable that information conveyed by disparate media can justifiably be called *the same* or *different*.'[9]

Instead, she proposes the concept of 'mutual implication', music and image working together in a '*combinatoire* of expression'.[10] Similarly, Kathryn Kalinak uses the conceptual model of music and image sharing power in a mechanism of interdependence.[11]

In dance, which can draw usefully upon film theory here, some choreographers have clearly recognised the power of music. Thus Antony Tudor reminds us cheekily that without them realising it, most of the time, it is the music 'sending' the audience and not the choreography (see Ch. 1, p. 3). He makes the point about power exaggeratedly (we are made conscious of the device) when, in a famous moment in *Jardin aux lilas* (1936), the emotional climax of the work, he keeps his entire cast in a photograph freeze, while the music roars forth (see Ch. 5, p. 287).

Humphrey admits the same musical power when she notes the potential for domination of dance by large orchestral forces and complex symphonic forms, also when she describes the game of ringing the musical changes on the same dance sequence. Process reveals the point:

> Music can also completely distort the mood. Suppose the dancer has a sequence arranged which is quite serious, a small segment of one of life's major encounters. Accompany this by trivial music which patters along without any depth of feeling. The result is that the dancer does not become stronger by contrast; rather he seems empty, silly and pretentious. Such is the power of the sound to set the mood. This same sequence, accompanied by jaunty, slightly jazzy music, can make the dancer look cynical; he is pretending to be serious, but actually it is all bluff, and he believes in nothing. The variations on this kind of thing are endless.[12]

The implication here is that music infects the dance so deeply that it looks different as a result: movement is not seen for its own independent values. This is one 'whole' experience, music and dance inextricably combined (see Ch. 1, pp. 16–17). Humphrey also notes the power of music when the effect is more of separation or disjunction between music and dance, in other words, of two opposing voices:

> If soft sound supports strong movement and vice versa, a curious effect is produced. The music seems to be antagonist; the figure of the dancer fights to be strong without encouragement; and in his more vulnerable moods the music seems to seek to destroy and dominate him.[13]

These examples refer to music as a site of meaning, which I will elaborate upon in the next section, first in terms of music by itself, and then as its meanings are brought into combination with dance.

Music as Meaning

Music, sometimes considered the most abstract of arts, is nevertheless a site of meaning, and choreographers have consciously or unconsciously taken this into account when interpreting scores. Time and time again over the years, theorists have considered the issue of music as emotional metaphor – Hanslick, for instance, in the nineteenth century, considering the analogy between musical dynamics and tempo and emotional patterns: 'intensity waxing and diminishing . . . motion hastening and lingering'.[14] And in this century, Suzanne Langer writes of music reflecting 'the morphology of feeling',[15] while Stephen Davies argues that music possesses 'emotion characteristics'.[16]

It is interesting that, in the seventeenth and eighteenth centuries, music tended to be discussed primarily in terms of meaning, affect and rhetoric, rather than structure. On the other hand, Stravinsky, with whom Balanchine, as we shall see, often preferred to take side, played down artistic expression and meaning. There is the famous exposition in his autobiography of his philosophy of enjoying art for itself, not for what it expresses.[17] He had changed his reading of his own *Le Sacre* (1913) score, first seen as music that depicted narrative, later, according to his developed modernist aesthetic, for its architectural values (see Ch. 1, p. 11). This is not to deny that music provoked associations and feelings for Balanchine and Stravinsky, but that, in the tradition of absolute music (and Hanslick too agreed with this), the musical fact is of prime importance rather than such associations and feelings. Many choreographers have been more ready than Balanchine to read clear, expressive, mood and emotional qualities in their music, sometimes, indeed, drawing upon these qualities to form a concrete narrative in their dance.

The expressiveness in music stems from such characteristics as dynamics, tempo and tonal tension, which have a psychological impact, stimulating the human nervous system. However, a large degree of the expressiveness of music is the result of convention or code. Theories of *Maniera* and *Musica Reservata* in the sixteenth century and *Affektenlehre* in the eighteenth century attempted to codify the possibilities for expressing meaning. At various points in musical history, different keys have been seen to possess different symbolisms, although, significantly, the symbolism changed over the years, and the meanings of individual keys shifted. Indeed, much of the semiotic content of music which we take for granted, in both 'pure' and programmatic music, stems from seventeenth-century opera. Originally grounded in words as 'word painting', musical devices have held on to the meaning from such grounding.

Even the formal device of tonality has narrative implications. Susan McClary explains that it emerged as 'a way of arousing and channeling desire in early opera', after which 'instrumentalists quickly adopted its procedures for their own repertories'.[18] Thus, the nineteenth-century theorist Ludwig Tieck described instrumental music as 'insatiate desire forever hieing forth and turning back into itself'.[19] The tonic pitch is suggested as a goal, withheld, then finally reached as a point of release. Sonata form, the signature formal model of late

eighteenth-century and nineteenth-century music, developed the tonal narrative further in terms of establishing a primary identity with a first tonal area and
'masculine' theme, questioning it with a secondary 'feminine' theme and tonal
area, and finally securely re-establishing the primary identity. According to
McClary, in the nineteenth century, many of these themes 'draw on the semiot-
ics of "masculinity" and "femininity" as they were constructed in opera or tone
poems'.[20] It is easy to see why, in terms of today's social critique, sonata form has
been read as a vehicle for showing conflict between masculine identity and the
feminine Other, or a metaphor for authorial power and domination.[21] Here too,
we see how musical narrative might be linked to ideology: thus, as an example,
McClary's reading of Brahms' Third Symphony as presenting 'tonality and
sonata in a state of narrative crisis', taking on and attempting to derail Enlight-
enment assumptions of a rational, ordered, world.[22]

Referring to other nineteenth-century theory, Anthony Newcomb points out
in his study of Schumann's Second Symphony (1846, Op. 61) that the nineteenth-century view of the symphony was predominantly a narrative view, the
work conceived as a sort of 'composed novel' (see Ch. 1, p. 12). This demonstrates how music can lose the meanings through which it was originally understood; in other words, again, the point about music being expressive through
understood conventions or codes. Yet Newcomb maintains elsewhere that music
still is heard narratively by many listeners, even if certain codes are no longer
understood: 'as a mimetic and referential metaphor, the mimesis involved is of
modes of continuation, of change and potential.'[23] Borrowing from narrato-
logical theory, including the work of Jonathan Culler and Paul Ricoeur,[24] Newcomb contends that, as in reading literature, we process musical events in relation to paradigm plots (like sonata form), shifting back and forth, recollecting,
developing expectations and so on. These processes, 'the temporal aspect of the
perceiver's activity as he proceeds through the unrolling series', lie at the core of
narrativity.[25] Thus, too, he reminds us of the emergent meanings from the individual work, which is always more than the sum of its parts.

Both McClary and Newcomb demonstrate the fact that form in music is not
'pure'; it is not devoid of meaning. The point is supported by the fact that formal
devices are seen to contain meaning in other representational arts. In novels,
paintings, theatre and television, conventions and stylistic devices are seen to
have narrative meaning, as much as the level of character and story. For instance, with respect to narrative, Stuart Hall has written:

> meanings are already concealed or held within the forms of the stories them-
> selves. Form is much more important than the old distinction between form
> and content. We used to think form was like an empty box, and it's really what
> you put into it that matters. But we are aware now that the form is actually

part of the content of what it is that you are saying. So then one has to ask why it is that certain events seem to be handled, predominantly in our culture, in certain forms.[26]

Music has also been seen to suggest space, as up and down in terms of pitch, or near and far in terms of volume; colours, from different instrumental timbres; the passing of time, at different rates, or as time arrested; or physical gesture, as the dynamic character of a musical unit suggests the quality of an action. The question arises again as to whether any of these meanings stems naturally from music. Strictly onomatopoeic sounds are exceptions, like the thunderstorm in *La Fille mal gardée* (Lanchbery 1960), or the knocking on the door to Giselle's cottage. However, it is not unlikely that the other meanings are arbitrarily based, established at a specific historical moment for social or religious reasons, but have become 'natural' through consistent application of the code. Even the painting of high/low in pitch, to Western musicians an 'automaticized associative result', is not certain to have had a natural basis.[27]

For us here, it is particularly important to consider certain occasions when music is used to evoke contexts and situations outside itself, again through established conventions. Certain instruments, for instance, carry, or used to carry, associations of particular social contexts and countries. Davies provides a useful list: 'horns accompany the hunt; the oboe, cor inglais [*sic*], and panpipes invoke rustic settings; muffled snare drums suggest state funerals and executions; pipes and drums go with marches; bagpipes are bound to call Scotland to mind; organs now have religious connotations.' He goes on to indicate that styles of music also conjure up particular contexts. Fanfares can mean the hunt, dance pieces can indicate social class as well as dancing situations, and folk idioms can signify particular countries.[28] Sometimes too music can suggest a situation or meaning by quoting a well-known reference: like the 'Dies Irae' plainsong melody, which refers to Judgement Day and which appears in numerous works, some used for ballet. It is used somewhat blasphemously by Berlioz in his *Symphonie fantastique*, the programme of which Massine borrowed for his eponymous symphonic ballet (1936). It also appears in Rachmaninov's *Rhapsody on a Theme of Paganini*, set by Ashton (1980) to include aspects of Baryshnikov's (and Paganini's) 'satanic' virtuosity, and at one point the male soloist mimes playing the violin. Both works use the connection between the melody and the words it sets. Within an individual work, the device of leitmotif can function as signal for a person or situation, a reminder of something or someone perhaps no longer present. Obviously, the most specific connotational reference can be generated in music with overt dramatic content, a programme title, a frame of reference that can be reinforced by 'naturally' established devices for meaning.

Another point suggested by some theorists is that music can contain or express motion. This is obviously a point that has direct implications for dance. Roger Sessions was in no doubt that music was a metaphor for the movement that is our primary life impulse:

> What music conveys to us – and let it be emphasised, this is the *nature of the medium itself*, not the consciously formulated purpose of the composer – is the nature of our existence, as embodied in the movement that constitutes our innermost life: those inner gestures that lie behind not only our emotions, but our every impulse and action, which are in turn set in motion by these, and which in turn determine the ultimate character of life itself.[29]

Considering the evidence that Stravinsky conceived his music in terms of physical realisation, Roger Shattuck concludes that Stravinsky's music contains the physical impulse of movement as a crucial element of his style.[30] It is, as Balanchine put it, *musique dansante*.[31]

Now Balanchine would say that the *dansante* aspect of musical expression was what he wanted most from music. Other choreographers of course look for musical meaning beyond this and are at liberty to make the meanings that they read in music more or less specific according to their choreographic treatment. Thus they might ground the emotional content that they hear, or respond with simultaneous dance gestures to musical gestures, which are more or less explicit according to the nature of the musical stylisation or context. There is also the tradition of music representing speech, the 'recitative' to accompany mime in some nineteenth-century ballets. Or choreographers can make use of the spatial connotations of high/low pitch and volume changes. Of course, the composer writing especially for dance is likely to be alive to the possibility of linking aural and visual meanings – Stravinsky, for instance, in the last Pas d'Action of *Orpheus* (1948) creating musical gestures depicting physical gestures of anger and violence: the Bacchantes attack Orpheus and tear him limb from limb.

The associations of certain instruments with particular social situations are reinforced in any number of dramatic ballets. So too instruments and dynamics have been regularly used in music written especially for ballet to signify gender or to bring out the qualities of particular steps: gentle dynamics and high-pitched instrumentation favoured for women, louder dynamics and lower registers for men, pizzicato strings for intricate pointework, tutti chords to articulate a man's *entrechats*. Choreographers using existing scores have often structured the casting of specific sections according to such instrumental conventions: Massine, for example, setting a solo for a woman to a flute solo in *Choreartium* (see Ch. 1, p. 55). The solo violin has had a particularly important place in ballet instrumentation. This stems perhaps from the nineteenth-century practice of having one or two violins (rather than a piano) accompany rehearsals. But the violin is also important as an instrument that was considered especially emotionally expressive, close to the human voice in its ability to 'sing'. No wonder then that Ashton took over Tchaikovsky's Entracte music in *The Sleeping Beauty*, with its lengthy violin solo, for his new Awakening *pas de deux* (choreographed for the 1968 Peter Wright production) – in other words, for a personal statement.

Other semiotic conventions used in nineteenth-century ballet and carried over into some twentieth-century work are the motto theme and *air parlant*. The motto theme, forerunner of the leitmotif of opera, is a musical theme associated with a character or situation and brought back to remind the viewer, and perhaps a character on stage too, of this association. In this way, Hilarion and the audience think of Giselle at the opening of Act II as they hear one of the tunes associated with her in Act I; in her Mad Scene, Giselle herself (and her audience) are reminded, again musically, of happier moments in her relationship with Albrecht. More recently, John Lanchbery developed this thematic device for various characters and situations in his new score for *La Fille mal gardée* (1960) (see Ch. 4, p. 242). The *air parlant* is a familiar theme taken from outside the ballet, a popular song or a tune from an opera, its original connotations brought to bear within the new situation of the ballet narrative. In Hérold's *La Fille mal gardée* (1828), for example, Lise's entrance on tiptoe so that she does not wake her mother is aptly illustrated by the opening chorus from Rossini's *The Barber of Seville* (1816), 'Piano, pianissimo'. This was incorporated by Lanchbery into his later arranged score. A modern example is Charles Mackerras' use of 'Twenty love-sick maidens we' from Sullivan's *Patience*, in John Cranko's *Pineapple Poll* (1951), to exaggerate the despondency of the girls enraptured by Captain Belaye.

Both the context in which the music was made and the one in which it is now heard contribute to meaning. Whereas some meanings are shared because of common ground between the cultural contexts of composer and listeners across the years, others derive from the differences between these contexts and the tradition that the music has generated (see Ch. 1, p. 13), and every individual brings her/his own particular associations to the music. The choreographer enters this multi-textual arena to demonstrate a particular understanding of the music, and to add an extra layer to our understanding of it.

Of course, in the case of 'story' ballets, whether the idea of the narrative was prompted by the music or vice versa, a range of specific narrative resonance opens up. Period situations and characters can resonate with the gestural and dramatic potential in the music. They can also resonate with the personal history and cultural context associated with the composer. The world of Chopin is, for instance, evoked in Ashton's *A Month in the Country* (Chopin, 1976, see Ch. 4, p. 247).

Thus, musical meaning is an integral part of our experience of a ballet. But there is a further point to be made about music offering a voice distinct from the dance or dancer, at particular moments. The music might add a separate layer of meaning. Or music and dance together might forge a special relationship that suggests quite a different order of meaning from those suggested in surrounding passages. In both circumstances, there could be striking effects of incongruence or difference.

This raises the question similar to that already raised by theorists with regard to performers and actors in opera and film, as to whether the dancers on stage always hear the music (metaphorically speaking). When music is built into the actual story of an opera or film (as so-called 'diegetic' music[32]), there seems to be little doubt that the performers are meant to look as if they hear the music, for instance, on the various occasions when Carmen 'acts' singing (in Bizet's *Carmen*, 1875), or when musical instruments appear within a film's visual imagery. Thus too, as ballet examples, Juliet picks up and plays a mandolin on stage in accompaniment to Romeo at the ball where they first meet, horns indicate the arrival of the hunting party in *Giselle*; or the sound of an action, like the knocking on Giselle's door, becomes musicalised as onomatopoeia. But the question as to hearing music that is not embedded in the story, non-diegetic music, has given rise to debate. This is the case even though, in many instances, within the terms of artistic convention, we have grown accustomed to such use of music and to shifts back and forth between diegetic and non-diegetic music.

Suffice to say here that the norm in dance is for us to understand that dancers do hear their music, as accompaniment to their dancing or as part of the world in which they dance. This is pointed up in certain ballets where musicians appear on stage, like Balanchine's *Duo Concertant* (1972). *Airs parlants* would now be seen, though not necessarily in the nineteenth century, as odd moments of disjunction, when a dancer might not hear, or at least, does not hear the same meaning that we do. In Louis-Jacques Milon's ballet *Clari* (Kreutzer, 1820), the heroine looks longingly at the Duke, hoping that he will marry her as promised. There is the quotation from Salieri's opera *Les Danaïdes* 'Descends du ciel douce Hyménée'.[33] The music then is Clari's thoughts. Possibly these are like a theatrical aside, 'unheard' by the Duke. But audiences at the time, who were expected to recognise the quotation, would have had the opera plot suddenly evoked as an extra field of resonance for them to enjoy. In *Romeo and Juliet* (1935), Prokofiev underscores Juliet's first meeting with Paris with a theme associated with her tragic death. This is a musical premonition that we understand, but that Juliet could hardly be aware of at this point in the story. She does not hear the same meaning that we do.

We are moving into the area of subtle 'crossings' or disjunctions within the musical/choreographic text. I am influenced here by the thinking of musicologist Carolyn Abbate in relation to moments of incongruence within opera and music of the nineteenth century – 'musical voices that distance us', 'unsung', narrative voices that speak across the overt 'plot' or sensuality of what we are hearing.[34] She is not referring here to narrative in terms of a linear succession of events. Indeed, one such moment perceived in Dukas' *The Sorcerer's Apprentice* (1897) is one of 'narrative synthesis, a musical moment that reinterprets musical actions from a time already finished'.[35] Abbate claims that there are potentially multiple voices operating in a work. Moving away from the concept of the author-composer's authority (Abbate takes her cue from the post-structuralist programme), these voices may not necessarily be those of the composer (nor, in my context, of the choreographer) – they are embodied within the performed work. The concept of dissonant, 'unsung' voices, Abbate traces to Barthes' 'grain of the voice' as he proposed the rebirth of an author 'inside' the art work. Barthes' grain, Abbate maintains, is 'something *extra* in music . . . conceived as a body vibrating with musical sound – a speaking source – that is not the body of some actual performer'.[36]

Within Lakmé's Bell Song to entertain the holiday crowd in Delibes' opera *Lakmé* (1883), there is an example of a dissonant voice emerging from a virtuoso passage that has nothing to do with the overt content of the text or plot. Significantly, it attracts the attention of her lover, who is apparently too far away to hear her words.[37] Then, introducing an example within instrumental music, Abbate focuses on the *Totenfeier* tone poem as it is incorporated into the first movement of Mahler's Second Symphony. She interprets the E major theme of the *Totenfeier* as a moment of 'fissure'. In a sketch, Mahler marked off this moment as a 'Gesang' (song), and we do not need to know the tone poem's background plot of Adam Mickiewicz's play *Dziady* to understand the signal of song and story at this point. Abbate's thesis is that Mahler has created 'an unmediated juxtaposition of two unrelated musics' here.[38] Such 'fissures' become 'sites of hyperbolic musical disjunction . . . With the "Gesang" there is not merely a musical *contrast*, but a registral shift to musical discourse that signals a *singer* and a *song*.'[39] Abbate's work encourages me to consider that there are musical and choreographic moments in ballet too that cut across the overt story and that we can interpret as flashbacks, devices of insertion, moments of mild distancing or bold dissonance, 'fissures'.

Until recently, musicologists have tended to resolve and discount these perceived dissonances within reductive analyses that demonstrate unity and coherence. However, there are a number of musicologists working against the old model of closed, unified systems, focusing on what is disjunctive and dissonant. In his critique of recent Brahms research, Kevin Korsyn insists on the ideological motivations that are behind our making exaggerated claims for unity, as such unity is a direct reflection of the consoling, comfortable unity and stability that we would wish for ourselves (broken, according to post-structuralist notions of the decentred self). He illustrates how Brahms' work can be seen as open and ambiguous, creating a more fragmented sense of self.[40] Likewise, George Edwards, in his 'The Nonsense of an Ending: Closure in Haydn's String Quartets', exposes Haydn to the dialogic, polyphonic models of the literary theorist Bakhtin and finds Haydn a master of collage, even a post-modernist.[41] Today, within advanced critical thinking across all the arts, such dissonances are treasured as 'hermeneutic windows', and it has proved useful to keep the curtains open on them during my own analytical process.[42]

Structural Categories for Relating Music and Dance

Always so sensitive to rhythm and musical issues, the critic Edwin Denby has suggested that 'The more ballet turns to pantomime, the less intimate its relation to the music becomes; but the more it turns to dancing, the more it enjoys the music's presence, bar by bar.'[43] Certainly, it does make sense that story ballets concentrate our attention on the narrative content at the expense of the music, and this question will be explored later in relation to specific ballets. Nevertheless, all dance bears some kind of relationship to music, however much it does or does not attend to the detailed internal mechanisms of the score.

There are a number of categories for defining structural relationships between music and dance and an understanding of their distinctive characteristics helps us to gain an enriched sense of musical-choreographic style. These categories too contain meaning, and it is an important fact that such concepts and devices are shared by our broader culture and are the means through which we understand artistic experience. Across the arts, for instance, we understand patterns of climax and dénouement, the hierarchy of structural units (phrase, periods, paragraphs, and so on), concepts of return as a method of closure (with a refrain or in an ABA structure).

I am not entering into the theoretical debate as to why we perceive interrelationships between music and dance – I am taking the fact that we do as a given, as so many others, including choreographers, have done.[44] Take, for instance, the concepts of *music visualisation* or 'Mickey-Mousing'. Rhythm is an area where especially strong analogies can be drawn between music and dance, hence my particular attention to this area as well as to ideas of *parallelism* taken from visualisation principles. In fact, the rhythm focus promises a broader project than might at first be expected, as rhythm overlaps readily with the other aspects of music and dance.

Dance and music are seen to operate dialectically, informing each other, rather than in a one-way relationship between a leading and an accompanying force. Given this, the *parallelism/counterpoint* model (see p. 64) remains useful in a consideration of structural relationships between music and dance. It is used

here to evoke the concept of a continuum rather than of two polarities of parallelism and counterpoint.

I have not ventured into the extremes of esoteric musical analysis. Certain
details of musical structure documented in musicological literature are primarily the products of a highly specialist analytical training. Some of these structures are, I would contend, 'unhearable', and the techniques that reveal them
are themselves the products of unifying models recently questioned by the world
of musicology itself (see pp. 72–3). I do not claim to know exactly what choreographers and their audiences grasp from musical structure: to this knowledge, I
cannot possibly have access. But I have incorporated into my thinking the theoretical evidence of musical matters provided by the choreographers discussed.

I am being careful here to draw the distinction between the term *visualisation,*
which refers to a choreographer's musical technique, and *parallelism,* which is
the resulting relationship within a ballet text. Music visualisation, the term invented by Ruth St Denis (see Introduction, p. xi) is a useful term for expressing
the technique of creating concurrence or imitation between music and dance.[45]
There are many different possibilities for visualisation, according to the different
elements that make up dance and music. Put simply, it is possible to visualise
many different aspects of music: rhythm and form; dynamics; texture, instrumental layout, thick or thin chord structures, or polyphonic/homophonic
sound; pitch contour; staccato and legato articulation; timbre, using established
associations between a dancer or particular sex and an instrument or instrumental group; energy pattern, patterns of tension and relaxation. Rarely has a
choreographer even attempted, let alone succeeded in, following all the above
possibilities, although probably St Denis and her partner Ted Shawn took these
principles further than most. Choreographers can choose to take on several
musical features simultaneously, or just one, or none at all. Most vary their
approach regularly during a piece, avoiding predictable relationships of close
concurrence and encouraging interest through variety. However, this is not to
say that regular music visualisation can never be lively. Mark Morris has proved
the point that this 'rule' against overdoing the device can be broken, demonstrating through his extreme density of visualisation the various ways in which
music can be listened to. And too, through judicious movement invention, he
shows us the ironies and fun of Mickey-Mousing.

Denby has written perceptively about the power of choreography to present a
particular point of view of musical structure as it chooses to highlight particular
features:

> The visual action . . . makes particular stresses in the music more perceptible,
> and continuities more clearly coherent. Watching the sweep of the dance
> momentum, you feel more keenly the musical one, and the visual drama can

give you an insight into the force of character of the score. A dance happily married to its score likes to make jokes without raising its small voice, and the thundering score likes it too . . . Inside the labyrinth of complex musical structures, you see ballet following the clue of the rhythm, you see it hearing the other musical forces as they affect the current of the rhythm, as they leave or don't leave the rhythm a danceable one. You see the dance listening and choosing its own rhythmic response.[46]

would argue the corollary, that music too can present us with a particular view of dance structure.

Parallelism between music and dance usually stands out as such from the surrounding context, most of all when the relationships between music and dance are especially close (when several musical features are visualised, and especially when details of rhythm pattern and pitch are imitated). It creates a kind of meaning, drawing attention to itself as special, as music and dance seem to clarify each other. The fresh legibility creates a sense of security, perhaps quiet, perhaps triumphant in effect. There is a clear example of close parallelism to quiet, lightly humorous effect in Balanchine's *Agon* (1957) Pas de Deux. Here we see a series of staccato isolated gestures when the woman is in *penché* with one leg around the man's shoulder: they release the right hand clasp (1), she touches the floor with her free hand (2), he releases his left hand to take his arm back high (3). The gestures follow the rhythm and pitch contour of three notes in Stravinsky's score. They stand out as one of several 'special' moments within the Pas de Deux (see Ex. 2.1).

Another example is from Balanchine's *Symphonie Concertante* (1947). Here, close relationships between music and dance are the style of the entire piece, two women soloists dancing the solo violin and viola respectively. In this example, one of them, the 'violin', matches the fast-slow continuity of Mozart's music: the

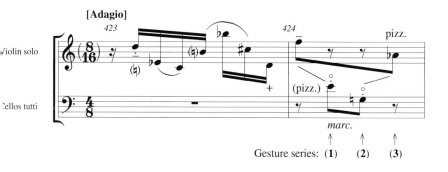

Ex. 2.1. Stravinsky, *Agon*, Pas de Deux.

[Allegro Maestoso]

Ex. 2.2a. Mozart, *Symphonie Concertante*, first movement.

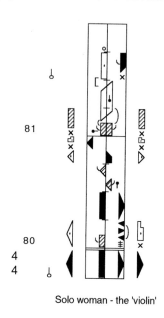

Solo woman - the 'violin'

Ex. 2.2b. Balanchine, *Symphonie Concertante*, first movement.

petits battements, the *pas de bourrée* and *soutenu* turn 'go with' the semiquavers and the rise and fall in pitch (see Exs. 2.2a, 2.2b). At the beginning of the slow movement, the corps 'accompaniment' enter with a lilting step into *plié* at the start of each beat, reflecting the accompanying musical figuration with its root notes similarly 'on' the beat (see Exs. 2.3a, 2.3b). Another possibility is for dance to anticipate or reflect the music rather than to match it simultaneously. If the gap in time is not too long, a clear relationship between music and dance can be established. Music also has the capacity to infect both our seeing and the dancer's performance, so that we perceive dance accentuations to musical accentuations, even when they are hardly, if at all, built into the dynamics of the movement. Again, there is the impression of parallelism.

However, even the closest parallelism contains more subtlety than we at first think. Denby notes some basic distinctions between music and dance. Even when dance accents correspond with musical accents,

Ex. 2.3a. Mozart, *Symphonie Concertante*, second movement.

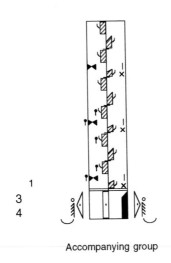

Accompanying group

Ex. 2.3b. Balanchine, *Symphonie Concertante*, second movement.

their time length is rarely identical with musical time units. (A leap, for instance, that fills two counts may end a shade before, and the next movement begin a shade after, the third count.) The variations of energy in dancing around which a dance phrase is built are what make the dance interesting and alive; and they correspond to a muscular sense, not to an auditory one . . .

Keeping time at all costs destroys the instinctive variability of emphasis; it destroys the sense of breathing in dancing, the buoyancy and the rhythmic shape of a dance phrase . . .

The edge in accentuating a bodily gesture (which underlines its correspondence with the musical beat) is a device that rapidly becomes monotonous to the eye and that tends to dehumanize the look of a dancer onstage. A dancer onstage is not a musical instrument; she is – or he is – a character, a person. The excitement of watching ballet is that two very different things – dancing and music – fit together, not mechanically but in spirit.[47]

In the same way, even when the phrase beginnings and endings in music and dance seem to correspond, there is often in reality overlap, a blurred synchronisation, energies awakening and trailing to rest at different times.

We are now turning our attention to *rhythm*, and here, we are talking about both imitative and contrapuntal relationships between music and dance. At this point, it is useful to identify and provide specific definitions for the various rhythmic concepts referred to in this book. Rhythmic categories can be divided logically into four strands, and I am indebted here to music theory for its development of rhythmic concepts.[48] The less easy concepts are given more detailed explanation after this tabulation:

1. Categories that refer to duration and frequency: note or move (the basic unit of duration in dance and music); beat; rubato/breath rhythm (the kind of rhythm which avoids or plays against a motoric beat); speed, for instance, tempo (the rate of beats), the rate of consecutive notes or moves, harmonic rhythm (the rate of harmonic change), or the rate at which space is covered.

2. Categories of stress: (a) dynamic stress occurring across more than one note or move (like a gradual crescendo); (b) accents, the stress of single notes or moves, for instance, metrical accents (the accent of downbeat, the first beat of the bar, or strong relative to weak beat); syncopation (the shifting of the metrical accent to accent a point that does not coincide with either a beat or strong beat); rhythmic accents (when a movement or note stands out through lasting longer than those around it); dynamic accents (accents produced by physical energy in both dance and music). Some categories of stress are particular to music: accents through ornamentation, melodic accent (created by a marked difference in pitch of the accented note from surrounding notes) and harmonic accent (an accent of relative dissonance). Particular to dance is accent created by change in level of weight, for instance, the shift to pointe or to *plié*.

3. Categories referring to the grouping of sounds or movements through time, the interaction of (1) and (2): metre, metrical hierarchy, hypermetre, polymetre (the use of different metres simultaneously); units (of grouped notes or moves), downbeat and upbeat units, unit hierarchy.

4. Energy pattern, the patterns of tension and relaxation across a work, section of a work or smaller unit.

The basic unit of duration in music and dance is the first concept to discuss, and here we see further fundamental differences between music and dance. We generally accept that a note or chord expresses the basic unit of duration in sound: a note or chord begins with a sound impulse and lasts until the next or until sound gives way to silence. The issue is more problematic in dance. Music is built from discrete units. Units of sound and units of duration concur: sound impulses begin both. This is not the case in dance, where impulses often do not occur at the beginning of a movement. Impulses can occur at the onset of motion after stillness, but they can also occur within a continuum of motion (for example, within a swing) or at the end of a continuum of motion.[49] However, it is the impulses still that determine our grasp of duration in dance. In the case of a step, the spectator perceives an impulse or moment marking a point in time. The precise timing of the moment is hard to establish in movement terms. However, there is no doubt that we do perceive a moment: it is obvious, for instance, when a dancer is 'behind' or 'off' the expected impulse. The counts that dancers use are further evidence that we perceive a moment in time. The counts mark these moments. In normal steps, the moment is probably the point in time when the dancer reaches stability, the vertical norm.

We perceive time in dance as divided into units that begin with either an impulse or an onset of stillness, regardless of the beginning of a movement. This conclusion is reflected in the conventions used in notating dance rhythm. For example, in the Labanotation of steps, a step symbol does not begin with the initial leg gesture, but rather with the moment when the foot first touches the ground,[50] an approximation of the moment of perceived impulse:

For the sake of simplicity, I am using the word 'move' here as synonymous with what we perceive as the basic unit of duration in dance.

Fundamental differences between dance and music also emerge when we consider *speed* as rate of notes or moves. Physical limitations determine that, in a given period of time, the maximum number of events possible is smaller in dance than in music. As a result, choreographers often choose, if they want to create an effect of parallelism, to reflect changes in musical speed in a generalised rather than precise fashion, and if we look closely, the number of moves in the *petits battements* and *pas de bourrée* in the *Symphonie Concertante* example does not match the four-semiquaver figures exactly (see Exs. 2.2a, 2.2b). Or choreographers reflect broad contrasts in continuity, in other words, whether musical notes form a continuous series or are broken with rests. Furthermore, speed changes can occur within a single dance movement, while there can be no equivalent to this in music. A note is just a note, but a dance movement, by its very nature, has slowing and quickening built into it. Dance constantly fluctuates in speed, and because of this, the effect of rubato in dance, the slowing, delaying and then catching up with the beat, can arise from within as well as across individual moves.

Different styles encourage us to read rhythmic patterning in music and dance in terms of a number of separate lines or as a summary of all the different lines. For instance, chordal or homophonic music encourages the summary reading, polyphonic or contrapuntal music encourages us to hear separate lines. Dance manifests such textural differences in its own way, in terms of a contrapuntal or 'homophonic' stage picture, but also within the body. Ballet styles generally encourage us to take the body as a whole into account. Steps, the transference of weight and the particularly articulate footwork of the style are of primary importance in establishing rhythm and relationship to music, with impulses in torso and limbs coinciding more or less with steps. But when we look more carefully, we often see extra impulses in legs, arms and hands that decorate the framework of the step rhythm – their impact less strong perhaps, but no less important in adding piquancy. The apex of a jump (unsupported or in a lift) can often become an impulse when marked by a leg or arm gesture or beat. Occasionally, there are no steps at all, and arms and upper body feature prominently, creating their own rhythmic patterns.

The matter of impulse is complex. The most subtle impulse may not be choreographed at all, but more a matter of interpretation. Or the effect may be to disguise the moment, a movement starting imperceptibly perhaps, shapes carved without the definition of points of departure along the way, or a series of steps being more about flow than separation.

We make sense of music and dance in terms of patterns of linked beats, notes and moves. When we consider the linking of beats, we are dealing with the concepts of *metre* and *metrical hierarchy*. Both these are established concepts in music theory, and can be borrowed usefully here for dance. If the fundamental metrical unit is the bar (measure), which groups beats in twos, threes, fours, and so forth, with a metrical accent at the beginning of each group, similar grouping and accenting is seen to occur at sub-bar and broader levels, the hierarchy extending from the length of the smallest note or movement values. Thus, a bar of 6/8, which is a grouping of two beats (dotted crotchets), contains two sub-bar groupings of three quavers. Then, several 6/8 bars may group together into *hypermeasures*,[51] each bar lasting one hyperbeat. Metrical accents become stronger the broader the level in the hierarchy; in other words, they are strongest at the hypermetrical level. The following example shows metrical organisation in 6/8 time with the bars grouped into four-bar hypermeasures:

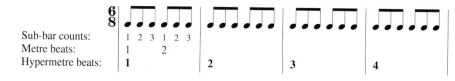

Sub-bar counts:	1 2 3 1 2 3		
Metre beats:	1 2		
Hypermetre beats:	**1**	**2**	**3**	**4**

Hypermetre does not always exist in music and dance, but when it does, it is usually regular and perceived either as a result of regular notes or moves every two or more bars, or successive units grouping notes or moves, each unit of equal length (two bars or more), most strongly when dance and musical material repeats, exactly, or with an element of variation. Hypermeasures can sometimes indicate units that we might call phrases. In dance, the counts that dancers use in rehearsal demonstrate the grouping of bars into a hypermetrical structure, counts that are sometimes marked in Labanotation scores. As befits what is most useful to the particular medium, dancers and musicians customarily count differently, dancers at a slower pulse rate than musicians. Balanchine's *Valse fantaisie* (1967) provides an example of hypermetre. Glinka's first theme, which is repeated many times during the piece, is constructed in four three-bar hypermeasures (of 3/4 metre), forming a twelve-bar phrase. This construction is shared by the choreography at the beginning of the ballet, where the material forms three-bar units, and the hyperbeats are revealed by the counts in the Labanotation score (though extended here into six-count units over two hypermeasures) (see Exs. 2.4a, 2.4b).

The grouping together of individual notes and moves into *units* (see the *Symphonie Concertante* example) results from our perceptual habits and our drive to make sense of the larger shapes as well as detail of what we experience. Thus, we group elements together in terms of their proximity and similarity and perceive rest, contrast and repetition as factors of separation between units. If repetition (or varied repetition) underlines the distinct identity of a unit, simultaneous matching of musical repetition in dance further reinforces that distinctiveness, and there is an effect of parallelism (whether or not details of musical rhythmic pattern and pitch contour have also been visualised). The parameters of metre and units grouping notes or moves operate separately, sometimes congruently, but not always so.

The terms *downbeat* and *upbeat units* describe the relationship of notes and moves to metre: they are units that begin on or before the downbeat respectively. Here, for upbeat units, I am not referring to the breath preparation before a dance impulse, which has no equivalent in music (see p. 79). Choreographers have the option of toying with the distinction between upbeat and downbeat units, and this can be very effective. These different units are illustrated by Ashton's Sarabande solo, created in 1968 for the Prince in *The Sleeping Beauty*. In both music and dance, a downbeat unit of material is followed by an upbeat unit. However, in the dance, the material of the second unit is a repetition of that in the first, the result being that the movement changes its relationship to the barline. The example indicates the positioning of the opening *developpé posé fondu* in *arabesque* (a) followed by a step back (b). When we first see this, the high point is the strong downbeat of the bar, and the step back occurs on the second beat of

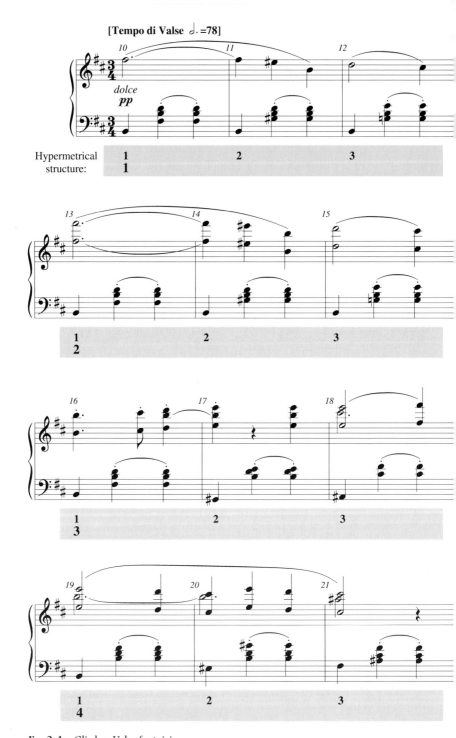

Ex. 2.4a. Glinka, *Valse fantaisie*.

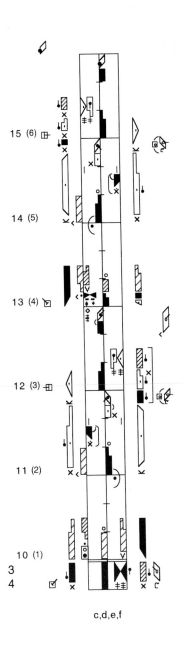

Ex. 2.4b. Balanchine, *Valse fantaisie*.

Ex. 2.5. Tchaikovsky, *The Sleeping Beauty*, Sarabande. a = *posé fondu* in *arabesque* (beginning of step unit). b = step back.

the bar. On repetition, the *posé fondu* occurs on the third and final beat of the bar, and the step back meets the downbeat of the following bar (see Ex. 2.5).

Position in relation to the bar-line affects the look of dance material (as well as the shape of what is heard). Fokine illustrates this:

> The same movement can convey a totally different impression depending on whether a dancer is descending or rising on her toes on a certain musical beat. In the first instance, when she is on the downbeat of the measure or part of the measure, she expresses self-assurance; in the second instance, while rising into the air or on her toes, she is expressing lightness, airiness, the ethereal quality of a fantastic being.[52]

Denby embellishes further:

> Take a specific ballet step. An assemblé looks different if it lands on one of the measure or if it lands on four; an entrechat looks different if the push from the floor comes on the downbeat, or if on the downbeat the legs beat in the air. A promenade en arabesque done at the same speed looks different if it is done in three-four time or in four-four. The stress of the measure supports a different phase of the step; it gives the motion a different lift and visual accent and expression.[53]

Unit hierarchy results from smaller units of notes or moves combining to form larger units. These in turn combine to form still larger units up to the level of the macroform, the first division, of a piece. We are talking here about a 'high' level of rhythmic organisation across a large timespan. In music, an established nomenclature exists for units that are either part of specific forms (for instance, exposition, variation, episode, fugue subject) or common to all tonal forms (phrase, period, theme or motif). In dance there is no such fixed nomenclature, except for the titles for individual dance numbers (e.g. variation), and motif, which is the term for an arrangement of movements that is characteristic of and particular to a work, more a term about individual appearance than about any conventional unit of time. The term phrase has been frequently used for dance, but in a variety of ways and rarely defined. I will use it here to convey the idea of a short dance unit, but will clarify what this means within a particular context. In ballet, there is a prevalence of symmetrical units of structure which together form a larger unit. These derive from the symmetrical structures of much eighteenth- and nineteenth-century music, but also from the structure of the body. So often, a musical unit is repeated or answered by a unit of related length; the dance unit is repeated on the same or opposite side of the body. Ballet choreographers can also make a point of affinity with the styles of nineteenth-century ballet by using such symmetrical patterns.

The terms *mobility* and *closure* refer to the processes of continuity and breaks in continuity that define units and articulate music and dance at various levels. They are widely used terms in music and literature and also well suited to dance. Broadly speaking, these processes are deeply intertwined, but mobility can be said to derive from developmental devices, closure from separation in time (sustainment or rest), completion of a progression (like the end of a pathway, or a musical cadence), or a major change that marks off as finished what has just been heard or seen. Simple, immediate repetition without rest or break has dual mobility/closure characteristics, indicating continuity through relationship to what has just been seen or heard, while closing off the previous material. There are different degrees of mobility and closure.

Music and dance can play off against each other in terms of mobility and closure. A choreographer or dancer can choose to draw attention to the long line of a section of music or to dissect the music in order to show its internal units. The dancer Richard Colton illustrates this in a discussion of Twyla Tharp's different approaches to two musical adagios, the Haydn in *The Bix Pieces* (1971), the Mozart in *Mud* (1977):

> You may emphasize either the seamlessness of the adagio music or the component rhythms that make it up . . . The choreography to the Mozart incorporates even the staccato movements into one long harmonious dance which emphasizes the long line of Mozart's music. The dance to Haydn has us constantly breaking long phrases into little segments . . . and that emphasizes all the facets that make up the Haydn music.[54]

During the slow movement *pas de deux* of *Ballet Imperial* (1941), the ballerina is drawn around the stage in a big circle, her series of *relevés* in *arabesque* matching repeating figures in the music. Kyra Nichols of New York City Ballet has been unusual in approaching the big circle as one long, silky, uninterrupted thread of mysterious motion, emphasising the larger sweep of the music rather than its repetitions.[55] Similarly, Suzanne Farrell's solo in *Tzigane* is a marvellous example of sustainment of dance pressure through any number of breaks in Ravel's unaccompanied violin solo. In reverse, Tudor once requested his class pianist not to play a musical repetition during a continuous sequence of movement, because it signified a break, opposite to the effect that he was trying to achieve through the class exercise.[56] Music can encourage us to perceive links across dance fragments or, the opposite, to fragment a continuous dance line. Matching musical closure in dance appears to emphasise the effect of closure, to reinforce the sense of completion.

Return is a particular form of closure. Signalling a concluding or terminal event, return articulates larger structural units and provides a major effect of closure, a sense of coming-home stability. We see this in any number of musical forms, such as sonata (the recapitulation after exposition and development), ABA and rondo (ABACA etc.), and the effect of closure is especially strong if the recapitulation is an exact repeat of what happened before, and in the home key. Similarly in dance, recapitulation can be made more or less exact as repetition, and therefore more or less emphatic.

Whether or not the choreographer decides to match a musical recapitulation is important. Dealing with sonata form structure, for instance, choreographers can choose to create a more or less powerful sense of return by repeating the familiar steps and formations of the exposition with the music, from the beginning of the recapitulation and onwards (the most powerful), or at a later point in the recapitulation, by introducing merely some kind of variation on the familiar steps, or, the least powerful of all, by making no clear reference whatsoever to the steps that we saw in the exposition. It is all a matter of degree, and the choice can have a decisive effect upon our experience of closure and the convincing re-establishment of the primary identity. Masking the straight emphatic return can give the feeling of an open ending, perhaps evoking the nineteenth-century romantic principle of continual evolution, or Becoming. This is opposed to conforming to the eighteenth-century classical principles of closure. These classical principles have been much more fully debated by musicologists than by dance writers. In music, we find implicative or causal structures such as antecedent-consequent, suggestions of the absolute necessity of rational resolution within form, tonal imperative for closure and return as metaphor for confident authorial power (see p. 67). We have begun to see that the different approaches, matching or masking musical return, have implications for meaning. Twentieth-century choreographers, choosing to use existing scores from previous centuries, also have to negotiate a relationship with the representations of these different pasts.

A final rhythmic category, *energy pattern*, is the pattern of tensions and relaxations, of climaxes and releases across a piece, a section of a piece or even within a much smaller unit. This is perhaps the most nebulous of concepts that can be housed under the umbrella of rhythm. A precise characterisation would need lengthy discussion. Suffice to say here that we recognise energy fluctuations in Western music and dance and that they are brought about conventionally through the application of a number of variables: for instance, dynamics or volume, instrumental or dance forces, speed, dissonance and consonance, and rhythmic regularity and irregularity. We might experience, for instance, the rise and fall in tension across a musical phrase and particular points of emphasis within it, through harmonic, melodic, rhythmic and dynamic means. Without any separate matching of these musical elements, we could still perceive a similar shape of rise and fall in an accompanying dance phrase.

Choreographers can take up opportunities for *counterpoint* against music as well as for music visualisation. I have already briefly discussed a kind of counterpoint of form, with reference to choreography masking return in musical form, but there are other, more obvious types of rhythmic counterpoint. There is the notion that rhythmic tension exists when conflicting rhythmic systems occur. Simple syncopations, when metrical and rhythmic accents conflict *within* either music or dance, already create a sense of tension – two rhythmic systems in conflict, the underlying metrical framework against the rhythmic pattern supplied by notes or moves. Here is a simple musical example: the main accent is displaced from the bar-line, to the second beat of the bar, the minim being longer that the crotchet:

However, rhythmic conflict can also be created *between* music and dance, with their separate accent patterns crossing, and sometimes this is the result of metrical or hypermetrical incongruity. A number of Eastern European anthropologists, for instance, undertaking the analysis of folk dance, have observed the tension from metrical incongruity, a conventional device for creating tension, with musical and dance accents crossing in rapid succession. Raina Katzarova describes the effect in such passages of metrical incongruity as of a continuous chase between music and dance.[57] An example of incongruity at the metrical level is the woman's solo in Balanchine's *Tchaikovsky Pas de Deux* (1960). The music remains in 2/4 time, but a dance combination introduces a passage of 3/4 time against the music, although sharing the beat: *piqué*, close in fifth position, *entrechat trois* performed four times, the passage lasting for six bars of music. The step seems to aerate the solo, freshening it after a series of square, regular rhythms (see Exs. 2.6a, 2.6b). Balanchine's *Valse fantaisie* contains a number of examples of incongruity between music and dance at the 'higher' hypermetrical level, four- and five-bar dance hypermeasures crossing the three-bar musical organisation (see Ch. 3).

Different degrees of tension are created by different types of counterpoint. The effect of tension is diminished the further apart the crossing accents, for

[Allegro]

Music counts: 1   2   1   2   1   2

Ex. 2.6a. Music for *Tchaikovsky Pas de Deux* (Balanchine). (Note: bars numbered from beginning of sequence, not from beginning of solo.)

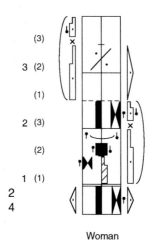

Woman

Ex. 2.6b. Balanchine, *Tchaikovsky Pas de Deux*, woman's solo.

example, when there is hypermetrical as opposed to metrical conflict; or, in syncopation, the greater the timespan between downbeat and the rhythmic accent that creates syncopation. It is also diminished when the crossing accents interact at regular intervals, or the less emphatic the accentuation.

Choreographers can, of course, devise material that rides freely across the musical pulse. Time and time again simple runs and walks are allowed to happen in this way, and with no apparent effect of tension between music and dance. However, some choreographers devise dance steps that ride across the musical pulse, sometimes with a shift in energy level that seems to pull the dance away from the music. This can create an effect of tension, as if there is antagonism between two independent forces.

To summarise so far, we have considered the choreographic technique of visualising music and some of the effects achieved by that technique: broadly, effects of security and relaxation for the eye and ear. Meanings, we will see later, can be much more varied than this suggests, depending upon the context of an individual work. We have also considered the opposite device of counterpoint between music and dance, counterpoint of rhythm, form and energy pattern. Counterpoint, like visualisation of music, contains implications for meaning. However, it is important to remember that it is misleading to indicate strict polarities, because parallelism and counterpoint both operate along a continuum.

Finally, it is relevant that certain devices from music have simply been taken over into choreographic practice, like variation techniques, contrapuntal textures, cross-referencing of material over time (all of which might be termed 'symphonic' devices). Established musical forms have also been used in dance. Sometimes these ideas might have entered dance quite independently; at other times, they are the direct result of musical precedents. After all, these devices were welcomed as soon as choreographers started to develop more ambitious and continuous structures than those of nineteenth-century ballet.

Ballet as Choreographic Text and Performance: Identity Issues

Establishing the identity of the ballet that we are watching, hearing and examining, we soon realise that dance, as a performing art involving interpretation, is elusive and slippery. There is also the problem of documenting the choreographer's intentions: dance notation, if it exists at all, is written by a notator, hardly ever by the choreographer, and sometimes when the choreographer is not even around. Much has been written about this problem, especially as the notion of the dance work, the choreographer's creation, and with it notions of ownership and copyright, have become more important during this century. The work has become a more important part of the equation than it was in the nineteenth century, in inverse relation to the dancer who performs it. I am not arguing the identity debate here, merely summarising some of the issues that arise in determining the identity of a work and are important to my musical focus. Although a number of problems are shared, dance poses far more problems than music. The dance tradition celebrates an unusual degree of freedom: dance is not easily pinned down.

There is the choreographer him/herself who may make changes in a dance to suit new dancers, because s/he cannot recall details of the first version, or to improve upon what existed before. Sometimes s/he might create a number of alternative versions for particular passages in a work. Choreographers are more or less concerned about setting and limiting their performance texts. Jerome Robbins has been notoriously pernickety about details remaining exactly the same between revivals, controlling every small move, far, far more than Ashton and Balanchine. Perhaps it is significant that he choreographed unusually slowly. Some choreographers allow changes even during the process of creation. Is this evolution or slippage? Elizabeth Cunliffe, Benesh notator with the Royal

Ballet, asks 'Does the choreographer notice? Does he care?'[58] Other people in rehearsal might be able to act as memory aids, but unplanned changes can still arise. A choreographer may consider that some aspects of a dance are far more important to preserve than others, perhaps particular movements, or the rhythm pattern (see Ch. 3, p. 126).

The notator, if there is one, has to overcome a number of awkward problems. Any notation is an interpretation of the choreography, but every notation score, as does every music score, also takes certain stylistic conventions for granted, to preserve legibility (to avoid cluttering the score) and to save time. Cunliffe points out that the notator pressing for detail can endanger the choreographic process where overview might be more important than detail; and does s/he record the choreographer's intentions and demonstration, 'nuances through the body', or the dancers' approximation? If there is slippage during the creative process, which 'version' should be recorded? The notator's art is one of compromise and intelligent decision-making, based preferably on acute knowledge of the choreographer's style.

Dancers, of course, offer interpretation too, their own view of the choreography, but other factors contribute to the particularities of their performance: body shape, training, performance style, all of which can shift between generations and stylistic traditions. Then, between the dancer and the work, there is the stager, who may or may not be the person who wrote the notation score; a video record, which presents just one interpretation for copying, and maybe with performance mistakes or other stylistic problems; a rehearsal director or *répétiteur* (ballet-master or mistress). All these mediate interpretively between the dancer and the work.

I will now go into more detail about the identity issues that involve music. All the ballet company personnel already mentioned, together with the music staff (conductors, rehearsal pianists and orchestral musicians), contribute in some way to the musicality of a ballet. However, many of the nuances that I consider here are highly subtle, and their detail is not generally recorded in dance scores. This does not mean that they are unimportant.

The choreographer imposes a view on musical interpretation, whether consciously or not, depending on how acutely s/he hears music and identifies changes in its performance and the dancers' responses to it. This is not entirely a question of precise musicality, rather that some choreographers allow more leeway than others in performance interpretation. Some choreographers are open to change from one performance or rehearsal to the next, to the creative freedom of the performer, whether dancer or musician. Again, Robbins tended to press for an unusually fixed text, from both the dancer phrasing a role to the music and the accompanying musician. The conductor Robert Irving recalls: 'Jerry is a tremendous player of records and is a little apt to think that somebody's version is *it*, instead of somebody's version of it.'[59] It was Robbins' practice to give precise performance instructions to his musicians. The Royal Ballet pianist Anthony Twiner recalls the difficulties of this approach, rehearsing his Chopin piano ballets according to an interpretation that was not his own, although admiring greatly Robbins' musicality.[60] He had a similar experience working with Hans van Manen on his ballet to the Adagio of Beethoven's 'Hammerklavier' Sonata (*Adagio Hammerklavier*, 1973). Van Manen had choreographed precisely to the Christoph von Eschenbach recording of the music, although, unlike Robbins, he had no idea of the layout of the musical score in terms of metre and beats and the performer's rubato in relation to the written score. Twiner had to compromise.

> I took the record home, and I listened to it, and I played along with it, memorized it, and marked my own copy as to how long this or that note was held by this man . . . I said, 'Well, it's not impossible. It may not be my personal interpretation but if that's the way you want it played, it can be done.'[61]

These examples indicate a particular choreographer's extreme fixing of a text, but most choreography, by its very nature, limits the musician's interpretation to some extent. Some choreography stretches the limits of current styles of musical performance practice. Today's 'correct' musical tempo might destroy the sense of the piece. Barry Wordsworth recalls that in 1991,

> Sylvie Guillem was dancing a solo [*La Luna* by Béjart], to the slow movement of the Bach E major Violin Concerto, which had been choreographed to a recording which I had not heard . . . That was very difficult because one tends to have very strong ideas about Baroque music and, with the change of fashion that we've had recently in how Baroque music ought to be played, this created a big problem for me. It was choreographed to a recording which is frankly out of fashion now, and it was absolutely essential that one took the tempo that Béjart had choreographed to in order to keep the whole essence of the piece.[62]

Or the issue might simply be to do with the history of a work's creation. All three movements of MacMillan's *Concerto* (1966) are performed at tempos slower than those marked in Shostakovich's score: the piece would be radically different if the music were performed at these tempos. Twiner suggests that this arose from early rehearsals: 'the pianist found it a bit much playing the outer quick movements, or maybe the process of the choreographer slowed the pianist down, because it was so cut up in short phrases'.[63]

We now turn to the dancers, all of them with different interpretations of music, though how different depends to some extent on their background, how much leeway they are given by a choreographer and whether they dance as soloist or member of the corps de ballet. A number of factors affect interpretation.

There is the matter of musical awareness, how much a dancer hears in a piece of music and how well acquainted s/he is with it. This is not necessarily the result of formal musical training, reading music, playing an instrument or analysing a score, although any of these experiences might help. Neither Margot Fonteyn nor Suzanne Farrell had formal musical training, but they are both widely acclaimed for their musicality. Many dancers go through musical preparation at home, listening to recordings, and getting to know the orchestrated version of a score, which is especially important when they rehearse to piano reduction and union regulations prohibit the use of recordings in rehearsal. Piano and orchestral versions of a score can sound surprisingly different. Dancers today are far better educated in dealing with difficult twentieth-century scores than they used to be, as a result of practice with this repertoire, and because techniques have been developed to help them. But, as we shall see, these are not necessarily techniques that encourage acute listening.

Traditions of musicality vary. There are the different traditions of dancers leading musicians or musicians leading dancers, which, in extreme circumstances, can mean distorting the music or choreography. Usually, musicians and dancers settle on compromise. Constant Lambert made the following generalisation:

> In classical ballet, such as *Giselle* and *Swan Lake*, the customer is always right, the customer in this case being the dancer. Unless tempi are grossly changed, it is the conductor's job to follow the dancer's physical idiosyncrasies. In modern ballet it is, on the whole, the job of the dancer to follow the more or less symphonic interpretation of the score by the conductor, but of course one can't make hard and fast rules in either case.[64]

It is widely agreed that the nineteenth-century scores written for dance can be treated with the most musical freedom. But Irving, a supporter of Lambert in his insistence on respecting musical flow and tempos, felt that, even here, musical continuity should be preserved. He writes of *Giselle*:

> The basic problem is that in many of the dance sections the same piece of music has to be played at three or four different tempi to suit the steps, and when the many varieties of tempo have been assimilated, the question remains how much to wait and how much to lead. In my early years I was an over-diligent waiter and follower . . . A return visit by Markova shed some new

light, as she seemed to maintain a greater fluidity of movement, and did not like the music cut up into so many small sections. The great revelation was the first visit of the Bolshoi Ballet in 1956, with Ulanova dancing and Yuri Fayer conducting. There was plenty of stretch and give in the tempi, but they seemed to move with a continuity which we had not achieved.[65]

Irving became known as a conductor who favoured brisk, strict tempos and the principle of music leading the dancers, which is absolutely in tune with the Balanchine aesthetic. He left the Royal Ballet in 1958 to join New York City Ballet. Returning to guest with his former company, he felt that tempos had slackened and that Lambert's model was no longer respected.

Different traditions and styles dictate different approaches. Russian companies are now the most notorious for following the dancers' whims at the expense of the music. Yet, the Kirov production of *Les Sylphides*, seen in London in 1988, faster and with more rhythmic impulse than most other productions, gave the work a welcome momentum and life. In Stravinsky-Balanchine, not only is the musical continuity respected, but dancers are required to bring out the motoric emphasis. Nevertheless, this style is not straightforward, and there is still room for give and take. As Balanchine himself said, 'A good instrumentalist, Milstein, for instance, or a resourceful dancer, can give the feeling of rubato in Stravinsky's music without blurring the beat.'[66]

Dancers use different techniques to co-ordinate with music. Do they listen, or do they count? The counting technique has become increasingly widely used. Some choreographers base their choreography on counts – MacMillan, for instance, would ask his musician to give him counts from the musical score and then made dance phrases to these counts, not directly to the music.[67] It seems that there are national and company traditions when it comes to counting. American and British dancers use counts more than, for instance, Russian dancers. Irek Mukhamedov never counts, not even to the difficult score by Brian Elias for MacMillan's *The Judas Tree* (1992).[68] However, counts are useful pegs for rapid learning in times when rehearsal schedules are extremely tight, and a useful mechanism for keeping dancers in unison or co-ordinated with difficult music.

There is much debate and difference of opinion about the value, disadvantages and effects of counts. It does seem likely that they affect musicality and phrasing, even if they disappear once movement is secure within the body. If dancers count when they perform, they do not necessarily hear musical detail or subtle changes between one musical performance and the next. More than one Balanchine dancer has expressed worries about today's rapid count-bound learning and dancing of Balanchine. Farrell, for instance, emphasises the importance of acute listening. Her intention when dancing was to leave herself open to the present and 'to hear what has to be heard. If you dance to only what you want to hear, you're dancing an opinion.'[69] She relished the challenge of a tempo that she did not quite expect or of a particular instrument sounding unusually forceful. Although she perhaps drew on previous performances more than she ever realised, it is Farrell's appetite for discovery, from keen listening, that is important. And discovery is what she taught. Thus, she mapped out the steps of *Gounod Symphony* (1958) for the students at the School of American Ballet and then, for the run-through, said 'Now do it again and do it differently than you did before.' And then again, at the next run-through, 'Do it differently from the way you just did it.' It is not that Farrell totally denies the value of counts. Indeed, she devises count sequences carefully when teaching steps, to bring out niceties of phrasing. But afterwards, she stresses release from them, release into listening and spontaneous response.

All the same, counting, which leads dancers to refer to beat rather than melody, probably suits the Balanchine style better than most. It is interesting that Balanchine changed tack for different dancers, because he understood the look that counts gave. Barbara Walczak recalls that in the 1950s Balanchine would say,

'Don't listen to the music, just count.' He was afraid that we would begin emoting . . . I heard an interview a few years ago with Joe Duell, and he said that Balanchine had told his dancers, 'Just listen to the music, don't count.' I was flabbergasted. But the company had changed.[70]

Fonteyn told James Monahan that she never counted, which freed her to be aware of phrase, proportions between one musical unit and the next, and what would happen later in the music. He remembers her saying that

when she danced she was aware, not primarily or deliberately of the beat (she took this for granted), but of the phrase or the sequence of phrases; she had found that, on the whole, she was so thoroughly conscious of the music's phrasing that she could usually measure, well in advance, the requisite movements, slightly spacing them out or compressing them according to the little vagaries of the orchestra on the particular occasion. She could, in short, listen well ahead.[71]

Occasionally, listening and responding directly to what is heard can defeat choreographic intentions. The choreography might be about working against the music. It is all too easy for dancers to let themselves slide into the rhythms and dynamics that seem most 'natural'. This is what happened in a passage of Ashley Page's *Two-part Invention* (Prokofiev and Robert Moran, 1996), where the smoothness that he wanted had turned into the sharp, punchy dynamics of the music even by the dress rehearsal.[72]

The manner in which dancers are taught phrasing is also important to interpretation, to their musical response. This is the case, even though they may then go on to adapt for themselves what they have learnt. Different dancers teach different rhythmic and dynamic shadings of movement. Most of the time, dancers learn through copying the moves of another dancer, supported by verbal clarification. Counting often changes: the counts may not necessarily be those that the choreographer used, if she or he ever used them at all. But counts do indicate phrasing, even if a dancer stops using them after a while. The count of one, the beginning of a count sequence, indicates the beginning of a new dance unit, and the close of the previous one. It is significant that Balanchine insisted on correct, 'musical' counting to Patricia Neary when he observed her staging *Agon*.[73] The least controversial position is that of the dancer who creates a role, hearing the phrasing of the choreographer her- or himself, and often collaborating in the production of the choreographic ideas and their response to music.

We are beginning to consider the musicality of the individual dancer, which can transcend traditions and stylistic generalisations. Indeed, excellent examples of this are the distinctive musicalities of Baryshnikov and Makarova, both of them Kirov-trained dancers. The class pianist Lynn Stanford compares their approaches, considering them both highly musical, but in contrasting ways:

The curious thing about Misha [Baryshnikov] is that he's very quick, impatient and all that. He's always running slightly ahead of the music. You can't watch Misha when you are playing for him and try to be 'with' him, because he's always slightly anticipating everything. But he is very *consistent* . . .

Now Natasha Makarova, on the other hand, is kind of laid back and languid, retiring and sylphlike. So Natasha is always – curiously – slightly behind the music. Just *slightly*. The music sounds, and she moves, but it is in such a consistent way that it all works, because it is always all *about* the music. It's never 'in spite of' the music.[74]

Another difference between Makarova and Baryshnikov: she likes to slow the music down to suit her languorous tempo – some musicians have been highly critical of her distortions of the music – whereas he is far more game to dance to the musician's tempo.

Coming to the vexed question of the dancer's rubato, we might ask: is it planned ahead by the dancer or a spur of the moment decision? Does it happen at every performance or as a one-off? Or is it choreographed and not in fact rubato or interpretive choice at all? Sometimes technical considerations enter

Ex. 2.7. Tchaikovsky, *The Sleeping Beauty*, Act I *Pas d'action*, Rose Adagio.

the picture. Rubato might well be the outcome of a chance situation, falling off-balance early, or holding a balance for longer than ever before, and then phrasing after that moment accordingly, delaying or catching up with the music during the next movement. Clearly, one video recording of a dance will never prove anything about rubato. Some dancers make an issue of rubato surprises. Wordsworth remembers the fun that he had working with Brenda Last:

> She didn't always dance bang on every note . . . she would linger and then catch me up. We used to play terrific games with one another, because after a time, we got to trust each other. In the middle of a performance she would suddenly rush for four bars and then wait for me, or I would do the same back to her . . . And that was only possible because she was so assured with what she was doing – she was so on top of everything technically that you could really relax and make a performance.[75]

Farrell, who listened so carefully to her music, said that 'dancing for me and Mr B was not etched in stone . . . I always lived every performance as if it was the only one that existed.'[76] She produced remarkable, expressive effects through her rubato. Richard Colton remembers:

> In *Mozartiana* . . . there was a great moment, a turn in back passé, and it seemed suspended in time by sheer – it looked like sheer emotion. And Farrell gets behind the music for the remainder of the phrase but then she speeds up, heightening the movement quality in a logical way, and ends with the music, in harmony.[77]

Dancers sometimes illuminate a moment in the music by selecting for visualisation an accent, rhythmic pattern or melodic shape. Observers see and hear these moments and enjoy them. Langdon Dewey noticed such moments in

Ex. 2.8. Tchaikovsky, *The Sleeping Beauty*, Act I *pas d'action*, Coda.

Fonteyn's *Sleeping Beauty*, about a third of the way through the Rose Adagio
(see Ex. 2.7):

> Fonteyn performed the low-sweeping circles of the arms and hands while
> beating tiny stationary steps on her toes . . . The accompaniment in the bass
> was the key . . . and the very phrase markings denote a prolonged emphasis
> on the second and fourth beats of the extended measures. These, she actually
> delineated for her audience, sweeping the circular gestures to end *with the*
> *phrases* on the first note of the following beat. She did this with such consum-
> mate artistry that it was impossible to know whether the musical line followed
> the dancer, or the dance line followed the orchestra.[78]

Later, in her Variation Coda, just before she dances with the spindle (see Ex. 2.8):

> The audience has heard the theme and rhythm a few moments earlier. Fon-
> teyn took that rhythm and made a spectacular entrance . . . The effect was of
> speed and marvellously controlled power. But she did something even more
> important: she singled out those accented bass notes for pointing the forward
> foot. The leaps were powerful; but the exact timing within the rhythm of the
> pointing gesture gave an illusion of extending the descending arc.[79]

The French dancer Violette Verdy, who, in her later career, danced with New
York City Ballet, similarly inspired observers to spot connections between what
they saw and what they heard, like Edward Villella watching her performance in
the *Tchaikovsky pas de deux*: 'In the passé, it's not just the foot and leg moving up
from the stage to the knee: she brings them up as though they bounced right
from the music.' And in the first movement of *Episodes* (1959):

> I didn't understand the score; but when I watched her I could understand the
> music and could see what Balanchine was after. Certain lunges didn't make

sense – choreographic sense – to me when I saw someone else at rehearsal just lunge and turn, lunge and turn. Then I saw Verdy do them, and I said, 'Of course.' When she lunged and turned I saw a motivation for the lunge and turn – both in visual terms and in relation to the music.[80]

Sometimes, like any other detail of dance, that kind of connection, established by one dancer, can lead others to follow suit. In other words, though not choreographed, it finds its way into the ballet. Verdy was unusually conscious of making connections with musical detail. On several occasions she has spoken of responding to timbre of voice or musical instrument, and, in *Liebeslieder Walzer* (1960), it is a conventionally gendered response:

> I felt I was many persons, because my dances were with different singers. Naturally I had some of the light, soprano passages, which had a delicate, tremulous quality, but I also had tenor – romantic and tender, but with a little more of a man's authority. And then I had one or two with the baritone that gave me a sense of dramatic force and urgency, because the singing was very inquiring and demanding. Then I would impose myself on my partner, I would be domineering, while when I followed the soprano I would abandon myself to him, fragile and helpless. With the mezzo, I would have a complaining, wounded quality, relying on my partner, but retaining my own pain. I would take on the color of the voice.[81]

Verdy, so often singled out for her musicality (she could read music and play an instrument) is an interesting case study. Here is someone who did not fit neatly into the New York City Ballet mould. Robert Garis welcomes the legibility of her phrasing, its 'drama', her pointed articulation of the shape of the dance material in relation to music:

> Its pointedness seemed old-fashioned compared with the subtle inflections within a single tempo I had come to love in Toscanini and in Balanchine's normal style. But the distance between Verdy's style and what surrounded her for me created a highly pleasurable tension of variation, which was of interest in itself and something I was proud of appreciating.[82]

Verdy confesses that Balanchine sometimes wanted to 'clean up' her dancing and make it plainer,[83] yet he clearly relished her stretching him beyond his usual stylistic framework. The dancer again is a musical collaborator.

Apart from leading or following the dancer on stage, the ballet musician has many other important areas of responsibility, decisions to make about general interpretation as well as response to the moment in performance. The job is far more complex than a matter of following a composer's metronome marking. Some decisions are a matter of practicality: height of the dancer, which can guide tempo (taller dancers tend to prefer slightly slower tempos); injury, which may require tempo adjustment at a point of technical difficulty; size of the stage (bigger distances might require a slight slowing of tempo); type of dance floor (for their own safety, dancers might well be inclined to jump small, and therefore faster, on a hard floor); dealing with changes in acoustics and changes in size of orchestra as a company tours different venues and orchestral pits.

Other responsibilities for the musician are a matter of artistic judgement. Composer (if the work is a commission), conductor, rehearsal pianist are all at some point in negotiation with the choreographer, but one especially important stage is the move from rehearsal room to stage and orchestra. How can you transfer to the stage the nuances that have grown up, perhaps unconsciously, in the rehearsal room, the slight slowings and accelerations, the holding back at the end of a phrase, which might be part of the pianist's original interpretation or the choreographer's vision as the dance develops, or a subtle mixture of both their opinions? Often, conductors attend rehearsals and get to know the developing work before the move to stage and orchestra. On the other hand, conductors need the freedom to keep their musical interpretation individual and alive, and their decisions are a matter of negotiation with choreographer and dancers, as time permits. Twiner is both pianist and conductor:

> When I'm conducting for principal dancers, I prefer to play my own rehearsal. I have something in my hands which transfers to my body, the speeds which they would like and which they can dance to. When I pick up the stick, there is something already in my body.[84]

When playing in the orchestral pit for performances, Twiner and Philip Gammon (another Royal Ballet pianist) both use monitors on the side of the piano, enabling them to maintain the direct visual link with the dancer from rehearsal room into the theatre.

'Something already in my body . . .' – the ballet conductor and pianist must have a well-developed sense of movement, a physical empathy with the dancers. Gammon breathes with the dancers in *Rhapsody*, for instance, with the ballerina's cadences, to match precisely with the beginning of her last solo, or to time the final chord of the *pas de deux* to the moment *just before* the male soloist lifts the ballerina into the wings. He had freedom to develop his own interpretation when learning the piece for Ashton's first rehearsals, but now choreographed, his timing is automatically less free than he would enjoy in concert performance.[85] Sir Thomas Beecham's response to the dance movement in Tudor's *Romeo and Juliet* (1943) deepened the more he became acquainted with the ballet. According to Denby, he conducted the Delius score at the first perform-ances as if in a concert, sumptuously and as if a showpiece, but his 'legato obliterated the landmarks they were used to'.[86] Movement flow is especially hard to track in this score with no 'groove' provided by the beat. However, by the last performance, Beecham had fully understood it:

> The dancers not only recognized their cues, they could find in the musical phrase they were cued to the exact impetus which suited their momentary phrase of dancing. Tudor had counted on these correspondences of impetus from the first. But only Sir Thomas understood completely on the stage and in the orchestra what aspect of the score it was that Tudor had counted on, and he made this aspect musically plausible and expressive.[87]

Markova (Juliet) applauded the momentum of Beecham's accompaniment, all the more surprising because the overall timing under his conducting was very slow. Tempo and continuity flow do not correspond straightforwardly. 'The mu-sic did not disintegrate. He had a supreme gift for sustaining its momentum, and the orchestra responded with superb playing. I was in seventh heaven at such inspired accompaniment.'[88] Clearly, Beecham made a major contribution to these performances of Tudor's ballet. We can take this idea further, that a clever conductor, when faced with a weak choreography, can weld it together and make more of it by musical means.

Conductors, like dancers, operate as part of distinct traditions. Performance customs have had a powerful effect on dance accompaniment, the trend during this century, for instance, towards a less romantic, drier, more modernist style of performance for works from previous centuries. Just as Toscanini 'cleaned up' opera in this respect, the New York City Ballet, governed by the aesthetic of Balanchine and Robert Irving, presented their ballet scores largely in tune with the new performance customs. There have been repercussions in other companies.

Another curiosity about musical practice in ballet is the tendency for the per-formance of scores to slow down over time. Concert performances of music used in ballet are often faster than ballet performances, the Chopin of *Les Sylphides* (1908) being perhaps the most obvious example of this. Dancers, possibly with-out realising it, prefer a comfortable tempo, even though this works against the general tightening of musical tempos during the twentieth century. Sometimes the slowing down occurs during the creative process, the 'natural' result of cre-ating dance movement in chunks, phrase by phrase, and then of having to com-promise on tempo in order to cope with stamina limitations. In contrast to this, the ballets *Agon* and *Apollo* (1928) are known to have gathered speed over the years, and eventually had to be slowed down again.[89] Stravinsky himself requested the change for *Agon*, but musicians can complicate the issue: they are not infallible, and they change their minds about the way in which their music should be interpreted; witness Stravinsky's own five recordings of *Le Sacre du printemps* and his published reviews of other performances of the work.[90]

Philip Ellis, who conducts for Birmingham Royal Ballet, points out how conducting style needs to be adjusted to compensate for the pianist's tendency in rehearsal to want to move on (because the piano is not a sustaining instrument), whereas the orchestra tends to hold back the tempo. He also recognises how, with the move to the stage, dancers have to cope with hearing their music later than before (because sound takes time to travel); hence the occasional use of upstage speakers in ballet to convey the orchestral sound to performers more quickly.[91]

For all this – compromises, dangerous uncertainties, and, most of all, time pressures that preclude optimum discussion – the magic of the moment of performance itself can still remain. Furthermore, in looking at any dance, we are confronting something with a highly complex and shifting identity that we can never fully grasp or control. We might indeed celebrate this, although, when we look closely at a dance on one video recording (usually only one recording is easily available, if that), it is all too easy to forget the multiple identities of a dance.

Sources for Analysing Music and Dance

The sources of film, video and scores (of both music and dance) are the backbone resources for any detailed musical-choreographic analysis. But there are problems and limitations with these sources, which we have to recognise. Ballets exist as a number of performance interpretations.

The film or video recording of a ballet not only represents just one performance interpretation of the work, it is also in itself a translation of the ballet. Some of the movement may well be lost from camera, the original spatial orientation of the dance on stage is often distorted, the dance dynamics are frequently altered (whether enhanced or diminished), and the practice of editing creates its own rhythms on top of those of the music and dance. A professional, commercial or television video recording of a ballet might well seem more alive to the viewer than a poor rehearsal film record made for in-house company purposes, but it is far more likely to distort the stage dance for the sake of televisual liveliness. Post-production editing may also disturb the synchronisation between music and dance. There may be large, obvious discrepancies in timing or much smaller, subtle ones that affect how the dancers meet the beat (on it, slightly before it, or after it). Furthermore, film or video recordings often include errors:

they may not be the best representation of a dancer's performance. Any attempt at deciphering the movement of a supposedly unison group of dancers immediately illustrates the problems of analysing from film or video. The dancers all look different. Whenever using film or video, we have to get behind the film process in order to see the stage piece, and we have to access as many 'versions' of a ballet as we can.

Benesh and Labanotation scores, invaluable as they are, also have their limitations. Again, there is some loss of information or change of meaning: the score represents the notator's interpretation of the taught dance. The timing of movement is often written with a degree of approximation, using conventions or omitting fine detail, and dynamics are often treated in even less detail. Yet scores usually provide a clear account of how choreography fits the framework of beat and metre, which is vital to my work and often much less clear and 'interpreted' in a film/video source. Scores vary considerably in their state of completion. Some exist simply in sketch form; others are highly detailed and with useful verbal material supporting the notation itself.

Supplementing all these resources for the analyst are live performances, rehearsals, her/his own reconstruction of the dance movement and music – getting to know the movement and music from the inside can be highly revealing – as well as information from written sources and interviews. It is enlightening to get hold of a wide range of information about choreographic changes and how they came about, about the dancers' contributions, about original musical sources, the recordings and scores used by the choreographer, and about musical interpretations.

In recommending that we are alert to such a range of sources, I am not advocating any attempt to establish an ideal text. It is important that dance texts grow and change with new performers and over time: they generate their own tradition. But I am suggesting that we use these resources during the analytical process to argue our case for style, to open up the argument. Subtle differences between versions of a text can have important implications for musical-choreographic style. They affect the interdependent structures of music and dance, they affect meaning, and most important of all, they tell us just how much life and energy can be gained from refined interpretive strategies.

Part 2

3

George Balanchine

Mention music and choreography, and Balanchine's name is probably the first to come to mind, for a number of reasons: an array of celebrated works whose *raison d'être* was their music, his extraordinary and unparalleled collaboration with Stravinsky, and a behind-the-scenes musician's training, a professional training, that enhanced every work that he made. Other choreographers might have shared his sentiment: 'I cannot move, I don't even want to move, unless I hear the music first',[1] but Balanchine is nevertheless the musician choreographer *par excellence*. Sometimes, he even suggests the superiority of this companion art form:

> The composer is able to give more life to a bar, more vitality and rhythmical substance than a choreographer, or a dancer for that matter. The musician deals with time and sound in a highly scientific way . . . The choreographer will never be able to achieve such precision in the expression of movement as the composer through sound effect.[2]

Balanchine's musical background has been well documented. He trained in piano, composition and music theory at the Petrograd Conservatory of Music alongside his studies of ballet, and soon after his arrival in America in 1933, he was still filling in time 'freshening up on counterpoint and harmony with his friend, the composer Nicolas Nabokov'.[3] During his career as a choreographer, he continued to develop his knowledge of the musical repertoire and of music theory, and remained an active pianist and composer of the occasional song or piano miniature – according to his friend, the violinist Nathan Milstein, 'he sight-read freely'.[4] There are many references to Balanchine conversing in sophisticated musical terms with composers, conductors and rehearsal pianists. Throughout his life, too, he made his own piano transcriptions of orchestral scores, many of which are now housed in the Balanchine archives of the Harvard University Theatre Collection. Thus, he worked on the Webern symphony used for *Episodes* (1959, see Ex. 3.1). As it has for many composers, such workmanlike enterprise would have given Balanchine an especially secure

Ex. 3.1. Balanchine's transcription for piano of Webern's Symphony Op. 21.

knowledge of a score, its structures, proportions, thematic ma-
nipulations, contrapuntal textures and orchestration. Certainly, even if he apparently kept silent on the subject of musical structure with dancers, everyone
who worked with him testifies to his firm grasp of a musical form, as background
preparation to creating steps in the dance studio. Furthermore, Balanchine's
musical interests led him to prioritise the values of musical performance: he
pressed for and won for himself one of the finest ballet orchestras in the world,
directed in his own time by Leon Barzin and Robert Irving.

It is hard to generalise about Balanchine's use of music, for there are so many contradictions and exceptions; he constantly avoids categorisation. True, certain musical styles suggested certain movement styles, moods and costumes. Twentieth-century atonal music gave rise to the most severe disruptions of the classical style, leotard ballets featuring parallel as well as turned-out placement, flexed as well as pointed feet, and angular, acrobatic moves. Nineteenth-century music inspired a closer reference to the classical tradition in steps, body line and tutus. Yet, numerous ballets do not fit the general rule. Then, if we note a general progression towards plotless ballets using musical titles, we can still find story ballets in his late career. But it is the plotless or 'storyless'[5] (or more or less so) music ballet that undoubtedly epitomises Balanchine, and which will be the main focus in this chapter.

There are signs that Balanchine was to move towards this kind of work even in his earliest career in Russia. There, he developed a profound admiration for Fokine's *Les Sylphides*. The dancer Petr Gusev recalls: 'Balanchine called *Chopiniana* his favourite ballet and often by himself performed various dances from it.'[6] Because of this admiration, undoubtedly, he suggested the revival of the piece to piano for New York City Ballet in 1972. While still in Russia, he also saw Duncan dance to large-scale symphonic music. During this early period, Balanchine also danced in Lopukhov's *The Dance Symphony* (see Ch. 1).

Musical Choices

The range of musical scores used by Balanchine is wide: this includes not only his ballets, but also his extensive work in opera, musicals and films. Whilst he was bold in his choice of contemporary music, he often used the music of previous centuries. There are surprises and oddities in his selections, and there are also favourite composers, above all Stravinsky and Tchaikovsky. Most of Balanchine's choreography in Russia was set to short pieces of music, unsurprising nineteenth-century and early twentieth-century choices. However, there are a couple of larger, more ambitious selections. An early work that is often referred to by Balanchine's contemporaries in Russia is the *Marche funèbre* (1923, to the second movement of Chopin's Sonata No. 1 in B-flat minor). With its solemn processions and sculptural groupings, it was evocative of funeral ceremonies, but its tone was of generalised emotion, and abstract choreographic values were controlled within a three-part musical structure, 'strictly subordinated to the music'.[7] Less well documented, the following year, according to the catalogue of Balanchine's work, he choreographed a *pas de deux* to the slow movement of Glazunov's Violin Concerto in A minor. Balanchine had plans too for an ambitious work to the music of Scriabin, and in 1924, the year in which he left Russia, he began a ballet to Stravinsky's *Pulci-*

nella.[8] Had he not had to abandon the project, this would have been his first large-scale work to contemporary music.

A survey of Balanchine's music over his career after leaving Russia suggests a clear pattern of change. The years in Europe (1924–33) were the years of collaborative ballets, works with stories or themes (often written by a separate individual, such as Boris Kochno), and with commissioned scores and designs. For the Ballets Russes, Diaghilev would match up the collaborators and make the musical choices himself. Much of the music that Balanchine used (for Diaghilev and immediately afterwards) was by contemporary French composers, although he also made a seminal contact with Stravinsky's music when he choreographed *Apollon Musagète* (*Apollo*) (1928). In the US, Balanchine tells us that he 'reacted rather violently in the direction of the classics';[9] by the 1940s, when Balanchine was in his late thirties and early forties, the series of plotless ballets using musical titles begins, the kind of ballet with which we most immediately associate Balanchine today. By the mid-1950s, such ballets (and now often without any major commissioned design element) dominate Balanchine's production.

It was in the 1950s that Balanchine also began to use highly complex twentieth-century music. There were the twelve-note scores by Schoenberg, Webern and Stravinsky (the commission *Agon*, which was partly twelve-note). Stravinsky and his assistant Robert Craft were instrumental in encouraging his interest in this genre of music. He also used Charles Ives for *Ivesiana* (1954). In the 1960s, most notably he set Xenakis (*Metastaseis & Pithoprakta*, 1968), stochastic music, in other words, using devices of chance and mathematical ordering; three scores that incorporated a jazz element – for *Modern Jazz: Variants* (1961, Schuller), *Clarinade* (1964, Gould), *Concerto for Jazz Band and Orchestra* (1971, Liebermann); two pieces of electronic music – for *Electronics* (1961, Gassmann/ Sala) and *Variations pour une porte et un soupir* (1974, Henry); and the music of the Japanese composer Toshiro Mayuzumi for *Bugaku* (1963).

The proportion of musical commissions lessened during the American years, partly perhaps for financial reasons, but perhaps too because collaboration became less important for Balanchine. Primarily inspired by listening to music, he enjoyed getting to know its form in detail, and existing scores guaranteed this opportunity. Commissions provided an occasional, welcome change. For obvious reasons, they were also his preferred method of working when he had a specific idea or theme as starting point for a ballet.[10] The most important of the commissions are the Stravinsky series, *Jeu de cartes* (1937), and then the much closer collaborations *Orpheus* (1948), *Agon* (1957) and, for television, *Noah and the Flood* (1962). Also noteworthy is the continuing collaboration with the Italian composer Rieti, which began with two pieces for Balanchine during the Diaghilev years, and extended into his American career, including the 1946 *Night*

Shadow. Then there is the single full-length commission of Balanchine's career, the three-act *Don Quixote* (1965) composed by Nicolas Nabokov (according to Arlene Croce, Stravinskian pastiche[11]). Important too is Balanchine's work in introducing many musical scores to the American public. Ballet was a very useful platform for music, for contemporary music, but also for 'new' nineteenth-century scores like the Bizet Symphony and Gounod's First Symphony, which had both been lost for about a century.

Stravinsky was not only Balanchine's most important collaborator, but also a major influence upon his entire career. *Apollo* was, he more than once recognised, 'the turning point of my life',[12] and Stravinsky's music, mostly of the neo-classical, post-Russian period, inspired three festivals of ballet, in 1937, 1972 and 1983. As for Stravinsky, he claimed that, 'In classical dancing, I see the triumph of studied conception over vagueness, of the rule over the arbitrary, of order over the haphazard . . . I see in it the perfect expression of the Apollonian principle.'[13] Balanchine used Stravinsky's music more regularly than that of any other composer, although it often seems surprising that they officially collaborated on only four occasions.

After Stravinsky, Tchaikovsky was Balanchine's most regular choice of composer: he was given special attention in a New York City Ballet festival in 1981, which presented works by several choreographers. Both the qualities of the music and the link with the Petipa tradition must have seemed appealing. Balanchine choreographed Tchaikovsky's ballet music – most notably *Swan Lake* (1951) and *The Nutcracker* (1954) – as well as several of his concert scores. Ravel was likewise given major treatment in a City Ballet festival in 1975, although there were some reservations about his compatibility with the company style. Irving had firm views: 'The trouble is he puts too much beauty and elaboration into the music to make it easy for a choreographer.' But, he went on to say, the 'slenderest pieces were exquisite, like [*Le*] *Tombeau de Couperin* [Balanchine] . . . Those are light, dry pieces'[14] – dry, like the neo-classical Stravinsky.

Balanchine's statements explain something of his musical principles and interests. At the time of the 1972 Stravinsky Festival, he singled out Delibes, Stravinsky and Tchaikovsky for their *musique dansante* – a particular rhythmic quality suited to dance was of paramount importance. 'They made music for the body to dance to. They invented the floor for the dancer to walk on.'[15] A year later, he added Mendelssohn to the list.[16] That rhythmic quality, which is to do with vibrancy and clarity of impulse, rhythm in the foreground, was an obvious reason why Balanchine often used music actually written for dance. This was not only music by Delibes and Tchaikovsky. For instance, there are his selections from Glazunov's *Raymonda*, to which Balanchine set new choreography as well as reworkings and borrowings from Petipa.

At other times, Balanchine mentions the inspiration of Verdi, whose opera ballet music he choreographed on a number of occasions. Verdi taught him 'how to handle the corps de ballet, the ensemble, the soloists – how to make the soloists stand out against the corps de ballet and when to give them time to rest'.[17] But he only once chose his music for a ballet of his own, for *Ballo della Regina* (1978). He also greatly admired Webern, whose twelve-note music was introduced to him by Stravinsky. Martha Graham and Balanchine choreographed separate sections of his complete orchestral music in the collaborative ballet *Episodes* (1959). Yet, Balanchine adds on Webern: 'The songs were the best of all, but they were written to be listened to. The orchestral music, however, fills air like molecules: it is written for atmosphere. The first time I heard it, I knew it could be danced to.'[18] Not all Webern, indeed, not even the 'best' music does he see as suitable for dance.

The case of Mozart is unusual, for Balanchine seems to have changed his mind about the suitability of his music for dance, although he remained a favourite composer. In 1954, Balanchine and the writer Francis Mason claimed 'Although Mozart wrote no music for ballet, of all composers his music is most adaptable for ballet, of all composers his music is the most danceable.'[19] In a 1959 interview, he was still enthusiastic.[20] Yet, in 1982, he maintains exactly the opposite, that most of his music does not have the dance element at all. Now he is resigned to Mozart's 'best' music (like Webern's) not being suitable for dance, citing as examples the operas *The Magic Flute* (he choreographed dances and directed staging in a 1956 production) and *The Marriage of Figaro* (for which he choreographed the Act III Fandango in 1948).[21] Apart from the Tchaikovsky orchestration and arrangement of Mozart in *Mozartiana* (1933, rechoreographed in 1981), Balanchine stopped using Mozart in the 1950s. This is not the only inconsistency that we come across in Balanchine's statements about music or between what he says and what he actually does.

Certainly, Balanchine is convinced that some music is best listened to, complete in itself, and not danced. Stravinsky's *Le Sacre* and *Les Noces* are other examples.[22] Or there is chamber music which, he feels, is of primary interest to performers rather than listeners.[23] On a couple of occasions, he cites specific principles. In the 1959 interview, he claims that the music of Beethoven and Brahms is representational, seeming to paint pictures, or, at least, to encourage people to build their own pictures from personal feelings. Instead, he wants their minds to be free of imagery in order to be open to the dancing. He says, 'Mozart and Stravinsky and Webern – this is a different kind of music. It is like a rose – you can admire it deeply, but you cannot inject your personal feelings into it . . . Your mind will be free to *see* the dancing.'[24]

Certain music (again he cites Brahms) requires a freedom in musical performance that is not possible when it has to accompany dance.[25] Yet, he did use the Brahms *Liebeslieder Walzer* (1960, actually, following up someone else's suggestion[26]), presumably attracted here by its basis in dance rhythms. And perhaps because of his admiration for Schoenberg, he warmed to the idea of setting Schoenberg's orchestration of Brahms' Piano Quartet in G minor Op. 25, introduced to him by Craft (*Brahms-Schoenberg Quartet*, 1966).[27]

Over the years, we can build up a list of the composers whom Balanchine considered not right for dance: Beethoven, Brahms (most Brahms), Mahler, Sibelius, Dvořák, Shostakovich, Bruckner, Bartók (the last's rhythms he considered banal). Only a little Prokofiev was, he felt, suitable.[28] It seems that he was generally averse to the romantic-scale, multi-movement, nineteenth-century construction, and he was highly critical of Massine's selection (and use) of Tchaikovsky's Fifth and Brahms' Fourth Symphonies (see Ch. 2, pp. 50–5).[29] Length might sometimes have been a major drawback. For instance, he removed the first movement of Tchaikovsky's Third Symphony when he choreographed the *Diamonds* section of *Jewels* (1967).[30] But perhaps most important of all was whether the music contained the *dansante* quality. Much of Tchaikovsky would seem to have that quality – many parts of the symphonies, indeed, have a buoyancy and danciness of rhythm that reminds one of his ballets. It is churlish to generalise, but one can appreciate if Balanchine found Bruckner and Mahler rhythmically unsuitable, as well as long-winded, for dance.

That a work was a well-known 'masterpiece', by a 'great' composer, did not prevent Balanchine from setting it. His use of Bach for *Concerto Barocco* in 1941 was unusual and controversial at the time (see Ch. 1, p. 14), the score suggested to him by Milstein.[31] *Balanchine's Festival of Ballet* simply recommends that the choreographer should be 'careful, as he acts on this inspiration, not to interpret the music beyond its proper limits, not to stretch the music to accommodate a literary idea, for instance.'[32] One senses again the figure of Massine as an example not to follow. *Barocco* is Balanchine at his most abstract, using a musical title. So, significantly, are most of his Mozart pieces, like *Symphonie Concertante* (1947), *Divertimento No. 15* (1956, and the earlier choreography *Caracole* to the same score), and the lesser-known *Concierto de Mozart* (1942).

No survey of Balanchine's music is complete without acknowledging his use of downright popular music, familiar tunes guaranteed to be easy on the ears and minds of his audience, like the Hershy Kay commission *Western Symphony* (1954), which is a medley of American folk tunes, and Kay's orchestrations of Sousa marches for *Stars and Stripes* (1958) and of Gershwin songs for *Who Cares?* (1970). One style that Balanchine could not tolerate was rock 'n' roll: 'It is awful, dreadful, mindless'.[33] But highbrow and elitist he certainly was not in his tastes. When he selected some Hungarian gypsy songs by Sophie Menter, orchestrated by Tchaikovsky, for the 1981 festival, he was unapologetic: 'Why does all music have to be the best? Let's have some cheap restaurant music.'[34]

Artistic Principles and Working Methods

What did such variety of music offer Balanchine as a choreographer? What did he want from it? Study Balanchine's numerous statements about music, written and spoken, and it immediately becomes clear: time is the factor that preoccupies him above all others. Although Balanchine is highly sensitive to the properties of melody and timbre, most important, music provides the crucial time/rhythmic foundation and limitation for choreography.

> Music is time. It's not the melody that's important but the division of time.[35]

> Music puts a time corset on the dance.[36]

> In my choreographic creations I have always been dependent on music. I feel a choreographer can't invent rhythms, he only reflects them in movement . . . The organising of rhythm on a grand scale is a sustained process. It is a function of the musical mind.[37]

We note again the deference that he shows to music as the superior art. On a less grand scale it is the musical pulse, which provides rhythmic drive, that Balanchine finds important. Indeed, he once said that what he 'mainly' expects from a composer is 'a steady and reassuring pulse which holds the work together and which one should feel even in the rests'.[38]

The importance to Balanchine of this organisational principle of pulse cannot be overestimated, nor the fact that pulse is unusually strict in his view. He attends to it positively in his own dance rhythmic organisation. Indeed, it is the tautness of pulse-driven rhythms that he so often singled out in his appreciation of Stravinsky, 'an architect of time'[39] – the silences, pregnant because the pulse continued through them, 'life goes on within each silence'; the strictly pulsed fermata, 'always counted out in beats'; and rubato, 'notated precisely, in unequal measures'.[40] Balanchine's composer friend Nabokov, who was also a spokesman for Stravinsky's work, considered pulse the central organising principle of Stravinsky's rhythmic style. Thus he wrote in 1944, 'Look at any one of [Stravinsky's] bars and you will find that it is not the measure closed in by barlines (as it would be in Mozart, for example), but the monometrical unit of the measure, the single beat which determines the life of his musical organism'.[41]

To Balanchine too, ballet music meant pulse-based music, as Stravinsky himself joked: 'But are the *Movements* [1959, for piano and orchestra, set by Balanchine in 1963] ballet music? Barbarous locution to Balanchine! What he needs is not a pas de deux but a motor impulse.'[42] We might recall the motor, machine impulse in the 1913 *Le Sacre* (see Ch. 1, pp. 39–42).

Of course, there are, as always with Balanchine, exceptions, several pieces set to music that has no firm undercurrent of beat, strict or otherwise. In *Ivesiana*, dancers often move 'through' seemingly 'pulseless' music, creating their own tempos between signals, walking, swaying or, in the 'In the Night' section, shuffling across the stage on their knees. Then, there is the strange *Variations pour une porte et un soupir*, which is a precise visualisation of *musique concrète* gestures, the female dancer as the door, the male as the sigh. The piece features a huge black cape attached to the woman by strings held from the wings. The programme note tells us that the duet 'depends upon measured vibrations of sound removed from the usual eight- or twelve-tone scale. The manipulation of the cape is also on a strict metrical count, the rhythms of which are elastic but precisely indicated.' Even though Balanchine knew where the pulse lay, it is not at all clear to the ear, and Karin von Aroldingen found it 'impossible to work with counts'.[43] Or there is the first section of *Metastaseis & Pithoprakta*. Significantly, Merrill Ashley mentions this as an unusual piece in her book *Dancing for Balanchine*, a ballet with 'difficult music,' without dance counts, and, directly related to that, no pulse base in the music itself.[44]

Far more of Balanchine's ballets are set to musical styles that demand some slight give-and-take in tempo, in other words, rubato (elongation or quickening of the pulse). The majority, too, of the scores he used have a less percussively pronounced pulse than those of Stravinsky. The scores of Tchaikovsky, Delibes, Glazunov and Glinka, indeed most of Balanchine's nineteenth-century composers, are of this kind. Yet, the important point here is that give-and-take is only effective as such when the pulse drive is already firmly established. In this respect, Balanchine is well known for having tightened up performance of the Tchaikovsky ballet scores, in other words, for being unusually strict about being 'on time', and not pulling out tempos to suit individual dancers. His version of *Swan Lake Act II* preserves the pulse impetus far more exactly than in most traditional ballet performances, and a result is that the relations between musical units of varying proportions and dynamics become much clearer.

The pulse drive is celebrated too in the movement style, most clearly with change of weight and in the work of legs and feet. That is why Denby wrote that New York City Ballet company dance 'on top of the beat', which 'builds up pressure. They dance with a rhythmic thrust that is quick and exact.'[45] He is excited by this, even though he notes the inherent danger of 'bluntness in the rhythm . . . marching-style meter . . . sameness of attack'[46] in the style. Indeed, one does not have to look far to find any number of examples of regular articulation of pulse in the choreography, whether or not to music that defines the pulse quite so regularly.

The opening moves of *Agon* are one instance, where Balanchine sets up a motor motion by choreographing each beat. At the very opening of the work, the four men turn around in silence. Understanding the rhythmic style of *Agon*, Denby perceived this moment, a 'soundless whirl', as 'a downbeat that starts the action'.[47] However, there is another downbeat marked by a rest which is the actual beginning of the musical score, and this silent moment is articulated in movement by a *plié*. The dancers then continue to articulate every beat, including further silent beats, clarifying an ambiguous sense of musical pulse and metre. Soon, under a sustained chord (bars 7–8), the dancers press on, with steps that are literally heard plainly articulating the beat above the musical sound (see Exs. 3.2a, 3.2b).

But this preoccupation with and particular treatment of pulse, shared by Balanchine and Stravinsky, is an important reflection of the modernist thinking of the time. The discipline of pulse is a part of the modernist aesthetic to which they both subscribe. Quite different from the nineteenth-century 'vitalist' romantics, who sought to harness the supposed potential for art to be a 'language of the emotions' – and, in relation to this, romantic music emphasised fluctuations in tempo and intensity – Stravinsky and Balanchine tend to play down meaning and expressive qualities in their art. In this respect, they inherit the tradition of Hanslick (see Ch. 2, p. 66). Balanchine explains that his choreography is 'not abstract', but rather 'concrete': 'A duet is a love story almost.' Yet, he then asks: 'How much story do you want?'[48] Recall him too admiring the kind of music that is 'like a rose – you can admire it deeply, but you cannot inject your personal feelings into it' (see p. 110).

Both Stravinsky and Balanchine belong to a broad modernist trend which led eventually to the extremes of abstraction, the American tradition, proposed by Clement Greenberg. A number of proponents of this thinking advocated emotional detachment, order and precision, stability and solidity after the extreme disorder and decay of the early years of the twentieth century, which marked the death-knell of the romantic movement. Hence, Ortega y Gasset's classic article 'The Dehumanization of Art' (1925)[49] and Eliot's article 'Tradition and the Individual Talent' (1917), in which he proclaims that 'the emotion of art is impersonal'.[50] The latter, interestingly, became the bible of Lincoln Kirstein, cofounder with Balanchine of the New York City Ballet. But there are echoes of this philosophy too in the writings of Ezra Pound, from those involved in the Neue Sachlichkeit movement and many others. This thinking also had implications for creative process – Stravinsky and Balanchine, on their own admission, working as craftsmen, moved, rather than inspired, to make material, and, in their own collaborations, speaking in the straightforward terms of exact requirements: time-lengths and bar numbers. As for Balanchine, it is not unlikely that earlier Russian experience, alongside the constructivist and acmeist poetic movements, had already pointed him in this direction.

Roger Shattuck characterises modernist art as an 'art of stillness' that mani-

Ex. 3.2a. Stravinsky, *Agon*, Pas de Quatre.

fests itself in different formal terms. At the two extremes, there is the art of juxtaposition rather than transition (see Ch. 1, p. 19), in which case, heterogeneous parts were to be comprehended according to a concept of 'simultanism' (as in collage), and there is the art of homogeneity, 'the continuous present' of similar or reiterated elements (as in, for instance, the work of Gertrude Stein).[51] I am also reminded here of the musicologist Richard Taruskin's references to Stravinsky's non-linear structures, his techniques of immobility through ostinato repetition and collage.[52] Certainly, there are many examples of collage in

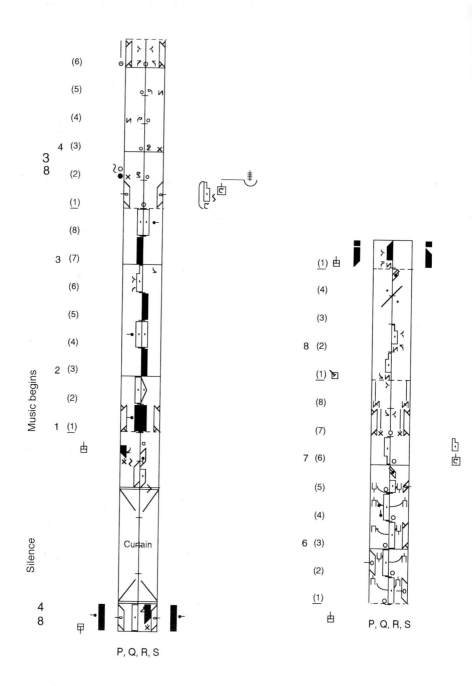

Ex. 3.2b. Balanchine, *Agon*, Pas de Quatre.

the work of both Balanchine and Stravinsky, but they clearly both lean towards the aesthetic of homogeneity, and control through homogeneity, in their discussions of the seminal *Apollo*. This is the turning point in Balanchine's career – significantly, it is a composer who confirms Balanchine's direction of the future. It is a well-known fact that both he and Stravinsky saw the ballet as an exercise in elimination, gestures selected according to 'family relations',[53] set to a strings-only accompaniment. After this work, Balanchine's statements begin to sound remarkably like the neo-classical, 'post-Russian' Stravinsky of the *Poetics of Music* (first published in 1942). Neo-classicism is one branch of modernism (see Ch. 1, p. 7). Stravinsky argues for unity rather than variety:

> Contrast produces an immediate effect. Similarity satisfies us only in the long run. Contrast is an element of variety, but it divides our attention. Similarity is born of a striving for unity . . . Variety is valid only as a means of attaining similarity . . . Similarity is hidden; it must be sought out, and it is found only after the most exhaustive efforts. When variety tempts me, I am uneasy about the facile solutions it offers me. Similarity, on the other hand, poses more difficult problems but also offers results that are more solid and hence more valuable to me.[54]

Listen to the tone of Balanchine's debt to Stravinsky in 1947: '[His] effect on my own work has been always in the direction of control, of simplification and quietness.'[55] And only a few years later: 'To achieve unity one must avoid separating elements similar in blood and essence . . . One's artistic feeling and experience can decide on their similarity.'[56]

Important to our discussion of time and pulse, Stravinsky draws from an article by his friend Pierre Souvtchinsky and applies these notions of unity and variety to the organisation of time.

> There are two kinds of music: one which evolves parallel to the process of ontological time, embracing and penetrating it, inducing in the mind of the listener a feeling of euphoria and, so to speak, of 'dynamic calm.' The other kind runs ahead of, or counter to, this process. It is not self-contained in each momentary tonal unit. It dislocates the centers of attraction and gravity and sets itself up in the unstable; and this fact makes it particularly adaptable to the translation of the composer's emotive impulses. All music in which the will to expression is dominant belongs to the second type . . . Music that is based on ontological time is generally dominated by the principle of similarity. The music that adheres to psychological time likes to proceed by contrast. To these two principles which dominate the creative process correspond the fundamental concepts of variety and unity.[57]

Strict pulse, motoric similarity, are surely major features in Stravinsky's view of unity and solidity. As Virgil Thomson, the American composer-critic, put it, the new music represents 'equalized tensions . . . the basis of streamlining and of all those other surface unifications that in art, as in engineering, make a work recognizable as belonging to our time and to no other.'[58] And together with a mechanical uniformity of motion, there is the image of speed, literal speed and a sense of speed through intensity of statement, both characteristic of Balanchine's style. Boris Asafiev writes that the new modernist music 'has always been unavoidably influenced by the impetuous current of our lives with its . . . fast tempi, and its obedience to the pulsations of work'.[59]

It is noteworthy that the very term rhythm denoted modernity during the early decades of the century; indeed, it became the title of a short-lived avant-garde British journal started up in 1911 (*Rhythm* was edited by John Middleton Murry and Katherine Mansfield) and devoted to the modern movement: the summer editorial that year stated that artists were now 'composing lyrics in colour, lyrics in line, lyrics in light to the new deity rhythm.' We recall too that Stravinsky's vision of dance was as an extension of the musical impulse: 'a form of rhythmic gymnastics' (see Ch. 1, p. 30). Yet rhythm is in the foreground despite its apparent contradiction with an 'art of stillness'. Perhaps, as Shattuck suggests, stillness or arrest is achieved in these circumstances 'not by absence of power to move' (read rhythm), but 'by an equilibrium of forces'[60] – surely Thomson's notion of 'equalized tensions' once again. The irony of the speedy, motoric style is that it often subverts images of progress and development. Insistence upon the present is no more apparent than in the many plain pulsing sections of *Episodes* (1959). To Webern, another archetypal musical modernist, Balanchine clarifies the individual moments, and most emphatically of all in the final Ricercata. Here, in the composer's idiosyncratic orchestration of Bach, musical lines are fragmented into two-note units that are given separate instrumental treatment. Balanchine likewise draws attention to moment rather than to phrase or sweep through time. The fugue subject notes are danced separately, often isolating body parts – a lunge on to pointe, a swing of the arm, a step to the side, a turning in of the knee, man and woman alternating and together.

Information about Balanchine's class teaching would support this discussion. He preferred, for instance, to eliminate exercises in 3/4 time, at least for a while during the late 1940s and 1950s. 3/4 time allows for a sense of swing, freedom, indulgence in an 'extra', 'wasted' beat:[61] it is not a precision time-signature. We hear too, how Balanchine would sometimes count an exercise '1, 1, 1, 1'[62] to train dancers to think, where necessary, of beat and moment rather than phrase.

It is fascinating to see just how acutely aware the renegade Gelsey Kirkland was of this aspect of Balanchine and Stravinsky style, 'confounded,' she says, by 'their steps and notes' (in other words, construction by moments): 'As a dancer I rebelled against rhythm ... I needed more than the propulsion of a beat ... Stravinsky replaced the thematic development of classical music with a range of sensations that alternately jolted or lulled the mind.'[63] Kirkland, of course, presents an extreme interpretation of this style, and does not admit that it is still possible to phrase, even in Stravinsky/Balanchine.

The modernist view has affected musical performance practice during this century, not only performance of contemporary music, but also performance of music of the past. This might well have prompted Balanchine's view of certain pieces of music. Richard Taruskin refers to the 'sewing-machine style' of modern Bach performance. The person he cites as bearing a major responsibility for this is none other than Stravinsky himself. 'I would go so far as to suggest that all truly modern musical performance ... essentially treats the music performed as if it were composed – or at least performed – by Stravinsky.'[64] Elliott Carter writes vividly about this Stravinsky style:

> What always struck me every time I heard Stravinsky play the piano – the composer's extraordinary, electric sense of rhythm and incisiveness of touch that made every note he played seem a 'Stravinsky-note', full of energy, excitement, and serious intentness.[65]

Again, Carter draws attention to the moment, the individual note. Stravinsky's own performance style of 'execution' (Balanchine's equivalent instruction was to ask his dancers simply to dance the steps) became enormously influential amongst musicians during the 1920s and 1930s, exactly at the same time as his philosophy of music was becoming widely publicised.

This provokes my observation that *Concerto Barocco* is an incisive demonstration of the new modernist aesthetics. The date, 1941, is significant: Balanchine had by then not only set a number of works to Stravinsky, he would also have been aware of Stravinsky's performance style. In the outer movements certainly, Balanchine seems to have heard the dawnings of the new Bach and glimpsed a new machine age for choreography, a more extreme assertion of modernism in choreography. Hear what Denby saw: 'powerful onward drive ... syncopated fun and sportive jigging ... its coolness and its simplicity are not [yet] in the current fashion.' Most compelling of all, he singles the work out as the especially good example of percussive beat-emphatic choreography, in which the sound of feet is important.[66] He all but uses the word 'jazz'. Others since have certainly done so. Jazz, sometimes filtered through Stravinsky, sometimes not, is another source for Balanchine's rhythmic style. John Taras makes the interesting suggestion that, in the case of *Barocco*, Balanchine had been influenced by the playing of the club pianist Hazel Scott, who was popular in New York at the time for her jazz versions of classical music.[67] Rehearsing the ballet in 1996 with Marie-Jeanne, the original leading soloist, Taras brought back the lost jazziness into the movement.[68]

Kirkland takes the extreme view again, but her comments are nevertheless revealing. She writes of Balanchine's 'mechanical interpretation of the score. It was as if he were constructing a clock on the stage, each of us keeping time like a cog in the mechanism.'[69] Certainly this is the new, sewing-machine Bach. It is also the Bach of neatly interlocking, hierarchical components of beat, hyperbeat and sub-beat, and, significantly, Balanchine has singled out for admiration 'the mathematical basis'[70] of Bach's music. These are the terms of twentieth-century rather than baroque music theory. Dancers map out different rates of beat simultaneously or at different times. They do so again and with even plainer precision in the Bach/Webern Ricercata of *Episodes*.

From what I have proposed, therefore, it is not surprising that Balanchine tightened up the performances of Tchaikovsky's music, just as Toscanini had done for opera. Neither is it surprising that he firmly criticised interpretations of Stravinsky that looked backwards to the previous vitalist aesthetic. According to Hugo Fiorato, conductor at the New York City Ballet, he loathed Stokowksi's treatment of *Firebird*. He called it 'Disgusting . . . anti-Russian. You know where that comes from [the *Firebird* tune]? A male chorus'; and of the tune near the end of *Apollo*, which some musicians tend to over-romanticise: '[Stravinsky] was thinking of *Gaîté Parisienne* when he wrote that!'[71]

On the other hand, Balanchine is not an inflexible modernist, nor must we overemphasise the point about strict motor pulse. It is the acidic twentieth-century scores that bring this out to an extreme in Balanchine's work. Balanchine's verbal statements, fewer and more concise than those of Stravinsky, do not press so fervently for such notions as solidity and stability. There are important freedoms in a good deal of his choreography and in the manner in which he wanted it (and its music) performed. We must remember too his close association with neo-romantic and surrealist movements in the visual arts, stemming from his career in Europe, and a continuing thread of romanticism through his choreographic career.

There are any number of legato, flowing Balanchine adagios, or occasions when Balanchine introduces a major contrast with pulse drive, as we shall see, in the *Agon pas de deux*, which uses breath rhythm around a regular, but quietly pulse-based Stravinsky framework. Some works give particular freedoms in timing to soloists: *Ballet Imperial* (1941), for instance, says Balanchine's pianist Gordon Boelzner, is not 'nailed to the floor'.[72] In *Mozartiana*, Balanchine called for both music and dance to be free in the Adagio with its many cadenzas, and wanted an unusually liberated, romantic account of the music by today's style of performance practice. Likewise, he insisted to Fiorato that the last movement of *Serenade* (1934) 'must be free – don't be afraid of rubato'.[73] It is his romantic conducting of the work that dancers (and apparently Balanchine too) have particularly enjoyed.[74]

Irving, on the other hand, seems to have been more hard-line than Balanchine, more strongly against sentiment, and a lover of quick tempos. It is pertinent to consider one comparison with his forerunner Barzin: 'Irving's performances are infinitely more elegant, better balanced, easier on sensitized ears, closer to the letter of every score . . .'[75] But his quick tempos could provoke friction with Balanchine, sometimes disrupting the latter's more flexible view of the music. One notorious example of this is the second movement of *Concerto Barocco*, and here, Fiorato, too, is in disagreement with Balanchine's later perceptions of the music. The stories about this movement are confusing. Irving reports that Balanchine borrowed his idea of tempo from a particularly slow, sentimental Menuhin/Enescu recording of the Bach double violin concerto.[76] It is true that Balanchine created the ballet to this 1933 recording, but it is definitely neither slow nor sentimental in style. In fact, the musical performance is much faster than in later performances of the ballet. Did Balanchine perhaps start to think of the music in slower, more lyrical terms as he later rehearsed it with more long-limbed dancers than Marie-Jeanne, the original interpreter? This is Taras's suggestion, and that Balanchine's view of the adagio style changed: he looked more and more for line, rather than for the energetic, weight-indulgent qualities of the 1941 version, and the tempo slowed particularly when Suzanne Farrell took on the role in the 1960s.[77] When he joined Balanchine in the late 1950s, Irving urged him to adopt a more bracing, contemporary, and less sentimental tempo once again, which now created problems for some sections of choreography in the new style, especially a particular passage containing a lift in *grand jeté*. Irving recalls that Balanchine eventually took his advice, and 'now I know how to manage that place [the lift]: I just give it a little stretch and it doesn't spoil the music.'[78] However, it appears that the tempo issues in *Barocco* have never been entirely resolved between musicians and dancers.

Barocco is a good example of Balanchine not being inflexible in approach. Our picture of him is the more interesting if we do not fall into the trap of simplifying a complex reality. There are times when the musical classics seem to have led the choreographer away from the Stravinsky aesthetic, to negotiate another kind of relationship with them and with their period. There are times too when music, both contemporary and of the past, appears to have opened his imagination to make something that is about freedom and fantasy rather than control and strict family relations. Balanchine was forever breaking his own rules. On odd occasions, he even asked for a 'schmaltz' style of performance, 'like restaurant!'[79]

But what does Balanchine say about how a choreographer should use music? There is the famous statement about perfect integration of the two elements, his creed, to make the audience 'see the music and hear the dancing'[80] (see Introduction, p. xiv). Generally, however, Balanchine is remarkably unspecific if not downright cryptic. Suki Schorer, a former dancer, who now stages Balanchine works and teaches at the School of American Ballet, muses upon Balanchine's comment on *Movements for Piano and Orchestra*: he described it as the most 'in-the-music ballet' of his career to date.[81] He did not explain himself further, advising her simply to watch the piece. She remains unsure exactly what he meant. Another remark seems misleading. Interviewed by Jay S. Harrison in the *New York Herald Tribune* (1959), Balanchine discusses his approach almost as if it is an attempt (if necessarily compromised) at literal music visualisation, rather like the formula method that Denishawn promoted. Perhaps he was being tongue-in-cheek here, or perhaps this was simply a way of telling the layperson that dance could be conceived in abstract terms like music. Advocating that a choreographer should not simply listen to the music, Balanchine says

> The printed notes give you a picture of that music – the way it rises and falls, the patterns it makes. Then you create a body movement that will roughly equal the flow of the printed notes. It is not a photograph of the printed score, of course; remember that for the larger parts of the body the maximum number of movements is six per second. If music goes at the rate of sixty notes per second, we cannot duplicate it, but we can make a gesture that gives the impression of that kind of rapidity.[82]

Certainly, Balanchine does not practise what he appears to preach here as a working principle, and his other statements are much more about independence and dialogue. Of *Concerto Barocco* in *Balanchine's Festival of Ballet*:

> The girls correspond to the music the orchestra plays, but not in any strict or literal sense; they do not mirror the music . . . The dance picture tries to tell something independent of an exact, bar-by-bar, rhythm-by-rhythm, mirror image of the music.[83]

It is pertinent that this is also how Stravinsky sees the relationship between music and choreography:

> Choreography, as I conceive it, must realize its own form, one independent of the musical form though measured to the musical unit. Its construction will be based on whatever correspondences the choreographer may invent, but it must not seek merely to duplicate the line and beat of the music.[84]

His notion of 'a struggle between music and choreography'[85] to bring about harmony and synthesis (with which Balanchine agrees) also suggests a strenuous working together of two independent forces. Could this be why Stravinsky proposed that he would write *Agon* as a 'concerto for the dance',[86] a striving interaction between the two media (using the Italian derivation, *concertare*, to strive)?

Balanchine also believes that choreography should not damage musical clarity:

> When I choreograph Stravinsky's music I am very careful not to hide the music. You see, usually choreography interferes with the music too much. When too much goes on on stage, you don't hear the music. Somehow that messy stuff obscures the music. I always do the reverse. I sort of subdue my dances. They're always less than the music. As in modern architecture [he uses the words of the high modern architect Mies van der Rohe], you rather should do less than more.[87]

This sounds like the principle that Balanchine adopted in *The Four Temperaments* (1946). A programme note reads: 'I have attempted to design a kind of stereoscopic choreography for Hindemith's strong score; my dances form a negative to his positive plate.'[88] The principle is similar to that in the second setting of the Stravinsky *Variations* (1982, to his *Variations for Orchestra*), which Farrell describes as underplaying the music, and much more pared down than before.[89] We can safely assume that concepts of close interaction and dialogue were in Balanchine's mind when he made work, allowing the viewer the space to both 'see' and hear the music.

In terms of working process, Balanchine first of all acquainted himself thoroughly with the music, making his own piano reduction if necessary. Tanaquil LeClercq remembers this as an extraordinarily rapid process:

> When I was married to him, I never could find out when he invented anything . . . He'd be at home, I'd be at home, he would go through the music, maybe play it once or twice, and the next day he'd have a whole thing [section of choreography worked out].[90]

Sometimes, he also used recordings in order to familiarise himself with the orchestral sound, especially important if he was using a modern score. We know, for instance, that he used the Stravinsky/Samuel Dushkin recording of Stravinsky's Violin Concerto in preparation and rehearsal when he first choreographed this music: *Balustrade* (1941).[91] Several early dancers have reported that recordings would occasionally be brought into rehearsal,[92] and *Concerto Barocco* is one obvious example (see p. 121) where this was the case.

In an article for the music magazine *Listen*, Balanchine makes a major claim about faithfulness to the musical score: 'I believe that music for the ballet should follow the composer's directions as to tempo and dynamics and phrasing . . . In my ballets, I never leave out parts of the original music, I never change tempi or in any other way disturb the continuity or shape of the music.'[93] But this is not entirely true. Part of Balanchine's initial process was to consider whether he wanted to use a score in its entirety, and he was no purist. Far more than is often recognised, he made his own cuts, some short, some long. Complete musical movements are cut from, for instance, *Scotch Symphony* (1952, Mendelssohn), *Divertimento No. 15* (1956, Mozart), and the *Diamonds* section of *Jewels* (1967, Tchaikovsky's Symphony No. 3). We shall see that he reordered the musical movements in *Serenade* and the 1981 *Mozartiana*. Within movements too, though less so in the later part of his career, there are omissions, a bar or two, a phrase, or even a section, and these are not necessarily straightforward cuts of musical repeats. Sometimes, Balanchine would fill in a cut with choreography at a later date, as in *Serenade*, or the *Emeralds* section of *Jewels*, into which he added the missing movements of the two suites *Pelléas et Mélisande* and *Shylock*. Perhaps he did this in response to the movement towards purism and authenticity in the musical world. But he did not always do this, and sometimes, for reasons of injury or noting that dancers became overtired in a work, he would insert a cut after the premiere. Then again, for practical reasons, he asked for the opening, curtain-up bars of *Emeralds* to be repeated, observing that the audience inevitably covered them the first time with applause.[94] Balanchine's own ideas about musical form usually work well, probably because he was a trained musician.

A complex example of Balanchine's cutting is the *Tchaikovsky Piano Concerto No. 2* (formerly *Ballet Imperial*). Here, Balanchine used the already abridged version of the score by Tchaikovsky's pupil Siloti, and he made further cuts of his own. Thus, in the first movement, he removed 11 more bars at one point, and 20 or 22 bars (he changed his mind) later, in the *pas de deux* cadenza. From the *pas de deux* in the second movement, he extracted six further bars. Here, the ballerina is drawn round the stage in a big circle, her series of *relevés* in *arabesque* leading to a climax of intensity, followed by a lessening of tension in a series of supported *jetés* travelling backwards on pointe. After this, in the Siloti score, there is a tonal diversion with rippling piano figuration: Balanchine seems to have preferred to bring the *pas de deux* simply and more quickly to a conclusion. But this is an occasion where Balanchine's musical seam is not totally comfortable, and Philip Gammon, pianist for the 1993 *Ballet Imperial* production of the Royal Ballet, sharpened a note in the bass line to soften the harmonic link.[95]

Balanchine's role in assembling different musical scores for certain works was in itself a creative act. *A Midsummer Night's Dream* (1962) was an unusual patchwork of Mendelssohn pieces and the nearest that he came to composing a score himself.[96] To suit the story line, he used not only the familiar overture and incidental music, but a number of other overtures and the first three movements of the early Symphony No. 9 for Strings. The joins between different sections of the music seem rougher than usual here, but the dance historian Jane Pritchard usefully suggests that Balanchine looked back to nineteenth-century structural precedents in this ballet, to what he grew up with in Russia.[97] At that time, he would have known ballets to musical scores involving interpolations from various sources, and, also model for his *Dream*, full-length ballets with a complete act of divertissement after the main action had finished. Later, in setting the *Divertimento from 'Le Baiser de la fée'* (1972), Balanchine devised his own musical shape, using excerpts from Stravinsky's concert suite as well as the earlier full-length ballet score. Many other works incorporate complete pieces simply placed end on to each other, as in the *Emeralds* movement of *Jewels* (see p. 124) and *La Valse* (1951) (which juxtaposes Ravel's *Valses nobles et sentimentales* and *La Valse*). After 1966, Balanchine regularly programmed *Monumentum pro Gesualdo* (1960) and *Movements for Piano and Orchestra* together, which introduced a violent contrast between courtly harmony, with references to a distant past, and jagged fragmentary motion that belongs entirely to our own time.

There is no conclusive information about the detail of Balanchine's musical analysis. We can imagine that he drew from his early studies of harmony and counterpoint, an educated structural sensibility, and then heard what he chose to hear as he began to develop visual imagery. Fiorato is certain that he would not have ventured into the highly specialised detail of recent musical analysts.[98] Yet it does seem that he was intrigued to acquire an understanding of the intricacies of twelve-note music – evident, for instance, in his consultations with Stravinsky – and we know that he spent a great deal of time working with the Webern scores for *Episodes*.[99] Perhaps that is why we find the most cerebral examples of music visualisation in the twelve-note pieces, surely creator's conceits of which few listeners could possibly be aware. There are, in *Episodes*, the famous upturned *entrechats* that match the inversion of the tone row, and in *Movements*, 'Near the ending of Stravinsky's *Movements for Piano and Orchestra* I have dancers marking the composer's returning twelve-note row . . . . but now slowed down, spread and stretched out.'[100] Perhaps these are Balanchine's private games, as he came to terms with a new musical logic. It is significant that he adds here, 'These certain things I do, naturally, but as little as possible. I don't imitate the notes of a piece.' However, there is every evidence that, whatever the music, Balanchine was especially well acquainted with its rhythmic aspects, and this means rhythm not only as it is heard, but also as it is visible in the score. Later, several instances that demonstrate Balanchine's knowledge of the written score will be discussed.

When he reached rehearsal – and it is widely known how he never choreo-graphed steps before rehearsal – Balanchine's method was to sing musical pas-sages, to demonstrate physically and to speak the dance rhythmic patterns and accents (like '*Yah* da da *dah* da da'). Thus, his dancers had the opportunity to grasp his particular phrasing. Without them consciously registering the fact, his phrasing could become part of their performance. From what dancers say, Balanchine tended to resort to counts only when learning proved very difficult otherwise and when working with complex rhythms (Stravinsky's *Agon*, for instance.) Rhythm was also the key framework for Balanchine's step combi-nations. Arthur Mitchell remembers how

> Many times when he was choreographing he would work rhythmically and then put the step in. If you were looking for a step, it wouldn't be there. But if you got *dah*, da-*dah-dah-dah*, it would come out. The rhythm was always the most important. The choreography was set in time and then space.[101]

Many dancers have confirmed this focus on rhythm in the rehearsal room. Maria Tallchief recalls times when Balanchine looked not at the whole dancer, but just at the feet.[102] Farrell remembers that Balanchine would sometimes pre-fer not to watch the dancers at all, but 'he'd tell by the sound of the feet whether we had the rhythm right'.[103]

Sometimes, Balanchine's own impression of the music would become advice to the accompanying musicians. Creating the 1981 *Mozartiana*, we hear that he would get to his feet and imitate the violin cadenzas, with verve, 'in a frenzied Paganini imitation',[104] to indicate feeling and precise accenting and timing to Lamar Alsop, the violinist. The Royal Ballet pianist Philip Gammon remembers Balanchine demonstrating a musical moment for him directly at the piano.[105] At other times, Balanchine would enter into dialogue. Fiorato does not remember any unwelcome interference, just the occasional idea expressed in precise, musi-cianly terms:

> like the piano piece in *Cortège* [*Cortège Hongrois*, 1973], to the conductor, a note for the pianist 'to play like cymbalum'. Or tempo issues. Near the end of *Apollo*, he suggested thinking of four rather than two in a bar to stop it run-ning away . . . Or there is the *piano* towards the end of *Rosenkavalier* [the Rich-ard Strauss score used in *Vienna Waltzes*, 1977], a moment which nobody seemed to play quietly. And he loved to hear this *piano*.[106]

As for faithfulness in tempo, Balanchine is again more flexible than he sug-gests, although he was precise and sometimes brought a metronome into re-hearsal. Hardly surprising, he admitted some flexibility to suit different dancers' physiques, but sometimes it is the nature of the music or choreography that is the determining factor. It has been suggested, for instance, that *Serenade* (or at least its Waltz movement) is played slightly slower than in a concert performance of its music.[107] Then there is the complicated incident of the slow movement of *Concerto Barocco* (see p. 121). An interesting point about several Balanchine works in the *Dance in America* television series is that the tempo was deliberately speeded up for the camera. According to director Merrill Brockway, the new tempo caused some consternation for Irving and some of the dancers, but Balanchine had quickly become aware of the particularities of TV timing (as did Merce Cunningham), that the screen has a slowing effect upon real, physical timing and energy.[108]

An examination of dance and music scores reveals further surprises. An extremely bold tempo adjustment was made for one section of *The Four Temperaments*. The Labanotation score of this piece, written in 1985 (only two years after Balanchine's death, as a record of Victoria Simon's staging for the Cleveland Ballet), indicates a major change in the Phlegmatic section.[109] This is the third of the four temperaments, the one representing solemnity and sluggishness. The metronomic rate of 100 (or 96–100) beats per minute indicated in the 1940 Hindemith score has plummeted to 'about' 64 or 68 beats per minute. A 1961 recording of the music with Hindemith conducting speeds up the final allegretto scherzando section from 100 to 112 beats per minute, further exaggerating the difference between concert and dance performance.[110] Much less obvious to the listener, but nevertheless in deliberate contradiction with the composer's stipulations, the Variation 7 and Coda of Webern's Symphony (used in *Episodes*) are indicated in the 1959 Labanotation score 'Steady tempo. Do not observe retards.'[111] However, in comparison with ballet practice elsewhere, the Balanchine tradition remains for the most part unusually faithful to the wishes of composers. For example, if he choreographed the Arabian Dance in *The Nutcracker* to a much slower tempo than Tchaikovsky designated, he later tried adopting the written tempo. In the event, he had to compromise, but today's speed remains far closer to Tchaikovsky's original intentions than that of performances by most other ballet companies.[112]

Now, as we examine specific Balanchine works, it is important to remind ourselves of the shifting identity of these works, sometimes as a result of Balanchine's own changes, which so often respected the needs of different dancers, sometimes through inadvertent alterations in revival. To demonstrate major textual changes, there is no better example than *Serenade*.

Serenade

Serenade altered more substantially during its history than most other ballets by Balanchine. Familiar is the story of how it was made for the earliest students at the School of American Ballet, in 1934, as a training ballet, and how Balanchine approached his task pragmatically, according to the availability of his dancers. He started working with a group of women. Men began to arrive as he formed the piece, and they were included. A woman arrived late one day, and the lateness was put into the ballet. Someone fell down; that moment too was incorporated. Process was part of the ballet from the start. Balanchine did what he could with whoever was available. In 1934, Balanchine choreographed only the first three movements of Tchaikovsky's Serenade for Strings, the Pezzo in forma di Sonatina, Waltz and Elegy. Later, there was time as well as new dancers with whom to develop the piece further.

Serenade is interesting to us both as a changing text and as a piece that speaks of different times. It is revealing to consider how music plays its part in that changing text. A consideration of music can enrich our understanding of a different cultural situation during Balanchine's early career, a time of different musical performance practices, and a time when America was not yet familiar with Tchaikovsky's work (except for the first Piano Concerto).[113] The evolution of *Serenade* might reflect Balanchine's response to the developing purism of the musical community around him. It is also important to consider how the musical score and the way in which Balanchine used it contributes to the different identities of the work, its changing structure, and the changing meanings implied by that changing structure. Yet, as much as we are aware that *Serenade* has its roots in 1934, it would be wrong to put it down as a relatively youthful and therefore simple work: in some respects, it is one of Balanchine's most sophisticated musical-choreographic structures.

Seen in historical context, *Serenade* is one of Balanchine's earliest symphonic pieces, a large part of it driven by abstract rather than narrative motives. The tradition for this kind of ballet was still quite new in 1934: *Les Sylphides* remained an unusual precedent in the repertory, and Massine's recent *Choreartium* (1933) had caused major controversy. Tchaikovsky's *Serenade* had already been used by Fokine in Russia for *Eros* (1915). This was a ballet about a girl dreaming of a statue of Eros come to life and of a painted figurine of an angel, both battling for her heart; in other words, terrestrial against celestial love.[114] Similarly to Balanchine, Fokine had used the first three movements of the Tchaikovsky, ending with the Elegy, and omitting the Tema Russo. That is probably as far as the link went, because Balanchine tells us that he did not like this Fokine ballet; he much preferred his *Les Sylphides*, which we now see has far stronger links with *Serenade*, in terms of dance ideas and as a *ballet blanc* that referred to nineteenth-century models. But it is possible that the three-movement *Serenade* score was the score that Balanchine knew first and best, and besides, it would hardly have been controversial to make selections from an unfamiliar piece of music. Perhaps too, as Claudia Roth Pierpont has suggested in an important essay on Balanchine's romanticism, he may have been motivated by the dying-away ending of Tchaikovsky's Pathétique Symphony.[115] *Serenade* is an all-string piece, like Stravinsky's *Apollo*. It is not unlikely that Balanchine found in it the same inspiration to eliminate, to be economical in tone.

The major changes in the *Serenade* text can be summarised.[116] The first alteration was the addition of a man to the Waltz, probably during later performances of the 1930s. In 1940, for a new production staged for the Ballet Russe de Monte Carlo, Balanchine gave all the female solo parts before the Elegy to one woman, Marie-Jeanne. At the same time, the missing Tema Russo (known choreographically as the Russian Dance) was added, in Balanchine's own heavily cut version of the score. The Elegy was kept at the end of the work; Balanchine's final vision was to remain intact. Later, Balanchine restored the cuts in the Russian Dance, a gradual process through the 1960s,[117] completed c. 1970–71, although he was cavalier about which version of the dance was taught, and Pennsylvania Ballet carried a cut version through to 1982.[118] Photographs of the 1930s *Serenade* testify almost invariably to the same dance images that we still see today, despite additions to the choreography along the way. Costumes, however, and the physicality of the dancers changed radically over the years, from calf-length dresses and short tunics of varying colours (even red, white and blue for a South American tour) to, in 1952, the long, diaphanous, tulle white-blue skirts that are familiar today on performers who are much sleeker and broader in their movement scale than those in the 1930s. Barbara Weisberger, who watched Balanchine create *Serenade* in 1934, remembers distinctly Heidi Vosseler, the woman carried 'to Heaven' in the last movement, wearing a veil over her head, an image that suggests tragic, religious meaning.[119] In the late 1970s, Balanchine called for the solo women to wear their long hair free during the Elegy.

As for the musical score, at the very first open-air performance, it was played in four-hand piano arrangement. Later, it was played in an arrangement for small orchestra by George Antheil, composer of the score for Balanchine's 1935 *Dreams*. By 1940, there is no mention of the Antheil arrangement being used any more.

Changes in choreographic text and costume play their part in the important dialogue between abstraction and drama, form and content, academic and symbolic movement in this work. For as much as the *Serenade* ballet begins with the full band of women in a potent gesture of the right arm up to the side, shielding their eyes from the light, they then move to the real starting position for dance, first position of feet and arms, a moment of poignant simplicity, symbol of the beginning of a classical dancer's life. Then there is pure dance, with mere hints of narrative, until a major thrust into narrative during the Elegy: a woman has fallen down, she rises, struggles with another woman, the 'Dark Angel', to gain a man, and then, abandoned, is carried heavenwards. Balanchine was often reticent about the meanings in the ballet. However, early programme notes and sketches for them, whether or not Balanchine himself had much to do with them, clearly guided the audience towards dramatic significance, a little hesitantly in the 1930s, quite overtly in the 1940s (see opposite). Audiences perhaps welcomed some narrative explanation of *Serenade* in those early days of the plotless ballet. Balanchine, on the other hand, probably played down narrative implications to his dancers, in order to achieve the special subtlety and ambiguity of *Serenade*, especially at the Ballet Russe de Monte Carlo, a company steeped in a culture of role-playing.

As I argue later in terms of musical structuring, it is in the 1940s that drama and narrative drive in the work might well have been at their strongest. Jack Anderson has already observed that the piece became more dramatic when Marie-Jeanne featured in all the solo roles in 1940;[120] this single-soloist pattern remained for some years. Listen too to Denby's reminiscences of 1952. Through *Serenade*, he notices the shift in New York City Ballet's expressive and rhythmic style:

> I would prefer it danced, so to speak, demi-caractère, not straight academic. Done as it used to be before the war [to Americans, prior to December, 1941], with a slight 'Russian' retard and dragging in the waltzing, that tiny overtone of acting gave the whole piece a stylistic unity and coherence in which the beautiful gesture images (from the one at the opening to the very last, the closing procession) appeared not extraneous but immanent in a single conception.[121]

In any case, from what we know about his preferred performance of the music (see pp. 120–1), Balanchine clearly kept returning to the romanticism of Tchaikovsky as a strong component of the work. As Pierpont says, he 'chose to italicize the conventions of romanticism' by freeing the women's hair in the 1970s.[122]

There remain many unknowns in the history of *Serenade*. How might the choreography of the first movement have changed over the years? Was what we see today a direct result of the original piecemeal working process? How did the woman fall down in the Waltz before the Russian Dance was choreographed? What was a pragmatic, on-the-spot choreographic decision and what was planned from the start? However, sources from different periods give us plentiful information about different versions, and different meanings can be gauged from these.

6–8 December 1934 Producing Company of School of Ameri- can Ballet	Without an implicit subject, the music and its thematic development indicate the tragic form of the primarily feminine ballet. Its lyricism is the large fluent sentiment of Tchaikovsky shifting from the fresh swiftness of Sonatina, the buoyant accumulating passage of the Waltz, through the sustained adagio of the Elegy. The classic dance has been used here in conjunction with free gesture, developed logically for the whole body's use. The corps de ballet as such scarcely exists. Each member is inseparable from the schematic design in personal individual meaning. The soloists crown the action alone, their tragedy prepared by the frame of the previous dances.
17 October 1940 Ballet Russe de Monte Carlo	Just as symphonic themes integrate and flow one against the other, so this ballet uses three types of movement in counterpoint. The sonatina and waltz are designed in ceaseless linear patterns danced on the 'points' and in the free plastic medium. The sonatina, a sombre adagio, calls forth two girls and a boy in a tragic pantomime against the background of the corps-de-ballet. *This is the note in Ballet Russe de Monte Carlo programmes through the 1940s, some of which indicate the separate movements of the ballet. All these programmes are incorrect in mentioning only three movements (the Tema Russo had already been added). Furthermore, except for temporary correction in 1942, the last sentence equates the sonatina with the final adagio.*
June–November 1941 (South American tour): American Ballet Caravan	La belleza sencilla de la Serenata para Instrumentos de Cuerda de Tschaikowsky se refleja en estos bailes de naturaleza tierna y romántica. Aunque el compositor encontro inspiración para sus melodías en canciones rusas, la música transciende cualquier característica puaramente eslava.
Sketches for a Note (n.d.).	Music by Tchaikovsky. Story and choreography by George Balanchine. The action of the ballet is symbolic and represents the futile search for mutual understanding between two people and the final realisation that each person must carry eternally the burden of his loneliness. The search is represented first by a Girl and later by a Boy. In the first section the Girl attempts to identify herself with a group. She takes her place among them, adopting the same attitudes and gestures. By their variations they indicate their differentness and their separateness from her. In the middle section (The Waltz) the Girl tries to achieve understanding through love, but this too ends in failure and she is left abandoned on an empty stage. In the last section the Boy enters, Hanging upon him, her arms encircling him like tentacles, her hands blinding his eyes, her feet following his steps more closely than a shadow, is a dancer who represents all the forces within him which make it impossible for him to give himself completely in love. He attempts to break away from this inseparable part of himself and is temporarily able to believe that he can find happiness with The Girl. But inexorably the tentacles reclaim him, the hands again blind him and he is pushed away from happiness back into himself. The Girl is again abandoned on an empty stage and is finally carried off, still seeking, but hopelessly. *The note is typed on the back of a City Center of Music and Drama Inc. order form and also appears in French translation. As Balanchine staged* Serenade *for the Paris Opera Ballet in 1947, this could well be the date of this note.*

Table 3.1. Sample early programme notes for *Serenade*.

Original Tchaikovsky Score		Ballet Score with Repetitions added by Balanchine	
A	bars 1–72 (a b a)	A	bars 1–72 (a b a)
B	bars 73–113 (a a)	B	bars 73–113 (a a)
A	bars 114–188 (a b a)	A	bars 114–133 (a)
Coda	bars 189-223	B	bars 134–174 (a a)
		A	bars 175–249 (a b a)
		Coda	bars 250–283

Table 3.2. *Serenade, Waltz.*

We turn first to the musical text. When there were only three movements, the Waltz preceding the Elegy must have constituted a much less emotionally substantial precedent to the final drama than we know now. It has, after all, a delicate, dying-away ending. This point is not undermined by the fact that Balanchine, most unusually, made his own insertion into this Waltz, creating a rondo ABABA out of an ABA structure and adding 60 bars to the existing 223 bars (see Table 3.2).[123] The Russian Dance provides a much bolder run-up to the Elegy, containing too its own drama with a sudden switch in tempo immediately before the rushing Coda to recapitulate the passionate Andante non troppo theme (here Molto meno mosso) that opens the entire *Serenade* (see Ex. 3.3). Shifting the Russian Dance into third place interestingly affects our reading of it within the ballet. In concert, it is a joyful, boisterous finale, relieving the tensions of the Elegy. In the Balanchine work, it is still passionately energetic, but the tone is different: it supports an impatient, mass striving rather than celebration through dance, which is reinforced by the tightening of the triple time swing rhythms of both Sonatina (6/8) and Waltz into duple time (no 'wasted' beat here, see p. 118). As Alastair Macaulay observes in his perceptive article on *Serenade*, there is nothing jarring about Balanchine's forged connection between the end of the Russian Dance and the beginning of the Elegy.[124] However, the decision does eliminate Tchaikovsky's special stroke of continuity, the high D at the end of the Elegy, which links with the opening D of the Russian Dance.

Ex. 3.3. Tchaikovsky, *Serenade*, I. Pezzo in Forma di Sonatina.

	Introduction	Exposition	Development	Recapitulation	Molto meno mosso	Coda
Original Tchaikovsky score	1 — Andante	43 44 — Allegro con spirito — 83 84 — 123 124 167 168; 1st subject / 2nd subject / Codetta		255 256 — 295 206 — 335 336; 1st subject / 2nd subject / Codetta	385 386 413 — Theme from Andante non troppo (1st mvt.)	414 449 — Tempo I Allegro con spirito
Bars cut by Balanchine	31–8		4 × 4 bars: 188–91, 196–9, 204–7, 212–5	264–359	380–409	
Dance: current version	5 female dancers		Build to full group	Pas de deux (main female dancer and partner) · Four more female dancers arrive · Ensemble. Soloists leave bar 283	Ensemble, including solos for male and female dancers	Ensemble. Ends female dancer alone, fallen to floor

Table 3.3. *Serenade*, Tema Russo (Russian Dance).

Balanchine's cuts in the Russian Dance directly affect the dynamic contour of this movement, and consequently its narrative drive. We can glean information about this from a 1957 film of *Serenade* and from Ann Hutchinson's notation begun during the 1950s and added to when Una Kai staged the work for the Royal Ballet in 1964.[125] Remember that the cut version of the Russian Dance was inserted at the time when only one female soloist led *Serenade* (until the Elegy). Tchaikovsky's form in this movement is sonata form: slow introduction, then exposition presenting two subjects or themes, development, recapitulation (three main parts), Molto meno mosso interpolation and coda. In Balanchine's original version of the music, this became introduction, then exposition and development (two main parts), a snatch of recapitulation, leaving out the second subject entirely, and a coda without the Molto meno mosso before it (see Table 3.3). This means that, unlike now, once the soloist has returned to the stage for the *pas de deux* that opens the development, she never leaves it; we feel the consistent pressure of her presence. It is as if Balanchine made his cuts in order to preserve musical pressure too. With no Molto meno mosso, and no recapitulation of the second theme, speed and fortissimo can be retained without a break once the dance forces begin to gather. In the slow introduction to the Russian Dance, choreographed for a line of five dancers, Balanchine cut eight bars. This is the passage later choreographed as a second winding into a tight line to face upstage, two tilts of the head one way and then the other, a pause, and then a winding out into a more spread line, heads tilting again, and pause. Without those slow eight bars, the five dancers descended quietly to the floor, linked hands, rose again, then gathered momentum in runs and *bourrées*. They huddled, intertwined and pulled out into line just once, not twice, choreographic resolution to musical resolution (on the unison note G), followed straightaway by steps preparing for the Allegro. Clearly, Balanchine once had a much more efficient view of the music of the Russian Dance.

Another example of musical compression occurs in the development *pas de deux*, when Tchaikovsky sustains a sequential passage for an unusual length of time, 32 bars, a four-bar phrase drawing from both first and second theme material, repeated eight times at four levels rising in pitch, heard twice at each level. Because of its length, the passage soon draws attention to itself, as if a diversion from the main thrust of the score, and then it builds pressure through repetition. When he first choreographed the Russian Dance, Balanchine simply discarded every other four bars (the exact repetitions at the same pitch, see Table 3.3), the dancers made a big circle, the man in pursuit of the woman, in four repeating four-bar phrases, and there was no sense of structural diversion. When he filled in the cuts, Balanchine simply carried on the repetitions in the dance (with a variation after 16 bars). The effect is now almost obsessive, especially given the unusually close visualisation of musical rhythm and pitch contour in this passage. Balanchine's original join across the recapitulation leading from bar 263 to bar 360 is the only one that is jarring. Most of his cuts are completely sensible in terms of a local musicality.

During the 1940s, clearly, musical issues were very important in supporting Balanchine's concern to develop the narrative and personal aspects of *Serenade* in preparation for the Elegy. This was the period when structure most strongly supported narrative drive. It still does to some extent, especially as there remains a strong sense of a leading protagonist – the woman who arrives late to join her companions at the end of the Sonatina is the same one who finds a man, is abandoned, and then carried heavenwards in the last movement – but changes have slightly lessened the dramatic impetus. In 1950, in order to give more chances to more dancers when showing the company for the first time in London, Balanchine once again shared out some of the solo material.[126] Three female soloists eventually became the norm for *Serenade*. A growing respect for the full form of the music led him finally to Tchaikovsky's original, more expansive version of the Russian Dance.

If comparisons between versions of *Serenade* highlight changes in its structure and meaning, we can now see that Balanchine's distribution of material and response to musical return or recapitulation also create meaning. Response to return, between the extremes of reiterating the device choreographically and of totally ignoring it, has a major effect upon our experience of closure. In my discussion of material, I am not referring to conventional, repeating classical steps that are like the canvas of the piece, most obviously the *temps levé* in *arabesque*, often with a *temps de flèche*, which also characterises *Symphony in C* and *Ballet Imperial*. Rather, I am referring to motifs, either combinations of conventional steps that together create individual character, or the more striking movement images of *Serenade*.

There is one very clear example of recapitulation of dance with music in *Serenade*, the Andante non troppo from the opening (see Ex. 3.3), to which the dancers move from shielding their eyes to academic first position. But it is treated developmentally nonetheless, the second time at the end of the Sonatina, as the opportunity for the solo woman's late entry, and then finally, near the end of the Russian Dance, for her partnered version, enlarged and doubly sorrowful with the addition of her leg extension *à la seconde*. Most other musical recapitulations in *Serenade* are treated in a decidedly more evolutionary manner. They are masked rather than emphatically reiterated by the choreography.

The musical structure of the Sonatina is classically symmetrical, opening and closing with the Andante non troppo material, and, in between, there is an Allegro moderato sonata form without development section. Tchaikovsky's biographer David Brown reminds us that this movement was 'a deliberate imitation of Mozart's manner'.[127] But these formal qualities are nowhere apparent in the

Allegro choreography, which continues to develop throughout, to unsettling effect. We shall, of course, never know whether this is the case because of Balanchine's unusual working process. Groups constantly assemble and dissolve, splinter and grow, chamber groups and large masses, with some solos in isolation or the briefest image of a soloist dashing through the ensemble or turning amidst a small group. Like weather formations, nothing lasts for long in this Allegro, and there is no return to a previous situation. The first half of the sonata form ends with the mass of dancers peeling off from a huge diagonal, the second with them in a series of *piqué* turns. Similarly, in the Waltz, despite Balanchine's own added musical repetitions, he avoids emphatic return of dance with music.

The Russian Dance (in its complete version) presents an entirely different picture. Here, not only does Balanchine make much more of a point about bringing back dance steps with their original music, but he reassembles amidst new material many dance images from the previous two movements. The characteristic much-repeated step to the second theme, the big, plunging hops with the upper body rocking backwards and forwards, comes back at the corresponding point in the music within a new formation of dancers, and other less novel movement ideas likewise. Then too the little hops in *arabesque* performed by a big group in unison (surely a memory of the massed *arabesques* of the Wilis in *Giselle*) create strong closure, at balanced, emphatic moments that end exposition and recapitulation respectively (just before the Molto meno mosso) and in the Coda. Dance material too is treated more symphonically in this movement, reworked, fragmented, recontextualised and counterpointed. Repetition of these various kinds could be said to rest our minds at this stage of the piece, although this is combatted by the rushed, panic nature of much of the recapitulation. Whatever the case, Balanchine does establish a marker point here, a means of separating off by formal as well as dramatic means the very different Elegy. The Elegy is like an apotheosis, by virtue of both formal device and 'expressive means shifting'.[128]

Balanchine regularly underlines the larger sections of musical organisation, like the shift from first to second subject or from exposition to development. Likewise, he responds to broader dynamic contour, to gathering tension and climax with a corresponding increase in dance forces, dynamics, complexity of stage picture through counterpoint, and so on. But Balanchine's approach to musical detail is no more a matter of simple mirroring than his approach to large structure. He might take on a textural idea, question and answer, for instance, but he might not take it on quite in the same way or at the same time as the music, and he might choose to bring out only one part of a texture. These are not characteristics special to Balanchine: many choreographers would have treated the music in this way. What is striking however, is the variety of Balanchine's treatment,

Ex. 3.4a. Tchaikovsky, *Serenade*, I. Pezzo in Forma di Sonatina. (Note: bar numbers given as in Eulenberg miniature score).

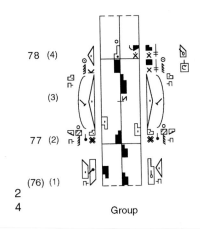

Ex 3.4b. Balanchine, *Serenade*, first movement.

and his capacity to refresh both eye and ear by constantly changing his approach, for instance, by reflecting music more closely at some points than at others. Thus, in the Sonatina exposition, immediately after the slow introduction, the group dance to the speed of the melody, then they run to a semiquaver accompaniment which starts up; a while later, they ignore the semiquavers to bring out the melody line more emphatically than before, now responding closely to its pitch contour, rhythm and repeating pattern (see Exs. 3.4a, 3.4b). Rather than adhering strictly to all the repetitions in the music, Balanchine keeps to the pervading hierarchy of two-, four- and eight-bar units of material. Sometimes, he elects to show us the short unit, sometimes the sweep of several linked together.

There are some passages where the close rapport between what we see and hear is suddenly very striking. Near the end of the exposition and recapitulation in the first movement, Tchaikovsky introduces powerful accents across the 6/8 flow of the music, creating a cross pattern of 3/4 (a device known as hemiola). Balanchine emphasises the strangeness of this device on two occasions, first

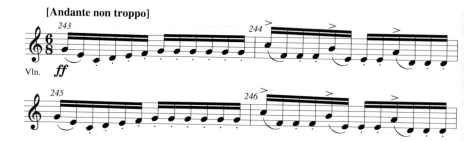

Ex. 3.5a. Tchaikovsky, *Serenade*, I. Pezzo in Forma di Sonatina.

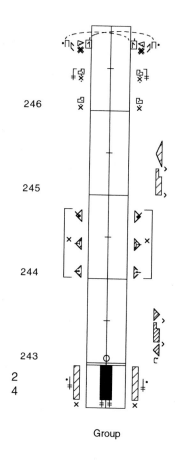

Group

Ex. 3.5b. Balanchine, *Serenade*, first movement.

with the arms circling forwards one after the other (bar 127 second time round in the Eulenberg miniature score), more obviously and extensively when the same music is recapitulated. Now, the device is visualised first time round and on its repeat. The dancers kneel in a semi-circle around one who has fallen to the floor (bars 244, 246; see Exs. 3.5a, 3.5b), and their arms first open from fifth overhead and then cross the chest in freeze-frame stopping and starting style. The tautness of the action and the sudden switch to the arms to foreground rhythm create a sudden, marked contrast to the flow of the previous allegro. (In early versions of the Russian Dance, Balanchine recapitulated these arm movements in varied form, another choreographic recapitulation, just before the Coda, bars 410–13 in the Eulenberg score.) The two *pas de deux*, when the leading woman and her partner have the stage entirely to themselves, also reveal musical detail clearly, and partly perhaps because there is no distraction here from other dance material: the opening *pas de deux* in the Waltz and the repetitive *pas de deux* in the Russian Dance (see pp. 134–5). Balanchine might simply have happened upon one moment of visualisation when he filled out the cuts in the Russian Dance. He repeats the first Allegro dance theme at the end of the recapitulation with the corresponding musical theme (bar 356), and then finds that its continuation, sharp *relevés* in *arabesque* and close in fifth, now coincides exactly and triumphantly with the up-down melodic structure of the musical continuation (bars 360–3, see Ex. 3.6).

However, these occasional effects of close music visualisation do not have important structural significance beyond playing their part in the ever-changing texture of music and choreography. Some effects, rightly so, come and go between interpretations, as dancers discover their own personal connections and use to advantage the contrast between tight connection and freedom. In a 1990 television broadcast, Darci Kistler as the leading woman and Maria

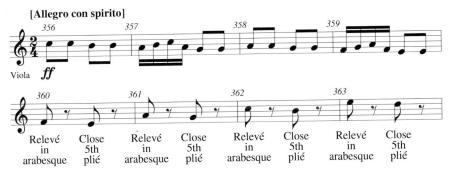

Ex. 3.6. Tchaikovsky, *Serenade*, IV. Tema Russo.

[Allegro moderato]

Ex. 3.7a. Tchaikovsky, *Serenade*, I. Pezzo in Forma di Sonatina.

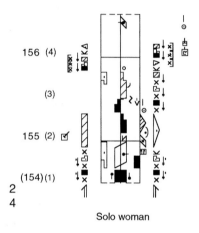

Solo woman

Ex. 3.7b. Balanchine, *Serenade*, first movement, 1984 Laban score. Note that the rhythm of the steps differs between versions. All other versions consulted (such as the examples below) show the *sissonne* landing before the bar-line and the following step with the left leg occurring on count 1 of bar 155 in the musical rhythm ♩ ♪ | ♩.

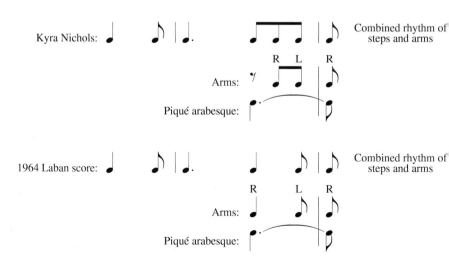

Calegari as the Dark Angel both reveal rhythmic niceties in certain passages by crisp use of the feet, but lightly, without over-emphasis.[129] Not all interpretations reveal those niceties – which appear as sudden spicy moments – and the Kistler material has a lazier, more even timing in both Labanotation scores that exist of this piece. Both these dancers present an attitude, a point of view about their music, whilst not overstating the case. These are instances too where steps might change over the years, because someone, perhaps a dancer, discovers a connection between what she does and what she hears, and others then follow the lead.

Typically, Balanchine articulates the musical pulse of *Serenade* with a compelling force, that is, when the dancers are not simply running into a new dance passage, or clearing the stage, or making picture images in slow sections. Indeed, he will often choreograph a pulse that is scored as a rest in the melody line. The first musical theme of the Sonatina not only suggests pulse (in 6/8 metre) but also the skipping rhythm that pervades the entire dance: ♩ ♪. On many occasions, Balanchine choreographs its pulse during rests and held notes, and thus he assures continuity. Dancing the opening of the recapitulation (see Exs. 3.7a, 3.7b), Kyra Nichols has taken the fast quaver pulse into her arms during the held note, after *piqué arabesque*, three arm swings alternating to fifth position overhead: the movement becomes a rhythm rather than the more rhythmically unspecific swirl through space that we tend to see today and that is notated in the 1984 Labanotation score. Precise but light in attack, her rhythm adds tautness at this point, an extra tension after the slower main pulse, and it seems to resonate with rhythmic figuration that we have heard a while earlier. But is this Nichols' 'discovery'? The 1964 Labanotation score also indicates rhythmic clarity and very precise resonance, but of another kind, a more immediate echo, of the long-short musical rhythm. (The score indicates in words 'pause' – on the *piqué*, with the right arm overhead with the *piqué* – 'then windmill arms' left and right.)

Macaulay observes the contribution of pulse to the aspect of impersonal ritual in *Serenade*, while pointing out that, even here, Balanchine varies his method: 'You feel the difference between dancers carried by a rhythm – as with the couple at the beginning of the Waltz – and dancers stepping into it – as with the two diagonal lines of dancers which cross behind the advancing soloist near the end of the same movement.'[130] In fact, this crossing passage is one of the few examples of metrical incongruence in *Serenade*. The dance step here disrupts the two-, four-bar hypermetrical system which continues in the music (see Ch. 2, pp. 80–1). The lines of dancers move across in three-bar units that mark three hyperbeats (the downbeats of each musical bar): *soutenu* turn (hyperbeat 1, bar 1), kneel (hyperbeat 2, bar 2), a step with push of the arms forward (hyperbeat 3, bar 3) (from bar 227 in Balanchine's enlarged musical score, to the last return of the opening Waltz theme, see Ex. 3.8). The mass effect is strong, and made more

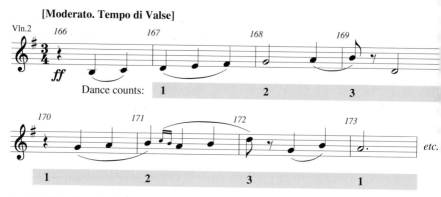

Ex. 3.8. Tchaikovsky, *Serenade*, II. Walzer.

complicated by the fact that the lines perform in canon, one hyperbeat apart, juxtaposing the *soutenu* pivot on pointe with the kneel.

Another passage of hypermetrical incongruence occurs in the development section of the Russian Dance, a major contrast after the obsessive attention to musical structure described earlier. The two soloists embark on a three-bar cross-phrase, step *temps levé*, step and beaten *jeté*, *soutenu* turn (three times, from bar 232), whilst the contrapuntal texture of the music creates extra metrical ambiguity at this point. Meanwhile, four dancers have entered behind. Returning to the regular two- or four-bar system of hypermeasures, Balanchine now uses the discrepancy between up on pointe and down in *plié* to contrast soloists and backing group, and the result is a rapid alternation of dance accents. At this point in the music, there is a high degree of harmonic tension, through modulation and chromaticism. Balanchine adds to this tension. However, such counterpoint of accents and metre is not a major feature of *Serenade*.

Balanchine singles out the Elegy for special treatment, emphasising flow, sweep, long line, once the poco più animato gets going, removing much of the pulse-driven and additive, unit-based style of the earlier movements. He was probably encouraged by the legato melodic impetus and accompanying quaver triplets here (flowing across two-quaver units in the 2/4 written metre). It is fascinating to see how he treats the passage where Tchaikovsky drops the triplets for semiquavers and reinforces the melody line across first and second violins an octave apart. The music seems suddenly restrained. Balanchine uses this moment to reintroduce a public element and to put the drama temporarily aside. The ensemble of men and women enter (significantly, these women still wear their hair tied up), and suddenly the choreography is formal, upright and freshly clipped to musical pulse, small phrase structure and repetitions. The passage begins with supported pirouette by four women, then they stop, their partners race to support another four similarly – then back again, two more supported *pirouettes* across the two alternating groups, then *arabesques* taken off balance, the first four women, the others, the first four again. Following this, the men lift one group aloft like pencils, legs together, hiding the men's faces; then these women support the other four in *arabesque* beneath them. The passage stands out from the rest of the Elegy, as Macaulay has observed: 'The shunting of these men between their women is so much an exercise that the scene can appear comic . . .' He then proceeds to rationalise the scene in terms of its relationships to the rest of the work:

> The cross-echoes in this picture are multiple. We recall how the hero is caught between two women . . . we foresee the final lift of the heroine ('like a saint's figure in procession') by three men; we recall the Dark Angel's arabesque that hid the hero who supported it. It is as if Balanchine was multiplying the central drama of the Elegy and thus rendering it abstract.[131]

But the passage also stands out, as we have seen, for musical reasons, and I would suggest that it is more remarkable for its disjunctiveness in this odd, fitful piece than for its cross-references, for the devices that sharply distance us from 'story' at this crucial moment in the drama. Fascinating to speculate whether the passage stood out quite so much in the pre-war, 'acted' *Serenade* that Denby remembered.

Long line is most emphatic of all at the conclusion of the Elegy, with the 'endless' procession, the rising to the heavens to the rising melody. Like the D chord in the music, literally lifted into higher octaves and into the 'elsewhere' territory of string harmonics, the woman is established aloft in the men's arms and then taken on her journey towards the light, embracing its warmth with a huge opening out into backbend as she goes (see Ill. 1). This is, in one sense, answer to the sad arm gesture pulling down from the light at the start, to the falling musical line of the Andante.[132] Thus, Balanchine's decision to keep the Elegy at the end of *Serenade* could be said to create visual and aural symmetry. However, looked at quite another way, his is far more an expression of romantic openness, evolution, Becoming. Subverting normal nineteenth-century practice, Balanchine's Tchaikovsky ends unfinished, literally in a different key (C) from that in which he began (D). So does Balanchine's choreography.

                    *   *   *

Serenade confirms the statement that 'the dance picture tries to tell something independent of an exact, bar-by-bar, rhythm-by-rhythm, mirror image of the music'. Yet there are occasions when connections between musical and dance structure are very strong, sometimes several musical features imitated, which reminds us of that strange interview when Balanchine talked about creating 'a

Ill. 1. *Serenade*, New York City Ballet, choreography by George Balanchine.

body movement that will roughly equal the flow of the printed notes'. Both are
important, because Balanchine's work, perhaps more than that of any other
choreographer, stresses the play between visualisation and counterpoint, the
extremes of both as well as the continuum between them. Together, music visualisation and counterpoint between music and dance are major content for Balanchine, a recurring theme across his work.

Some ballets make an issue of very close relationships between music and
dance as the foundation of their style. *Symphonie Concertante* (1945) is the most
spectacular example, with dense attention to musical ornamentation as well
as ground structures and clear association of one solo woman with the violin,
one with the viola. Perhaps this was seen as a 'teaching piece' for both dancers
and audience, a lesson in music and classical dancing, in listening as well as
watching. It was created for a programme of the National Orchestral Association called *Adventure in Ballet*, 'to show the relationship between a classical
symphony and classical dance'.[133] Maria Tallchief, who danced at the premiere,
said, 'I always wondered whether Balanchine had done it as a learning exercise
because there were no furbelows or frills. It was like taking your medicine every
day.'[134]

It is the sonata form first movement of *Symphonie Concertante* that presents the most extreme visualisation of all, an academic revelation of musical structures. There is the musical recapitulation section, which, in terms of thematic material, is an exact repeat of the exposition, except for an expanded coda and an added cadenza. Likewise, Balanchine keeps the dance steps the same: he simply swaps the roles of the two soloists when Mozart swaps the violin and viola parts. A passage in the development features one of the soloists in an *adage*, supported by three women from the corps; the musical passage is repeated, and so is the choreography, using the other soloist and reversed, danced on the opposite side of the body. Consistently enough for us to feel that this is the *raison d'être* of the ballet (but not so much as to become predictable), steps reflect the detail of the music too, its melody, rhythm and accompaniment pattern (see Ch. 2, pp. 75–6). Musical-choreographic relationships loosen a little in the second and third movements.

Early critical reaction to this work was mixed. Some, undoubtedly because of this special concentration on musical matters, found it untheatrical, like Robert Sabin: 'An exhibitionistic exercise in the most brittle and empty academicism.'[135] On the other hand, the critic of *The Times* (London) considered that 'Though over-energetic and lacking repose, it follows Mozart so intelligently that had other choreographers showed equal consideration for the music on which they based their talents we should have none of the controversy about symphonic ballet.'[136]

Other works that feature unusually close relationships between music and dance are *Ballet Imperial* and *Allegro Brillante* (1956), but nevertheless, not as much so as *Symphonie Concertante*, and in terms of detailed attention to the musical structure rather than regular matching of large repetitions. The most exciting dancers can, of course, play with and against the music in their interpretations of such ballets, not exaggerating the close relationships, by not 'nailing' themselves to every note. Even for the obvious repeats in *Symphonie Concertante*, Tanaquil LeClercq had an imaginative answer in her performance. Pat McBride says, 'When the repeats came . . . she had an intuitive sense of how to vary them so that maybe the step was done in a smaller way, or was more amusing, slightly tongue-in-cheek.'[137] To very different *musique concrète*, in the *Variations pour une porte et un soupir*, Balanchine sets up mirror relationships between dance and musical gestures, here to somewhat comic effect, the woman as the Door, the man as the Sigh. As the sound elements overlap, so do the statements of the man and woman.

Movements for Piano and Orchestra, apparently the most 'in-the-music' piece that Balanchine made, likewise reveals musical structures with a high degree of regularity: during its ten minutes, individual notes are picked out, their separateness thus emphasised, aphoristic phrases are clipped to a close with complementary dance gestures, and clusters of accents are reinforced. There is some association of soloists with the piano and the ensemble of six women with the orchestra – more to make a point about difference – but, typical of Balanchine practice, this is not a consistent feature. Every Interlude between the five musical movements is carefully delineated by being given to the ensemble. Even Stravinsky's twelve-note row is visualised at the end, a slow account of it. Each of the six ensemble dancers takes one note (covering the first six notes of the row), turns to face the audience, and starts to *bourrée*; the later notes of the row are also choreographically accented. At the same time during *Movements*, Balanchine often chooses to clarify the musical pulse, different rates of pulse, even through musical rests (as at the beginning of *Agon*). This is especially striking in the fourth movement, and the Interlude that follows ends in a musical rest, during which the dancers slap their thighs emphatically. This clarification of pulse is probably the reason why Boelzner talks of Balanchine 'scanning' the music, because he

> can visually clarify the meter. Of course there's a lot of silence in that score, but Stravinsky never gave up rhythm even though you don't hear it so much in this sort of shattered, twelve-tone music. But you can see it. It's all being ticked away for you on the stage.[138]

Perhaps it is one of the reasons too why Stravinsky was moved to write his piece 'Eye Music':

> To see Balanchine's choreography of the *Movements* is to hear the music with one's eyes ... The choreography emphasizes relationships of which I had hardly been aware ... and the performance was like a tour of a building for which I had drawn the plans but never explored the result ... The ballet ... might also have been called *Electric Currents*.[139]

Richard Moredock, another rehearsal pianist with New York City Ballet, has suggested a new subtlety in Stravinsky's remark. Stravinsky was really referring here to Balanchine's response to the technical layout, the look of his musical score, not to visualising what you hear, but to what you do not hear.[140] My reading, indeed of the phrase 'in-the-music', is that Balanchine was doing both these things. *Movements* is the most intensely analytical of all the Balanchine works that I know in picking out both surface and hidden structures of the music, bringing to attention the smallest detail, helping us to come to grips with the mechanics of this difficult score. Any emotional aspects are very quiet. If Balanchine considered his *The Four Temperaments* choreography the negative to the music's positive, or 'less than the music', then the roles in *Symphonie Concertante* might be considered equal, and they must surely be reversed in *Movements*.

Generally, Balanchine's method is not to emphasise regularly either big block repetitions in a score, entries of solo instruments (matched by solo dancers) or frequently repeating musical themes. His connections with the music vary considerably as a work progresses, in both manner and intensity. Moments of intense imitation stand out, and they can produce a variety of effects: surprise, the pleasurable relaxation of simplicity, resolution of conflict, even triumph.

Balanchine also borrows structural devices from music without necessarily mirroring the music at the same time. We saw examples of this in *Serenade*, and perhaps Balanchine responded in this way as a result of his musical studies: there was, after all, no comparable taught or written choreographic theory. But he might too have gleaned ideas from analysing a work like *Les Sylphides*, or the theme and variations dance of Swanilda and friends in *Coppélia* (which Balanchine much admired).[141] As others setting plotless dances to music understood at this time, new ways had to be found for structuring these dances, some of which were of large proportions. The 'symphonic' approach from music was useful to adopt, in terms of an intricate network of thematic ideas, cross-referencing within and across movements, the counterpointing, reworking and fragmenting of material. We must remember too Balanchine's debt to Verdi, whose deployment of chorus and soloists in his operas gave him models for choreography.

By the time of *Concerto Barocco* (1941), Balanchine's symphonic style is already much more highly developed than in *Serenade*. It relates directly here to baroque structures of ritornello form: a body of material is presented at the start, returns during the course of the movement, but is also broken down so that individual ideas from it appear separately and within new contexts. Thus, in the first movement, the combination of step-*tendu devant*, step-*tendu devant* and a series of small *temps levés* in *arabesque* (the third bar of the ritornello material that was originally performed by the corps of eight women) is later pulled out by itself and repeated with variations. The two step-*tendus* find another context within the soloists' 'chicken step' (bar 42), now followed by a step and sharp bending forwards over parallel *retiré*, the arms flashing out behind the body. Later, the *temps levés* are found at the end of another unit that begins with *piqué arabesque* and a *grand pas de basque* (bar 51). Internal repetitions within the original motif are added and removed so that the count length of the dance unit constantly changes: 5, 4, 3, 4, 2, 2 (bars 71–5). This was indicated appropriately in the 1963 Labanotation score as the 'sandwich step'.[142] *Barocco* is a network of thematic ideas and relationships within movements and, transformed in tempo and spirit, across movements.

Serenade also gave us insights into the different ways in which Balanchine uses large musical forms, particularly his approach to return or recapitulation. There is plenty more to say about this (in, for instance, sonata, ABA or rondo forms), which is one of the most fascinating aspects of his approach to music. In *Serenade* there was the tendency to mask the straight, emphatic return, dance with music, in favour of evolution and openness, which epitomises the romantic sense of Becoming. But this is not always the case. Contrast Balanchine's use of Bizet in *Symphony in C*, of Mozart in *Symphonie Concertante*, and of Bach in *Concerto Barocco*, where, in the first movement, for instance, four out of six of the ritornello repetitions receive more or less the same choreographic treatment. All these choreographies respect the convention of musical return and closure with far more regularity than in *Serenade*: in them, there is far more long-distance repetition of dance with music. But there is also a far greater tonal imperative for closure in baroque and classical than in much romantic music, and generally a greater period respect for convention (Bizet looks back to the classical period here). *Symphony in C*, *Symphonie Concertante* and *Concerto Barocco* would seem to be much more 'formal' works. Even *Apollo* and *Agon* appear frozen in time and formal, by virtue of the recapitulations within their separate dances and, in the case of *Agon*, across the whole (the men's *pas de quatre* is repeated at the very end). Thus *Apollo* tells its story not straight as a story that seemingly happens during the time of the piece, but more in the spirit of a story that has already happened and is now recalled. *Le Tombeau de Couperin*, contains several examples of large-scale repetition: in the Prelude, the opening section (29 bars) is repeated, both dance and music, and, in the Forlane, there is an early repetition of dance with music and a recapitulation of the same visual-aural material again near the end. Here, the formality and simplicity of the big repeats seem appropriate to the formal, 'social' style, the court dance reference of the piece.

The case of *Symphony in C* is interesting. Balanchine rid himself of several of his plainest big repeats over the years. The Labanotation score of the first American version in 1948 (one year after the French premiere, when the ballet was called *Le Palais de cristal*) proves just how much Balanchine changed his mind.[143] The original repeat of the exposition of the first, sonata-form movement (repetition of both music and dance, just as in *Symphonie Concertante*) was simply dropped after a while.[144] The exposition repeat in the last movement was sometimes dropped, sometimes included, an exact repetition performed by the dancers brought back from the first movement, and then, after a while, this music was totally rechoreographed for these first movement dancers. While the music is heard twice, the choreography now added something new. Today, the only straight large repeat that is left in this work is in the Scherzo third movement. Yet, even so, there are still a number of briefer, but nevertheless striking, recapitulations with the music. At the moment of musical recapitulation in the outer movements, for instance, dancers refer back to the corresponding point in the exposition. In the first movement, the corps accompaniment comes back; in

the last, all four ballerinas dance the original solo material. In this last movement, the second theme jumping phrase of the men also returns with the same
music in the recapitulation. The triumphant, formal closure at the very end is
enhanced by a number of references back to earlier movements of the piece: it is
'a kind of dance summing up of all that has gone before'.[145]

Balanchine provides two especially intriguing examples of large repetition of
dance with music. In the slow movement of *Concerto Barocco*, he underlines the
fact of recapitulation by exact reference back in the choreography, but, just
here, this makes the moment strange. The opening of the movement he had
treated like a transition (of two bars), the second woman soloist leaving to give
way to the man, after which the dance proper began, the *pas de deux*, with all its
associations of centrality in ballet. He makes a normally insignificant preparation the moment of musical beginning, rather than the opening of the *pas de
deux* itself, the real point of this movement. The net result is an odd switching of
positions just before the big theme recurs in the recapitulation, a brief return to
the stage of the second solo woman, only for her to depart again, and a brief
withdrawal of the male dancer; in other words, to bring us briefly back to where
we were at the beginning of the slow movement. Such eccentric, 'purposeless'
behaviour draws unusual attention to this structural landmark. It also reminds
us of the fundamentally formal, abstract drive of the ballet as a whole.

The treatment of recapitulation in the slow movement of *Scotch Symphony*
is odd in another way. Here, referring back to the nineteenth-century *La Syl-
phide*, we see a sylph in a romantic encounter with a Highlander, their meeting
pompously and suddenly interrupted by a group of Highlanders marching in to
shield her from him. But soon, just as suddenly, they bow out to allow him to
reach her again. There is something of a plot here. When the interruption music
returns again, the same drama recurs, this time reversed to the opposite side of
the stage. But why should a story recur with such formal exactness? The exactness of the repeat, underlined by its repetition to the same music as before,
freezes the drama into mere decoration and reminds us that we should not take
it too seriously. Indeed, the very pomposity of the men (and the style of the
accompanying music) gives the passage an almost comic air. This is not really a
story ballet after all, and it is a structural, musical-choreographic device that
reminds us of this.

Can we rationalise these differences in Balanchine's approach? I have often
heard the explanations that Balanchine repeated dance material because he
was short of time or because he liked what he had made and wanted to see it
again. Shortage of time may well have been a reason for the big repeats in the
first version of *Symphony in C* (not I think any attempt to answer Beaumont's
bizarre criticism): 'When a composer repeats a section of his music he does it
because that is how his composition develops, but when a choreographer re-

peats a section of his composition there is always a suspicion that he could not invent something new to go with the music.'[146] But could we also suggest that Balanchine's choreography negotiates a relationship with the different sensibilities of different musical choices? Balanchine clearly saw some musical structures as more ready for open choreographic structures than others. Certainly, the results of his different approaches to large musical form contain a range of meanings.

A fascinating example is *Ballet Imperial* (from 1973 called *Tchaikovsky Piano Concerto No. 2*), for I have always sensed that there is something unbalanced about this ballet.[147] It is a comment on the nineteenth-century Petipa tradition, and the concerto has three separate movements or frames. There is the major ballerina and her partner, as usual, but what is striking is the emphatic weighting of the second ballerina towards the end of the first movement. It leaves an effect of 'dissonance' unmatched by Tchaikovsky, who recapitulates what we have already heard in the exposition and signifies closure. She appears in a trio with two 'new' solo men taken from the group just for this section; it is a surprisingly long trio and it begins in a strange, quiet mood. After this, the end of the first movement, which brings the first ballerina back (minus her partner), seems rushed and inconclusive.

My reading is that Balanchine was exploring the tension between the overarching narrative, which is about the changing relationship between the first ballerina and her partner, and the 'abstract' principle of three distinct frames or musical movements in *Imperial*, and, over the years, he went on exploring this tension, at various times cutting the mime elements in the second movement and the *Imperial* decor. Most important, his relationship to large musical structure, particularly with regard to return, is crucial to the relative effect of mobility or closure and thus to narrative. In this respect, he seems determined to keep the first frame relatively open, and operates in counterpoint with the musical structure. But there is also a gender issue here, with the stress on the second, 'other' ballerina, who is dressed appropriately in black in Eugene Berman's designs for the Royal Ballet, and is choreographed as an independent force for much of this ballet. There is another dissonance late in the third movement, a solo for the man, rather like an afterthought. It is interesting that critics have concentrated on the 'positive' aspects of Balanchine's references to Petipa in *Ballet Imperial*: they have not alluded to these odd, underside, deconstructive, unbalanced aspects of the ballet.

The analysis of *Mozartiana* will include further discussion of Balanchine's approaches to musical form. But first, we will turn to *Agon*, which demonstrates other aspects of Balanchine's play between music visualisation and counterpoint.

Agon

Agon (1957) has often been cited as a key composer-choreographer
collaboration. Balanchine's match to Stravinsky's brilliant musical score, with
its bitter edge, twangy instrumentations and mischievous courtliness, has made
Agon one of the seminal ballets of the century. It was also a turning-point work
in the careers of both collaborators. Whilst both music and choreography contain reference to a number of traditions, including nineteenth-century classical
ballet, jazz and baroque, the piece is important as one of Stravinsky's transitional essays in serialism or twelve-note music. Part of it is written in the new
mode in which he could express his principles of elimination and unity: 'A series
is a facet, and serial composition a faceting, or crystallizing way of presenting
several sides of the same idea.'[148] Devised by Schoenberg as a compositional
method after what he perceived as the breakdown of tonality, the principle behind serialism is that a sequence of notes (taken from all twelve degrees of the
chromatic scale) governs the development of a piece of music. Agon was also
Balanchine's first work in this musical genre.

Agon took a long time to materialise.[149] Stravinsky seems to have felt no particular urgency to write a ballet. Kirstein had asked for a third Stravinsky ballet
as early as 1948, to make a triptych with Apollo and Orpheus, but it took until
1953, by which time various mythological themes had been suggested and dis-
pensed with, before Stravinsky finally settled down to writing. He had at last
been inspired by de Lauze's seventeenth-century dance manual Apologie de la
danse (1623), which Kirstein had sent to him. Stravinsky chose the Greek title
Agon (meaning 'contest') and decided to base his writing loosely on the seventeenth-century dance forms. It was agreed that there was to be no story content.
The Prelude was written in 1953 and was revised as the rest of the ballet slowly
developed. The project was shelved at the end of 1954, taken up again in 1956,
and completed in 1957.

It has been suggested that the number twelve, which was initiated by Stravinsky and became the number of sections and dancers in Agon, stems from the
twelve-note basis of part of the score. The musicologist Irene Alm has argued
that this is not so, and that the number of sections and casting of the piece had
been determined before Stravinsky introduced serial writing to Agon.[150] There is
evidence that Balanchine and Stravinsky had established the large plan of the
work, including lengths, character and tempos of individual sections during a
working period in Los Angeles in the summer of 1954. Stravinsky continued
after that time writing several sections in tonally-derived style, only composing
the first twelve-note section, the Coda, at the end of the year. However, it is
important that he had been moving towards serialism since 1952, before starting work on Agon. In their planning, Balanchine and Stravinsky also agreed

Musical Structure	Dancers
Section 1	
Pas de quatre	4 men
Double pas de quatre	8 women
Triple pas de quatre	4 men/8 women
Section 2: First pas de trois	
Prelude	1 man/2 women
Saraband-step	1 man
Gailliarde	2 women
Coda	1 man/2 women
Section 3: Second pas de trois	
Interlude (variation of prelude)	2 men/1 woman
Bansle simple	2 men
Bransle gay	1 woman
Bransle double (Bransle de Poitou)	2 men/1 woman
Section 4	
Interlude (variation of prelude)	1 man/1 woman
Pas de deux	1 man/1 woman
Section 5	
Four duos	4 men/4 women
Four trios	4 men/8 women
(Coda: recapitulation of opening pas de quatre)	4 men/8 women

Table 3.4. Structural layout of *Agon*.

that, as the audience would find *Agon* difficult, it must contain repetition and not be too long.[151] I can find no evidence of any choreographic parallel to the note sequence technicalities of Stravinsky's serial procedures.

The sources analysed here span the period of time from the premiere of *Agon* (1957) to the present time, after Balanchine's death: six recordings of New York City Ballet performances (between 1960 and 1993) and two Labanotation scores, one written during the making of the piece, the second completed in 1987 after a 1985 staging.[152] These sources demonstrate that the work has changed very little since 1957 – much less, in fact, than many other Balanchine works. Although there are some changes in details, the two Labanotation scores indicate remarkably similar dance counts. Therefore, this analysis refers to a work with an unusually persistent identity.

The musical structure of *Agon* is analysed here as sixteen dances grouped into five sections, with the dances in the second and third sections based on seventeenth-century dance forms (see Table 3.4). Balanchine's choreography closely follows this musical structure. At the end of the work, the Coda repeats exactly the music of the opening Pas de Quatre. Balanchine created new choreography for the first part of this Coda and continued to use the twelve dancers from the previous Four Trios. However, responding to the idea of musical recapitulation, he proceeded to repeat the corresponding choreography of the opening dance for the four men alone.

In an enlightening doctoral dissertation on *Agon*, the musicologist Robynn Stilwell has referred to interlocking structures of music and dance that create increasingly larger orders of form. Tracing the use of serial techniques, tonality, classical and modern ballet styles through the ballet as a whole, she finds *Agon* like 'a sine wave that dips into the past with a complementary curve into the modern, beginning and ending with the neo-classical – a fusion of the old and the new.'[153] The interlocking at lower levels is explained by drawing upon Balanchine's own analogy between a ballet and a cabinet, choreographer and cabinetmaker:

> There is the skeleton frame [the outer repetitions of the Pas de Quatre]; there is the division into panels or drawers [the groups of dances]; then there is the inlay work which is so invested into the structure that it is never merely decorative or rhetorical.[154]

However, as soon as we get past the skeleton frame, *Agon* reveals 'symmetrical asymmetries'[155] in both music and choreography:

> The primarily tonal Double and Triple Pas-de-Quatre with some serial elements balancing the primarily serial Four Duos and Four Trios with some tonal elements . . . The gender separate buildup of choreographic forces in the Pas-de-Quatre movements balances the multiplication of a male-female duo by four, and the addition of a second girl to each duo to form the Four Trios.[156]

It is relevant that other divisions than mine, into either three or four (as opposed to five) sections, for example, have been rationalised. The large structure of the ballet is essentially dynamic and ambiguous. So is the more detailed structure, from a single dance, like the Bransle Gay – ternary in music interlocking with a choreographic structure that is more like binary – down to contrasting moments of musical mimicry and counterpoint with the choreography.

Stilwell points out how music analysts have striven to find unity across the score, putting it down as eclectic and disparate as such unity evaded them. However, an issue that I take up later, she sets out to demonstrate that the ballet as a theatre event does demonstrate unity, and partly through the consistency of its irregularity and diversity at surface, 'inlay' level.[157] On this point, Balanchine's choreography illuminates the music.

Most of the major musical divisions within each of Stravinsky's dances are marked choreographically by a change of either dance material or of patterning of dancers within the stage space. There is a more subtle point to be made here about the nature of these structural divisions. With the exception of the Pas de Deux, which, in many ways, stands apart from the rest of *Agon*, Stravinsky's music is constructed as a series of formal cells or blocks. These occur without breaks between them, contrasting in material and sometimes also in metre. The opening Pas de Quatre, for instance, begins with a fanfare (bars 1–6), stops short for a rumbling passage for lower strings under a shrill clarinet and oboe chord (bars 7–9), which is in turn interrupted by a passage for harp, mandolin, piano and strings (bars 10–13). All these are discrete cells that recur, sometimes in varied form, later in the movement: for instance, the fanfare in bars 14–19 and 30–4, the rumbling passage under a chord in bars 20–2 and 35–8, the harp/mandolin passage in bars 23–25. Balanchine choreographed according to the same plan, as Denby describes: '[The different units of material] fit like the stones of a mosaic . . . Each is distinct, you see the cut between; and you see that the cut between them does not interrupt the dance impetus.'[158] Perhaps this structuring principle is the reason Balanchine described *Agon* as 'more tight . . . than usual'.[159] The piece exemplifies collage perfectly, the art of juxtaposition rather than transition (see Ch. 1, p. 19).

Both music and ballet were conceived in 'chamber' style, with small forces, many solo and small ensemble passages, the full body of dancers and instruments rarely used. The larger ensemble dances framing the work contain the fullest orchestration. Women dancers tend to be associated with flutes when they dance alone, men with brass, classical ballet conventions perhaps determining such gender stereotyping here, and likewise in the use of strings and solo violin for the Adagio of the Pas de Deux. On several occasions, there is a connection between musical and choreographic textures. This is especially clear in the two duets within the Pas de Trois. In the outer section of the Gailliarde, Stravinsky introduces mirroring techniques: in the first section, flutes and double basses (playing harmonics) opposite violas and cellos, similarly in the last section, with an additional mirror canon between harp and mandolin. It seems more than coincidental that, for much of this dance, Balanchine sets one woman mirroring the other. In the Bransle Simple, Balanchine sets two men in exact canon following the canonic lines of two trumpets. This orchestration had been inspired by the de Lauze *Apologie de la danse*, which contains an engraving of two trumpeters accompanying a Bransle Simple.

Examining small-scale details of *Agon*, we find numerous instances of music visualisation. Balanchine gives particular stress to the arrival of the final Coda, a key point of recapitulation which matches the opening music of *Agon*. There are four repeated, heavily orchestrated chords, with strings playing pizzicato under the trumpet fanfare (bars 561–3), and to each chord, Balanchine has choreographed a dance accent: an *entrechat* for the eight women, a *pirouette* for the four men, a *sissonne* for the women and finally a dragging step for the men. The accents for the women occur with the height of the jump, the thrust out of the dancing group. Interestingly, the timing of four separate dance accents in precise correspondence with the music is much clearer in the original 1957 Labanotation score than in the later one. Balanchine treats the occasion of recapitulation as especially important for emphasis, and logically so. There are both musical and choreographic devices which invite the audience to anticipate this recapitulation. Immediately preceding the Coda, a horn fanfare sounds like a distant recollection of the opening trumpet fanfare; Balanchine brings the four men in a line out front, with movements accentuating the ball of the foot and the heel, recalling images from the opening male Pas de Quatre.

Four castanet bars in the Bransle Gay provide another example of visualisation with a structural purpose. In them, the castanet ostinato rhythm (which is also clapped by the two framing men) is suddenly exposed, alone: ♪♪♪♪ . Castanets give the distinctive timbre to this solo. (Denby writes that their sound is drawn attention to stylistically as well: 'now and then one arm held high, Spanish style.'[160]) These castanet bars are the moments of transition, clarifying phrase structure and also offering moments of simplicity and respite within a rhythmically complex dance. For the first two (bars 310 and 315), the female dancer simply takes two steps, first forwards, then backwards on repeat; for the other two (bars 320 and 335), she gestures playfully, arms alternating up and down crisply in a precise imitation of the musical rhythmic pattern.

Yet a number of instances of visualisation arise out of nowhere, as startling moments, even question marks or jokes. Sometimes these are punctuating points, a staccato musical-choreographic gesture marking the end of a dance or section of a dance. In the Bransle Simple, which is in ABA form, the moments of visualisation emphasise the end of the two outer A sections. To the same sustained, accented chord (bars 287 and 308), the first time, the men extend an arm towards each other; the second time, they take up a standing position side by side and fold their arms. Then, at the very end, in a surprise extra gesture, replicating a much more strident musical accent, they strike a histrionic locked-arms sculptural pose, the real ending immediately after the 'false' one; or is it an ending? One of the men reaches inconclusively up and away from the other. It is interesting how, at the end of the Bransle Double, the woman is thrown up in the air extending in *arabesque* as if she is trying to escape upwards (again to a musical accent, but here in ironic opposition to the downward motion as the accent introduces the bass register). She gets further than the two women near the close of the first Pas de Trois in *their arabesques*. Balanchine and Stravinsky avoid obvious closure on a number of occasions. Even at the end of *Agon*, Balanchine does not match the end of the first Pas de Quatre exactly. In their combat lunge gesture, on or nearly on the last musical exclamation mark, the first time round, the four men face each other as two against two, looking towards stage centre. The second time round, they face each other in pairs, a much more confrontational gesture, and with two centres, not one. So the contest (*agon*) continues? In the 1960 film, this is how they ended the ballet. They never resolved the gesture back into the opening pose of backs to the audience that we now see in the silence after the last chord, and that Stravinsky indicates in his score. Other moments that visualise music occur within dances. Eight women perform an immaculate *plié* up and down in fifth position only to cave in, out of the blue, collapsing, with legs turned in, to a violin glissando (bar 82). Then there is the jerky bumping shoulders and bending into a huddle to a phrase of descending accents in the Coda of the first Pas de Trois (bars 241–3). Again, these moments stand out as eccentricities, adding to many others, exaggerated through musical mimicry and unresolved during the continuity of *Agon*.

Some instances of music visualisation are so subtle that the musical-choreographic relationships did not emerge in my early viewings of the dance. There are moments created by individual dancers' interpretations of the music. Other subtle moments arise out of a sequential relationship between musical and dance gesture – the dance anticipates or echoes a musical feature. This latter device creates tension – the effect of music and dance racing or chasing each other, or movement can seem like a late reverberation of a sound feature. In the Coda to the first Pas de Trois, the ironic gigue rhythm articulated by the solo violin from bar 193 (see Ex. 3.9) has already been 'heard' in the dance in the skipping and 'soft shoe' steps that begin at bar 187. In the same trio, there is a striking passage where a series of *entrechats* springing down the line of dancers (bars 201–2) anticipates four shrill repeated B-flats on the flutes (bars 202–3). Further accented kicks and *relevés* then become echoes or reverberations of those high notes. Effects like these, which emerged after repeated viewings of the dance, encourage the notion that notes and moves, 'moments' in music and dance, though created at different times, do not exist in isolation from each

Ex. 3.9. Stravinsky, *Agon*, First Pas de Trois, Coda.

other in *Agon*. Rather, the music and dance are in dialogue in a dynamic relationship.

In addition to points of music visualisation in *Agon*, Balanchine introduces a variety of other kinds of relationship between music and dance. In terms of metrical structure, he discovered a wealth of possibilities for musical-choreographic interaction. Stravinsky's score is already highly complex, with its irregular accenting and shifting metres. There is nearly always a strong sense of driving, underlying pulse, whether or not it is always articulated, and Balanchine reinforces this sense of drive. When the rhythmic pattern is ambiguous or unstressed, steps and gestures articulate pulse and metre, sometimes coinciding with the musical notes, sometimes not (see p. 114).

Often, there is an even pattern of moves, each step or gesture indicating a beat. Indeed, much of the choreography in *Agon* was built this way. This might seem dull – a surprising fact, since the *Agon* collaboration is acclaimed for its rhythmic interest. However, with such extraordinarily varied rhythms in the music, additional complexity in the dance movement might have muddled the choreography and created insurmountable rhythmic problems for many dancers. Moreover, moving to every beat does not in any way preclude the gradation of accent. Balanchine takes full advantage of this possibility. There are also jazz-style freedoms in the rhythmic style of the dance: the slightly 'offbeat' stepping of the men in bars 5–6 is an early example.[161] Balanchine often achieves rhythmic tension through counterpoint, especially when he introduces a different metre from that of the music. Passages of polymetre are a common feature of the dances in *Agon*. There are one or two passages in all but two dances, including the Prelude and two Interludes, where musical metres counter choreographic metres for a few bars. Balanchine introduces this device in different ways, although it is usually through repetition in the movement that the impression of a strong, independent dance metre is obtained. In the second half of the Saraband-Step, the male soloist performs a jumping and turning step combination in four counts (equivalent to two musical beats, 2/4). This is performed four times against three bars of 3/4 in the music (bars 158–60). In the closing section of the Gailliarde, Balanchine introduces counterpoint between the musical barlines (bars 181–3). The music is heard most clearly as 3+3+3 beats within each bar of 9/4. Balanchine introduces a 4+5 structure (in a *posé* in *attitude* or *arabesque* combination with transition steps).

The Bransle Gay makes an interesting example of metrical counterpointing. A sense of heightened energy or small climax near the end of this dance results from the interplay of musical-choreographic rhythmic organisation, which contributes significantly to the shape of this little solo. The dancer pulls further and further away from the rhythmic structure of the music as the solo progresses, drawn back to it temporarily during the castanet transition bars (see p. 155). For a while, the solo shares the clear, shifting 3/8, 5/16, and 7/16 metres of the music and is counted accordingly, although Balanchine creates his own independent rhythmic patterns. The first two phrases of this binary dance (see p. 153), which constitute Section A in an AB choreographic structure, illustrate this point. The shared metrical structure is as follows:

Introduction (castanet ostinato)   3/8 (bar 310)
Phrase 1   7/16 5/16 5/16   7/16 (bars 311–14)
Transition (castanet ostinato)   3/8 (bar 315)
Phrase 2   5/16 7/16 7/16   5/16 (bars 316–19)
Transition (castanet ostinato)   3/8 (bar 320)

In the music, bars 316–19 are a reshuffling of the four 'modules' that make up bars 311–14 (see Ex. 3.10).

In dance Phrase 1, the woman articulates each beat in turn and with minimal decoration in between them, a clear example of 'dancing to the beat'. Some dance movements are slightly accented, and these, more often than not, coincide with the longer, rhythmically accented notes in the flute line. Dance Phrase 2 is different in terms of both steps and rhythm. The articulation of every pulse loosens, and there is now marked change between accented and non-accented moves. The main rhythmic stress occurs with the sustained moves, the first three on *relevé* – in *arabesque*, twice, then with the working leg in *attitude* unfolding into *arabesque* – and the last on a dragging step. A *cabriole* in bar 319 introduces a 'dotted' rhythm for the first time. Written in musical notation, for ease of comparison between dance and music, the dance rhythm looks like this:

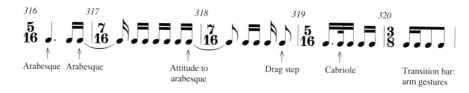

Here, the dance accents do not fall in the same places as the flute accents. Balanchine creates a counterpoint of accents, whilst his own rhythmic pattern is irregular and complicated.

Next, in Section B, the dancer establishes her own definite five-beat metre with two repeating units of material (one unit moving sideways across the stage, performed four times, one moving backwards, seen three times, bars 321–7). The music is written in a corresponding 5/16, but it seems far less clearly metred than the dance, and the music and dance accents are independent. In bar 331, the soloist starts a brilliant five-count (5/16) turning sequence, which she per-

Ex. 3.10. Stravinsky, *Agon*, Bransle Gay (Section A).

forms three times, moving directly towards the audience. At this point, she diverges from the musical bar-line, establishing metrical counterpoint and creating an unprecedented touch of tension within this solo: crossing the musical bars 332–4, which are a repeat of bars 311–13 (7/16, 5/16, 5/16). Finally, in bar 335, this tension is resolved, as the soloist simply imitates the castanet ostinato with her arm gestures.

   If this sounds like a tight, comfortably rounded dance, then we might now recognise its off-balance surprises. In Section B, just before the turning sequence, the woman drops into second position *plié* on pointe from *échappé*, twice,

Ex. 3.11. Stravinsky, *Agon*, Bransle Gay.

with a few steps in between (bars 328 and 330). The *pliés* 'sound' a little like a falling motif on the clarinet that is then immediately echoed by the flute (bars 328 and 329), but also like a chord on harp and strings played three times (bars 330–1, see Ex. 3.11). The chord is odd, like a punctuation point. There is nothing else like it during the Bransle Gay (it is the only use of strings), and Stilwell points out the musical significance that bars 328–31 'interpolate' the row from the Bransle Simple.[162] Likewise in the choreography, the *pliés* are 'new', bold, open, symmetrical, exaggeratedly so in Wendy Whelan's 1993 performance as she plunges deep into them with her arms flashing high over her head. Nothing is straightforward around this point. There are no exact rhythmic coincidences between music and dance ideas, and the beginning of the woman's turning sequence overlaps the third chord. The first *plié* cuts in unexpectedly after only three repetitions of the step unit backwards (four would balance the sequence preceding it). Similarly, after his 'interpolation', Stravinsky does not give a complete repetition of Phrase 1. The Bransle Gay is, after all, an ambiguous dance.

The canon device is important in *Agon*, a Balanchine trademark, occurring in countless works and here on numerous occasions. As canon at the distance of one beat, it creates two important rhythmic effects. It underlines pulse, the 'moment', in a work wedded to the instant as much as it projects powerful momentum (see p. 118). It can also simulate beats in a metre: each stressed movement passing down a line of dancers creates a beat, and the first one in the line, the downbeat. Thus, in the Coda of the first Pas de Trois, the 'metre' of three canon passages is three beats to a bar (created by the three dancers), against two beats in the 6/8 musical bar (bars 201–8, which are repeated bars 222–9; a different canon passage, bars 234–40). The contrapuntal effect between music and dance is very clear because the dance beats are marked by strong accents: *entrechats*, leg kicks, sharp *relevés* in *attitude*, and/or *pirouettes*. The effect is especially restless in the closing section of this Coda (bars 234–40). This canon begins with the man in the centre, shifts the eye to the right and then to the left, to the women on either side of him.

We have seen so far that Balanchine's rhythms at times visualise Stravinsky's rhythms and at other times counterpoint the music. Interestingly, in the Gailliarde, the movements draw attention to the musical part-writing and bring out the unusual, piquant orchestration (see p. 154). The choreography shifts between high and low spatial levels. In the first section, the dance accents are usually at the high level – *entrechats* and *relevés* – and they connect with the syncopated flute and string lines. In the central section, the dancers emphasise a descending three-note pattern in the piano line, again with *relevés* (bars 171–2). Then, the dance accent goes down to low level with *pliés*, marking the two-beat grouping of the music for a while (in bars of 6/4). Here, the mandolin and harp writing seems to emerge more strongly. Rhythmically, the Gailliarde is intriguing. It demonstrates that, although dance steps can be neutral in accent, the music invites the viewer (and perhaps the dancer) into perceiving an accent that is in some way complementary to, or harmonious with, itself.

Balanchine's choreography introduces a further important aspect of musical-choreographic structuring which is concerned with speed. Changes in speed of motion contribute to the ensemble climax of the piece. While the final Coda music moves towards a peak of chromatic tension, the choreography gradually gathers momentum with double *pirouettes* and a quick five-count series of steps that crosses the musical metre. Then, a rapid half-turn upstage and reverse back again leads to a climax of stillness as the entire ensemble freezes in a crouched position. All is still between bars 596 and 598, reflecting, for the first time, the depth of the rumbling double basses. The movement up to this point is much faster and more brilliant than the movement for the four men to the same music at the beginning of *Agon*, although Balanchine responds to the chromatic tension on both occasions. The canons (dubbed 'Petrushka canons' according to the 1987 Labanotation score, because of the trumpet scoring) recur from the opening Pas de Quatre, but in presto variation. In addition to this, Balanchine shifts the viewer's eye frequently and rapidly in the Coda, more than anywhere else in *Agon*. In the second Petrushka canon, leg kicks and *pirouettes* catch the eye as they are performed in canon, taking the eye into the centre, darting it to one side, to the opposite side, and in towards centre again (bars 592–5). Against any musical suggestion, Balanchine invented new choreography in the Coda, using 'dangerous' extremes of speed, sounding the alarm against obvious closure, leaving only a brief (and potentially uncertain) conclusion for the four men (see p. 156).

So far, we have observed Balanchine's handling of musical-choreographic rhythmic structure by discussing the detail of separate dances. But his procedures also have implications for the larger shape of *Agon*. It is possible to perceive sections of relative tension and relaxation, the least tension perhaps in the solo dances and male and female duets, a peak of tension on either side of the Pas de Deux, in the Bransle Double, and then through to the Coda. Use of space, group organisation and counterpoint support this contour.

The tension surrounding the Pas de Deux only emphasises its unique qualities within the work. Musically, this is perhaps the most complex and cerebral section. Freely serial, it inspired some of the most imaginative, unclassically-styled movement. Diana Adams, who created the woman's role, recalls that Balanchine wanted to start with the choreography for the Pas de Deux, perhaps because 'it would give him the key or approach to the rest of the work'.[163] Arthur Mitchell, her partner, remembers Balanchine taking two weeks to make it and saying: 'This is the longest it's ever taken me to choreograph anything . . . because everything has to be *exactly* right.' It was 'one of the few, or the only, time I've [Mitchell] ever seen him take things and throw them out.'[164] Here, for the first time in the work, the tempo is Adagio. After a long opening section which sets the tone of the duet, short, faster episodes follow, including solo variations, and finally another Adagio (Doppio Lento). The structure of the whole Pas de Deux is shown in Table 3.5. The dance speed reflects the musical tempo, except at 'A tempo' (bars 452–62), where the dance speed becomes allegro.

Another major difference in the Pas de Deux is the breath rhythm, manifest in

Section	Metronome marking	No. of bars	Orchestration
Adagio	♪ =112 (bar 451 Più Lento =86)	411–51	Strings
A tempo	♪=112	452–62	Strings
Male variation	♩ =126	463–72	Horns and piano
Female variation	♩ =126	473–83	Flutes and strings
Male refrain	♩ =126	484–94	Horns, flute and piano
Coda	♩ =112	495–503	Strings, trumpet, trombone, piano
Doppio Lento	♪ =112	504–11	Cello and violin solo, mandolin, harp

Table 3.5. Balanchine, *Agon*, structural layout of Pas de Deux.

the long sustained lines of intertwining and stretching motion. The lines are peppered with staccato gestures, but these do not override the main legato attitude. Mitchell referred to the Adagio as 'one long, long, long, long breath'.[165] The music too is structured differently here: no longer a series of jaggedly contrasting motoric formal cells, but a number of fragile short gestures – some bounded by rests, or passages of a gradual piling up of sound. For the first time, Stravinsky introduces the lyrical qualities of the strings. The effect of the change cannot be overestimated. There have been earlier hints of breath rhythm in the dance (sustained slow motion in the second half of the Double Pas de Quatre and at the end of the Prelude, first Interlude, and Bransle Double), but its impact is not stressed until the Pas de Deux.

The performance timing also seems more personal in the Adagio, as if the dancers provide their own continuity, being in touch with the music but no longer disciplined by its pulse.[166] Thus, Denby noted that 'you hear the music gasp and fail, while the two dancers move ahead confidently across the open void'.[167] The dancers are literally more in charge of their own timing. There seems to be general agreement that the Adagio sections are basically without dance counts,[168] and the incompatibility between dance scores for the passages that are counted, confirmed by variations in performance, suggests that performance latitude was given for this part of the piece. Lack of counts means that, though the dance still co-ordinates carefully with the music, there are new leeways for rhythmic detail and interpretation. The biting, aphoristic statements that penetrate the two Adagios bring back the driving pulse, although, oddly, these statements prove more rhythmically erratic between interpretations than any other section of the work. They only highlight further the return to Adagio (Doppio Lento) for the close of the Pas de Deux, to even more sustained, drawn-out dance timing. Here, apart from a final gesture of passionate embrace, there

Ex. 3.12. Stravinsky, *Agon*, Pas de Deux.

are no staccato dance moments at all. Stravinsky's collaborator, the conductor and musicologist Robert Craft, referred to the Doppio Lento as the high point of the *Agon* score.[169] Perhaps Balanchine too felt that this section was special in some way, saving for it his most sustained use of breath rhythm.

The Pas de Deux contains a series of powerful images: the man helping the woman reach her head up and back to meet her foot, he suddenly dropping stretched out at her feet while supporting her risky *arabesque*, or the woman pitching over the kneeling man to rest her head on his breast. However, just as important to the organisation of this dance are the moments of connection between choreography and music. Some staccato, some more sustained, these moments punctuate the Pas de Deux like a series of highlights, structuring it rhythmically without diminishing the sense of continuity. These moments are important in renewing our aural and visual awareness. Some of them, it seems, are choreographed, present in most or all interpretations; some seem to be more personal, 'found' by a dancer; others appear to have emerged during the history of the piece. And, for those passages of the music that are repeated, new choreography reveals new aspects of the music.

Examples of choreographed connections between music and dance are as follows: deliberate gestures of linked arms and hands at the beginning, mirroring the rhythm pattern and pitch contour of the music (bar 414, Ex. 3.12); the staccato isolated gestures of the woman in *penché* with her left leg around the man's shoulder (see Ill. 2: they release the right hand clasp (1), she touches the floor with her free hand (2), he releases his other, left hand to take his arm back high (3), while she stretches her left leg into arabesque – following the rhythm and pitch contour of the last three notes of bar 424, Ex. 3.13; see Ch. 2, Ex. 2.1); or, breathing with a sustained chord, the travelling lift and lowering to pointe down the diagonal, the woman's legs in second position (bars 427–9). At the end of the Pas de Deux, the woman prepares to extend her leg backwards into *arabesque*, stepping on to pointe and holding the ankle of her raised leg (bars 443–5). The potentially difficult movement is pinpointed by a gentle gesture on the cellos and double basses. Perhaps this is the 'moment' to which Denby was referring when he wrote, 'The mutual first tremor of an uncertain supported balance is so isolated musically it becomes a dance movement.'[170] When the man stretches flat

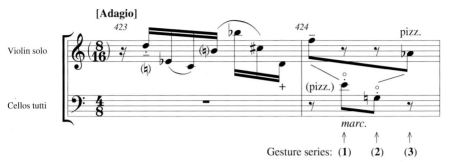

Ex. 3.13. Stravinsky, *Agon*, Pas de Deux.

supporting her *arabesque*, he scoots clockwise with his feet in order to turn her on pointe, accompanied by an anxious, stuttering violin tremolo (bars 447–8). This action to the poignant violin sound seems to be one of the clearest instances of Balanchine's avowed response to Stravinsky's timbres.[171]

In the 1960 film, Diana Adams exemplifies the performer's latitude in responding personally to the music. Her high *attitude* as she wraps her leg around the man's shoulders is timed to the B-flat peak of the violin motif (bar 423, Ex. 3.13; the movement culminates in the position in the photograph, Ill. 2). It is as if her movement, including the *pirouette* that precedes the *attitude*, 'sings' with the musical motif. Other later recorded interpretations do not draw attention to the motif contour in the same way. Otherwise, Adams' performance seems to be one of the leanest, the least charged with personal, rhythmic highlights of all the interpretations consulted. On the other hand, Suzanne Farrell, in the 1982 video, finds a multitude of possibilities for musical-choreographic connection (much more so than in her 1966 performance), details of pitch contour and dynamic difference – some gently referred to, others more directly emphasised. Even the action of extending her leg upwards in order to step out of the man's arms 'sounds' like the rise to a pizzicato A-flat at the end of bar 424 (see Ex. 3.13, the second time round, during the repeat of the section from bars 416–28). Perhaps this kind of response is what Arlene Croce alluded to when she wrote of an overaccented, overpunctuated *Agon*, Farrell (and her partner Peter Martins) 'broadcasting their effects'.[172] But there is another way of viewing this. Farrell underscores the Doppio Lento in her approach. She introduces big contrasts and dramatises the even longer rhythmic lines of the final Doppio Lento: here she draws out her backbend in counterpull with Martins, and rolls her torso powerfully towards her standing leg to extend the action of her final *penché arabesque*.[173] For Farrell, breath evolves and deepens. It is as if she too sees the Doppio Lento as a 'high point'.

Some musical-choreographic connections in *Agon* might well have been introduced during the later history of the piece. In the 1983 broadcast, Mel

Ill. 2. Allegra Kent and Arthur Mitchell in the Pas de Deux from *Agon*, choreography by George Balanchine.

Tomlinson exaggerates the letting go of Heather Watts' ankle to a pizzicato cello C (bar 441). The exaggeration is documented in the 1987 Labanotation score. In the earlier interpretations consulted, the action is achieved more simply. Likewise at the end of the opening Adagio, Farrell and Watts lower their left arms in a gesture that reflects the falling two-note musical motif (harmonics passing from cello to double bass, bar 451). Farrell (1966) and Allegra Kent (1973) draw their arms upwards. In the 1960 film, Adams makes no gesture at all.

Analysis reveals the range of detailed interplay between music and dance in *Agon*. It also reveals a major contrast in style between the Pas de Deux and the rest of the work. Rhythmic organisation plays an important role in determining the contour of the work as a whole as well as ensuring the liveliness of its detail. It is as if choreography and music mesh together in *Agon* like interlocking parts in a sophisticated piece of machinery, a rare example of deep interdependence disciplined by a shared motoric drive. Yet the machine metaphor must be applied sparingly. The excitement of *Agon* is that shifting and volatile musical-choreographic relationships continually enliven our visual and aural awareness. They also contribute to the irregularity that is such a marked feature of the work. As much as Balanchine's ballet cabinet demands a stable frame, the inlay fights to upset that frame. If Stilwell finds unity in the consistency of diversity and irregularity in *Agon*, what I enjoy increasingly is its overriding effect of *inconsistency*. We must not underestimate the power of its electric shocks, the tantalising difficulty of its questions. The final statement is that the contest continues.

*   *   *

A major difference between *Agon* and *Serenade* is the advance in complexity of rhythmic relationship between music and dance, and particularly the increased counterpoint of accents and metres. There are early examples of the latter in *Serenade*, and there is evidence from Millicent Hodson's reconstruction of *Cotillon* (Chabrier, 1932) that Balanchine was employing rhythmic counterpoint even earlier than *Serenade*.[174] But soon, Balanchine was taking this principle much further, and Marie-Jeanne remembers specific exercises in cross-counting in Balanchine's ballet classes.[175]

Sometimes, as we have seen in *Agon*, Balanchine simply keeps the dance rhythm plain against a complex musical texture (perhaps not to overplay the difficulties). At other times he adds syncopations of his own, and a frequent device is the canon, which creates a flurry of accents that have no single, fixed relation to the metre of the music. Often too in Balanchine's work, a familiar step is made unfamiliar by rhythmic manipulation. When repeating a step, he might displace it in relation to the bar-line, so that what originally coincided with a strong beat now coincides with a weak beat, and vice versa. Thus, the step becomes differently inflected, its own accent pattern shifted, or, in the new context, it appears to cut a cross-accent pattern against the music. The device often creates the effect of double-take, ambiguity, as our memory of the original relationship to the metre is carried over into our reading of the new situation. One of the clearest examples of this occurs in *Concerto Barocco* where, at the start of the first movement ritornello (see p. 147), the ensemble perform accented *relevé* in fifth position (on the strong beat in the music) and a drop to the side leaving one leg stretched in *tendu*. Later, Balanchine reverses the step rhythmically, placing the drop on the strong beat of the music. Later still, he adds to the point by pitting two groups of dancers against each other performing both versions of the step in canon one crotchet beat apart. Another example, in the twelfth variation of *Donizetti Variations* (1960), shows the men performing *sissonnes*, the first time beginning them on the musical count of 1, on repeat, ending them on the count of 1. Again, the effect is of double-take.

Polymetre or metrical incongruity is one of Balanchine's standard rhythmic devices. Most of his works contain at least one polymetrical passage, so far as we know from those that have been preserved in some form or other. Women's variations often contain one or two such moments; in the *Tchaikovsky Pas de deux* (1960), for instance, across 2s in the music, the woman performs a beaten step in 3s – *posé* 1, close in fifth 2, *entrechat trois* 3 – (see Ch. 2, Ex. 2.6), and there is a final *piqué* turn combination down the diagonal in 5s. There are far fewer examples in men's variations, which tend to be kept more square, or regular, with the music. The effect of the device varies: in the Tchaikovsky solo, a light spicing (the step in 3s); or brilliance (the final combination in 5s down the diagonal); or fun, which sensitive and musically clear dancers have been able to bring out; or building tension, as when suddenly and climactically, at the very end of *Theme and Variations* (1947, Tchaikovsky), all the men and women perform a *posé* in *arabesque* step (with *tours en l'air* for the men), men in canon with the women, all in twos against the musical three to a bar. It is pertinent that Farrell reinstated such a moment when she revived the 1958 *Gounod Symphony* for the School of American Ballet. The 'crossing' of metres had been lost during the history of the piece. The original moment, performed by Diana Adams and captured on silent film, had seemed more musical to Farrell than its later version, and she felt that it had the freshness that Balanchine would have preferred.[176]

While Balanchine often chooses to 'plug' the dancers simply into the pulse in passages of complex music (as in *Agon* and *Episodes*), there is evidence to suggest that the devices of crossing metre appear most frequently when the music is already rhythmically irregular. In other words, again, Balanchine takes his cue from the music. These are mainly pieces choreographed to twentieth-century music, in particular, middle- and late-period Stravinsky. Those from Balanchine's later career show the greatest metrical complexity of all, partly perhaps because later generations of dancers were more finely trained in musical sophistication. However, there are striking examples that use pre-twentieth-century music.

In *Valse Fantaisie* (1967), for instance, hypermetrical play might be said to provide the main substance and liveliness of the piece. Glinka's hypermetre is already a little wayward for waltz music, as he builds generally in three-bar, as opposed to the normal four-bar, hypermeasures, thus creating larger phrases of either twelve bars (3 + 3 + 3 + 3), or eight bars (3 + 3 + 2). There are many passages where Balanchine takes the rhythmic mobility a stage further, setting two, four, and occasionally five-bar hypermeasures against the music. An example is the opening step for the small corps which, at its first appearance, not only keeps to the three-bar hypermeasure of the music but also visualises pitch contour with a *développé, tombé* and *temps levé* in *attitude* (see Ch. 2, Ex. 2.4). That especially close relationship between music and dance established, Balanchine sets out to loosen it. After a transition, the opening musical theme returns (bar 52) and the soloists enter, now with a five-bar variation of the opening three-bar step, incorporating a lift. The next time that this musical theme is heard (bar 123), the solo woman dances another variation to it, establishing a four-bar hypermeasure. But throughout *Valse Fantaisie*, the rhythmic lines of dance and music are in flux, meeting occasionally, only to set up their independent lines again. It is as if music and dance playfully swim through each other. It is interesting too, that Balanchine uses the principle of hypermetrical play in the adage of his one-act (white act) version of *Swan Lake*. In at least two places, he rephrases the Ivanov choreography to cross the musical units.[177]

There are times like in *Movements for Piano and Orchestra* when Balanchine quite clearly responds to the technicalities of a musical score rather than to the resulting musical sound. Perhaps the most striking demonstrations of Balanchine's visualisation of the musical score are those involving metrical ambiguity, the written metre conflicting with what is actually heard. Balanchine is clearly as sensitive to metrical principles as he is to pulse. For the 1977 television version of *The Four Temperaments*,[178] Balanchine changed a passage in the Choleric section so that it matched the written musical metre (12/8, four beats to a bar). The passage extends from bar 134 to bar 142, beat 1: 29 dance counts in total. This is exactly where Hindemith eases from 12/8 to 6/4 and then shifts back again to 12/8. Here, the composer alters the metrical structure *between* the bar-lines, in other words, without changing the time signature. Originally, Balanchine choreographed to complement these changes that he heard in the metrical structure of the music but, according to the conductor Robert Irving, he altered the dance rhythm to 12/8 throughout because 'Balanchine's musical integrity took possession of him and he couldn't stand that he was walking across the [written] beat and not with the beat.'[179]

The conflict in the later version between choreography and sound (the 1977 television version was then preserved for the stage) is especially hard for dancers, who have so often to step between the notes. They are instructed (in the 1985 Labanotation score): 'Do not listen to music. Count, or watch conductor.' The metrical conflict creates a highly unsettled effect here. It helps to create the image of a mass pressure building consistently over time, a determination against all odds. In contrast, much of the previous material in this section is distinctly fragmented or broken up. The pressure is released – a relief – by the Choleric soloist bursting in to calm the proceedings before the apotheosis of the work. This passage of metrical conflict is also an excellent example of clarifying beat by moving sharply and steadily once per beat. There are 28 moves in 29 counts: one move, when the downstage group of women are lowered to the floor, their legs stretched out in front of them, occupies two counts.

The final Doppio Movimento sections of the first movement of *Rubies* (Stravinsky, 1967) are similar to this passage in *The Four Temperaments*. What is *heard* here is a 3/4 metre articulated by an ostinato on timpani, piano, cellos and basses. The score, however, reveals that this ostinato is, in fact, off the beat throughout and, furthermore, that the written metre is 4/4, with which woodwind and horns correspond (see Ex. 3.14a). Balanchine has made many of the

Ex. 3.14a. Stravinsky, *Capriccio* for Piano and Orchestra, first movement.

steps conform to the written metre rather than to what is most readily heard. Sometimes he picks up on the offbeat pulse. For instance, from one bar after [31] in the score up to [32], a group of eight women step and jab their pointes into the floor, two groups in canon, four of them syncopating between the beats articulated by the other four, in other words, dancing to the off-beat pulse (see Ex. 3.14b). Yet Balanchine still choreographed the movements in 4/4 rather than 3/4.

The last movement, the Capriccio, of *Stravinsky Violin Concerto* (1972) is notable for its ambiguities and shifts between 2/8 and 3/8. In the Presto Coda, there is a 42-bar passage ([123]–[129]), written in 3/8, Stravinsky's original metre, but which most strongly suggests 2/8 to the ear. Having looked at and listened to the score, Balanchine visualised the metrical tension that is at the heart of this music. The soloists he choreographed in 2/8 and the corps in 3/8, and later vice versa. His response is as a musician, using musicianly devices.

Balanchine's exploitation of metrical ambiguity quite clearly contributes to the larger dynamic outline of this Capriccio. From plain beginnings, counter-metres and -accents become an increasingly important feature, whilst the full

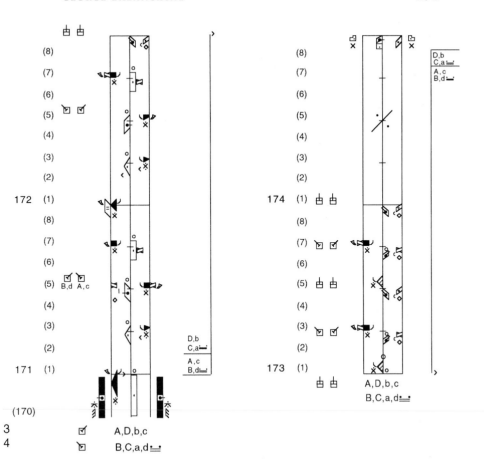

Ex. 3.14b. Balanchine, *Rubies*, first movement.

cast gradually assembles on stage. A clear hierarchy of pulse rates is also demonstrated, one, three or six beats articulated per bar. At one point, near the middle of the Capriccio, Balanchine creates three rhythmic layers against the music ([116]–[118]). The music is in an ambiguous 3/8 metre. The soloists in the centre of the stage perform a slow lilting and intertwining dance as a foursome and as couples, a step counted in fours. Meanwhile, two blocks of women upstage mark a slower pulse (like a hyperbeat, at half the rate and rather like semaphore): one arm swinging across the body so that the hand clasps the shoulder (1), swinging up and out again (2), the knee turned in (3), and then out (4). Two blocks of men frame the soloists with a similar slow pulse dance unit, performed kneeling on one knee. Downbeats or beginnings of units in music and dance frequently occur at different times. The effect is strangely unsettling, just before the soloists pick up energy and continue the drive towards the final climax of the piece. Rhythmic tension peaks during the Presto Coda, after [129], with constantly shifting metres shared in music and dance (2/8, 3/8, 2/8, 2/8, 3/8, 3/8, 2/8, 3/8 etc.) as well as further examples of counter-metre, until the tension is released in the final eight bars. Balanchine's devices for building to a flamboyant conclusion include gathering his dance forces, increasing tempo (with the music), and criss-crossing groups in the stage space. He counterpoints groups of dancers performing different material, as well, before allowing their resolution into final, triumphant unison. However, devices of rhythmic tension also make a powerful contribution to building climax. At this point in Balanchine's career, they are especially sophisticated, giving the work a particular flavour, an essential aspect of style.

There are other kinds of rhythmic complexity to consider in Balanchine's work, related to the patterns of moves and syncopations. Balanchine's tendency to mark pulse plainly in some works has already been noted; at other times, he introduces simple, easy-to-read repeating rhythmic patterns. But there is always plenty of variety in the weighting of steps, and, furthermore, the most advanced, twentieth-century scores may already provide the liveliness of highly irregular rhythms. When faced with very regularly phrased, repeating waltz rhythms, Balanchine is careful not to underline them slavishly. In *Liebeslieder Walzer*, it is as if he has encouraged dancers to muse across the beats, or he might introduce weighting of the second beat of the bar for a passage. And in *Vienna Waltzes*, the basic plain rhythm of the waltz step is pointed differently, decorated with frills of steps crossing the beats, or pared down into skeletal outline. Added to Balanchine's rhythmic style is the influence of jazz, touches of which also infuse much of Stravinsky's music, and the effects of free-hipped stepping which can slightly anticipate the impact of beat. After all, dancing 'on top of the beat', which Denby borrowed for his description of the New York City Ballet style, is a jazz expression. The net effect of all this is tremendous rhythmic vitality.

It is in Balanchine's late work that we find the most developed rhythmic intricacy, rapidly produced syncopations and more complex patterns made by steps. There are isolated touches of this intricacy in earlier works – even in *Apollo*, there is an irregular jazzy step in Terpsichore's variation – but intricacy becomes part of the general style of later works. *Who Cares?* is important in this respect, infused by ideas from tap and soft shoe dancing. Another key work is the 1976 *Chaconne* (Gluck), a reworking of a piece made in 1963, with re-accented roles for Farrell and Martins. Croce interestingly observes a rococo style that she believes would not have been present in the 1963 version of this work.[180] The virtuosity here is largely achieved by rhythmic means.

Mozartiana is an extreme example of this kind of rhythmic intricacy, and here the rhythmic shocks are often paced, or simply unrepeated, in such a way as to avoid your grasp, in other words, 'unreadable' at first viewing. *Mozartiana* is the model too of a work that celebrates interpretative values, the more ephemeral aspects of musicality that Balanchine encouraged. The Pas de Deux in *Agon* raised the issue in a context where pulse becomes quiet. But individual rubato is just as important an issue where pulse is clear, and even in Stravinsky's music. After all, whatever Gelsey Kirkland might have said, Balanchine wrote: 'A good instrumentalist, Milstein, for instance, or a resourceful dancer, can give the feeling of rubato in Stravinsky's music without blurring the beat.'[181]

Mozartiana

Balanchine cast *Mozartiana* as a vehicle for Suzanne Farrell. The ballet is a late collaboration (after many others) between the choreographer and dancer, and musical issues are of paramount importance in an analysis of this collaboration.

Mozartiana was presented as the opening ballet of New York City Ballet's 1981 Tchaikovsky Festival. For this occasion, Balanchine returned to a piece of music that he had first used for the short-lived Les Ballets 1933 in Paris. He had been relieved at that time to return to a classic after Diaghilev's preference that he should work with contemporary scores. Here, in the Suite No. 4 in G major Op. 61, 'Mozartiana', is Mozart refracted through Tchaikovsky (who revered Mozart), and now Balanchine. Tchaikovsky had selected four unrelated works by Mozart and formed them into a suite, hoping, by doing this, to introduce fine but little-known pieces by the composer to a wider public. The lineage is further complicated in that one of the works, Ave Verum Corpus, a motet for chorus, strings and organ, had been transcribed for piano by Liszt, who added an introduction and postlude; Tchaikovsky turned not to the original Mozart in this case, but to the Liszt transcription, for his source. The other three works had originally been written for piano.

The pieces used by Tchaikovsky are as follows, in the order of his Suite:

Gigue in G, K574 for piano (1789)
Minuet in D, K355 for piano (1780)
Ave Verum Corpus for voices, strings and organ, K618 (1791), transcribed by
    Liszt for piano (1862) – renamed Preghiera
Variations for piano (1784), on 'Les hommes pieusement' from Gluck's comic
    opera *La Rencontre imprévue* (1764)

Tchaikovsky's decision was to respect Mozart's text. Without using the full-blown romantic orchestral sound, he modifies texture and sometimes adds his own harmonic detail. He makes more extreme the contrasts in dynamics (Mozart's scores contain simple dynamic indications), adds more shadings of his own, but only rarely goes against Mozart's directions. The cadenzas in the Ninth and Tenth Variations needed to be rethought for violin and clarinet, but these are the only points where there are major changes in musical notes. The book by Robert Maiorano and Valerie Brooks on the process of making the 1981 *Mozartiana* tells us that Balanchine rehearsed to the Mozart (and Liszt) piano pieces, the ready-made piano reduction,[182] but kept in mind the implications of Tchaikovsky's orchestration.

Balanchine clearly had a new vision of the music when he rechoreographed it in 1981. The most important change was his repositioning of the Preghiera at the beginning of the work, as a prologue prayer. This was the same kind of formal risk with the music that he had taken in *Serenade*, although here the fact that he was dealing with four Mozart pieces originally conceived entirely separately might have inspired his freedom. The choice of black for the costumes was also significant. The 1933 ballet (which remained essentially the same piece in various versions through to the 1950s) sounds very different. It featured various characters meeting in an Italian square: a village eccentric in the Gigue, a group of women villagers in the Minuet, a veiled woman in white supported between two figures draped in black in the Preghiera, whilst the Theme and Variations introduced two lovers and various characters from earlier in the ballet and ended with a gypsy scene. Many of the costumes were in bright colours. Denby was deeply impressed by the ballet in 1933 – 'It wouldn't stay out of my mind'[183] – but he found the 1945 Ballet Russe de Monte Carlo production had a new 'sunny' quality.[184]

Even if Rouben Ter-Arutunian's 1981 *Mozartiana* costumes make reference to the early ballet (in fact, they make much stronger reference to Balanchine's *Harlequinade* of 1965[185]), brightness is certainly no longer an issue, except in the conclusion, and then with a different tone. The Preghiera is sombre; the Finale is gently sparkling. The 1933 ballet, as Paul Parish, has suggested, might have been a parody of religiosity.[186] The 1981 *Mozartiana*, when Balanchine's own death was not far from his mind, had serious religious content. Significantly, Farrell, who remembers singing the Ave Verum in church as a girl, tells us that Balanchine got her to recite its words for him in rehearsal,[187] and Parish suggests that Balanchine attended closely to the meaning of the words in his interpretation of the music:

Ave verum Corpus natum de Maria Virgine: Vere passum, immolatum in cruce pro homine: Cujus latus perforatum fluxit aqua et sanguine: Esto nobis praegustatum, mortis in examine.

Hail, true body, born of the Virgin Mary; (who) Truly died, sacrificed on the cross for mankind; Whose side, pierced, flowed with water and blood: Be by us tasted in death's trial. [Parish's translation]

Ill. 3. Suzanne Farrell in *Mozartiana*, choreography by George Balanchine, New York City Ballet.

The 1981 *Mozartiana* is organised as a pyramid in praise of Balanchine's senior ballerina. She was supported in the first cast by Ib Andersen, a small, light male dancer, perhaps a sort of Mozart figure, a *demi-caractère* soloist, Victor Castelli, who projects a witty *commedia* air, four younger women and four little girls, representatives of earlier stages on the balletic echelon. Arlene Croce has noted the diffusion of characters in the ballet:

Andersen doesn't even enter until the final section – the Theme and Variations, which he dances with Farrell. The rest of the dancers . . . aren't defined in their relations to each other until the finale [Tenth Variation]. The little girls flank Farrell in the opening number, then disappear. The four women [of the Minuet], who might be their grown-up counterparts, aren't identified with either of the men. Balanchine has avoided setting up the obvious correspondences and turnabouts. Although we sense the connection between the big and the small girls and between them and Farrell (for one thing, they're all dressed alike), it's an elusive and mysterious connection. And who is the second man [in the Gigue]? You might think that Balanchine would cast this lone male dancer in contrast to Andersen, but in fact it's Victor Castelli, another lightweight.[188]

There is a courtly feeling to the whole work, but also a light buoyancy about it; the style for the men, particularly, is Bournonville-rococo, in other words, closer to Mozart in spirit than a neo-Petipa style would have been. The Farrell-Andersen relationship makes no point about romantic bonding.

Maiorano and Brooks saw the practical reason for putting Farrell's Preghiera first in the work: to give her rest before the demanding Variations,[189] which had been shared between more dancers in earlier versions of the ballet. Not that the dancers, nor perhaps even Balanchine, knew until late in the rehearsal period that the Preghiera would begin the work. Maiorano and Brooks tell us that Balanchine decided to begin by choreographing the Theme and Variations, which is where Tchaikovsky commenced his orchestration.[190] The working order for the ballet was as follows:

Theme and Variations 1–9
Minuet
Gigue
Minuet (finished)
Variation 10
Preghiera
Variation 10 (finished)
The last twelve bars

The Preghiera serves to set the emotional tone for the rest of the ballet, like a prologue front curtain, but the style that it sets up is totally separate from the rest of the ballet. *Bourrées* are the norm to which Farrell continually returns, long waves of them, and broad legato gestures of prayer and beseeching. Balanchine responds to the general meaning rather than detail of the words that lie behind the music, and more obviously to the ebb and flow of harmonic tension: when this tension increases, Farrell breaks out of *bourrées* to descend into a huge kneel and arch backwards in prayer, or, at the two climaxes, she makes a more etched series of steps and *piqués* stretching upwards in *arabesque*.

After the Preghiera, a '*Mozartiana* style' develops. From now on, there is an exceptionally high density of ideas, including ideas about interrelating music and choreography. The characteristic musical form is straightforward binary, AABB, the traditional baroque/classical musical form for dances. Often, there are exact repeats of each 'half', A and B, and the expanded B section refers directly back to the material of A. Balanchine does anything but follow these repeats in the Gigue and Minuet. Indeed, he makes us hear different things in the same music when it comes back, picks up on the rhythmic irregularities in the score and adds more of his own. A feature of the Gigue is its limited number of presto dance ideas constantly refreshed as they appear in new dance contexts set to different points in the music and re-rhythmicised. As in folk style, there are many cross-accents between music and dance, even some steps that race between the musical beats. In the Minuet quartet, rhythm becomes a group issue, and what a texture it creates! We are back to 'symmetrical asymmetries' (see p. 153), geometrical outlines and, embedded within them, an abundance of fantastic figuration which is lively largely as a result of rhythmic play. There are the usual polymetrical devices. There are also canons, as question and answer from one bar to the next, in simple, slow, deliberate steps or *sissonnes* articulating off-beats 2 and then 3, in a heady rush down a line, or within hot-pursuit travelling passages in double time. Balanchine sometimes takes his cue from the bar-line, sometimes from the upbeat beginning of a musical gesture (which is not so usual for Balanchine), now from an underpart, now from the dominant melody. The pressures constantly shift.

The Theme and Variations are the centre of gravity of the ballet and rebuild this density of information from simple beginnings. Mozart's musical structure develops with varied, written-out musical repeats (within the binary forms) in Variations 4, 6–10; Variation 8 is 'unfinished' and races into a cadenza, leading into Variation 9, an Adagio overflowing with cadenza figuration for solo violin, and Variation 10 develops into a more freely structured allegro broken by two cadenzas for clarinet. The choreography is far more freely structured than the music. It constantly evolves. Rather than building upon and relating back to any obvious theme, Balanchine's method is to develop an intricate language of pointe steps ('rapid small needlework'[191]) and *terre à terre* allegro to contrast with large-scale moves. *Bourrées*, courtly bows and certain arm positions refer to earlier sections of the work, but the emphasis in assembling this language is on change rather than similarity, distant rather than close relationships. Motivic values are small. After the Theme and first Variation, there is no straightforward major repetition of dance with music, in other words, clarification of the repetition form of the music.

The fourth Variation for Andersen is a fascinating example of transformation through variation. Balanchine radically changes the architecture of the opening dance sequence by casting a different dance movement to the major musical accent each time it occurs. The sequence contains *temps levés* in *arabesque* and in *passé*, beaten *assemblé* and *pirouette*. The big blast two bars into the Variation (see Ex. 3.15) coincides first with the landing from the beaten *assemblé*, then with the spring into *temps levé*, finally with the step preparation for the beaten *assemblé*. Each accent is differently harmonised by Tchaikovsky, but Balanchine's treatment is to make us virtually forget where he started from. Thus too he demonstrates the importance of rhythm in establishing the architecture of a dance phrase.

The *Mozartiana* set of Variations is far more experimental than Balanchine's

Ex. 3.15. Tchaikovsky, Suite No. 4 in G major, 'Mozartiana', Variation 4 of Theme and Variations.

others. *Theme and Variations* (1947, Tchaikovsky, Suite No. 3) is a more overt acknowledgement of the conventions of musical formal structure, with large repetition and return of dance with music and clear similarity relationship stressed across the ballet. Development from the simple step-*tendu* dance theme progresses slowly, Balanchine guiding us through almost pedagogically, and the dance movement is much easier to remember. The variations in *Divertimento No. 15* (1956) have a fixed relationship to the musical form, with the opening four bars of nearly every variation repeated with the music.

The *Mozartiana* Variations nevertheless do demonstrate their own clear line of development, to which musical issues make a major contribution. There is an immediate conversation, contrapuntal ingenuities as well as matching of small rhythms and accents in music and dance. As an example, in section B of the Theme, both Mozart and Balanchine introduce a dotted rhythm, but Balanchine introduces his at points different from those in the music. Balanchine shows the following rhythm in his steps, four times:

The 'dotted' rhythm (long-short) steps are like an anticipation and then an echo of the similar 'hiccups' in the music (see Ex. 3.16). Then, in the first Variation for Farrell, Balanchine refers back to these dotted rhythms in little steps on pointe or steps followed by punctuating toe taps. Again, this is not simultaneous music visualisation, and these dance rhythms occur at irregular intervals, so that their appearance is always unexpected and surprising. Counterpoint between music and dance soon becomes much more forceful than this, and there are moments of crossing metre in each of Variations 3–6. In Variation 8, there is a welcome return to simplicity and the plain walking characteristic of the Theme, before the wildest freedoms of all in the Adagio Variation 9. The final Variation 10 proposes a harmonious relationship between music and dance once again, with one wicked touch, a foretaste of the skip step to the final, plain return of Mozart's theme, except that this step is first seen in a three-count version crossing the music before its final resolution in four-count metre with the theme.

Ex. 3.16. Tchaikovsky, Suite No. 4, Theme of Theme and Variations.

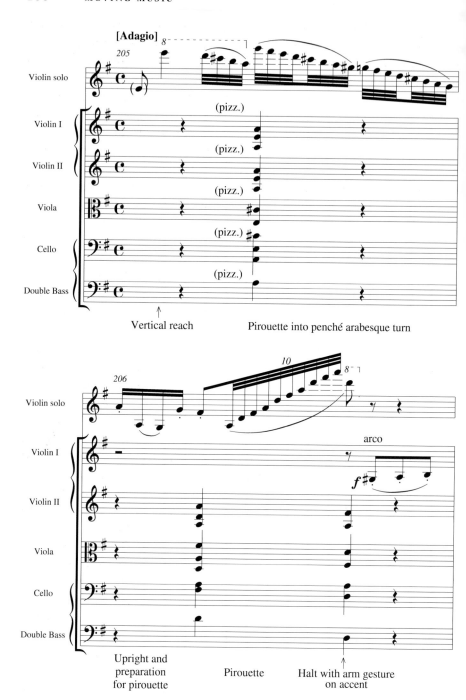

Ex. 3.17. Tchaikovsky, Suite No. 4, Variation 9 of Theme and Variations.

Balanchine still wants us to note the larger shape, the 'binary form' outline of the Adagio Variation 9: the cadences are moments of quiet and simplicity. Yet this Variation represents extremes of freedom and contrast in *Mozartiana*, extremes partly embedded within the cadenza character of the music itself. Recall that Balanchine mimed the violin part in rehearsal 'in a frenzied Paganini imitation' (see p. 126). The Adagio is a series of billows, squalls, moments of calm, and a veritable storm near the end: to a passage of unusually strong dissonance, Farrell reaches vertically, performs a *pirouette*, driving straight on into a *penché arabesque* turn on her heel, plunges downwards with the musical figuration while Andersen races round her, widening the circular emphasis – he brings her up with the music into a *pirouette* – they both stop dead, side by side (see Ex. 3.17). This Variation is marked by huge dynamic contrasts, movement surprises, some musical anticipations in the choreography, some echoes, other movement ideas springing out of nowhere amongst the musical detail, fits and starts that sometimes become longer spreads of energy. But freedoms are at the same time constrained by sharp discipline. Dance phrases, like the one described, are clipped tight to the end of violin breaks. Croce puts it well: 'It's about the flowering of form within form.'[192]

The Variations are also playful in their orchestration of gender. The surprises are for Andersen, No. 6 characteristically 'feminine' in its lightness, for flutes, oboes, clarinet and bassoon, and in No. 8 a tinkling glockenspiel and pizzicato strings mark his return to dance with Farrell. But such ambiguity has been suggested earlier in the ballet. Back in the Gigue, Castelli's opening moves bear the 'stamp' of flutes, violins and clarinets, an airy image that remains despite all sorts of other orchestrations later in this dance. Not that this is the first time that Balanchine has questioned the gender conventions of ballet instrumentation. Denby observed 'girls dancing hard and boys soft'[193] in *The Four Temperaments* and the exchange of themes and soloist/accompaniment arrangements between men and women in this ballet destabilises the relationships that we tend to read according to convention. Orchestration helps to make the point, the lyrical, solo violin and viola given to both male soloists, Melancholic and Phlegmatic, whilst Choleric, a woman, gets the strident roaring piano and furious string tutti.

Farrell's performance in *Mozartiana* is remarkable for bringing out musical subtleties. How much these precise points of timing are actually choreographed, or simply Farrell's interpretation, or even Farrell in just one performance, we may never know. We may never know too how much of her timing was affected by chance rather than decision, by, for instance, falling off pointe a little earlier at one performance than at another. We do know, however, from Brooks and Maiorano[194] and from what she herself has said, that Farrell made her own discoveries in rehearsal, and some of these became part of the piece. In a public seminar, Farrell spoke of a moment in Variation 1, at the end of Section A. In the

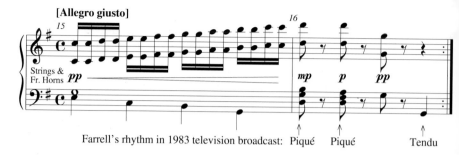

Ex. 3.18. Tchaikovsky, Suite No. 4, Variation 1 of Theme and Variations.

1983 broadcast of the work,[195] she performs *piqué, piqué* and hold for two beats in *relevé*, accenting the second, weak beat of the bar, and coming down from pointe to *tendu* with the bass note on beat 4 (see Ex. 3.18). Originally she came down on beat 3, continuing to dance to the melody line, but she then heard the bass note on timpani and cellos/basses, discovered the other opportunity, which kept the dance impetus alive a little longer, and knew that she had a choice between two versions.[196] Indeed, in a video of a rehearsal at Saratoga, New York, in 1981, six weeks after the premiere, she still favours completion on beat 3, with the melody.[197] Another example, in an Adagio passage, Farrell walks on pointe to a series of repeating D quavers (bar 185), stepping out on every other one, choosing on-the-beat notes in the 1983 broadcast, off-the-beat notes in another record film shot the same year.[198]

A special moment that Paul Parish singles out from the 1983 broadcast is the second, and largest, climax of the Preghiera, when, to the passage of maximum harmonic tension, Farrell performs four sets of *piqué arabesque*, each *arabesque* followed by a step forwards on pointe and another one down and across the body in preparation for *arabesque* in the opposite direction. The passage is a perfect illustration of Farrell's subtlety of phrasing. Parish describes it thus:

> Farrell inflects each set differently: the big drama in the second set is the pause in attitude effacée (the working knee partially bent, the foot half-way in to the knee). In the third set it's the foot reaching down from passé, in the fourth it's the hold in passé as her hand comes down in front of her mouth as if to cover a sudden intake of breath.[199]

I would add musical details here. Baldly speaking, Farrell's step rhythm changes during this passage, whether or not this was specifically choreographed. The analysis of steps in terms of musical notation can only be approximate: changes of weight often involve slight anticipations or delays in relation to beat (see Ex. 3.19). The change in bar 3 has musical significance, for it occurs as soon as

Ex. 3.19. Tchaikovsky, Suite No. 4, Preghiera.

the peak of musical tension has been reached. On the downbeat of the bar, Farrell marks the melodic peak with the first direct reaching and looking upwards in *arabesque*. Then, immediately, she seems to forecast musical resolution, as her step on pointe, placed with exquisite precision, draws the attention downwards, taking some of the rhythmic weight away from the arabesque and responding to the new crotchet movement in the melody. In the other 1983 record film, Farrell sustains the arabesque once more in bar 4, a final delay of resolution, like a gasp before literally falling backwards (instead of forwards) into the next step on pointe (minim–crotchet–crotchet again). Farrell sustains a sense of edge right through this passage, but her dancing not only introduces difference, it also makes us hear the ebb and flow of musical tensions. As Croce observes of Farrell in *Mozartiana*, hers is 'dancing that points out the broad musical sense of a passage only to dive inside the elastic mesh of its infrastructure.'[200]

Although it seems that she was able to get away with more than other dancers, Farrell provides a salutary reminder of the subtlety and ephemeral nature of the performer's musicality that Balanchine encouraged, dynamic qualities so hard to convey in notation, and so dangerously solidified by video. Her own description of the end of a turning sequence in the *Diamonds* duet (from *Jewels*) is revealing and reflects back on the processes in her *Mozartiana*:

After a building tremolo, the music reaches a climax and ends almost in silence with a haunting echo following in its wake. Sometimes I finished my turns on the music and let the echo follow me, sometimes I became the echo, sometimes I was both. In other words, 'musicality' to me was not defined by hitting the turns and finishing on any specific climactic notes, but in shaping the physical sequence into the musical one in any number of legitimate or even illegitimate ways. But there was always one connecting factor: in dancing one is in the energy business, and music is the senior partner. Sound is not music's sole attribute, it has an energy of its own, and sometimes that energy requires more time.[201]

Farrell's edge also contributes to the unusually tenuous sense of coherence in *Mozartiana*. I have emphasised difference within the distinct dances, sometimes violent contrasts, and transformation rather than relationships that stress similarity. It is perhaps not surprising that Farrell speaks of experiencing an initial awkwardness in the movement: 'many stops and starts, and the energy seemed to build backward instead of forward'.[202] Croce and Macaulay have both remarked on the larger issues of form in the piece, the unexplained, loose relationship between the characters, the structural diffusion, the lack of connection between movements.[203] As Croce says, 'its parts don't come together until the end, and when they cohere it's not so much through the mutual gravitation of structural components as through the cumulative sense of the dancing.' She really wills that unity: '*Mozartiana* is transcendentally coherent.' I am not so sure about this.

Here again are musical issues. The Preghiera, by dint of starting the ballet (Balanchine's decision), establishes a gravity that hangs over its entirety, renewed when we see the Preghiera dancer Farrell return for the Theme and Variations. The intensity and personal force of those Variations are never resolved into easy happiness. When the ensemble unites into formal line-ups in Variation 10, it is twice disrupted by cadenzas: it barely establishes itself as a community before it is rushed towards the conclusion. It is as if Balanchine responded to the wilful and fantastic elements in this music, so often masking its formal proposals and going for its fragmentary and diverse detail. Cadenza is quite as crucial as form. We end up nevertheless hovering in the ether.

*   *   *

We have seen something of the range of Balanchine's use of music during his career, and how, even to the last, he surprises us by challenging himself in new ways, subverting expectations that we might entertain of his style. This only goes to show how inadequate are the frequent generalisations about Balanchine visualising music, statements that he often encouraged himself, like 'I must show them the music. The music must be seen!'[204] Not given to sophisticated analysis of his work (at least in public), Balanchine often ended up saying so little as to be misleading. Visualisation sounds on the face of it straightforward, but Balanchine's lesson to us in taking us round the different parts of a score, renewing our aural experience, clarifying certain particularities like a musical interpreter would, are anything but straightforward. Generalised statements about independence and counterpoint are none too helpful either, given the immense variety of methods that he developed for working in dialogue with music.

An enquiry into the sophistication of Balanchine's musical response has broad ramifications. The outcomes of such an enquiry could well be set in counterpoint against and could potentially undermine other current Balanchine analysis – discussions, for instance, about women, politics, passive performers, unity, balance, coherence of form. His musicality speaks of human energy, intelligence, imagination, risk . . . and agency. It is not merely about dry mathematics. It has meaning.

Many choreographers after Balanchine have recognised something of this, Balanchine having influenced the next generation (and some members of his own) more than any other ballet choreographer of the century. Around the world, choreographers have followed his example of making ballets (and modern dances) without stories and about their music, like Richard Alston, David Bintley, Eliot Feld, William Forsythe, Hans van Manen, Mark Morris, Ashley Page, Jerome Robbins, and Twyla Tharp. Few, however, have used as model any of the detailed aspects of his musicality. Perhaps this is because of his unusual depth of musical training, which offered an exceptional opportunity to engage deeply, not only with the classics but also with the most complex music of his own generation.

Balanchine's formal complications might well be said to have reflected developments within twentieth-century music itself; he was excessively modest in saying that a choreographer cannot invent rhythms and has to rely on music to do so. His own contribution has proved brilliantly inventive.

4

Frederick Ashton

'Taking one's lead directly from the music . . . this is the method which I now prefer,' Ashton wrote in 1948.[1] Time and again, we hear of Ashton immersing himself obsessively in a score: 'When I'm making a piece, I listen to the music incessantly, or other music by the same composer – nothing else.'[3]

Yet, unlike Balanchine, Ashton could neither play a musical instrument nor read a score, despite having had a mother who was musical, who, he tells us, 'played the piano very well'.[3] Balanchine was always disparaging about this gap in Ashton's education, and de Valois too once remarked 'It was a terrible nuisance that Fred couldn't read music' – affectionately, not to suggest any lack of musicality, and rather regretting that she could not use him as a role model for student dancers and choreographers.[4]

Other rather more surprising comments about Ashton's musicality appear in the dance literature. In his seminal book on Ashton, David Vaughan mentions that Ashton was one of the dancers beating their feet to emphasise the musical rhythm in de Valois' *Rout* (in a 1931 performance); he reports that 'the latter element was very troublesome for Ashton, in spite of his experience of dancing to counts with Nijinska'.[5] Marie Rambert recalls that when Ashton first came to her studio in 1924,

> He had a taste for music, but absolutely no idea of its theory and could not count a bar in waltz time. He found it difficult to execute even a simple enchaînement in time, probably because subconsciously he was composing something else to that same music (no doubt much more interesting than my purely educational exercise).[6]

Rambert may well have hit the nail on the head in suggesting that Ashton took off into the world of his own choreographic imagination. Certainly, it is hard to believe that he had any fundamental difficulties with rhythm. Perhaps too, he felt less than diligent about doing what went against his inclinations – like percussive rhythms – and a little loathe to obey the commands of two senior women. As we shall see later, counting was never his method in making or re-hearsing work: this is not how he 'heard' music.

Other comparisons with Balanchine stress the other-than-musical forces that generated Ashton's inspiration. As Lincoln Kirstein, Balanchine's lieutenant, put it, 'It is primarily a theatre style, not a musical one – his influence is not Balanchine but Sarah Bernhardt.'[7] Or Rudolf Nureyev: 'In the end [Ashton and Balanchine] knew as much as each other but they came at it differently. Some-how Fred was completely open: he made himself see how elements could influence him . . . He understood theatre very well. He was a theatre animal.'[8] Nureyev's reference to Ashton's 'openness' is interesting. This is a good word for Ashton's tendency to latch on to other people's impulses and ideas for his own artistic ends, whether dancers, lovers, répétiteurs (like Michael Somes and Chris-topher Newton), or musicians. Ashton's creative behaviour was like that of a performer who derives power from colleagues on stage with him, partly active, partly passive and 'open'.

Nevertheless, despite what Kirstein said, Balanchine was an important in-fluence on Ashton. He greatly admired Balanchine's early work and was cap-tivated by the neo-romantic Les Ballets 1933 (see p. 173). In the post-war decade, the influence showed most of all. As Ashton's biographer Julie Kavanagh indicates, during this period he made a similar point of naming bal-lets after their scores: Symphonic Variations (1946, Franck), Valses nobles et sentimentales (1947, Ravel), Scènes de ballet (1948, Stravinsky) and Illuminations (1950, Britten).[9]

More importantly, witness his 1948 statement, he now made a point about giving the lead to music, after his earlier tendency to use visual and literary sources to start himself off. In 1948 too, he claimed that music led him in his quest to make dance that is fundamentally about dance, not stories. Symphonic Variations was the turning point work in this respect:

> One gets the purity of the dance expressing nothing but itself, and thereby expressing a thousand degrees and facets of emotion, and the mystery of poetry of movement; leaving the audience to respond at will and to bring their own poetic reactions to the work before them. Just as the greatest music has no program, so I really believe the greatest ballets are the same, or at any rate have the merest thread of an idea that can be ignored, and on which the choreographer may weave his imagination for the combination of steps and patterns.[10]

Writing in 1959, Ashton has slightly relaxed his position and reaffirms his belief in the story ballet. Now, perhaps to emphasise his distance from Balan-chine's style, he insists that ballets without stories, popularly known as abstract ballets, though appearing to convey nothing but the exercise of pure dancing, should have a basic idea which is not necessarily apparent to the public, or a personal fount of emotion from which the choreography springs. Otherwise, in my opinion, a cold complexity emerges which ceases to move an audience.'[11]

After this, Ashton's tendency is still to stress music as his primary guiding force, but most of his ballets have stories, and a literary source sometimes gives him his initial impulse.

A hypothesis of this chapter is that Ashton found a way of enjoining the two concerns, music and theatre, so that his style is *both* musical and theatrical, and the musical is not necessarily diminished by the theatrical. Balanchine's practice cannot be the yardstick for comparison. John Lanchbery, Ashton's last conductor-colleague, sees no disadvantages in Ashton's non-analytical, non-specialist musical approach:

There's no big fuss over Fred's being musical. He doesn't sit at a piano and play. He doesn't even discuss the elements of music in any detail. But he has a massive, inborn instinct for what is right.[12]

He always had a chip on his shoulder, an inferiority complex about Balanchine reading and playing. But his approach made things much simpler in fact: he didn't embroil himself. He went directly to what he wanted and he had a wonderful gift for pinpointing what he wanted.[13]

As any aspiring choreographer of his generation would have done, Ashton attended concerts, listened avidly to the radio, purchased recordings so far as they were available (far less plentiful in his early career than later on) and noted scores that might be interesting for ballet. But major influences on his taste and collaborators in terms of his understanding of music were Ashton's musician colleagues.

By far the most influential of these musicians, indeed for the whole of British ballet, was Constant Lambert. It was he whom de Valois described as 'our only hope of an English Diaghilev',[14] broadly educated as he was across the arts. He later proved exceptionally versatile as not only composer, but also arranger, conductor and writer. He already had experience of the Diaghilev Ballets Russes behind him before coming into contact with Ashton, having composed the music for Nijinska's *Romeo and Juliet* (1926 – in fact, a revision of an existing Lambert score *Adam and Eve*). A year later, Nijinska used his music in *Pomona* for her own company in Buenos Aires. Formed again from existing music, the ballet score was to be used again by Ashton in 1930. Lambert became conductor for the Camargo Society in 1930, joining the Vic-Wells Ballet as music director in 1931, and remaining in that post until 1947, although continuing to conduct for the company after that date (he died in 1951).

In terms of Lambert's conducting, it is pertinent that, when the Sadler's Wells Ballet visited New York for the first time in 1949, Lincoln Kirstein wrote about him to the critic Richard Buckle:

A divine conductor . . . The greatest ballet man in the business.

The hero of the occasion, according to Balanchine and myself, was Lambert; he had a fine band and the score never sounded so well; he is a genius for *tempi*; absolutely on the note in every variation; no boring bits; and he supports the dancers on the huge stage by giving them assurance from his authority. He whipped people up into applause, purely by sound; when nothing was really happening from a dancer he seduced everyone into somehow imagining that she was divine. Anyway, he got an ovation; many people knew what he had done.[15]

Lambert's Diaghilev experience proved to be formative, although later he turned critical of his achievements of the 1920s. He promoted the impresario's early ideal of close collaboration and discussion between all the artists involved in a work.[16] The experience also had a major impact on his musical preferences: a particular openness to French and Russian music and a particular impatience with the nineteenth-century Teutonic canon (see Ch. 1, pp. 13–14) and what he perceived as its declining tradition of the symphony. Lambert's was a highly individual and complex personality; he was a robust romantic, strong in his beliefs, and always eager to promote the lesser-known that he found interesting. He was also very supportive of a number of British composers, like the following, who, under his auspices, were all involved in some way with Ashton's work: Lennox Berkeley, Lord Berners, Gavin Gordon, William Walton, or those who helped with orchestration or arrangement, Denis Aplvor, Gordon Jacob, Elizabeth Lutyens, Alan Rawsthorne and Humphrey Searle. Yet he was cosmopolitan in attitude, impatient with narrow insularity and had particularly stinging remarks to make about the nationalist trends in English music led by Vaughan Williams in the early decades of the century: 'that particular form of provinciality that has degraded nationalism to the level of the exotic'.[17] These remarks stem from his classic manifesto *Music Ho!* (1934), subtitled 'A Study of Music in Decline', which represented a largely pessimistic view of the state of concert music between the wars. Richard Shead, Lambert's biographer, presents a useful summary of Lambert's argument, which also testifies to his highly individual spirit:

Artificial attempts to cultivate a 'national' style (like the English folk-song school) are false and ludicrous. The great revolutionary upheaval in music which took place before the First World War, and in which Debussy and Schoenberg played crucial parts, is over; consolidation is less exciting than revolution, and few composers even try to consolidate. The majority prefer to fall back on devices like pastiche (Stravinsky in his neo-classic period, together with his followers) or on 'mechanical romanticism' (like Honegger's *Pacific 231*) or on facile note-spinning (Hindemith and his 'Gebrauchsmusik', which so far as Lambert is concerned consists in providing music of little or no value in the hope of supplying a need which does not exist) . . . The only hope for music lies in the kind of composer who, unconcerned with fashion, goes his own way, working out a musical style that pleases himself (rather than a coterie) and paying attention to the dictates of form rather than to those of mode. And Lambert gives Sibelius, Busoni and [Bernard] van Dieren [a contemporary British composer] as examples.[18]

Among the other composers whom Lambert particularly applauds are Borodin, Boyce, Chabrier, Debussy, Glinka, Liszt, Satie and Weill. It is an idiosyncratic, out-of-the-mainstream list, especially in terms of what turned out to be the dominant modernist tradition spearheaded by Schoenberg, Webern and Stravinsky. Perhaps most surprising is his attack on Stravinsky. Lambert professed admiration for the early collaborative ballets like *Firebird* and *Petrushka*. He spared his main attack for the 'time travelling', neo-classical Stravinsky of the 1920s (see Ch. 1, p. 20) and the late Diaghilev period that he had known as a creative participant. Now that the ideal of the *Gesamtkunstwerk* had given way to a 'scrapbook mentality', Lambert perceived the work of Stravinsky (and also that of the new generation French composers who wrote for the ballet during this period) as dry, mechanical and synthetic.

A pianist friend of Lambert's, Angus Morrison, who played at the premiere of *Symphonic Variations*, ventures that, for once, here, Lambert might have been swayed by the opinion of a close friend Cecil Gray, whilst trying to escape his own past: 'The whole section called "Post-War Pasticheurs" in *Music Ho!* has too much of the exaggerated indignation of the reformed sinner castigating his own erstwhile lapses . . .'[19] It turns out that some Lambert work has definite Stravinskian touches, certainly his last ballet *Tiresias* (1951).[20]

Also interesting and forward-looking to our own times are Lambert's broad tastes and anti-elitist views. Interested in jazz, popular music, and the lighter kinds of concert music, he incorporated ideas from the vernacular into his own work, for instance, into *The Rio Grande* (1927, set by Ashton in 1931). And he had a sense of social purpose, to reach beyond the academic purist or connoisseur to the man/woman in the street.

Lambert, it is commonly suggested, was largely responsible for Ashton's musical education, although, with the paucity of available recordings in the 1930s and 1940s, there was more obligation at that time for a musical advisor to be active in this kind of way. Lambert suggested existing scores that Ashton might use, discussed their structure with him, introduced him to the community of other British contemporary composers who might also write, arrange and orchestrate for the ballet, and insisted on standards of conducting that respected the sense and drive of the music. Vaughan points out that many ballets took their artistic as well as musical conception from Lambert,[21] like *Apparitions* (1936, Liszt, arranged by Lambert) and the ballets to Lambert's scores, *Horoscope* (1938) and *Tiresias* (1951). Yet, years later, in conversation with Kavanagh, Ashton was careful not to give too much credit to his colleague for moulding his musical taste: 'No one did that. But I would listen to his opinion.'[22] A letter from Lambert to persuade Ashton to get down to work on *Apparitions* teasingly suggests an element of compromise for a less musically advanced, more sweet-toothed Ashton: 'I want as far as possible to use only unknown pieces mostly from the latest period though I may allow you *Valse Oubliée* and *Consolation* as a sop to your feelings.' The piece was framed by two renderings of Liszt's lyrical *Consolation No. 3*. But Ashton is quick to point out to Kavanagh, '*Apparitions* grew from an equal appreciation of Liszt. We had been through all the music we liked long before – I was just as much pushing Liszt as he was.'[23] In later life, is Ashton perhaps a little testy about the reminder of so much musical guidance? In any case, it seems that Ashton became more independent of Lambert as time went on, and quite naturally so as his own experience and confidence increased. On a number of occasions, he went against his advice, particularly when it came to setting symphonic music – Lambert, we recall, wrote vigorously in counter to the symphonic ballet movement promoted by Massine (see Ch. 1, p. 14).

Ashton continued until the end of his career to nourish himself creatively from other musician colleagues and friends, who would guide him in getting to know a score, its structuring in sections and phrases, sometimes suggesting how to fit the incidents in the story to the music. Robert Irving, who became musical director of the Sadler's Wells Ballet (1949–58), was very much in the mould of Lambert, who gave him the model for conducting: 'to take things along at a pretty good clip . . . I tried to follow that.'[24] Again an advisor to Ashton, he was less instrumental than Lambert in shaping the company repertory, although an important legacy is his arrangement of the Glazunov selection for *Birthday Offering* (1956). Irving left Britain to become musical director of New York City Ballet. From 1960 to 1972, John Lanchbery was principal conductor of the now Royal Ballet; he formed an important creative partnership with Ashton that began with *La Fille mal gardée* (1960) and continued after he had left the company. The last ballet that he arranged for Ashton was *A Month in the Country*, in 1976, although it seems that there were ideas for further collaboration after this. Pianists too were important to Ashton, like Philip Gammon, who worked closely with him from the early 1960s. Gammon singles out Ashton from other choreographers of his experience, for incorporating the rehearsal pianist into his creative thinking: 'That's one thing I liked particularly about Ashton: he would welcome any comment I would like to make about the musicality of the choreography, the look of the step in relation to the music.'[25] And then, there was a late lover, Martyn Thomas, whom Kavanagh now reveals as a seminal contributor to some of Ashton's later projects. Although he had no formal musical education, Thomas nevertheless helped in the planning stages of *The Creatures of Prometheus* (1970, Beethoven); he co-ordinated dance events with music for *Rhapsody* (1980, Rachmaninov) and most importantly, as we shall see, *A Month in the Country*.

There were other ways in which Ashton's capacity for listening (the passive aspect in his makeup) mixed with a determination to make his own decisions on musical matters. Throughout his career, he had to answer to ballet company management, which sometimes rejected his ambitions, sometimes served as a stimulant. Alexander Grant recalls that Ashton sometimes provided a list of musical possibilities from which the Royal Opera House management would select, presumably making decisions according to the criteria of market popularity or programme balance. Ashton was pleased to relinquish a measure of responsibility.[27]

Musical Choices

For story ballets, the potential of music to provide sympathetic imagery, in line with the story, was naturally a guiding factor in Ashton's musical selection. Or the music might even suggest the story content in the first place, to varying degrees of detail. On a number of occasions, Ashton chose music that was likely to set up immediate, intended associations in the mind of the listener, or at least to provide an obvious complement to his own theme: as for *The Dream* (1964, Mendelssohn's Overture and incidental music are an obvious choice) or *The Wanderer* (1941, based on Schubert's Wanderer Fantasy, the theme of which came from a song of the same name). Although the late work of Liszt was not well known in the 1930s and 1940s, it is likely that the 'diabolical' associations of this composer would have been read by those who watched *Apparitions* and *Dante Sonata* (1940). Ashton was especially delighted to discover intricate connections between his music and other sources, like Liszt having had an affair with Marie Duplessis, the real woman behind the Dumas character in *Marguerite and Armand* (1963),[28] or the numerous overlaps between the worlds of Turgenev and Chopin (*A Month in the Country* – see p. 247). Or there might be personal resonance. Perhaps Ashton saw the lonely artist figure of Elgar in *Enigma Variations* (1968) as a mirror to himself, Elgar then being uncertain of public appreciation and later overtaken by a new generation of composers.

Although commissioned scores suit the timing of story ballets, they afford no such advantages of ready resonance, and indeed Ashton developed reservations about them. There are scores by Lambert – *Horoscope* and *Tiresias*; Lord Berners – *A Wedding Bouquet* (1937), *Les Sirènes* (1946) and *Cupid and Psyche* (1939); William Walton – *The Quest* (1943), *The First Shoot* ballet in the Cochran revue *Follow the Sun* (1935), and in 1983 he added a few bars at the end of his five lute bagatelles *Varii Capricci* specifically for the eponymous ballet;[29] Lennox Berkeley – *The Judgement of Paris* (1938); Malcolm Arnold – *Homage to the Queen* (1953) and *Rinaldo and Armida* (1955); Alan Rawsthorne – *Madame Chrysanthème* (1955); and Hans Werner Henze – *Ondine* (1958). For the composers who provided Ashton with original scores, Ashton's process was to give detailed instructions: notes published in Vaughan's book indicate the overall layout of sections, placement of climaxes, very precise time-lengths for each section (though not as Petipa did, an exact number of bars), tempo marks (using musical terms), occasionally time signatures and an indication of preferred instrumentation. The Ashton literature gives us the impression that these commissions did not result in the same intensity of dialogue and mutual understanding as evolved from Ashton's work with his own music staff. Stories of the difficulties in the collaboration with Henze are well known; dancers have since commented on the odd experience of having to dance an Ashton ballet using counts or thinking of music in terms of co-ordinating with a series of cue points. On several occasions, Ashton found the working process with a composer uncomfortably slow: for *The Quest*, he was forced to make up a portion of the dance in advance of hearing Walton's music.[30] Of course, the economics of commissions were another consideration, but Ashton worried most of all about the process: 'you can get a millstone around your neck. Unless I like the music I'm lost.'[31]

We can imagine too that he missed the possibility of detailed listening to a score from a recording, which he so loved doing, getting to know the orchestrated version of the music well before making the choreography. On a number of occasions, Ashton had a musical score in mind for a long time before setting it, like the Satie *Gymnopédies 2* score which he purchased in Paris in 1929 when with the Ida Rubinstein Company, many years before he used it for *Monotones* (1965/66).[32] Ashton more often settled for musical arrangement rather than commission.

It is conventionally believed that Ashton favoured above all the lighter music, often ballet music, of the nineteenth century. Scores for well-known ballets such as *Les Rendezvous* (1933, Auber), *Les Patineurs* (1937, Meyerbeer), *Birthday*

Offering (1956, Glazunov), and *La Fille mal gardée* (1960, an adaptation of Hérold) come to mind. The choreographer Richard Alston has suggested that such music, with its light and crisp rhythms, admirably suits the 'lightweight and feathery texture of the batterie and intricate footwork'[33] in Ashton's style. Alastair Macaulay proposes that Ashton used this music to look back to a world where 'romantic flirtation might combine with social formality more comfortably than in a twentieth-century setting'.[34] However, in a 1988 analysis of Ashton's musical selections, the critic Noël Goodwin stresses Ashton's eclecticism and points out that about half his composers were from the twentieth century, many of these British composers.[35] It is easy to overlook this, for many of the ballets that represent these composers have disappeared from the repertory. But there are no scores from the cerebral serial or post-serial schools that Balanchine took on for challenge, and this is significant in terms of Ashton's different inclinations. Ashton also set a number of pre-nineteenth-century scores, extending back to Couperin, Dowland and Purcell. He used selections from Bach cantatas (arranged by Walton) for *The Wise Virgins* in 1940, and, true to times when such a composer was considered sacrosanct, he was attacked by the critic for *The Times* for doing so.[36] The figure of Lambert looms large in many of these choices, also in the infrequency of major Austro-German composers. But in the final interview of his life, Ashton spoke of his own fear of using such big composers: 'Everyone always asks why haven't you ever done a Mozart ballet? – and I say because I find it impossible, I can't match up to it. It's too great, I can't scale it up there.'[37]

A composer who stands out as a favourite is Liszt (a Lambert favourite), and whose music accompanied *Apparitions*, *Mephisto Waltz* (1934), which was later rechoreographed as *Vision of Marguerite* (1952), *Dante Sonata*, *Marguerite and Armand*, *Hamlet Prelude* (1977) and a duet, *Oh, quand je dors* (1971). In guiding Ashton, Lambert introduced him to a number of the composer's lesser-known and often abrasive late works. Other Ashton favourites included Lambert himself, Lord Berners and Walton, whilst, perhaps inspired by the example of the Ballets Russes, he maintained a penchant for recent French music: he set Milhaud, Dukas, Satie, Poulenc, Debussy, and on a number of occasions Ravel. For his very first ballet, *A Tragedy of Fashion* (1926, Eugene Goossens), Ashton had proposed commissioning a score from Poulenc or Auric, but Rambert sensibly advised him against this, for reasons of his lack of experience as well as cost.[38] It is important not to forget Ashton's delight in Tchaikovsky, manifest in the number of contributions he made to productions of his ballets.

Ashton chose Britten's music on three occasions, most notably for *Illuminations* (created for New York City Ballet); he also worked with him on two operas as producer of *Albert Herring* (1947) and choreographer of the dances in *Death in Venice* (1973). Perhaps surprisingly, there were no commissions from Britten, although this was possibly not for the want of asking. Ashton was friendly with the composer, and was miffed that he chose to collaborate with John Cranko on *The Prince of the Pagodas* (1957).[39] Another story is that Ashton was simply not available to work on this ballet.[40]

Often considered the quintessential ballet composer of the twentieth century, Stravinsky's music was chosen by Ashton on three occasions, for *Le Baiser de la fée* (1935), *Scènes de ballet* and *Persephone* (1961). This is despite Lambert's disparaging views, although Irving recalls that it was de Valois who objected to Ashton's choice of *Scènes* in 1948.[41] Perhaps she was nervous of audience reaction to its acerbic qualities, perhaps guided by Lambert herself. At any rate, Ashton's admiration for the composer is in no doubt. He wrote in 1948, the year of *Scènes*:

Stravinsky has always been a favourite composer of mine, because I feel that he is among the few composers of today who thinks in a really contemporary way. He also has a greater understanding of the problems of ballet than any other living composer, having had a vast experience in composing for the medium.

Like Balanchine perhaps, the fact that *Scènes* was 'devoid of any literary or dramatic argument' appealed to him: 'It left me free within the limits set out by Stravinsky, to indulge my choreographic imagination to the fullest.' There is too the fact – perhaps here he was thinking back to *Apollo* – that the dance 'works up to a true apotheosis in the magnificent style so typical of Stravinsky.'[42] Ashton also choreographed the two dancing roles for the New York Metropolitan Opera's 1981 revival of Stravinsky's opera *Le Rossignol*.

A notebook of the mid-1940s contains a number of surprising ideas for ballet scores that were, in the event, never used, including Sibelius' *Seventh Symphony* (even if this was a symphony, perhaps one detects the predilection of Lambert here) and a Saint-Saëns Concerto; on another page, Ashton notes down Schoenberg's pre-serial *Gurrelieder*.[43] At the time of his retirement from the Royal Ballet, Vaughan tells us, the choreographer's prospective scores included the Gershwin Piano Concerto, and Tchaikovsky's String Sextet (*Souvenir de Florence*).[44] We know no more about his intentions, whether for instance he thought about having this music arranged, but these particular works are all especially noteworthy as large-scale, with developed symphonic movements – not, as they stand, what we most readily associate with Ashton. In any case, Lambert steered Ashton away from certain symphonic music. Debussy's *La Mer* is an example, but in the case of two other works, Ashton defied him: he went ahead with Franck's *Symphonic Variations* and Delius's *Paris Overture* (for *Nocturne*, 1936), despite Lambert's advice.[45]

Ashton created four three-act ballets: *Cinderella* (1948, Prokofiev), *Sylvia* (1952, Delibes), *Romeo and Juliet* (1955, Prokofiev, for the Royal Danish Ballet, because de Valois was against having another full-length Prokofiev score after *Cinderella* in the home repertory)[46] and *Ondine*. After these, Ashton created *Fille* and *Two Pigeons* (1961) in two acts, partly perhaps because of the shortage of large-scale ballet scores available, but also because he preferred to work on the smaller scale. All his other ballets, except for short divertissement pieces, are in one act.

Outstanding in the Ashton chronology is the number of arranged scores, a practice no doubt prompted by Diaghilev's precedent and Lambert's encouragement. Arrangements were especially useful to Ashton, tailored as they can be to fit the drive of a story, especially if short pieces are used. Lambert understood this well, using mainly dance music and short keyboard works. If we take *Apparitions* as an example, some of the Liszt piano pieces appear complete, but often with new endings that link with the next piece or support the thrust of the narrative. In others, phrases or sections are cut out along the way. Revivals of the ballet, including the last one for London Festival Ballet in 1987, reveal further processes of cutting from the original score.[47] In contrast, Lambert left the fifteen-minute symphonic score of *Dante Sonata* intact when making his own orchestral arrangement. In a radio programme, Lambert discussed how, impressed by the Diaghilev example, he had collaborated closely with Ashton to suit the score and its orchestration to the drama of the ballet:

Ashton suggested the theme of Dante's 'Inferno'. I, after various ideas, settled on the Liszt piano piece which is used. The general layout, by which I mean not the dancing as such, but the association of various characters with various themes, and the general dramatic sequence was then established mutually by Ashton and myself. I played the piano at almost all the rehearsals while the choreography was being created, so that when it came finally to orchestrating the ballet, I had the whole stage picture in my mind. I am certain that, apart from whether people like *Dante Sonata* or not, it has a visual-cum-musical unity which could only have been achieved by this form of collaboration.[48]

On a few occasions, Lambert made the musical arrangement and then asked another composer to carry out the orchestration, like Gordon Jacob for *Apparitions* and *Harlequin in the Street* (1938, Couperin), and Walton for *The Wise Virgins*. An interesting early arranged score was by Edwin Evans, the music critic and musical director of the Camargo Society. His selection of Mendelssohn pieces for *The Lord of Burleigh* (1931, orchestrated by Jacob) comprises a number of piano pieces, mainly *Songs without Words*, also, more surprisingly, movements from large-scale works such as a string quartet, and the well-known Octet and Violin Concerto. A glance at the ballet score reveals Evans' major cuts to both the Octet Scherzo and Violin Concerto finale – for example, only half the original concerto movement remains.

Ashton's later collaborative approach, which is detailed later, was of quite a different order, described by Lanchbery as 'welding',[49] and involving considerable reordering of sections of music. Ashton and Lanchbery did not hesitate to take on large-scale musical forms for *The Dream* and *A Month in the Country*, intertwining separate pieces as well as altering the original orchestration.

Artistic Principles and Working Methods

Ashton's early tendencies were, like Lambert's, towards neo-classicism and an artistic chic associated with the Diaghilev of the Parisian 1920s. In terms of music, he put it this way: 'At the end of the Twenties no one wanted Romantic, emotionally charged music, everything was Bach, Mozart, Poulenc, simplicity of orchestration, Stravinsky and all that.'[50]

The climate soon changed: a romantic revival was under way, hinted at during the 1920s through works like Nijinska's *La Bien-Aimée* (1928) and Balanchine's *Le Bal* (1929), later with Balanchine's *Cotillon* (1932), given major impetus with the repertory of Les Ballets 1933. The same year that this company operated saw the publication of Mario Praz's study *The Romantic Agony*, which stressed the more macabre, pathological aspects of romanticism and discussed the cult of the Fatal Woman. Sacheverell Sitwell's biography of Liszt was published in 1934. Significantly, Lambert had acted as advisor and corrected the original draft.[51] In programme notes accompanying the 1987 revival of *Apparitions*, the archivist-historian Jane Pritchard points out the trio of ballets on the romantic theme of artist-and-muse that faced Londoners during the 1930s, *Apparitions* (using the Fatal Woman theme of Berlioz's *Symphonie fantastique*), preceding by a few months Massine's actual setting of that symphony, and later, in 1937, for the Markova-Dolin Ballet, a revival of Nijinska's *The Beloved One* (originally titled *La Bien-Aimée*).[52] Ashton was rapidly drawn into this new tide and into what has been labelled neo-romanticism, a movement that featured particularly strongly, though not exclusively, in the visual arts. Ballet, it turned out, was a prime site for neo-romantic artists.

Ashton was in contact with two neo-romantic traditions. There was the French movement (1926–36) that included Christian Bérard, Pavel Tchelitchew and Eugene Berman, a reaction to the dominant modernist abstraction of Picasso, but which avoided the degree of menace and distortion developed under the banner of surrealism. A later British movement reached its peak of

importance in the 1940s (extending into the 1950s in the films of Michael
Powell and Emeric Pressburger). Ashton, Lambert and Cecil Beaton had much
admired the designs of the French neo-romantics and the choreography of Balanchine for Les Ballets 1933.[53] Works that they saw included *Cotillon* (Bérard),
a model ballet for Ashton, and *L'Errante* (*The Wanderer* – Tchelitchew). Another
version of the latter, to music by Schubert and on a similar theme of intellectual
and emotional journey, was made by Ashton some years later.

Paintings by the British neo-romantics evoked a sense of atmosphere and
feeling for place, most often with a current of melancholy, nostalgia for a threat-
ened landscape and a disappearing past. There was too a suggestion of isolation
and a withdrawal from the embrace of international modernist abstraction. Dis-
credited in the 1950s by Pop Art critics such as Lawrence Alloway, the movement was then destroyed by the onslaught of formalism and American abstract
expressionism. It has been viewed critically as 'a retrenchment in British culture', representative of a 'Centre Party' in British art and criticism, 'educated
gentry accustomed to some guardianship over and spokesmanship for English
art and letters'.[54] But John Piper, himself a neo-romantic who had once worked
with abstraction, says that he found this latter position untenable as World War
II loomed, and, indeed, it has been said that 'there was scarcely a painter in
England in the 1940s who was not subject to the Romantic impulse in some
degree'.[55] The movement has been reread through the framework of 'New Art
History' within the recent, more pluralist post-modern climate, and through a
series of exhibitions in the 1980s culminating in the Barbican's *A Paradise Lost:
The Neo-Romantic Imagination in Britain 1935–55*. Concerns of 'the body' and
'the land' are seen to have particular significance to our own times, as does the
theme of 'quest' explained in the *Paradise Lost* catalogue: 'a search whose object
is the shrine, an Eden or Arcadia; a quest made by artists sensitive to the spiritual loss of their day, a society which was to be broken by a tidal wave of war
carnage and subsequent consumerism'.[56]

Likewise, Ashton's work might speak afresh to us today, tangential as it too
has been to mainstream modernist trends. Certainly, given his personal inclinations, we can understand how the mystical and pastoral preoccupations of the
neo-romantics struck a chord with him. His work features the painters Michael
Ayrton (*The Fairy Queen*, 1946), Eugene Berman (*The Devil's Holiday*, 1939),
John Craxton (*Daphnis and Chloe*, 1951), John Piper (*The Quest*) and Graham
Sutherland (*The Wanderer*). Sophie Fedorovitch and Cecil Beaton, more regular
designers for Ashton, were both strongly influenced by the French neo-romantics. It is significant that, true to Ashton's artistic context, William Chappell
categorised *Symphonic Variations* (plotless as it was) as a romantic ballet in his
1948 book *Studies in Ballet*,[57] not at all in the same mould as the increasingly
hard-edged plotless style that Balanchine was developing in the 1940s (as in

Concerto Barocco and *The Four Temperaments*). Meanwhile, Ashton maintained a long friendship with Tchelitchew and there were plans to work with both him and Bérard (Tchelitchew the original choice for *Apparitions*, Bérard for *Illuminations*).[58] The romantic vein in design continues with Lila de Nobili (*Ondine*), and then David Walker and Henry Barden (*The Dream*), both pupils of de Nobili. Ashton never had any contact with the British movement that focused on the values of abstraction.

It is the neo-romantic movement that is perhaps the most closely attuned to the Ashton aesthetic, and yet the choreographer's values are by no means straightforward. There are the odd, late indulgences in youth culture, the chic of the 1960s and 1970s, like *Jazz Calendar* (1968) and *Lament of the Waves* (1970). More important is the figure of Petipa, and on any number of occasions, we see a tightening of the reins on formality and classical principles: in *Birthday Offering*, in his dances interpolated into *The Sleeping Beauty*, in a number of aspects of *Symphonic Variations*, most extreme in *Scènes de ballet*. Listen to Ashton's own description of this last work: 'a hidden beauty . . . a cold, distant, uncompromising beauty which says I am here, beautiful, but I will make no effort to charm you'.[59] And the composer Henze, in imperfect English, writes to Ashton in deep admiration for the ballet: 'This music: like steel, the dancers: like fanatic, apassionate appearances, the prezision of the movements, and this absolute beauty . . .'[60]

Far removed, it seems from these descriptions, are the values of emotional or personal impulse. But *Scènes* is exceptional. The romantic impulse soon returned, and remained strong, no more so than in the later work of Ashton, who is now an older man, feeling increasingly out of touch with modern times, and looking back. As Bryan Robertson sums it up:

> He was fundamentally an Edwardian – not a Victorian as people say – but an Edwardian, which has to do with this quality of nostalgia, of not being quite into the new century and with strong feelings about the one that's just slipped round the corner.[61]

Perhaps his most overtly Edwardian ballet was *Enigma Variations* (though the score dates from 1899, Queen Victoria's reign). This was his first collaboration with the designer Julia Trevelyan Oman, whose realist, decoratively detailed design accounts of the past well suited the romantic nostalgia of Ashton's later career.

Discussion of the broad aesthetic context of Ashton's work rationalises his musical choices and clarifies his preference for atmosphere, 'poetic evocation',[62] over cerebral modernism. It also helps us to understand his musical-choreographic style. This has often been discussed according to the terms of lyricism.

As we shall see, this should not necessarily mean any reduction in power, passion, wit, even menace. Yet it does mean a different attitude to pulse from Balanchine, a lighter and freer attitude. In descriptions of Ashton's rhythmic style, we do not find the words 'motor' and 'drive' being used, rather words like 'lyrical' and 'flowing'. Ashton wanted his dancers to 'melt into it and enjoy it [the choreography] and not have a warring element in it'.[63] Edwin Denby analysed the New York City Ballet style as dancing 'on top of the beat', which 'builds up pressure. They dance with a rhythmic thrust that is quick and exact.' He contrasted the Royal Ballet style, which is to 'follow the beat . . . with a tiny lag'.[64] Perhaps this is one more way in which Ashton looks to romantic nineteenth-century precedents rather than (and unlike Balanchine) contributing to the hard, machine style of modernism.

The beat is sometimes seen as a relatively unimportant framework in the creative process (see p. 202). Henning Kronstam, who created the role of Ashton's Romeo, reports: 'Fred told me that he never worked on the beat of the music. He always worked on the melody.'[65] Margot Fonteyn claimed likewise, that Ashton's musicality is 'not limited to the mathematical aspect of each measure, which in fact rather bores him'. Instead, he responds 'to the line, colour and overall significance of the work'.[66]

These generalisations can be misleading. Indeed, in his last interview, Ashton seems to contradict every one of these statements: 'I immediately get the rhythm: it's almost the first thing. Pulse: you see it's like Stravinsky . . . [you must get] the drive and the force of it.' So he even cites the arch-modernist Stravinsky! But he goes on to suggest the source of his own freedoms: 'Perhaps that pulse is the result of the period I was born in, jazz or whatever. Where there was more sense of rhythm and pulse.' This is a crucial point. Jazz works with and against pulse, and the playfulness and slipperiness of jazz heightens sensitivity to pulse. 'With pop music, there isn't that wonderful sense of rhythm that was in jazz.'[67]

Ashton shows a very secure, sharp relationship to pulse when he wants to, using the crisp dance rhythms of the nineteenth century, or, the most extreme example of all, using the motoric beat of Stravinsky's *Scènes de ballet*. We are talking about a question of degree, and again the comparison with Balanchine is a useful one. The pulse of Ashton is never as forceful. He also fills out the space more between the extremes of motor rhythm and creamy *adage*, making more of the gradation of dynamic qualities and the in-between range of accentuation.

We have seen that it was important to Ashton's musical understanding to seek advice from musicians. He also enjoyed collaboration with his dancers, and this too gives interesting clues as to how his particular musical style developed. It is well known that Ashton's working process was to ask his dancers to provide him with movement material for moulding in his own way. He would arrive in the rehearsal studio with the 'scaffolding'[68] worked out, the directions in space decided, but no movement settled. He might have a general idea about the kind of movement, and try out a few moves himself, or he might sit and give instructions to interpret before working on the material himself. 'I want something like a fountain . . . or a horse bucking' – Antoinette Sibley suggests the kinds of image that Ashton used as a starting point.[69] The whole of the Vera solo in *A Month in the Country* was mapped out on his notator Faith Worth: Ashton asked her to do *ballonnés* to a corner of the stage, *bourrées* round the room and *échappés* in the centre. Worth then taught the solo to Denise Nunn, after which Ashton 'fiddled about with the steps. He fiddled a lot after that.'[70] A major part of Ashton's fiddling was rhythmical. The first *ballonné* step, for instance, was made to finish quickly, so that there was hardly any jump left in it. Another issue is that improvisation in rehearsal offered Ashton phrases of dance material to fit not just onto but also *around* a musical framework.

Ashton indicated rhythm by physically showing it (as he grew older, tapping his feet as he sat in his chair) or by a kind of singing of the musical rhythm: 'chum, chum, chum . . . *Ya* da da da da', and so on. Or he might tell a dancer to try a step or short phrase faster on repeat. The main point is that Ashton did not count or refer to metre: he did not analyse rhythm himself, nor did he ask his musicians for counts. A musically precise assistant like Michael Somes might step in later and count for the dancers if it seemed helpful, but he too liked to impart nuances from singing phrasing, Cynthia Harvey recalls, 'with the emphasis on the note that he wanted you to make the clearest'.[71] The New York City Ballet response to Ashton's *Illuminations* is interesting. When Tanaquil LeClercq had to teach her role to Diana Adams, she was asked 'What are the counts?' a characteristic question from a City Ballet dancer. LeClercq replied that in Ashton style, 'When you hear this in the music you do *that*, then if you move a little faster on this next thing, you'll make it.'[72] Counting during the creative process could well have hardened the beat, emphasised it more regularly than Ashton wanted and prevented listening to music.

Nor did Ashton necessarily correct changes that occurred between rehearsals or revivals, unless he had been especially insistent about a particular point. A notator or dancer might be wise to such changes, but Ashton was more concerned with what seemed right on the day, sometimes, for instance, making minor alterations himself to suit a new dancer in a role. Dancers who were accustomed to rehearsing with him also knew how to work, indeed, when it came to new choreography, to virtually create, within his style.

Symphonic Variations will reveal further aspects of Ashton's rhythmic style. It is also important as a turning point in Ashton's career and a rare example of an Ashton ballet without a story to an uncut symphonic piece of music.

Symphonic Variations

Looking back in 1964, Ashton rationalised why he made *Symphonic Variations*: 'There seemed to be a clutter of ballets with heavy stories and I felt that the whole idiom needed purifying. And so I made *Symphonic Variations*, and it was a kind of testament.'[73] This was the first ballet that Ashton made after the war, and it was the one that prompted his first statements stressing the values of simply dancing to music. César Franck's *Symphonic Variations* for piano and orchestra gave him the initial idea of a ballet. The score had been introduced to him by the pianist Angus Morrison, who worked out initial ideas for the ballet with him.[74] The work was originally conceived in mystical terms, with a rather elaborate plot and many more dancers than the three men and three women finally chosen. Ashton had been inspired by his wartime reading of mystics such as St Theresa of Avila and St John of the Cross,[75] but his eventual decision was to pare down and remove all specific information about story or character. What remained was a 'poetic evocation', but with power given to the more formal aspects of dance, the interplay with music (using the name of the music was a significant gesture), and abstract designs by Sophie Fedorovitch: a huge sunny green backdrop enlivened by light black strokes and swirls, and Greek-inspired versions of white practice-costumes. The six dancers for whom Ashton created the work were Margot Fonteyn, Pamela May, Moira Shearer, Michael Somes, Henry Danton and Brian Shaw.

It is important that the process of working on *Symphonic Variations* was unusually lengthy and painstaking for Ashton. He had come to know the music very well during the course of the war. Thus, he says, 'I was able to ride on the music quite a bit . . . I'd always hoped I would get round to using it one day.'[76] The delaying of the premiere because of an injury incurred by Somes meant that he had further time to work on the ballet, and the process of paring down and refinement could continue. May recalls too how the dancers were exceptionally well prepared in their understanding of the music, which Ashton played to them again and again on a wind-up gramophone while they were on tour, before rehearsals actually began.[77]

The ballet was generally praised. However, Ashton's choice of 'symphonic' music met with opposition from some quarters. Lambert, for one, tried to persuade him not to use it, although he later agreed that Ashton's choice had been a good one. There were critics too who, while admiring aspects of Ashton's work, singled out for criticism his use of a concerto-style piece of music. The opera and sometime ballet critic Philip Hope-Wallace felt that no stage presentation could compete with the existing drama between piano solo and orchestra:

[This music] has its own spotlit soloist, the piano, and is conceived all through in terms of the stresses and expressive effects of a piano-concerto. The arpeggio stealing into the minor steals attention from the stage. The prancing passage work in the finale flashes like lightning above the dancers whose panting gyrations seem as pointless and unnecessary as would be dancing to accompany a big operatic aria.[78]

Or the problem was that Ashton had provided no solo counterpart in the dance to the piano, instead choosing a more democratic approach to his cast of six. The *Guardian* critic complained: 'The hard core of the problem is not solved; it is evaded.'[79]

An explanation of the original scenario for the ballet is useful in telling us how the final structure came about. Ashton's jottings in the programme of a concert at which the Variations were played suggest the early stages of an outline.[80] The entries in his notebook give a more developed account. They begin as follows:

Woman-Winter, Man-Summer . . . 12 or 6 girls, 6 men or 12 men; or 6 plus 1 man, 6 plus 1 girl . . . The women, the Winter, mourn the departure of the Men. The waiting period, the earth robbed of the sun. The moon period, the Underworld, darkness . . . The arrival of the Men, the sun's rays. The search for the male. The summer. The Earth, the light . . . the Dance of Union . . . the Festival.

Later, Ashton shows the structure as ABAB, with a clear rhyming relationship between the larger sections of the piece.

a) *Poco allegro* – Part 1. The Women, Winter, the period of waiting, the Moon period, the Underworld, the Darkness. The Earth, Venus mourning. The Virgin's faith.
b) *Allegretto* – Part 2. The arrival of the Men. The Sun's rays, the Summer, the World, the Heavens, the Light, Adonis returns to the Earth, Life, Love, the Lover excites the love of his Spouse.
a) *Molto più lento* – Part 3. The Search. The Wound of Love and Rapture caused by spark of love. The Dance of Union, Fertility.
b) *Allegro non troppo* – Part 4. The Call of the Bridegroom. The Festival. The Summer. The Marriage. The Heart's joy in union. 'Art and Faith united in one unseverable bond.'[81]

Ashton has taken the broad outlines of the music here as a basis for his division into sections:

Poco Allegro – a kind of Prologue
Allegretto – a Theme and five Variations on the Theme
Molto più lento, seen by Ashton as separating off the sixth Variation, which
leads into an Interlude
Allegro non troppo – the Finale

In the completed work, there is a case for seeing the structure more clearly in
terms of three sections, which is the view adopted here for the structural diagram (see p. 207): Prologue, Theme and Six Variations, and Allegro Finale.
However, we still perceive Ashton's plan. There is a focus on the women first, one
man soon joining them, then on all three men, who rapidly become part of an
ensemble with the women. A *pas de deux* follows, as symbol of searching for love,
and at this point the ballet begins to breathe more, with a new freedom and
openness of movement. There is a bonding of men and women to each other
and to the community, and finally a joyous celebration of harmony. The mood-
tempo alternation of slow-serious-wanting/fast-bright still provides the rhyming structure (ABAB) of the ballet. Thus, traces of the original meaning and the
structuring of that meaning remain, even though Ashton, by deliberately not
including any programme note, offered the opportunity for free interpretation.
The historian Beth Genné likes to see the three men posing quietly upstage at the
beginning of the ballet as part of the 'vegetal' world of Fedorovitch's backdrop.
Fedorovitch too, like Ashton, went through a process of abstracting her ideas
from more obviously referential beginnings. When the men come forwards, to
Genné they are 'symbols – as in Ashton's original scenario – of spring and fertility'.[82] Others may prefer a more abstract reading of such nature imagery,
although there is a considerable consensus of agreement about the overtones of
serenity, human bonding and hopefulness in this ballet, especially important
after the horrors of the war.

Much of the interest in *Symphonic Variations* derives from its formal values,
which also contribute meaning. The ballet is partly about space: areas, boundaries and relationships within and extending beyond the stage space are primary
content. Dancers often establish themselves in space in stillness as much as in
motion. At first, the choreography relates to the line of the backdrop, later to the
square that the dancers take turns to form as frame for the Variation dances.
Then, joining in kinship and joyous celebration of that fact, the dancers seem to
lose all roots and limits, and to bob and race freely in harmony with the movement suggested by the lines on the backdrop. There is also the cavern of space
which we occupy as audience. As Alastair Macaulay has observed: 'Above all,
Symphonics is a Vitruvian ballet – an exposition simply of how pure dance to
music, without props or scene changes, can radiate from the area of space
onstage into the larger, taller facing arc of an auditorium.'[83]

The six dancers look both charged and humble in context. As A. V. Coton has written, 'The disparity between these persons and the vast area of their action proposes an imagery of infinities.'[84] Is the world of these dancers a huge sunlit glade, or is it a cosmic arena? The Covent Garden stage has never looked more generous: we might imagine how it seemed to audiences watching their Sadler's Wells Company, after the war, on this stage for the first time, in a statement of such optimism and potential.

The end of the ballet comes as something of a surprise, leaving a sense of breathlessness, reverberations continuing, despite a sudden return to the opening arrangement – or, almost: the centre man is now not with his back to the audience, but reaching diagonally upwards and outwards to downstage right. (Earlier, turned to face the audience directly, this position is what Macaulay describes as the 'long, limpid gesture that aims past and above the women's zone into the theatre's heights'.[85]) There is no real resolution at the end of *Symphonic Variations*, although the final impact is of space suddenly closing in again, of reining in the energy that has spilled out of the dancers. Ashton had problems with the ending and tried many different versions. May remembers one when all the dancers ran from the stage holding hands in their chain motif, and apparently, he also tried another with the dancers lying on the floor.[86] Both these ideas suggest a dissipation rather than preservation of energy. The writer Geraldine Morris considers that the present ending has cyclical connotations, a return to start all over again,[87] like the cycle of the seasons that prompted the ballet in the first place.

Table 4.1 is a schematic layout of the music in relation to the choreography. Rather than detailing their separate structures, it gives sufficient information to highlight their points of connection. There is no firm agreement amongst musicologists about the structure of the Franck score, which does not fit any established concerto pattern. However, most agree with the basic outline given here of three main sections, the middle one of which contains a set of six variations.

An important feature of the choreography is its hierarchical structure, its clear proportions according to the three-section/movement structure of the music, which in turn encompasses its smaller divisions. In other words, we grasp the large proportions as well as the smaller ones defined by changes of cast and dance episodes. The original ABAB structure demonstrates that Ashton had had these large proportions in mind for a long time. And yet the overriding principle of both music and dance is organic, each episode or section leading into the next, a sense of onward momentum counteracting the effect of formal divisions. *Symphonic Variations* is like a flower with a fluent rhythm of opening and closing, expanding and contracting in a crescendo towards the sun. It is significant that Franck does not number his Variations in the score, which is conventionally a clear signpost of separation. In a sense too, the whole piece is about variation

Opening Tableau
Two lines, men close to the backdrop, women closer together, further downstage

1. Prologue *F-sharp minor, Poco allegro*

Music
A gruff fortissimo unison theme for strings (Theme 1) alternating with quieter piano pleading (Theme 2) forms the basis of the Prologue. Later, this duality eases into a rhapsodic passage for piano only, and when the opening pattern of conversation returns at the end of the Prologue, Theme 1 is quietened by the piano. In the centre of this section, there is an anticipatory entry, the opening of Theme 3 (the base of the later Variations).

Dance
Three women move to the piano entries, holding still to the string statements. Similar dance material returns, varied, with the return of the antiphonal opening music. At the entry of Theme 3 (equivalent to the first 8 bars), the centre man (Somes) joins the women. He remains dancing with them.

2. Theme and Six Variations *F-sharp minor, Allegretto quasi andante*

Music	*Dance*
Theme 3	Three men, antiphonally (Somes/Danton
Piano only	and Shaw) or in unison
Variation 1 (Variation of Theme 3)	
Orchestra and piano alternate	Men and women alternate
Variation 2	
Piano: staccato quaver figuration	Two women
Variation 3	
Piano: semiquaver figuration; syncopated	Two women and one man (Danton)
accents on the second beat of the bar	
Variation 4	
A new fortissimo and full orchestration	Solo man (Shaw)
Variation 5	
Piano: triplet figuration	Solo woman (Fonteyn)
Variation 6	
Molto più lento	Pas de deux (Fonteyn, Somes)
Legato, flowing piano figuration	
(F-sharp major), pianissimo	
Interlude	
Piano: arpeggios (Theme 2 in the bass), two	Three couples
'breath' climaxes, the second extending to	
trills leading into the Finale	

3. Finale *F-sharp major, Allegro non troppo*

Music
Sonata form basis:
Exposition (Theme 2: first subject; Theme 3: second subject bass accompaniment)
Episode in 6/8 Un pochettino ritenuto
Recapitulation

Dance
Exposition: organised mainly as central couple (Fonteyn, Somes) /two couples
Episode in 6/8 led by central couple; the others then join them
Recapitulation: three couples in unison forming one group

Table 4.1. Structural layout of *Symphonic Variations*.

Theme 1

Ex. 4.1. Franck, *Symphonic Variations.*

and relationship, not just the central Theme and Variations section: there are close thematic connections across the entire work.

According to Franck's cyclical principles, musical themes relate, or rather become closely related. Perhaps it was the symbolism of the reconciliation of the opening opposing forces (technically speaking the reconciliation of Themes 1 and 2, see Ex. 4.1) that had attracted Ashton to Franck's music in the first place. This question/answer passage of the musical score has often been compared to the slow movement of Beethoven's fourth piano concerto, which has been read

Ill. 4. The Royal Ballet in Ashton's *Symphonic Variations*. (Stephen Beagley, Wendy Ellis, Cynthia Harvey, Jay Jolley and Karen Paisey.)

quite literally in terms of the taming of orchestral forces of disturbance by a persuasive piano. Franck does not take the musical idea nearly as far as Beethoven does: he soon resolves the tension by integrating aspects of Theme 1 into other later material. The opening of Theme 3, the basis of the Variations, bears a relationship to the stepwise rising pattern that started Theme 1. Then, in Variation 4, the dotted rhythm of Theme 1 enters Theme 3. Theme 1, thus integrated, never shows itself again in Prologue form. In the Finale, after the Variations proper have finished, both Themes 2 and 3 put in additional appearances. Theme 2 is the first subject of this sonata form. Theme 3 is the second subject accompaniment in the bass, though the melody above also bears a strong relationship to Theme 3.

Plenty of thematic connections across the choreography make it, too, 'symphonic' in construction, a language of motifs, ideas that can take on new meanings in new contexts. The following are some of the characteristic images of the work. At the opening, the dancers stand contrapposto, with one foot resting on pointe crossed over the other. Soon they add to this a frozen body-shielding *port de bras*, arms in parallel lines pulling in opposite directions, one over the head, one across the chest (see Ill. 4). When this motif returns in the Finale, it takes on a totally different, lighter, dynamic spirit. The central couple first show us an *arabesque* or low *sissonne* lift with one of the women's arms curled around the head of the supporting man. Later, this becomes a motif of bonding for all three couples. Running in a chain round the stage, hands linked, becomes the signa-

Prologue: Opening of Theme 3

Strings (pizz.) and WW.

Ex. 4.2a. Franck, *Symphonic Variations*, Prologue: opening of Theme 3. (Note: bars numbered from beginning of sequence.)

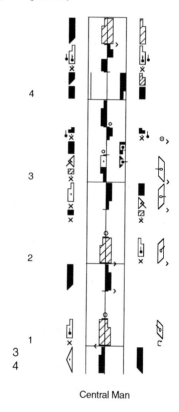

Central Man

Ex. 4.2b. Ashton, *Symphonic Variations*, Prologue.

ture of the Interlude, flowing across the musical phrasing and seen twice; it comes back a third time at the very end of the piece. A couple of images we see just twice. In a Prologue climax, the centre woman arches back from the arms of her partner towards the audience. At a climax during the Finale all three women do this. An image from the men's entry (Theme 3) is of the centre man, the outer pair, or all three in bold *changements* or *entrechats*; that too returns in the Finale.

We are now beginning to look at the more detailed aspects of *Symphonic Vari-*

ations.[88] Macaulay has rightly noticed how Ashton starts the work with 'movements . . . tied closely to the music's phrases'.[89] Later on, he frees up this relationship. In fact, the change seems partly to do with a change in the quality of the music itself. Musical phrases begin clipped and fragmented. Later they flow much more smoothly one into the next. Some visualisation of the music is brought out by a dancer's interpretive choice, but much in this ballet is quite clearly choreographed.

At the beginning of the ballet, the women stand absolutely still during the gruff string Theme 1. Then they dance precisely to the piano phrases. They plead, and plead again: we see the same movement twice, a drawing of the arms around the front of the body, then the frozen, pulled parallel arm position, which appears especially stark because it is timed to the silence immediately after each piano pleading. A third phrase is longer, but the choreography fits just as tightly. The phrasing in both music and dance is upbeat: two falling notes and the beginning of the arm gesture occur before the bar-line. Theme 1 then returns with more urgency. The women hold still. When the same piano pleadings recur slightly varied, in a new key, so does the dance material, but the parallel arm motif is now slightly softened by an accompanying chord. After this, when the piano figuration becomes lively, the women respond to its new continuity with a travelling phrase, their *bourrées* slowing – again, just when the melody slows – into half turns in fourth position on pointe.

The men too introduce themselves with clear visualisation of the music. The central man steps out from the backcloth to use the rhythm and staccato of his melody with surprising precision (the first two four-bar units of Theme 3 – only the first half of the Theme is heard at this point). He makes two steps forwards (upbeat to downbeat again), another two forwards, two back, a *rond de jambe* swing into another two steps (to the short-long rhythm), and a *temps levé*, which happens, unusually, after the last step has been completed, not using the step for impetus to leave the ground (see Exs. 4.2a, 4.2b).[90] This takes him into a run forwards towards the women, now to the piano arpeggiation – and he makes the limpid arm gesture. The effect of stepping so precisely, even studiously, to the short-long rhythm, and popping up on the last note, is to add the lightest touch of ironic humour. Recent revivals have tended to iron out this rhythm: the last step is joined directly and conventionally to the *temps levé*, and something of the oddity and jauntiness of the passage is lost. The dance rhythm of the third and fourth bars now reads:

When all three men enter to the full statement of this Theme (at the beginning of the Theme and Variations section), they follow meticulously its phrase structure and change in speed. Short phrases bounded by rests are introduced antiphonally, the central man against the outer pair, characteristically with a *rond de jambe* or *passé* into *arabesque* directly to the audience, arms separating in breaststroke fashion. The more developed phrases are danced by all three together. Spurts of quavers are treated with more mobility in the choreography. Later in the work, the choreography still draws attention emphatically to the musical structure, but now as part of the developing flow. Accompaniment movement more often than not visualises an under part in the musical texture. During Variation 2 (when two women dance to the staccato quavers of the piano) the other framing dancers walk back and forth, academically treading out the crotchet rhythm of the Theme beneath. It is a version of the simple step-step pattern that introduced the centre man. Cynthia Harvey did it with the image of 'smelling perfume . . . and the hand [held in front of the body] no higher than the heart',[91] but the effect of the treading below is again slightly odd, whimsical perhaps. The dancers remind us that the Theme is still the base of these Variations: it is easy to miss it. Harvey found the next Variation 3 'light, funny': she enjoyed being spectator to it. The two women dart to one side then the other, and one of the men jumps after them in echo, right on the accompanying string pizzicato. The framing dancers articulate the pizzicato too, raising one arm and lowering the other, then reversing for the second accent. Or, in two isolated moments during the *pas de deux*, the framing dancers gesture *développé*, then retract the leg across behind the body or back into contrapposto, picking out pizzicato chords under the rippling piano part. In the Finale, Ashton uses visualisation to build insistently at the onset of recapitulation. The women join in one by one at four-bar intervals, circling their partners in a series of turning *balancés*; they follow the music, which repeats every four bars, modulating and rising in volume. When the men prepare in emphatic *plié* to jump and land to the two pairs of big accents that follow, the women answer by still more circling, now *chaînés*, to the piano figuration.

There is no pattern of big blocks of material repeating, dance to music, either immediately or at a distance, as might be Balanchine's style. None of the choreography comes back, for instance, as recapitulation during the recapitulation in the musical Finale. Clearly here, ongoing development, a sense of continuing evolution is the point that Ashton wishes to stress. One striking idea recurs with its music in the Interlude. The three women start off in *bourrées* and are then supported in two lifts to yearning gestures in the cello line, the pleading Theme 2. They return upstage and repeat the whole sequence. Could it be here, exceptionally, that the repeat makes the point about the sense of time standing still (actually, from very slowed down harmonic motion) in this section of the music? But the continuation is strikingly different the second time round. The first time, the passage is released into the second of the running chains, with the dancers slowly pulling out into *arabesque tendu* on the first 'breath climax' of the music. The second time, with no prompting of musical change, the men immediately set off in gentle allegro with a leaping phrase round to the back of the stage. This turns into rapid crossings of the stage, women and men alternating, the women's *piqués* answering to the men's leaps. There is a feeling of continuous growth from this point onwards into the allegro Finale. The second breath climax in the music is simply absorbed into the crossings.

The most striking 'breaths' occur in the *pas de deux*, with two big arcing lifts, literally the highest moments of the ballet. 'The ballerina should really tear herself in two in those lifts,' Ashton once said.[92] Suddenly, vertical space opens up. The lift sequences end with an unusually powerful stillness in *arabesque*, the ballerina's head thrown back, her projection still extending upwards and beyond. Already, Ashton is thinking of longer continuities; the work has relaxed into occupying more generous spans of time. Within these, now, there are occasions of striking independence between dance and music. The onset of dance allegro in the Interlude, just described, is one example. There are also moments of sudden stillness at the end of the Finale exposition, to ever more intense music, a series of abrupt moves by the three women into frozen positions. Then, at a musical hiatus, they arch back towards the audience to hold again, this time with the music.

We have already seen that moments of almost academic contact with the music can seem slightly subversive. Despite its serious dramas, despite its quieter mystical secrets, an undercurrent of quirkiness is never far from the surface of *Symphonic Variations*. Often, this is the result of some gentle discordance or counterpoint. Spatial and design features of the piece contribute: symmetries against asymmetries or just-off-symmetries. The skirts of the outside women are identical, but longer one side than the other; yet the centre woman's skirt is totally symmetrical. The men's costumes all look the same, but all have one sleeve, one shoulder bared.[93] The opening arrangement on stage shows all three women standing in a unison line, looking down to the left. But behind, in their line, the outer men match symmetrically, and the centre man faces upstage, the only person to do so. When he dances with the three women in the Prologue, there are some remarkable off-kilter configurations: the central woman kneels in greeting to another woman diving towards her from an overhead lift, the third then running to complete the picture, or the same woman kneels and mirrors the arms of the other three dancers packed together tightly in attitude. When the framing of the Variation dancers begins, there is always some kind of oddity of pattern, spatial or gender-based, just the central woman motionless at one corner, or the same woman and three men forming the square, or two women at one corner, and the central woman opposite them. Certainly, the tendency is towards ironing out these asymmetries as the work progresses, but remember that even the final tableau contains its unexpected touch of off-centredness, with the middle man reaching to downstage right. The cleverness of the arrangements lies in the tension between force of pattern and minor subversion of it.

Many of the other small discordances have to do with relationship to music. May recalls how Ashton told the women that they were to dance the piano while the men represented the orchestra.[94] Certainly there is a tendency for this to be the case, enough for us to sense something of a pattern, and particularly in antiphonal passages (as in Variation 1 – strict alternations between orchestra/ men and piano/women). However, there are many times when this is not true at all. Theme 3, the entry for all three men, is set to piano, without any orchestral accompaniment, and later, appropriate to the narrative of the work, material is shared freely enough that any such duality in choreographic orchestration breaks down. On the other hand, Ashton does use the variety of timbre provided by the piano to underline the gender of the dancers. The means are conventional – percussive piano work given to the men, while the women dance to light figuration and the more lyrical passages.

The unison string Theme 1 that opened the work is danced by neither the women nor the men. It is interesting that Ashton leaves this first theme, the gruff, unison, exposed account of it, very much like a dissonant outside 'voice'. No one on stage is ever as dark as this. When it returns towards the end of the Prologue, the Theme catches and adds urgency to the frozen parallel arm gestures of the line of three women, first as one isolated fortissimo blast, the next time pronounced mezzo forte – the women then begin to control it and step out to its quietening voice. We never hear this voice again. The men bring a light which never dims from this point onwards.

Analytically speaking, the men are much more closely associated with Theme 3 than with any particular orchestration, first the centre man, then they all introduce it as the theme of the six Variations. Later, Theme 3 is much more boldly articulated, in other words, as conventionally noisy music for men dancers. When it dominates the texture in Variation 4, there is a male solo. In the Finale, now hidden as accompaniment to the second subject, it is again danced by the men. Morrison has confirmed this point, that the major link between gender scoring and music is thematic.[95] Now, we see too that the women are most closely associated with Theme 2, in the Prologue and recapitulation in the Finale.

Rhythmic asymmetries provide other small discordances in the work. As an example, there is the first Variation, characterised, just like it sounds, by upbeat-phrased *pas de bourrée*. But the timings, as well as other aspects, of these *pas de bourrée* keep on changing. This is clear from all revivals of *Symphonic Variations*, although significantly, with its odd timings, this is a Variation that shifts rhythmically more than most between revivals. The pattern here is for the two women to move more slowly than the three men, who seem to be urging them into action, accelerating them gently towards their fast, slightly dotty duet Variation 2. The men's rhythm tends to be this:

(see Exs. 4.3a, 4.3b).

The women first articulate the following rhythm, in *pas de bourrée piqué*:

Towards the end of the Variation, their pace has become a little faster:

Steps in this variation are often weighted differently in relation to the musical phrase (their place within the four-bar hypermeasure changes). Similarly, in the virtuoso Variation 4 for one man, certain steps are weighted differently in relation to the bar-line on repetition. There is the opening step and *fouetté* to *retiré*. The first time, the *fouetté* is accented by the downbeat; the second time, the preparatory step occurs on the downbeat, the *fouetté* on the second beat of the bar. Later, a *jeté renversé* lands first on count 2, then on count 3. These are steps that refuse to fit neatly into the regular 3/4. Ashton could either have been led by the nature of a step here, or by the desire for this rhythmic asymmetry. But the latter, as we shall see later, is a part of his style.

Perhaps the rhythmically oddest Variation is the one for the two women (Variation 2), apparently modelled on the Sapphic pair in Nijinska's *Les Biches*.[96] Ashton groups flat-footed *assemblés* and *sissonnes*, *pas de bourrée* and little *jetés* into constantly shifting timings. Apparently, these steps are usually counted out simply in sixes or not counted at all, but the following analysis (drawn from a number of video and performance sources) indicates the way in which they are organised:

Phrase 1: Upbeat phrasing	4	4	4	6	6			
Phrase 2: Upbeat phrasing	3	3	5	5	3	3	4	
Phrase 3: Downbeat phrasing	6	6	6	6				
Phrase 4: Downbeat phrasing	4	Upbeat phrasing	6	6	6	6		
Transition:	5							

Ex. 4.3a. Franck, *Symphonic Variations*, Variation 1, bars 1–2 and 16. (Note: bars numbered from beginning of sequence).

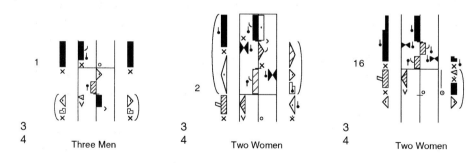

Ex. 4.3b. Ashton, *Symphonic Variations*, Variation 1.

The music can be counted as six quavers in a bar (3/4 time), equivalent to what is valued here as 6 dance counts. The women start and finish Phrases 1 and 2 with the upbeat phrasing of the piano, which sounds like downbeat phrasing here, as if the bar-line has been displaced. The same pattern develops again during the final Phrase 4. In the centre of the Variation, in Phrase 3, they shift to downbeat phrasing, just when the real, written bar-line begins to be felt again more clearly. We recall that the framing dancers step doggedly to the Theme throughout this Variation. They keep the sense of the written bar-line secure even when the two Variation women do not. Ashton responds to the musical ambiguity in this Variation, as well as to the rhythmic shifts that he hears, and, in Phrase 2, he adds yet more complications of his own: in the feet, metrical groupings of 3, 4 and 5 that are never heard in the music (confirmed by twists of the head and seesaw arms alternating up and down, see Exs. 4.4a, 4.4b). There are no two ways about it: this little Variation is a wild experiment in rhythm.

Similar rhythmic counterpoint occurs within the musical texture during the Finale exposition, different lines again out of synchronisation, the piano line weighting the halfway point, and the orchestra, the beginning of each bar. The two side couples are downstage. The women dance to the piano line, around their partners in bright *grands jetés* and *piqués*; the men keep with the orchestra, clearly picking out the separated notes in the accompaniment with *petits jetés*. The result is a puzzle of unpredictable articulations, an accent here, another there, constantly shifting the eye. On discovering how each part relates to the musical texture, the rationale behind the puzzle becomes clear.

I am mentioning these 'curiosities' in Ashton's *Symphonic Variations* not merely for their own sake, but because I believe that they are crucial to the sense of the work. As counter-tones, they enhance and refresh the major statements of symmetry, stability, serious intent and secret mysticism, just as an argument becomes the stronger for other points of view. The exploitation of such curiosities in revivals is important too to the buoyancy and life of *Symphonic Variations*: the clear, but unforced articulation of rhythmic jest, a sense of the musical irony when it occurs, and so on. It is all too easy for *Symphonic Variations* to lose this life in a quest to show it well-behaved. Respecting the special position of this ballet within the repertoire can mean sanctimonious performance.

Other subtleties of phrasing are crucial too. Harvey remembers that there were minor differences of opinion as Somes staged the ballet for American Ballet Theatre in 1992, between Somes, his assistant Wendy Ellis and the notator. But she also remembers the precision of his work, the care for gradation and quality of accent once a decision was made. 'The best ballet master I ever had,' she calls him.[97] In a fragment of film captured in rehearsal, Somes makes a lot of a 'squeezing into the knee . . . squeezing the orange'[98] for certain movements, a slight pressure and delay, as contrast to the following movements which were to

Ex. 4.4a. Franck, *Symphonic Variations*, Variation 2.

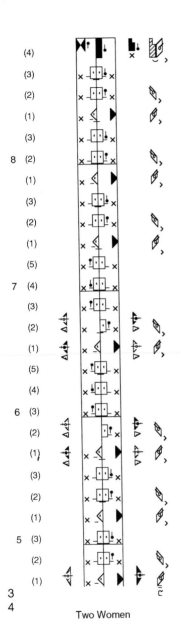

Ex. 4.4b. Ashton, *Symphonic Variations*, Variation 2, Phrase 2.

be performed straight. Some of Ashton's comments, on the other hand, have emphasised the breath and big passion in the work – 'she [the ballerina] should really tear herself in two.'

The musicians' interpretation is another important issue for this ballet. Certain concert interpretations do not work. The critic Cormac Rigby has observed that the music 'can legitimately be played quite brazenly', but that the ballet demands 'the gentler, more persuasive performances'.[99] Morrison shares his view. It was with his interpretation that Ashton worked closely as he made *Symphonic Variations*: '[It should be played] slightly on the slow side . . . [with] some emotional spaciousness . . . Now it's played more slickly and more sort of rattled through.'[100] And perhaps interpretation is one reason why the music critic Philip Hope-Wallace maintained his reservations about the ballet (see pp. 203–4). His view of the Franck score was not Ashton's view. In a letter, he congratulated Ashton on the new *Scènes de ballet*: 'Only about "Symphonic Variations" do I remain impenitent: I do not feel that the true "effect" of the music (pianistic, percussive and exciting on *those* lines) is rendered on the stage. But, seriously, I have never seen a ballet to a concerto which satisfied me.'[101] An understanding of details specific to the ballet is invaluable. Anthony Twiner, a Royal Ballet pianist, remembers a performance by one guest pianist, Valerie Tryon:

> She played it beautifully . . . but Ashton said to me, 'I don't like the way she plays it.' She was just sitting there playing it straight, as she had learnt it, like a concert piece: she didn't know what was going on on stage. But you can't always do that, because there are certain nuances – he wants the music to bend slightly or to relax, which is perfectly legitimate.[102]

*   *   *

Symphonic Variations stands out in Ashton's work as a plotless choreography of symphonic scale, in other words, taking on the challenges of large-scale musical form. Ashton's usual tendency is to let narrative lead him through a symphonic form, or, dictated by music built from a number of short sections or separate pieces, he opts for the same sectional structure in his choreography. *Symphonic Variations* is unusual too in employing visualisation of music as a structural device, a starting point from which dancers are later freed. Elsewhere, Ashton usually introduces this kind of visualisation in isolated moments, for emphasis, perhaps as a way of drawing attention to fast footwork. In the *pas de deux* in *Les Patineurs*, for example, Ashton contrasts the skating motif that smoothly sweeps the couple around the stage with two moments of little pricking steps on the toes, the pair circling tightly together, picking up their feet sharply. The first time, their steps are defined precisely by a passage of staccato in the melody, the second time without such musical support.

Ex. 4.5. Elgar, *Enigma Variations*, No. 6 (Ysobel).

In *Enigma Variations*, Isabel Fitton's motif anticipates the musical complement: across the bar-line, two little stutter jumps with feet together and a third spreading into second position. She tunes into the characteristic rhythm of this musical variation (see Ex. 4.5), but first she dances the motif across a legato moment in the music. Her rhythm only coincides with the music the second and third times round. Here, you can read the anticipation as an indication of character, a display of eagerness in love as she takes her opportunity to display her feelings towards her lover Richard Arnold.

Ashton gives definition to what must be one of his longest dance phrases ever at the start of Air's solo in *Homage to the Queen*. A diagonal of movement unfolds in one span, to be turned around and repeated back upstage. Ashton emphasises fluidity, with *bourrées* and legato swaying from side to side, creamy *épaulement*, his dance impulses starting before and continuing after the beat. Arnold's music is much more phrased within each span, with question and answer, symmetrical divisions and so on. However, at the end of each journey downstage and upstage, there is a meeting of forces and bright punctuation, the ballerina's *arabesque* leg alternating up and down in sharp correspondence to the staccato melodic motion.

As *Symphonic Variations* has already demonstrated, orchestral effects and texture fascinated Ashton. He took ideas from orchestral rehearsals as well as recordings. Even at a late stage, he would make changes to his choreography according to what he heard. Some of his responses are fairly obvious. He hears two harp gestures in the first of the *Gymnopédies* (used in the 'white' *Monotones*) and choreographs flourishes of the arms to them: these are gestures that Debussy added when orchestrating the Satie piano piece and Ashton would not have known about them from the straight piano score. The *Rhapsody pas de deux* offers a moment of quieter, more underground response to orchestration. Just as all seems to be calming down, the dancers quicken pace again, despite the music, or so it at first seems. When the ruminative piano part emerges alone from the orchestral texture, we realise that their steps and small jumps have been tracing the piano line. It is as if the reason for this little 'gust' in the choreography is suddenly revealed. In the *pas de deux A Walk to the Paradise Garden*, the music and dance concept is taken from Delius' opera *A Village Romeo and Juliet*. There is a wonderfully personal passage that stands out as a special 'moment' from the broad brushstrokes around it. We hear intimate and isolated musical voices: to a flute arabesque, the woman descends from a 'dead' lift, hands fluttering, feet quivering, melting soon after into *bourrées* to a more grounded, more 'bodied' solo violin (the scoring is from the Sir Thomas Beecham edition). Even if he did not analyse verbally what he heard, Ashton was acutely aware of instrumental timbre and part-writing. A number of these examples indicate Ashton's delicious unpredictability in suddenly sharpening our focus at a particular moment, through special contact between music and dance. By doing this, he also defines the moment within its larger context: detail reminds us of the whole work.

Ashton also reminds us of the whole work by creating a dynamic contour independent from that of the music. The plotless white *Monotones* is a good example, set to Satie's three *Gymnopédies*, two orchestrated by Debussy, the middle one by Roland Manuel.[103] Ashton's title says a great deal. The music is non-progressive, without any sense of climax, just a few louder, bigger moments, and in these circumstances, a simple harmonic change becomes 'important'. This quality of levelness derives from several features, the modal harmonic structure, the repetitive short-long, crotchet–minim rhythmic framework, and the sense that all three pieces are variations on one melodic idea always working back on itself. In *Music Ho!*, Lambert wrote of Satie's 'peculiarly sculpturesque views of music'. Passing from one *Gymnopédie* to the next is 'as though we were to move slowly round a piece of sculpture',[104] looking at something from many points of view. Possibly, Ashton was aware of Lambert's views on the piece. The dance is literally sculptural and, especially when the woman pivots on pointe, it seems that Ashton is taking our eye round his sculpture too.

However, whereas writers have tended to emphasise the peace, levelness, and celestial calm of the *Monotones* choreography, which is perhaps the lasting impression, occasions of independent dynamic contour (choreography in contrast to music) are important. Ashton frees up the third of these pieces with running passages and a larger, sweeping use of the stage space. If the music negates any sense of progression or climax whatsoever, the choreography gives us a sense of growth and then, made more effective by the contrast, Ashton provides a supremely tranquil ending. There have already been minor gusts during the second of the *Gymnopédies*. After four introductory bars, one of the men runs across the stage, marking the limits of his voyage with *pirouettes*, all free across the musical beat; meanwhile the woman, carried by the other man, subdivides the musical rhythm, two beats against three in the music, with scissor-like movements of the legs. Sharp moments stand out at various points in this *Monotones*: the arm flourish in the first piece to the harp gesture, or, in the last – and this time not suggested in the music – decorations of the plain, short-long, *plié*-stretch motif, extra steps, extra wing-like flaps of the arms up and down, crossing the underlying rhythm.

Why this independent contour here? Perhaps, without it, that sweet 'deadly-dull[ness]'[105] of the music with its ever-repeating short-long rhythmic base might well have turned into unbearable boredom. Whatever his title, the Ashton contribution has shape, dynamic contour, a sense of progression, far more than in Satie's music, and that shape gives a sense of wholeness.

There is a similar independent choreographic contour in Ashton's Sarabande solo for the Prince inserted into the 1968 Royal Ballet *Sleeping Beauty*[106] (see p. 232), and this time it suggests a range of personality and feeling. We are at the point just before the Prince sees Aurora in the Vision Scene. The musical structure is A B A A1, each section four bars long. In the centre of the solo, there is a suggestion of pulling back, checking emotion. Then, the broad, sweeping, galloping step that opens the final section of the solo and which takes the Prince in a big circle round to the back of the stage is restive against musical resistance, pulling away from what you hear – which is, after all, still calm, just a variation of the opening music. The Prince drives towards the musical-choreographic climax, a turn, with arms opening to second position, his eyes making contact with the audience for the first time, at the peak moment in the melody. My reading is that the Prince shows impetuosity, impatience here, after a more thoughtful opening statement; and, crucially, that new impetuosity is enhanced by going against musical implications.

Quite the opposite procedure, Ashton can also underplay musical implications. In the final *pas de deux* of *La Fille mal gardée*, he saves up his power, delays his fireworks to make them seem bigger by contrast when they do arrive. Now the opening music returns, underlining the achievement of happiness in love with fuller orchestration, but Ashton pulls everything back. Colas turns slowly away from Lise and pauses; she quietly moves to him and nestles close. Twice they do this, and only then do the turns and high lift erupt. Once more, the introduction of contrast heightens the effect of emotional peaks and troughs in a dance, clarifies the shape of the whole.

Time and time again, we hear that Ashton admired stillness and simplicity, especially at emotional and musical climaxes. Wagner opera, Kabuki theatre, Alain Resnais' film *L'Année dernière à Marienbad* all provided him with models.[107] The music of *Daphnis and Chloe*, he says, was

> so overwhelming sometimes that I felt that it was like waves that were going to submerge me, and I had great difficulty in keeping my head above it, especially in the last scene, where there's a great surge of music . . .
>
> Often the better the music is, the stronger it is, and the more emotional, the more you can stand still and do nothing . . . And I found at the time in watching Wagner's operas that same quality of standing still – when Tristan turns and sees Isolde and for what seems like half an hour they just stare at each other . . . [108]

Kavanagh describes an effect of tremendous power through simplicity, how 'To one of Ravel's most luscious surges of music, Chloe, gazing into Daphnis's eyes, slowly bourrées towards him through a frieze of corps. She hangs on his neck and he swings her around in slow motion . . . until she is flying around him horizontally.'[109] Perhaps the most striking parallel moment is in *Marguerite and Armand* when, to a fortissimo that marks the arrival of Armand, the first meeting of the lovers and Liszt's pivotal melody, the couple stand at opposite ends of the stage, rooted to the spot, suspended in time – Armand just slowly raises his arms. At the end of *The Two Pigeons*, Ashton stopped the dancing for the final big moment in the music: the Poet simply lifts the Girl through the back of the chair, the Lovers clasp hands, and a second dove flies in.

Ashton reacted similarly to music that had become big or climactic through association, like the Nimrod variation in *Enigma Variations*:

> I was very frightened of the Nimrod . . . That's such a big piece which is played as well as practically going through the incinerator, the Cenotaph and all these grand and solemn occasions. So this piece of music did rather alarm me . . . I did several versions and in the end I eliminated more and more and more and just let the music speak for itself and just created the mood.[110]

   Thus, the Nimrod is strikingly spare and frequently pedestrian, with isolated gestures emerging during the flow of a musical phrase: the contemplative trace of a foot on the floor, a gentle *piqué* in *arabesque*, a greeting between Elgar and Jaeger, a short walk, or perhaps the sketch of a more heated run. There is a good deal of stillness too. The pace quickens slightly with the arrival of Elgar's wife, but the lifts are generally restrained – two are 'dead', without any jump preparation and with her arms held to her sides. Then the big climax at the very end, when all three run directly to the audience on a drum roll, quickly disperses to nothing. They halt at the moment when the musical fortissimo is reached (count 1), the beginning of the climactic musical phrase. Their physical power drops away into quiet resignation, notably *while* the musical phrase continues to unfold and expand. Its volume increases further during count 1, towards an accent on count 2, before diminishing during counts 2 and 3 (see Ex. 4.6).

   At the 1994 Roehampton Institute Ashton conference,[111] a lecture-demonstration included sections from the fine Birmingham Royal Ballet revival of *Enigma*. Here, the trio started the run forward on count 1, but this later timing cancels out the rush of expectancy, the feeling of urgency, racing the music and then cutting out, so effective in earlier films. Elgar's music had not initially appealed to Ashton, but he found extraordinarily poignant, yet quiet, ways of using it in this work.

   Ashton's style of accenting moments with and against music also shapes his choreography. In an interview with Alastair Macaulay, Ashton spoke of rehearsing Fonteyn in the last *pas de deux* in *The Sleeping Beauty*, to bring out its drama, with pauses and sharpness, and positions registered:

With certain pirouettes, I said 'You've been shot in the back!' Bang . . . She runs into pirouettes. I made her hold that, you see. People now just go [*makes vague whirring noise to indicate bland pirouettes.*][112]

The effect of major accent is often to do with exaggerating beyond what is conventional and expected from a particular movement. Cynthia Harvey, also rehearsed by Ashton in *Beauty*, likewise remembers his vision of the Rose Adagio

Ex. 4.6. Elgar, *Enigma Variations*, No. 9 (Nimrod).

as 'a drama' of contrasts, getting her to hold back in *tendu* as long as possible before the *promenade* in *attitude*, 'holding back until you have to rush in.'[113] As Somes once said, Ashton 'will deliberately slow down a movement, if it is essential that it should be followed by a display of speed, in order to heighten the contrast.'[114] These contrasts are not prompted by anything in the music.

Anthony Dowell confirms that Ashton always wanted to avoid levelness: 'suddenly there would be something mad'.[115] We see the device with compelling clarity in the televised *Dream pas de deux* master-class. Dowell tells Karen Paisey and Philip Broomhead (Titania and Oberon) how Ashton insisted on a sharp *rond de jambe* cutting through the very quiet legato opening musical theme.[116] Complete with taut pulling back of her head, Sibley demonstrates the move so that it looks dangerous, an ecstatic swipe across musical implications. The duet is punctuated by spurts of impatience from Oberon. Late on, Titania dances piercingly quick *sissonnes relevés*. All these sharpnesses are in character, indicating wilfulness and power. There might also have been the danger of a sagging lethargy if Ashton had merely underlined the slow tempo and legato flow of the concluding music and not thrown accents across it. Sharpness creates dramatic contrast with melting quality and adagio, and makes the return of these latter qualities the more emphatic.

What is important to us here is that these dynamic differences are often not guided by the music, and are especially effective precisely because of this, although such musical discrepancy is probably one reason why Ashton's accentuation is so easily lost from his style. If the distinction is present, it can operate as a metaphor for personal energy, intelligence and wit; if not, the result can be prim, saccharine or merely indulgent. The early BBC film of *Monotones 1 and 2* (1968) is a revelation. Whether or not it really is speedier than most modern performances, it certainly has far more sharp articulation, and it indicates, as Sibley insists, that the first, 'green' *Monotones* has to show its rhythm (she means pulse drive), in order to contrast with the 'eternity' statement of its second partner piece.[117]

Showing rhythm is important too to the relationship between step sequences and metrical structure, and here as well, Ashton is always upsetting expectations, securing moments of piquancy even when the musical context seems at its most straightforward. Attention turns naturally to the feet and to change of weight for creating rhythmic patterning to musical metre, but with an important caveat: in Ashton's style, on many occasions, the eye is caught and absorbed by the upper body before the feet. Upper body and arms create the big, occasional stresses, the rapid ripples, or smooth swirls as counterpoint to the articulation of feet. The rich rhythms, for instance, of *Five Brahms Waltzes* are really in the torso and arms, not in the legs at all. We might envisage that this is because these dances are after Isadora Duncan, and not in classical style, but upper body choreography is just as integral to classical roles such as Titania in *The Dream* or Natalia in *A Month in the Country*. Indeed, it is significant that by far the most commonly remembered Ashton correction is 'Bend!', referring to the torso.

Ashton choreographs some steps to flow silkily or breathe between the musical beats. *Enigma Variations* provides some especially telling examples. In Lady Elgar's leitmotif – the *pas de chat* and *bourrée* step – the *bourrées*, articulated by shifting the feet in fifth (three shifts – right *devant*, left *devant*, right *devant*), fit between the notes of the music. There is a subtle resonance with the musical triplet, but the dance and music ideas do not happen simultaneously. Dorabella dances down a long diagonal towards Elgar, an irregular series of steps built from *pas de chat* and *ronds de jambe*. Ashton responds to both the melody line and the fragments of figuration above it. The diagonal begins: *rond de jambe, pas de chat, rond de jambe*, two *pas de chat*, *rond de jambe*, two *pas de chat* – but this time Ashton sneaks in the sketch of a third before the next *rond de jambe*, all within the same musical span as before (two beats), and the result is that the series of *pas de chat* is now thrown outside the pulse framework. Such rhythmic devices are expressive, suggesting a kind of anxiety, and in Dorabella's case, that she is a young girl with a stutter. On other occasions, Ashton suggests that his dancers should 'play with the music',[118] when a movement needs to be slowed down in order to register clearly, and then the next movement is quickened as compensation.

Syncopations across the music testify to Ashton's utterly firm handling of pulse. A trio in *Les Rendezvous*, two men and one woman, process with a series of *petits jetés devants*, but against the square eight-quaver count musical structure (two bars of 2/4), they alternate arms up and down as follows:

Phrase 1:	First 8 counts: On counts 1 (R arm up), 3 (L arm up) and 6 (R arm up); then 8 counts of plain *jetés* (arms still)
Phrase 2:	First 8 counts: On counts 3 (L arm up) and 6 (R arm up); then 8 counts of plain *jetés* (arms still)
Phrases 3 and 4:	Repeat as phrase 2

A crossing rhythm is already clearly present in an early silent film fragment of this piece (c.1937),[119] so the device is not an interpolation for a later, more sophisticated version of *Rendezvous*. When Ashton choreographed the 5/4 woman's solo on Georgina Parkinson in *Beauty*'s Act III Florestan *pas de trois*, Ashton suggested that thinking 'Rim-sky-Kor-sa-kov' to herself would secure her rhythmically.[120] The underlying musical accentuation is, after all , long-long-short, on counts 1, 3 and 5. But this does not mean that Ashton choreographs the long-long-short rhythm obsessively; indeed, he introduces one step that shoots a syncopation across it, accenting beats 1, 2 and 5. There are many other occasions when Ashton peppers simple, repetitive dance rhythms with cross-accents, especially enlivening as he often matches the symmetries of immediate musical phrase repetition, dance repeating to music as in so much nineteenth-century choreography. Pieces like *Les Patineurs* and *La Valse* need these syncopations to avoid predictability, and Ashton gives us plenty. There are crossings within the bar or, in more relaxed fashion, within the larger framework of a hypermeasure: a regular accentuation of the downbeat might suddenly be subverted to the weak beat of the bar or hypermeasure, perhaps prompted by a melodic accent, perhaps not. A comparison between Ashton's *Romeo and Juliet* and other productions of Prokofiev's score is especially instructive. Not only the neat pointework and crisp jumps, but also the syncopations, appear to lighten the texture of their music. Never did Prokofiev's music in the ensemble dances seem less ponderous, less square.

Metrical crossing is not at all the characteristic of Ashton's style that it is of Balanchine's, but this is hardly surprising, given his lesser preoccupation with pulse and metre. There is the odd crossing of two counts against three (as in the *Monotones* criss-crossing of the legs mentioned earlier), or vice versa, but only in some pieces, and rarely the delight in the odder dance metre of, for instance, five or seven against the music.

In his *Beauty* Garland Dance, Ashton introduces two against three as anticipation of a similar device in the music, a two-count metre breaking in and interrupting the waltz rhythm from time to time, 'hemiola' style. The music gave him the cue to introduce two hemiola steps, but these cross the music's waltz rhythms on first appearance. On repeat, they achieve rhythmic harmony, resolution with the accompaniment, which now matches the two-beat hemiola effect. The first step, for an inner group of dancers, occurs during the first section of the dance, a simple *posé retiré devant* and *coupé*, 1 2, repeated closing in fifth position, 3 4, and an *entrechat trois derrière* 5 6, allowing the complete step to be immediately repeated on the opposite side of the body (all accents are on the 'up' movements, on pointe or in the air – see Exs. 4.7a, 4.7b). The second step, moving on the diagonal in and out of stage centre, starts step *coupé fouetté*, followed by two runs and then step, *assemblé, changement*, the last three moves particularly accenting 1 2, 3 4, 5 6 (accents now down into the ground – see Exs. 4.8a, 4.8b). This step sequence is repeated at the very end of the Garland Dance (now with a *ballonné* replacing the *fouetté*), the persistent two-beat metre shared now between music and choreography and driving to the brilliant conclusion of this dance. Rhythmic touches such as these break up the flow of simple waltz steps and add an element of waywardness within an easy-going, stable sort of dance.

With sparkling wit, Ashton introduces the same kind of procedure at the beginning of the Scherzo in *The Dream*. Four fairies cross in a rectangular pathway round Puck, and as he bounds and turns to the basic 3/4 time, they travel in 2/4 with little springy beaten steps, small and fleet because of their quicker

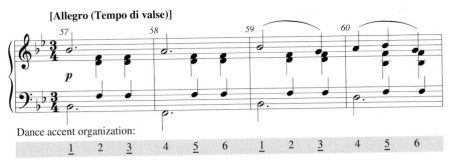

[Allegro (Tempo di valse)]

Dance accent organization:

1 2 3 4 5 6 1 2 3 4 5 6

Steps repeated fitting melodic rhythm:

1 2 3 4 5 6 1 2 3 4 5 6

Ex. 4.7a. Tchaikosvky, *The Sleeping Beauty*, Waltz.

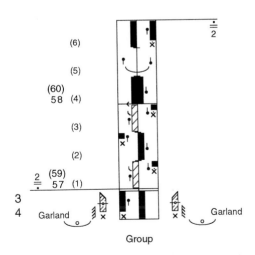

Ex. 4.7b. Ashton, *The Sleeping Beauty*, Waltz (Garland Dance).

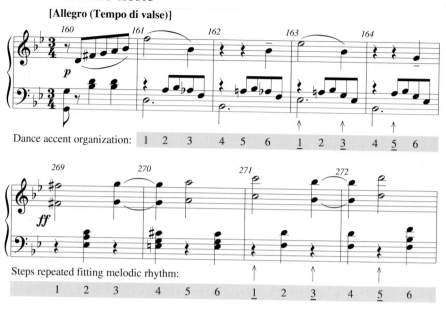

Ex. 4.8a. Tchaikovsky, *The Sleeping Beauty*, Waltz.

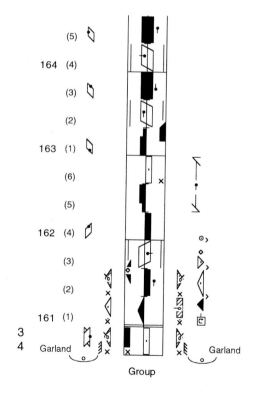

Ex. 4.8b. Ashton, *The Sleeping Beauty*, Waltz (Garland Dance).

rhythm and with, no less, but a different kind of, buoyancy. The landing at the end of a *pas de chat* is the delicious beginning of the next phrase. But Ashton knows a good deal about the fun that already exists in Mendelssohn's music, the melodic riffs in two-beat units crossing the established 3/4 framework, and the syncopations weighting the second beat of the bar. When they next dance together, it is these syncopations that the fairies choose to enjoy, matching them with sharp *relevés*.

As with the *pas de chat* in the fairies' phrase, Ashton shows a particularly acute understanding of the potential of upbeat phrasing. Most dance phrases, to all appearances, begin squarely with the bar-line and the downbeat in the music, except for breath preparations or disguised 'catch steps' that enable a dancer to transfer weight on to the correct leg or to gain momentum for the beginning of the 'real' steps. This is the structure of the majority of *enchaînements* that we learn in ballet class. Ashton's response is a likely result of his hearing first and foremost melody rather than bar-line. Phrases of the upbeat kind often have a gentler, less hard-edged opening than downbeat phrases, and thus contribute to a lyrical style. When, for example, the dance begins to develop in the Nimrod of *Enigma Variations*, the phrases seem to swell/sing spontaneously from the upbeats in the music. In *Symphonic Variations*, we have already seen a number of upbeat examples and how Ashton likes to show us the difference between upbeat and downbeat phrasing (see pp. 215–17). Harvey (who took Fonteyn's role in this ballet) remembers distinctly Somes counting her solo 3 1 2, 3 1 2, and she likens Ashton's upbeat practice to that of Twyla Tharp, unlike Balanchine, really '*using* the first note [the upbeat of the music] . . . a full step, full value . . . not just preparing on the first note'.[121] There are examples of upbeat phrasing throughout the Ashton repertory.

Astute use of upbeat contributes to one of the most tingling moments in *Monotones*. It is the little unison turning *changement* (on pointe/demi-pointe) and then stretch of the legs during the second *Gymnopédie*, a variation on an already very familiar *plié* and stretch of the legs (to the short-long rhythm of the music). This occurs to a shift in the musical harmony, and, in this plain context, a simple harmonic change becomes an 'important' moment. Arlene Croce wrote that the powerful effect of this moment in the ballet 'is out of all proportion to the humility of its means. It's like a shock to the senses.'[122] But the effect has something to do with the humility of dance means juxtaposed with the big moment in the music. It also has to do with rhythm. To a movement idea and a rhythm that we have already seen and heard many times, Ashton has suddenly underscored the first beat of the bar in a way that he has not before – with sharp pointes piercing the floor from the little jump, and an extra upbeat, the *plié* before the jump. A familiar idea is thus refreshed.

The plain rhythms of much of Meyerbeer's music in *Les Patineurs* are likewise nicely refreshed in the Blue Boy's first variation. Macaulay has pointed out that 'he executes his first jump (*hortensia*, an unbeaten jump in which the legs change position two or three times in the air) in silence; and the first brass fanfare begins as he lands.'[123] This is what Harvey means by a 'full step, full value' to the dance upbeat, except this time there is no accompanying musical upbeat, at least when we first see this jump. When the Blue Boy repeats his step sequence, we hear the upbeat with it in the music.

Look too at the beginning of that constantly fascinating *Beauty* Sarabande: the Prince inflects the opening phrase differently by starting it first on the down-beat, *posé fondu* in *arabesque* on count 1 (a), followed by step back on count 2 (b), the second time *posé fondu* on the upbeat count 3, step back on count 1 of the next bar (see Ex. 4.9). Both times, Ashton is guided by the opening of the melodic phrase.

This moment in the Sarabande also demonstrates Ashton's style of rhythmic asymmetry, his fondness for shifting the relationship of his material to the bar-line. Unlike with Balanchine, the effect is not to tease the viewer into questioning whether the bar-line has been displaced, rather it allows the viewer to experience a change in the quality of a step, a different inflection. Sometimes the shifting in the Sarabande involves going through the musical pulse. Bruce Sansom, who was taught this solo by Dowell, notes the number of steps that are repeated, faster, the second time round, and has found emotional logic in this.[124] But the steps also involve pressing on across the musical pulse in order to be in time for the next cue point within the musical phrase. Thus, for a *pas de bourrée* into *fouetté* into *arabesque*, there is a sense of pushing onwards, a restlessness, and, making the repeat a little faster, he can accentuate the harder-to-achieve 'tortured' position in *arabesque*, this time the arm on the same side as the raised leg sweeping forward across the chest (pulling the back against the leg). The first time round, the opposite arm to leg was used. With so little straightforward repetition of dance with music in this solo, the effect is of continuous change, process rather than finished, stabilised statement, a mirror to the Prince's changing feelings.

Ex. 4.9. Tchaikovsky, *The Sleeping Beauty*, Sarabande. a = *posé fondu* in *arabesque* (beginning of step unit). b = step back.

Thwarting expectations, the devices described also draw attention to rhythm. A perfect example of Ashton's interest in varying material by re-rhythmicising it is what is known as 'the Fred step', Ashton's signature step which he tells us was taken from a Gavotte that he saw Pavlova perform. The step, defined by Vaughan, is *posé en arabesque, coupé dessous*, small *développé à la seconde, pas de bourrée, pas de chat*. Ashton's signature step appears in nearly all his pieces and in constantly different guises.[125]

Often, Ashton's movement idea is quite brief and simple. In the first ballerina solo of *Scènes de ballet*, Ashton introduces a motif that stops dead with the musical motif, always in fourth position, sometimes legs straight, sometimes the front one bent, sometimes one arm overhead. When the musical motif returns, a step and hitchkick before the halt creates a dance unit that fits the rhythm of the musical gesture exactly:

Then, suddenly Ashton surprises us by fitting it into less time and ending the step unit with an added *relevé* and pull of the body and arms to one side, and the rhythm is:

Soon, he is back to fitting the musical rhythm again. Thus, Ashton wittily enlivens a rather marionettish dance idea.

During his first variation in *Les Patineurs*, the Blue Boy travels upstage on the diagonal in a turning, jumping sequence performed three times. It hints at a symmetry within itself, showing two landings in second *arabesque* on the first beat of bars 2 and 4 respectively. But their effect is subtly different. The first time, the shape is quickly diverted into *relevé* with the *arabesque* leg brought out *devant*, a syncopation weighting the second beat of the bar; the second time the *arabesque* is given greater weight, the effect of two whole beats before the transition turn into the repeating sequence. The sequence creates the following rhythm, which is not suggested by the music:

The sequence is also interesting in demonstrating the different qualities of emphasis upwards in *relevé* (in bar 2) and downwards in *plié* (in bar 4), the point made more firmly by its inbuilt symmetry (see Exs. 4.10a, 4.10b).

The shifting of the musical accent from up on pointe or in the air to down in

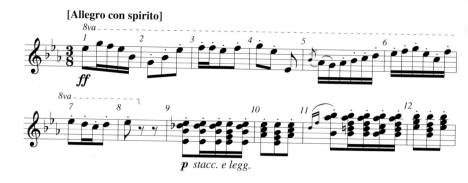

Ex. 4.10a. Meyerbeer, *Les Patineurs*, Blue Boy Variation. (Note: bars numbered from beginning of sequence.)

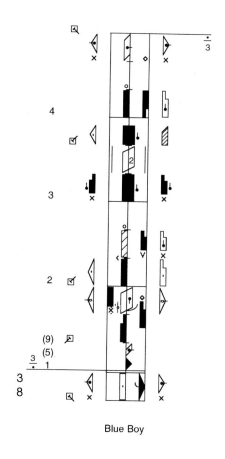

Blue Boy

Ex. 4.10b. Ashton, *Les Patineurs*, Blue Boy Variation (diagonal sequence).

plié, or vice versa, is another characteristic of Ashton's style (we saw it in his Garland Dance). It often produces a sense of surprise. In Lise's Fanny Elssler solo from *La Fille mal gardée*, she pulls from *plié* to *relevé* in fifth on the musical accent, the downbeat, in a short-*long* rhythm (Lesley Collier does this four times, Nadia Nerina three times[126]). Next, she jumps down into *plié* on the musical accent to pull up to fifth immediately afterwards, in a *short*-long rhythm. Nerina emphasises the distinction of the *plié*, adding pressure and slightly lengthening it. Again, because there is a clear relationship between the dance ideas, the rhythmic change, the change in quality of the dance accent, is emphasised.

In the opening section of *Beauty*'s Florestan Pas de Trois, the impetus is at first downwards: small *cabriole* preparation to *chassé* (down) *pas de bourrée*, luscious *pliés* concluding *grands jetés en tournant*, *assemblés* and *sissonnes*, and then, like a quiet trace of the opening step, *chassé pas de bourrée*, to one side and then to the other, a real diminuendo effect in dance terms. Now, to the repeat of the musical theme, we see the accent as up, with the unfolding of the leg high to second position and a spring up to *relevé*. That shift comes as a shock, and even more so because of the economy through which it has been achieved. Some dancers recognise this point and demonstrate it by sustaining the moment of lift ever so slightly. On the other hand, if they do not recognise it and bring it out, we are not likely to recognise it either.

Far more often than most choreographers, Ashton scores jumps with the accent at the apex of the leap. Denby noticed this years ago as a feature of the Jester's role in *Cinderella*,[127] and it is also a characteristic of Puck's dancing in *The Dream*. The effect of hovering can be miraculous. Rehearsing Puck's solo in the Scherzo, ballet-master Christopher Carr pointed out: 'He [the accompanist] catches you [the dancer] up in the air.'[128] More recently, Baryshnikov was given a number of spectacular jumps of this kind in *Rhapsody*. Faith Worth notes that this kind of emphasis easily disappears, as dancers find it out of the ordinary to perform. It is not how we tend to jump in ballet class. Whereas the fairies surrounding Puck at the end of the Scherzo were also taught originally to emphasise their jumps in this way, in keeping with Puck's earlier style and suggesting the airy, non-mortal quality that they share with him, she remembers that they were already dancing down on the musical accent by the time of the premiere.[129] *Les Rendezvous* is interesting in making a feature of different timings for the *grands jetés* at the opening, with the accent up, at the top of the leap, coinciding with the musical downbeat, or down, with the musical downbeat, in this case, the step and jump lasting either one or two bars (see Exs. 4.11a, 4.11b). The effect varies: light and soaring or boldly deliberate entries followed by fleet departures. The Labanotation here has been taken from a Sadler's Wells Royal Ballet performance (1979). The same timings are evident in a 1962 Royal Ballet television performance. Faith Worth's Benesh score (1964) shows different

Ex. 4.11a. Auber, *Les Rendezvous*, opening. (Note: bars numbered from beginning of sequence.)

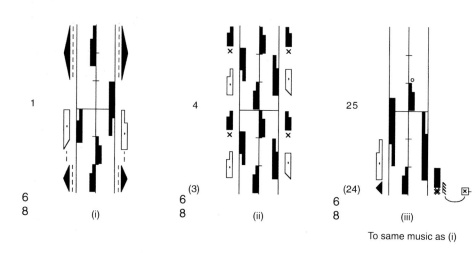

Ex. 4.11b. Ashton, *Les Rendezvous*, opening (*grand jeté* sequences).

timings for examples (i) and (ii); something of the variety of effect is lost, although, as in the television performances, the timings of the three *grand jeté* sequences are all different.[130]

Again, the early film of *Les Rendezvous* shows that Ashton already had the device of shifting rhythms clearly worked out by the 1930s. Indeed, all the above examples, from different periods of Ashton's career, testify to a total rhythmic security, and a high degree of sophistication in rhythmic and musical matters, however awkward he might have once appeared in Rambert's studio. Interesting it is too that, when asked to choreograph two training Solo Seal variations for the Royal Academy of Dancing, he packed them with rhythmic and dynamic subtleties and constantly changing responses to the music. These aspects, not just the movement difficulties, he saw as a crucial aspect of training.

Yet there are circumstances when Ashton's musical technique is plain, and to good effect. Often, when he has fun with character outside the classical style, his approach is to simplify, to incorporate mimicry, sometimes exaggeratedly, and to adhere firmly to musical phrasing. Of course, this has much to do with selection of music (or its arrangement) with appropriate qualities in the first place.

Lanchbery scored Alain's first solo in *Fille* for tuba, to achieve a grotesque effect. In *The Dream*, Bottom has a heavily accented 'hee-haw' motif in his melody line. Sometimes these characters dance their already heavy-footed music in very plain, 'Mickey-Mouse' style; on the occasions when they do not, they come across as muddled or incompetent, as if keeping with the music is just too hard for them. In *A Wedding Bouquet*, to show that they are types, Ashton has his characters move obsessively to Berners' accents and phrases, which are sometimes regular, sometimes pulled out of symmetry. The people at this party seem stuck in a groove (the regular phrasing). When they fall out of it, they appear suddenly dotty. The interpretation is a question of context: asymmetries elsewhere can look like flights of the imagination or clever surprises. *Enigma Variations* visualises music more closely and regularly than is usual in Ashton. Sometimes, it seems that the dancers identify closely with the distinctive character of their own musical variation, as if the music is speaking them. At other times, the effect is a sympathetic hint of eccentricity or humour, or an expression of the honest solidity of friends who know each other well enough to be straightforward and plain speaking.

We come now to *Scènes de ballet*, which Ashton singled out as his favourite piece, and which stands out from his others in terms of its musicality. It is companion to *Symphonic Variations* (created just two years earlier) in its plotlessness and symphonic construction, but it makes many different musical points. The choice of acerbic Stravinsky is unusual for a start, although this particular Stravinsky is a distinctly Ashtonian kind of choice. 'Featherweight and sugared' Stravinsky once characterised it,[131] the piece commissioned by the American impresario Billy Rose as a divertissement in a 1944 revue called 'The Seven Lively Arts'. Markova and Dolin starred in this divertissement; Dolin choreographed it. The music has often been evaluated as dubious Stravinsky, and rather vulgar, but Lawrence Morton saw it as a gently satirical commentary on Billy Rose's show. He describes the Pas de Deux:

> There is a trumpet tune of almost incredible sentimentality . . . Remove from it the marks of genius, make it four-square, give it a Cole Porter lyric, and you have a genuine pop-tune. As it stands, however, it is a solemnisation of Broadway, a halo for a chorus-girl, a portrait of Mr. Rose as Diaghilev.[132]

True, there is a sentimental, 'sugary', even nostalgic tinge to the music. Stravinsky himself called it 'a period piece, a portrait of Broadway in the last years of the War'.[133] All this suits Ashton, but it is also distanced, ironised, which suits another side of him.

Stravinsky's many rhythmic sophistications had attracted Ashton, who, Somes believes, learnt a good deal about music from dealing with the technical

complexities of the score.[134] It is likely that he would have had help from a musician. In the 1948 essay featuring *Scènes* as an example of the creation of a ballet,
Ashton mentions the use of counts in preparation and rehearsal, a rare procedure for him, according to the memories of most of his dancers and colleagues. He also explains that he wanted to match the pattern-making in the
music: 'In this ballet I set out to merge the rhythmic subtleties with the visual
counterpoint, and I wished my choreography to grow out of the music as a
flower grows out of the soil.'[135] Ashton devised his spatial patterns inspired by
the theorems of Euclid.

The following are examples of Ashton's response to the complexities of this
score. After the spare prologue for the five men, there is an ensemble dance, in
brisk 5/8 time, but with a 3/4 repeating horn motif striding over it on two occasions (see Ex. 4.12). A group of women [8], then a line of men [14], enter with
big jumps to this new slow pulse. Ashton analyses the different parts of the
texture in the final allegro ensemble before the apotheosis. Here, Stravinsky
writes the score in 3/8, but a 4/8 bass ostinato running throughout emerges
more and more strongly from the texture as the dance progresses (see Ex. 4.13).
The dancers all start out in 3/8 time, but the three intermingled groups, women,
men and solo couple, create three different rhythmic strands, each with accents
popping out of the texture at different times. Later, some of the dancers begin to
respond to the 4/8 ostinato, but there are still flashes of 3/8 material. Four men
jump up in a line across the back to mark this against everyone else (one jump
every two bars of 3/8). Straight afterwards, a point is reached when the listener
is now more likely to hear 4/8 rather than 3/8, whatever the score says: we hear
the 4/8 ostinato marked out staccato on the piano, but the men perform a
sissonne sequence towards us in 3/8 (the metre written in the score). Here, Ashton behaves just like the Balanchine of *Movements for Piano and Orchestra*, who
sometimes brought out what he read in the score rather than what is most easily
heard (see Ch. 3, p. 146). A number of analytical procedures in *Scènes* bring
Balanchine directly to mind, although perhaps Ashton's style is to focus rather
more than Balanchine on the melodic aspects of Stravinsky. Some of these textural interrogations are foreshadowed in *Symphonic Variations* (see p. 212).

The two ballerina solos in *Scènes* are marvellous, contrasting examples of
Ashton's response to musical form and detail. The first treats the music broadly
and like a crescendo. It features different versions of the 'marionette' motif that
stops dead with the music in fourth position (see p. 233). In a final, crazy variant
with the ballerina almost falling over her feet in excitement, she is no longer in
time with the clipped musical motif. The solo ends with her being escorted by two
men down the diagonal and exploding into a very high lift. There are restless
rhythmic asymmetries in the dance phrases throughout the solo.

The ballerina of the second solo has been described by Antoinette Sibley as 'a

Ex. 4.12. Stravinsky, *Scènes de ballet*, first Danses (corps de ballet).

Ex. 4.13. Stravinsky, *Scènes de ballet*, second Danses (corps de ballet).

black pearl'. There is something dark and manipulative about the solo: she is seductive, and Sibley's image for one passage is of her 'conjuring up spirits'.[136] But one of the most intriguing features of the solo is its play with Stravinsky's musical structure and the implications of this play. The music is in a tight ABA form, with a six-counts-in-a-bar (3/4 in the music) ostinato or repeating rhythm, and legato melody lines that wind freely and lazily around the established metre (see Ex. 4.14). This is the kind of music, like much neo-classical Stravinsky, that makes a pretence about its own mobility or destiny: it does not really go anywhere.

The dancer's style is sinuous too, with big free *port de bras* and play in the hips, whilst she keeps to the large phrase outline of the music and taps out the ostinato with her pointe at both beginning and end of the solo. However, she makes much more than the music of the tension between stability and instability. There are precarious balances along the way, but particularly important is her approach to the music, operating as an independent voice that constantly connects and reconnects with different aspects of the musical texture, sometimes selecting the ostinato rhythm, or just the underlying metre but not specifically the rhythm, sometimes the sweep or the detail of the melody. At one point, a luscious *port de bras* and backbend identify with the sensuality of two solo cellos. Bear in mind that melody and musical metre create very different groupings here (the 1 of 1–6 counts is not necessarily the 1 that is heard in the melody). It is the kind of restless musical analysis by the dancer that entangles your ear.

In the last section A, she does not repeat with the music. She drives on against musical implications, she takes her freedom and swims across the musical metre

Ex. 4.14. Stravinsky, *Scènes de ballet*, Variation (ballerina).

(six counts in a bar) in a fast waltz (three-count units across the back) and several series of little hops in *arabesque* (five-count units, the first beginning with the
long melodic upbeat of the cellos). Here, then, is an example of metrical incongruence, dance against music. I have seen different versions of these last phrases
performed with different crossing metres, but none of these are simply twos
against threes, which is Ashton's usual practice. Then, at the very end, after the
toe-tapping motif which implies closure, the ballerina extends a hand lightly to
her partner, turns away to print a quiet fourth position on pointe, but, as if her
ambiguity is totally planned and not a matter of partner power, she pulls away
with one arm extended diagonally upwards. The solo ends 'open', just a little,
tantalisingly so. The music too has an open edge.

I refer to meaning, and in respect of this, a most fascinating point for subverting musical implications is the centre of the solo, where two upward moving
intervals in a clarinet line are singled out by the choreographer as gestures for
special attention (see Ex. 4.15). It is important to remember the centuries-old
semiotic significance of moving upwards in pitch, meaning idealism, aspirations
heavenwards, overcoming earthliness, or literally just going upwards. At points
of major emphasis at least, choreographers over the years have tended to visualise this upward movement. But not the ballerina here. She cancels it out. On both
occasions, at [99] and [100], a *développé* to the side is emphatically folded down

Ex. 4.15. Stravinsky, *Scènes de ballet*, Variation (ballerina).

across behind the body into *tendu*. The second occasion needles with particular irony, with its wider interval in the music (breaking in before the bar-line) and checked tempo around this point. The imaginative interactions with Stravinsky in both these ballerina solos resonate with meaning. Nevertheless, *Scènes* remains overwhelmingly abstract as Ashton ballets go. His main course of development was narrative, increasingly so in his late career when his collaboration with Lanchbery became especially important.

Characterisation through music, the evolution of story and unfolding of emotional content, were uppermost in their minds as Ashton and Lanchbery worked on 'welded' scores. The *Fille* score was their first project, and it entailed their working together very closely and virtually writing the score anew. They used Hérold's 1828 ballet as a foundation, much arranged, reharmonised, its rhythms changed and numbers reordered. Lanchbery included interpolations from the original anonymous score used by Dauberval in the eighteenth century, and one tune from the 1864 Hertel score (for Widow Simone's Clog Dance), but he also composed whole sections of the score himself in the style of the period. The creation of this score has been meticulously recorded elsewhere.[137] It is enough to say here that it incorporates nineteenth-century devices. There are *airs parlants*, speaking tunes borrowed from other, opera sources that resonate with the story content in some way: like the opening number, which borrows from Martini's *Le Droit du seigneur*, the storm scene from Rossini's *La Cenerentola* (both in the Hérold score), and airs from Donizetti's *L'Elisir d'amore* which are used for the Elssler *pas de deux* (so-called because the music was interpolated for Fanny Elssler in 1837).[138] Lanchbery also established themes to recur as reminiscences for various characters and situations: such as Colas, Simone, love, and daughter-scolding.

The other major Ashton/Lanchbery collaborations were *The Two Pigeons*, *The Dream*, the film *The Tales of Beatrix Potter* and *A Month in the Country*. *Pigeons* was not such a close collaboration as *Fille* because Lanchbery was abroad during most of the preliminary creative process. The score uses the Messager ballet music *Les Deux Pigeons*, although Lanchbery took the liberty of incorporating a number from the composer's opera *Véronique* and added some bars of his own to improve the effect of the ending. *Beatrix Potter*, which was based on Victorian and Edwardian salon and theatre music, was unusual in that Ashton choreographed to the pre-recorded orchestral score.

In respect of Ashton, we should not forget Lanchbery's treatment of a number of nineteenth-century ballet scores, including *Swan Lake* and *The Sleeping Beauty*. For instance, he interpolated the Sarabande from Act III into Act II of Peter Wright's 1968 production of *Beauty*. It is now Ashton's solo for the Prince, a quiet, simple, ruminative little piece that was once intended for a much more extrovert group dance (see pp. 223, 232). The original piece is longer and moves into areas of rich orchestration, with contrasting material, canons, wild modulations and a forte chordal blast at the end. Lanchbery radically altered the music, transposed it from A minor to F minor, and repositioned it in the score to suit Ashton's needs.

In their welding collaborations, Lanchbery has likened his position, as it developed, to that of a 'tailor making a suit. I knew what he wanted, and he trusted me.'[139] Lanchbery often attended ballet rehearsals with Ashton, and they never hesitated to interfere in each other's territory if the fancy took them. At their numerous meetings on the structure of the *Fille* score, for instance, Ashton would make musical suggestions like 'Cut out the repeat of the second melody and give it instead an exciting sort of coda – rum-te-tum-TUM-that sort of thing . . . Can't the love theme come back there for a few bars?'[140]

It was Ashton who suggested the pauses that characterise Lise's Elssler *pas de deux* solo, pauses at the ends of phrases during which she balances on pointe. He had heard some Spohr on the radio[141] and told Lanchbery, 'It was awful, but there was a wonderful thing about it, the stopping and starting . . .'[142] He decided to introduce this device into the *Fille* solo.

The Dream involved reshaping large, symphonic forms to suit the dance narrative. Ashton had suggested to Lanchbery that he should feel free to select from beyond Mendelssohn's incidental music, like the *Songs without Words*, but Lanchbery feared that such impurities might be criticised, and he kept firmly to the composer's intended music, save one transition of a few bars which he composed himself. He also reorchestrated certain sections of the score. Virtually all Mendelssohn's incidental music makes an appearance at some point. Lanchbery is especially proud of his achievement. Some numbers he retained from the original more or less intact; the rest is a remarkable jigsaw with much reordering of Mendelssohn's sections, and bold cuts. In his programme note, Noël Goodwin has summarised aspects of the score:

the Fairies' march (no. 2a in the suite) for the entry of Oberon and Titania; the Song with Chorus, 'You spotted snakes' (no. 3); the A minor Intermezzo (no. 5); the Scherzo (no. 1) for Puck's undoing of the mischief; part of the Wedding March (no. 9), for the reconciliation of the lovers and of Oberon and Titania; the Nocturne (no. 7) for the Oberon-Titania pas de deux; and the Finale with Chorus (no. 12) . . . some of the Rustics' Bergomask Dance (no. 11) for Bottom's variation sur les pointes, and Titania dances with Bottom to the Funeral March for Pyramus and Thisbe (no. 10).[143]

Lanchbery (and Ashton always as close colleague) decided to use the Overture to bind the parts of the work together. He begins by going through it with mammoth cuts along the way, ignoring its sonata form, and then, after the curtain is up, goes back to it again. Mendelssohn himself quotes from the Overture in his own incidental music – for instance, Bottom's 'hee-haw' gesture is introduced in both the Overture and the Rustics' Bergomask Dance – but Lanchbery takes the principle much further. Parts of the Overture are interpolated throughout the ballet score, whether to introduce characters, or to underscore The Fog episode. Lanchbery employs the Overture music thematically, saving certain sections so that they can be associated with fairies, happy mortal lovers, quarrelling mortal lovers, Bottom and so on. Immediately, Overture music brings on the Fairies, in the first dance number. Then, signalled by Mendelssohn himself, who recapitulates ideas from the Overture underneath the Finale song 'Tro' this house give glim'ring light', Lanchbery brings back far more music from the Overture as a way of saying good-bye to all the characters. It is a nice touch that the theme for the happy mortal lovers is introduced for Titania and Oberon at the end of the ballet. At one point, when Titania awakens from her dream, Lanchbery uses a section from the Overture but turns it from minor to major key.

Although Lanchbery was especially pleased with this score, it is interesting that Irving, by this time musical director of New York City Ballet, has nothing but criticism for it. He speaks sniffily as if he had seen the patched score for himself:

> It's all put together like a film travelogue . . . it's dreadful. I'm very sorry I've never seen anyone disparage it in a notice which surprises me. Those are set pieces of great renown and quality and . . . to cut them up in little strips and tab them all over the place and join them onto one another and play them at what's more, a miserable tempi, was not at all to my taste. [At the New York City Ballet], we play pieces. We don't mutilate them.[144]

In fact, the music critic of *The Times* had referred to 'some unfortunate surgical amputation of Mendelssohn's incidental music'.[145] Irving was generally critical of what he called this 'snip-snip'[146] approach to scores. Contrast Ashton's view when a rehearsal pianist complained about the treatment of the music: 'Don't be such a purist!'[147]

In fact, Balanchine's own score for *A Midsummer Night's Dream* is just as much a concoction, even if of another kind, totally unrelated pieces stuck together, introducing the very impurities that Lanchbery sought to avoid. If we can be less purist about manipulating existing music, we might appreciate that the Lanchbery score suits the evolution of narrative excellently. There is a rapid initial sequence of events, followed by a slowing to highlight the Oberon-Titania *pas de deux*, and then a happy recapitulation of characters and themes to round things off peacefully.

The Dream is precursor in its 'welding' approach to *A Month in the Country*.

A Month in the Country

In *A Month in the Country*, the 'welding' approach resulted in an integrated musical-choreographic text carrying immensely rich resonance between what is seen and what is heard. The ballet score has been praised by most dance critics, indeed, as 'perfect' by Arlene Croce.[148]

A Month in the Country was 'freely adapted from Turgenev's play'.[149] The original programme note for Ashton's ballet is as follows:

> The action takes place at Yslaev's country house in 1850. Beliaev, a young student, engaged as a tutor for Kolia [Yslaev's son], disrupts the emotional stability of the household. Finally, Rakitin, Natalia's admirer [Natalia is Yslaev's wife], insists that he and the tutor must both leave in order to restore a semblance of calm to Yslaev's family life.

The plot of the play is reduced and simplified for the ballet. Ashton concentrates on the central situation, eliminating complexities that cannot be translated into dance and those characters who are considered to be extraneous to this situation.

The ballet opens with a tableau and variations for each member of the family. Beliaev enters for a fifth variation and then joins in a lively dance with Natalia, Vera (Natalia's ward) and Kolia. Beliaev has, we understand, already profoundly affected the two women of the household and, during Natalia's first *pas de deux* with Rakitin, she tells him of her love for the tutor. Vera expresses romantic feelings of love to Beliaev in the *pas de deux* that follows. Discovered by Natalia embracing Beliaev, Vera is admonished for her behaviour but Vera refuses to accept that her love is impossible. After a brief flirtation between Beliaev and the maid Katya, Natalia comes across Beliaev alone, puts a rose into his buttonhole and dances with him, a *pas de deux* of mutual love. They are discovered by Vera in an embrace and from this point the ballet draws to a swift conclusion as she tells the rest of the household what has happened and Beliaev's departure becomes inevitable. He steals back for a final farewell (a scene that does not occur in the Turgenev), but, although he finds Natalia alone, decides to leave without her seeing him, dropping near her feet the rose that she gave him. Natalia sees the rose after he has gone, and the curtain falls.

Ashton had great difficulty in arriving at a musical choice – here, the subject attracted him first, before the music – and considered various composers including Tchaikovsky, Glinka, Borodin, Balakirev and Cui. Ashton has explained that

> the Borodin quartet was too short; it would have meant too much decapitation of the play. We considered using Tchaikovsky's pieces written for each

month of the year [*The Seasons*, for piano, 1876] – Pavlova used 'December' for her 'Christmas' ballet – but that would have been too episodic, too bitty.[150]

Sir Isaiah Berlin finally suggested Chopin, at first to Ashton's dismay, even though he loved the composer's music: Chopin had recently been represented three times within Jerome Robbins' work in the Royal Ballet repertory, as well as, of course, in *Les Sylphides*.

The final musical selection is as follows:

Variations in B-flat major on a theme from Mozart's *Don Giovanni* ('Là ci darem la mano') for piano and orchestra, Op. 2 (1827).

Grand Fantasy in A major on Polish Airs for piano and orchestra, Op. 13 (1828).

Grand Polonaise in E-flat major for piano and orchestra (1830–31) preceded by Andante Spianato in G major for piano solo (1834) (published together as Op. 22).

The recording by Claudio Arrau of all three pieces confirmed the right order for the ballet, which also happens to be the chronological order of their composition.[151] With his friend Martyn Thomas, Ashton worked out a first draft of events in relation to music, making cuts so that the ballet was seven minutes shorter than its final version, but including two Chopin piano Preludes 3 and 17. The latter, which were later dropped from *Month*, had already been used twice before by Ashton in his early career. When Lanchbery arrived from Australia for a week's working with Ashton, he immediately noticed a resemblance to *Enigma Variations* in the first part of the ballet, a variation structure introducing the different characters which they preserved.[152] It is interesting then that Ashton had had *Month* in mind as a future collaboration with the designer Julia Trevelyan Oman when working with her on *Enigma Variations*. Lanchbery says that he found the new project 'very much handed to me on a plate' with the early Variations worked out in the most detail. There has been discussion since as to how much credit should go to Lanchbery for the 'welding' and how much to Thomas, who was acknowledged in the original programme for helping 'to construct the action of the ballet to accord with the music'.[153] Lanchbery was responsible for at least one of the musical recapitulations towards the end of the ballet. Give Thomas his due: later analysis demonstrates many subtle technicalities in the score organisation that could only be the work of a trained musician. Lanchbery remembers sorting out the final details of the piano score and carrying out the orchestration when back in Australia.

Earlier, I mentioned the power of resonance in this ballet between what is seen and what is heard. Whether all this resonance, all this multi-layered interaction,

Ex. 4.16. Chopin, Variations in B-flat major on a theme from Mozart's *Don Giovanni*, 'Là ci darem la mano', theme statement, opening (A).

was ever intended by Ashton, Lanchbery and others is unlikely. Ashton spoke very little about what he made and the process of making it. Yet, it is one of the most distinctive features of *Month*, combined with celebration of the duality between external appearance and internal feeling.

Perhaps it was simply fortuitous that the Arrau recording of the three Chopin pieces that Ashton used determined the right order for the ballet. Possibly fortuitous too is that one of the pieces is a set of variations on the 'Là ci darem la mano' melody from Mozart's *Don Giovanni*: 'Give me your hand' – the Don's song of seduction to Zerlina (see Ex. 4.16). Chopin adds an anacrusis, or upbeat, to the Mozart. The melody operates like an *air parlant*. Apart from Ashton's delight in having his 'two favourite composers' brought together, there is a certain irony here as we are asked to compare two characters who share the capacity for devastating impact on the women whom they encounter. But Ashton, we know, enjoyed connections between the different facets of a work. Kavanagh has pointed out the affinity Ashton discovered between himself and Turgenev in their philosophy of love, tendency to work outside current fashion and obsession with femininity; she notes the number of action details borrowed from Turgenev's novel *First Love*.[154] Ashton could also enjoy the evidence that Turgenev was friendly with Chopin and George Sand, whom Beliaev mentions admiringly in the play; the setting of the dance in 1850, when the play was written and only shortly after they were likely to have met; that the Russian upper classes looked west for cultural inspiration, commonly speaking French amongst themselves; and that Turgenev and Chopin both lived and probably met in Paris. Ashton also liked to think that the *Month* household could have been near the Polish border – nearer, in other words, to Chopin's homeland.[155] Vera, Natalia's ward, plays Chopin offstage according to a number of stage directions in Emlyn Williams' translation of the play that Ashton used (a copy is in the Ashton library at the Royal Ballet School), though not in the translation by Isaiah Berlin. Nor are these directions in the original Turgenev. Oman recalls that it was her idea to have the piano on stage, for Vera to play at the beginning.[156]

Prompted by this kind of information, some of which has, after all, been supplied to us through programme notes, I am intrigued by the ballet's connections with Mozart's *Don Giovanni*. Scenes from the opera decorate the walls of the set – another connection – as in the fashion of certain genre pictures and engravings of the mid-nineteenth century. That again was Oman's idea, but it encourages us to see connections between the Don and Beliaev. It is as if the Don's voice inhabits the work. After all, he has been variously interpreted as quarry or victim as much as pursuer, liberator of women and idealist rather than straightforward vile seducer. Croce compares Beliaev interestingly to the Kierkegaard figure of an unconscious Don, object of love rather than lover.[157] In his 1843 essay 'The Immediate, Stages of The Erotic or The Musical Erotic', Kierkegaard considers the abstraction of sensuality rather than the Don himself as the true seducer, epitomised, it happens, for him, in the musical Don Giovanni, not a speaking individual, but a voice, 'the voice of sensuousness, and we hear it through the longing of womanhood'.[158] In this respect, it is interesting that there are two possibilities for the ballerina at the very end of the ballet when Beliaev returns and drops near her the rose that she gave him. She can either glance at it and rush after him, trying to catch him, and then return to the rose, or – and this confirms the point about Beliaev as abstraction – she can stand pondering over the rose, in love with the idea of love rather than the person, and then run after Beliaev.[159] In performance, dancers probably choose from these options on the spur of the moment, and for practical reasons, such as whether or not there is enough music left to ponder before running. Nevertheless, according to their decision, the text can be read in subtly different ways, giving power to Beliaev as person or as abstraction of love. I return to this point later in the analysis.

The erotic force of Beliaev is focal within *Month*, and it is interesting – though again, I am not trying to argue unduly from the point of view of Ashton's intentions – that Ashton once toyed with the idea of calling his ballet *The Student*, after Turgenev's original title for *Month*.[160] Ashton, who created a *Don Juan* ballet in 1948 (using Richard Strauss' symphonic poem), was aware of at least one less conventional, more open, nineteenth-century, post-E.T.A. Hoffmann reading of this character. In a letter to the critic Edwin Evans, he begged for more information about the epic poem by Lenau upon which the Strauss is based, a poem which presents the Don as disillusioned idealist, the victim of his desire.[161] The use of the 'Là ci darem la mano' theme can therefore promote a fascinating range of imagery with which to enrich our view of the ballet.

Ashton tells us that the Mozart theme also suggested the operatic recitative/aria structure of the ballet to him.[162] At any rate, Ashton, Thomas and Lanchbery used their opportunities, reshaping and repointing the score to enhance the action.

Ashton was sensible in choosing little-known pieces by Chopin. As few would have any preconceived sense of their musical structures, he could be sure that alterations would not be jarring to the audience. The presence of an orchestra provides a larger scale to the piece than piano alone would have done, and the first two of the pieces are suitably sectional, conveniently marking off scenes in the action. This particularly clear-cut sectional structure enabled the changes in the order of events in the Fantasy to be made relatively easily. Indeed, abrupt transitions are absolutely appropriate during this part of the drama, bristling as it is with interruptions and dramatic confrontations. Each Chopin piece corresponds to a particular stage in the drama. The Variations, except for Variation V, are appropriately cheerful and bright, for they serve simply to introduce the characters of the household amusing themselves together before any dangerous emotional entanglements have developed. On the other hand, the Fantasy and Polonaise are restless and tonally unstable, suiting the darker moods that arise in the drama.

It is remarkable how well the music and dramatic structure fit together. Of course, much of the 'fitting' was a result of considerable manipulation, even at one point to the extent of taking two bars out of a section and using them to link two other sections. But the joins are convincing and, what is most surprising, very little music had either to be composed or even transposed in key. The orchestration is considerably modified, in fact improved. Chopin's orchestration is considered weak and Lanchbery has written pertinently on this subject in his programme note:

> Orchestral writing was never Chopin's strong point, and the original scoring of these fine compositions is at best slender and at times sketchy. I attempted to strengthen slightly the role of the orchestra since the music is now being used as part of a dramatic ballet, and furthermore since the piano of today is a larger and stronger instrument than the one which Chopin knew.[163]

The most significant alteration of the original Chopin structure occurs with the curtailment of the Polonaise and the ensuing return to material from the Variations and Fantasy; this material covers the official departure of Beliaev, Natalia's final solo and Beliaev's brief reappearance to return the rose that Natalia has given him. Two separate sections of music from the introduction to the Variations are heard (the 'Là ci darem' theme is clearly alluded to again, though we have not heard this actual section of the score before), and, finally, the part of the Fantasy entitled Thème de Charles Kurpiński returns, the theme to which Beliaev danced and during which Natalia returned to him before their love duet. That theme is therefore already associated with Beliaev and Natalia, and it is an obvious reminiscence motif, introduced for dramatic point, as is the other musical reference to the Variations. It is as if early memories flood back, and we and the main protagonists are called upon to summarise a recent past that is rapidly disappearing before our eyes (and ears). There are also the matching sketch references back in time in the briefest of solos for Natalia – she bursts in with short motifs, a little step, a *port de bras*, that refer back to both her duets with Beliaev, the early Polacca and the later Andante Spianato – and then her husband interrupts her privacy. Thus, Ashton, Thomas and Lanchbery have devised a 'whole' structure out of three originally distinct pieces, and suit the dramatic development at the same time.

Within the three pieces, the order of events is altered only for the Fantasy, as the following comparison shows:

Original Score	*Ballet Score*
Introduction: Largo non troppo	Air: 'Już miesiac zaszedl' (5)
Air: 'Już miesiac zaszedl' (5)	Introduction: Largo non troppo
Thème de Charles Kurpiński (12)	Presto con fuoco (13)
Presto con fuoco (13)	Lento, quasi adagio (14)
Lento, quasi adagio (14)	Molto più mosso (15)
Molto più mosso (15)	Kujawiak
Kujawiak	Thème de Charles Kurpiński (12)

However, cuts are frequent (there are a few repeats not marked in the original), particularly in the final section of each Chopin piece (the Polacca of the Variations, the Kujawiak of the Fantasy, the Polonaise itself) where large-scale repetitions of material and tonal diversions detract temporarily from the skeletal tonal structure. Such repetitions and diversions are so frequent in the Polonaise that we do not hear more than a small proportion of the original when they have been cut; nevertheless, nearly all of the most important musical material of the Polonaise is retained. The result of such cutting here is a new urgency.

Significant additions of 'composed' music include the opening, where the original orchestral introduction (eight bars) is more than doubled in length by repetition and tonal modulation using the original material. A brief phrase assists the awkward modulation from the B-flat major of the Variations to the A major of the Fantasy. The last four bars of the introduction to the Polonaise are transformed. In the original, they allow the tension of the previous crescendo to subside gradually so that the Polonaise enters quite calmly at first; for the purpose of the drama, it is better to preserve the tension and the suggestion of shouting and animated conversation that goes with this orchestral outburst, and Lanchbery sweeps us breathlessly into the Polonaise, treating the moment of its entry as a climax. The time length of the original score from the Arrau recording is fifty minutes; the ballet score, timed from the televised performance, lasts forty minutes.

If Ashton suggests that the Mozart theme 'Là ci darem' from *Don Giovanni* encouraged him to devise an operatic structure based on recitative and aria alternation, there are also moments of quasi recitative in Chopin's music. They are all used for silent action. In the Polonaise (bars 77–84), for example, the piano style is declamatory as Natalia's admirer Rakitin points to the rose that Natalia has given Beliaev and gestures to him to leave. Moreover the first part of Variation V is made up of a series of brief, contrasting musical phrases, to which Ashton fits Beliaev's entrance, the acknowledgements all round, a mimed gesture to each musical gesture and a new character for each change of orchestration (see Ex. 4.17). The style here is very much as in the earlier *Marguerite and Armand*, where Ashton fits musical gestures to the first meeting and greetings of the two lovers. Their respective genders are exaggeratedly reinforced by loud/soft dynamic contrast. Exactly the same musical gestures fit Armand's later accusations and Marguerite's pleading responses. The episode when Natalia chances upon Beliaev and Vera embracing, listens appalled to Vera's explanation, and eventually slaps her, is set to music that contains firm gestures; to histrionic effect, she opens and closes the double doors to the room on the piano arpeggios; chord accents mark the motions when first Natalia and then Vera pushes the other away aggressively. The musical exaggeration of the confrontation adds a touch of humour. A large cut is made in the Lento section, with the result that Vera's pleading with Natalia is kept appropriately short.

The conversational quality of these musical passages probably prompted Lanchbery to create a similar quality in some places where it did not exist so obviously, thus extending the idea of music-dance recitative. The original form of the music used to introduce the Vera-Beliaev *pas de deux* does not suggest recitative, but Lanchbery alters the orchestration and dynamic level to underline the interplay of character on stage and Ashton works a dance gesture to each short musical phrase. Chopin marks the ends of the first two phrases pianissimo after piano; Lanchbery increases the volume to forte instead of the pianissimo and holds back the string entry until this point. These are the instances when Beliaev moves independently of Vera, and the changes underline contrast in character and gender – gentle, appealing woodwind for Vera and firm, unison strings for Beliaev. Similarly, in the Polonaise, orchestra and piano are made to alternate in holding the main melody as if to underline the conversation, even though there is no attempt to associate a particular instrument with a particular character.

There are other occasions on which modified orchestration reinforces the dance structure. Sometimes in the set dances, Lanchbery holds back the piano entry until the dancers actually begin to dance: in the Kujawiak, for instance, which accompanies Beliaev's dance with the maid Katya, or in Natalia's first duet with Rakitin, where the piano enters at the variation of the theme 'Już

Ex. 4.17. Chopin, the first part of Variation 5, showing the relation of dance to musical gesture and significant modifications in orchestration. At [13], Natalia, Rakitin, Katya, Vera and Kolia are on stage.

miesiac zaszedl'. In the Andante Spianato for piano only, which is the music for the love duet between Natalia and Beliaev, Lanchbery transfers the Semplice section (a sort of interruption during the Coda) to strings. Now this is even more of an interruption, strings contrasting with the intimate qualities of the piano, given too that the piano, to Chopin more than to any other romantic composer, represents a specific world closed off from the rest of music. The device works well dramatically because Natalia, reminded of the social problems that their relationship will cause, stops dancing when the orchestra returns her to harsh reality. Then we return to the piano, to dancing, and to the abandonment to feeling.

The most drastic musical change in the entire ballet occurs with the treatment of the Kurpiński theme. In the early draft, Ashton labelled this 'Russian music' and already indicated the changes that were to be made.[164] In the Chopin score, the theme is presented as a fragment, simply and only once, a frail but jaunty little oddity in a piece that otherwise appears indulgent and full-blown (see Ex. 4.18). As well as transposing it into A minor (to blend more successfully with the end of the Kujawiak), Lanchbery transforms it into a large musical moment, repeats each half of it, plays it slower with a more sustained accompaniment,[165] romanticises it by altering the orchestration, and provides dynamic contrast, absent in the original. The music is barely recognisable in terms of the original, and it could be said that Lanchbery has taken the liberty of orchestrating it in a 'Russian' style more appropriate to the late than the early or middle nineteenth century. This belies his comment on 'strengthening slightly' the existing orchestration! Otherwise, the score that Lanchbery has fashioned not only clarifies structure but preserves intact the flavour of Chopin's music.

It has already been pointed out that musical dynamics as well as orchestration are altered in the introduction to the Vera-Beliaev duet. Generally speaking, however, each musical section is performed in accordance with the dynamic and metronome markings of Chopin himself. The interpretation of the music for the Vera-Beliaev *pas de deux* is carefully suited to the drama and is distinctly more tender and gentle than the Arrau interpretation with which Ashton originally worked. The dramatic context has clearly defined the possibilities. Nevertheless both interpretations are valid and in accordance with markings provided.

The piano itself plays a number of different roles in the work. At the outset, it is the domestic instrument, the Mozart theme mimed by Vera on a piano on stage, before the dance Variations begin. Soon however, it becomes very much the personal voice – allusions to the actual role that it played in nineteenth-century music, as the voice of romanticism. Liszt describes the piano as 'my eye, my speech, my life'.[166] Romantic music is often described as having a speaking quality, with listeners in the nineteenth century known to respond concretely rather than abstractly; Roland Barthes in our own times observes that

Thème de Charles Kurpiński

Ex. 4.18. (Left and above). Chopin, Grand Fantasy in A major on Polish Airs.

Schumann's music is always *a quasi parlando*.[167] We might be reminded here of how the piano 'pleads' at the opening of *Symphonic Variations*. There is too the romantic notion of the composer developing an individual style and expression, Chopin's, one of yearning, restlessness, and drawing-room intimacy. If the piano is like a voice, directly expressing feeling, Ashton goes further in making us feel that piano and dancer are one, and that dancer/piano sing as in an aria. As an instance of the piano indicating the highly personal, there is the *pas de deux* for Natalia and Beliaev to the Andante Spianato. It is in this *pas de deux* too that we see excellent examples of piano ornamentation, so easily read as musical gesture, become personal, become dance gesture. Indeed, the ornamented Chopin style becomes the dance style of much of *Month*, which is correspondingly more florid, lacy, here than in many of Ashton's works. Throughout the ballet, *bourrées*, intricate play of hands, swirling arm gestures and circling lifts, are a direct parallel to this piano style. At the beginning of her *pas de deux* with Beliaev, Natalia's style is immediately ornamented, even at a point when the melody is still quite plain.

Interestingly, at one key point, the piano could be seen to 'speak the dancer' less directly or at least ambiguously. I am influenced here by Carolyn Abbate's idea that music has the potential to speak with a voice that works against expectations or dominant patterns (see Ch. 2). Beliaev dances the second part of Variation V to the piano, which is gently warmed by strings, to Chopin at his most personal and lyrical and, speaking in terms of how Chopin is often gender-read, at his most feminine. The musical style here is far more Chopinesque than in the earlier Variations, which allow the Mozart theme to be heard much more clearly. The solo is a luscious adagio, with expansive *port de bras*. This is not typical male music in ballet, nor is typical male dancing set to it, and we can readily contrast the far more conventional differentiation of men and women in the scoring (*à la* nineteenth century) of, for instance *The Dream* or *La Fille mal gardée*. Witness Lanchbery's comments here on the construction of gender in *Fille*. At one point, he needed 'A typical "male variation" version [of a tune by Hérold]', and at another point, 'A soft trio passage of the original had to be made more four-square and masculine, since it was needed for male corps de ballet.'[168]

We see the male figure Beliaev dancing to the piano. But are we simply seeing a male figure here? It is crucial that, for this variation, unlike the others before, which are public and *en famille*, Natalia stands downstage with her back turned to the dancing tutor. Rakitin, who is also present, opposite upstage, is very much on the sidelines. Beliaev's solo, though often passionate, is oddly unfocused, directed everywhere and nowhere more than anywhere else. Is Beliaev not an emblem here, something in Natalia's imagination, a representation of love, again, 'the voice of sensuousness, and we hear it through the longing of womanhood'? Such a thing does not need to be literally looked upon – it can be heard, imagined, felt. Is he not another image of the androgynous dream figure in *Le Spectre de la rose*? He is after all free to be claimed by a number of women in this piece. For a while, at least, the meeting with Natalia means little to him – while she is immediately in love, he is out in the garden with her son during the next scene. Is not our ear coaxed into occupying a female position in this inversion of male gaze, with a woman 'looking at a man' through her imagination?[169] The newly lyrical piano might be heard here as Natalia's 'voice'. Other devices help us to read this solo as an entry to a different registral plane, a dream, her dream: the dramatic recitative introduction, complete with thunder clap, and the move for the first time in these Variations from B-flat major to the distant tonal world of G-flat major. The passage seems an important contribution to the empowering of Natalia within the piece, a strong woman as Turgenev's women so often are. The ballet is, in the end, primarily about her, woman, and love, rather than about 'the student' Beliaev.

It is significant that Ashton chose Anthony Dowell for the role of Beliaev, for Dowell never presented the conventional male ballet dancer all-powerful, strong-muscled image. In this solo, he brings out the 'other' element unusually strongly, supported surely by the piano scoring and the voice-like connotations of the piano. It would not be unreasonable to go further and suggest that, in this ballet as a whole, the piano is fundamentally the voice of woman. Later, significantly, Beliaev is scored 'as a man' to the orchestra without piano: in conversation with Vera before dancing with her, then in his solo to the Kurpiński theme.

Structurally too, Beliaev's Variation marks a turning point in this piece. At first, in the Variations on the Mozart theme, formality is emphasised through straightforward symmetry: Theme A (eight bars, see Ex. 4.16), which is repeated with minor variation, an alternative Theme B (eight bars), and then once more the variation of Theme A. Form is further simplified in that each eight-bar unit already contains repetition, in a classical eighteenth-century antecedent–consequent structure, and there is tonal imperative for full closure at the end of the theme (a 'classical' self-contained system):

A	A1	B	A1
8 bars	8 bars	8 bars	8 bars
4+4	4+4	4+4	4+4

The family atmosphere is informal, the music speaks of controlled emotion, learnt manners, socially acceptable behaviour, even if there is something of a pent-up excitement on stage. Mozart and the eighteenth century have a deeper meaning in relation to the narrative. It is interesting that the original Chopin starts with an extended introduction, turbulent with modulatory excursions (which Lanchbery introduces at the end of *Month*), and then settles into these formal and conventionally arranged variations. Significantly, Ashton and his collaborators chose to start the action with formality and tonal stability.

Also underlining stability – and this might simply have reflected the 'natural' tendency to level out and slow tempos in ballet – the speed of the variations remains virtually uniform through Variations 1 to 4, although Chopin stipulates the following metronome changes:

Music		Dance Variations
Variation I	♩ = 76	Natalia
Variation II	♩ = 92	Vera
Variation III	♩ = 63	Yslaev, Natalia's husband
Variation IV	♩ = 92	Kolia, Natalia's son

The ballet tempo is ♩ =76 throughout.

The first two dance variations generally match the immediate musical repetitions after every four bars, confirming choreographically the musical formality. Vera's variation is an example, Lanchbery believes, of Ashton responding at the late stage of orchestral rehearsal to a point that he would only have heard in the orchestrated score.[170] Punctuating accents from wind instruments (there is nothing in the piano score to suggest these) gave the idea of big lunge steps interspersing *bourrées* around the stage, but Ashton playfully introduces these steps first without the orchestral accents before we hear them marked out.

Formally speaking, everything rapidly opens up from Variation V onwards – Beliaev's entry, appropriately. Here, the old four-part form starts to shatter – this is the point where Chopin puts his romantic signature on a hitherto conventional set of variations. Lanchbery adds to the point by cutting the first written musical repeat – we do not need to hear the recitative music all over again (see Ex. 4.17), and the Variation ends 'open' in a different key from that in which it started. From then on, structures are rhapsodic, episodic, with plenty of tempo fluctuation.

We can now contrast the large form of the three main *pas de deux* in *Month*, Beliaev with Vera, then with Katya the maid, and finally, with Natalia. Vera's *pas de deux* with Beliaev, she in love with him, demonstrates a continuity: Ashton masks repetition, varied repetition or recapitulation in the music. The ballet has now opened out emotionally. At one moment of musical repetition, Ashton does anything but emphasise the musical point. The moment when repetition begins is underplayed with a 'dead' lift, which then contrasts hugely with a 'big lift': Beliaev turns Vera way above his head, her hands delightedly spinning around each other to the flurry of notes on the piano. The form of the music for this *pas de deux* is appropriately open, and it moves from A major to an unresolved dominant of F-sharp minor; the narrative of the *pas de deux* is likewise unresolved, emotionally unfinished.

The *pas de deux* with the maid is light-hearted rather than about feelings of love, and the response to the music is of quite a different order. The music, based on a dance known as the Kujawiak, is neatly closed off tonally, returning to its starting key, and the repetition of a particularly accented passage is matched with repetition of the so-called 'rhythm step' set to it. The choreography for this *pas de deux* meets up neatly with the syncopations in the music.

Very different yet again, Natalia's *pas de deux* with Beliaev is mutually passionate, and then stresses timelessness and reverie; more than half of it is musical coda (after a simple A B A1 form), a long, sensuous shimmer settling into tonic harmony, with a deviation in the Semplice section, only to emphasise the return of the shimmer (see Ex. 4.19):

Introduction:	bars 1–4
A:	bars 5–20
B:	bars 21–36 (modulating – based on theme of A)
A1:	bars 37–52
Coda:	bars 53–102 (Semplice: bars 67–84, 99–102)

Interestingly, the music is taken at a slower speed for the ballet than is indicated in Chopin's score. To the shimmer, Ashton choreographs gentle swaying lifts, side to side, and side to side again (see Ill. 5), and endless *bourrées*, seamlessly linking into the lifts, and finally stilled. The transient lurks, but the characters of this romance clearly want it to go on for ever. This static time sense makes the interruption of Vera seem startlingly abrupt and the ensuing *dénouement* alarmingly rapid by contrast.

Before this shimmering coda, the choreography demonstrates several points of independence from the music. The broader contours of the music are reflected, with two lifts at the two climaxes, one in the middle section B, one in the final section A1, but it is interesting to note how florid and passionate the movement seems at the outset (when the musical theme is plain); how the movement quietens of its own accord; and how, when the opening musical theme returns (bar 13), the movement to it starts much more peacefully than before, a simple, continuous promenade turn in one direction maintaining the *arabesque* that ended the last phrase and then incorporating smooth steps on the spot to *attitude* and back to *arabesque* again. The overriding image at this last point is of sustainment in time. For the recapitulation of section A, the movement is new, but the dynamic procedure is the same as before, hasty and then quieter and sustained, again independent of any change in the music. Often, too, the choreography shoots its own accents across the music. Sometimes musical ornament has a

Ex. 4.19a. Chopin, Andante Spianato in G major, Introduction and beginning of section A.

Ex. 4.19b. Chopin, Andante Spianato in G major, Coda (first part).

Ex. 4.19b. (contd.) Opening of Semplice section.

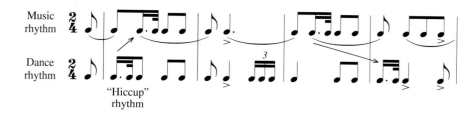

Ex. 4.20. *A Month in the Country*, Variation 1 (Natalia): rhythmic analysis of opening phrase.

Ill. 5. Anthony Dowell and Lynn Seymour in *A Month in the Country*, the Royal Ballet.

counterpart in the dance, sometimes the dance uses the musical idea, reflects it and carries it further. There is a flourish of linked hands with arching of the back, first with a musical flourish (bar 17), then performed by itself a bar later.

As often in Ashton's work, the choreography has its own shape of turbulence and quiet, but the dynamic contrasts are more extreme here than anywhere else in *Month*. The music seems relatively placid. The dancers pull against the music to create energy and added passion, until relative resolution with the music in the coda. Now, there remains a flutter of nervousness in the *bourrées*, but the primary image is 'for ever'.

Elsewhere too, *Month* is full of Ashtonian devices of independent dance rhythms and accents creating lively conversation with the music. Dowell has referred to the sudden 'mad'[171] *changements* in his early *adage* solo (Variation V), sometimes with legs spreading wide, his head twisting restlessly from side to side. We see too his motif of sharp *arabesques* directed to one side and then the other. Crossing any pulse, such madnesses look doubly wild against Chopin's continuing legato. The opening filigree phrase in Natalia's Variation wends its way deftly around the music, holding to its pulse but meeting and parting with its accent structure, and her little 'hiccup' rhythm cheekily anticipates and then echoes the same rhythm in Mozart (see Ex. 4.20). Seymour's performance is wonderful for its variety and gradation of accent, from the barely-present articulation of *bourrées*, toe taps and *petits battements*, to the dynamic swoop of body and arms. Or an *off* the beat *piqué* into a new direction, drawn out with a light breath, contrasts with the triumphant printing of an *on* the beat *piqué* accent with arms and head gesturing affirmatively. The solo is already restless with zig-zag changes of direction. Musical and rhythmic means contribute further to this impression.

Thus, even at the most detailed level, the forms of music and choreography work in dialogue to create meaning. *Month* has established itself as one of the richest integrations of music and narrative choreography in the repertoire.

*   *   *

Month also reminds us that we must not forget the role of the interpreter in the musicality of Ashton's work, and the dangers of analysing a dance from just one video recording. Ashton celebrated the individuality of his dancers, in musicality as much as in anything else. Margot Fonteyn, whom he considered profoundly musical, could take the capacity for choreography to breathe within phrase limits to surprising extremes. Her solos in *Daphnis and Chloe* and *Ondine*, even the very late *Salut d'amour*, are like improvisations, maintaining the pressure through long spans of time when she seems to play with, to pull against, even to taunt her accompaniment. But she is spot on with the musical triumphs and crises when she wants to be, when it really matters. Watching Lynn Seymour teach the role of Natalia in *Month*, the dancer Bruce Sansom observed that she probably did every show differently, given the variety of phrasing that she came up with in rehearsal.[172] A 'natural' dancer, she 'played with the music' (see p. 227) more than most.

Ashton was always ready to initiate changes in the choreography himself to suit different dancers. Dancers were taught different subtleties at different times. In coaching Sansom and Karen Paisey in the last *Fille pas de deux*, Ashton insisted on a passage of three shunts backwards being 'really clipped . . . as hard as he could get them'.[173] The dancers could soften their quality in the next phrase, a typical Ashton contrast. But Sansom thinks it not at all unlikely that Ashton would have taught other dancers differently.

The most respected *répétiteur* might make changes as well, whether consciously or unconsciously. Lanchbery recalls a passage in the Fairy Summer Variation from *Cinderella*: four little moves (jumps and shifts of weight from fourth to fourth position on the spot) to a four-note rhythm pattern in Prokofiev's music. Lanchbery feels sure that Ashton repeated the same step exactly, even though the second time round one of the notes is dropped from the musical pattern – Ashton not untypically moving against the grain. I cannot imagine that Ashton did not hear the musical change. This way, the original harmonious rhythmic relationship between music and dance is gently disrupted (by the musical change).

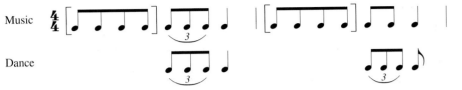

Somes has staged the repeated step with just three little jumps, matching the new musical pattern[174] – was this an Ashton change or a Somes change?

Anita Young, who learnt the solo from Ashton, continues to teach it in repertory classes with the four moves repeated.[175] This too is how we see Vyvyan Lorrayne perform it in the 1964 film of *Cinderella*.[176] Interestingly, in Elaine Fifield's performance in a 1957 film, there is yet another rhythmic version of this passage.[177] This time, there are only three moves, discrepancy between dance and music the first time round, resolved (by the musical change) as the step repeats.

In two versions of this dance passage, Ashton introduces a touch of contrapuntal spice into the relationship with music whilst he maintains choreographic symmetry. I believe this is significant.

My reading is that flexibility and capacity for change is part of Ashton's style, and yet Ashton at the same time had a very particular musical-choreographic style. Individual details can change, but there are nevertheless strong stylistic characteristics to preserve: sophistications of counterpoint against the music, nuances in phrasing style, oddities of dance rhythm that often make his dance material harder to read, more nervously unpredictable than that of Balanchine. It has been suggested here that much is lost if dancers do not indicate precisely the distinctions between timings of steps or if they even out the dynamics in narrative pieces. Over the years, the tendency has been to lose syncopations rather than to gain them. Former dancers Jean Bedells and Joy Newton worked on putting them back into *Façade* for the 1994 Royal Ballet revival. Bedells recalls that 'it had become bland: I remember Joy insisting on syncopation in a section of the Waltz, using the bass-line, *not* the melody.'[178] Dramatic contrapuntal contrasts also tend to get ironed out. Ashton's style all too often succumbs to the pressures of a natural levelling out of dynamics, the loss of accentuations when the music does not immediately suggest them, a settling back into musical forces (see Ch. 2, pp. 94–5). When the levelling happens, however, or when unusual, expressive points of timing are brushed over, Ashton the 'theatre ani-mal' begins to disappear and the sentimental romantic takes over. Details of musicality are integral to his consideration of dance as drama, whether this be a short variation or a full ballet.

The question arises: did these subtleties exist even in Ashton's earliest work? It seems likely that they did, despite changes over the years, given evidence from the 1930s ballets that have come down to us, what has been said about their early performances, and the silent film footage of *Les Rendezvous*. Trained in the jazziness of the 1920s, its rhythmic playfulness and risk with pulse, Ashton soon became secure and sophisticated in rhythmic and musical matters. Later, he became equally subtle in his approach to orchestral texture and timbre and the forming of 'welded' narrative scores.

Ashton's musicality is a thoroughly positive complement to his particular theatrical instincts. Was it a drawback then, his lack of formal musical educa-tion in reading and analysing music? For the music that he chose to use, never the very advanced twentieth-century scores that Balanchine handled, Ashton's developed sense of listening seems to have served him perfectly well. And per-haps too – or, at least, this could be one reason for the special flavour of Ashton's musicality (like that of many jazz musicians) – it is what it is *because* he worked free from the vision of those beats and bar-lines.

5

Antony Tudor

'The more ballet turns to pantomime, the less intimate its relation to the music becomes,' Edwin Denby once wrote,[1] and it is a theme of this chapter to examine whether this is true of Tudor's work. Balanchine was primarily a maker of plotless ballets. Ashton created a good many story ballets alternating dances and gestural episodes, although moving away from stilted mime conventions. Tudor went further in obliterating the divisions between gesture and dance steps, recitative and aria. The narrative drive is especially strong in much of Tudor's work, but it is also deeply embedded in the movement texture. The issue therefore that Denby raises is especially urgent in his work, and Denby's evaluations of the work over the years make a useful introduction.

Denby was admiring of Tudor's musicality: 'Tudor's musicality, like Balanchine's . . . is a marvel worth seeing'.[2] But he understands that the basis of this musicality is very different from that of Balanchine. This is evident in his writing about *Jardin aux lilas* (1936), a ballet about a woman who is forced to marry a man whom she does not love, and *Pillar of Fire* (1942), which tells of a woman's sexual frustration and guilt before reconciliation with the man whom she loves:

> One 'reads' the climactic moments in these ballets in a pantomime sense because from the outset Tudor has emphasized the pantomime aspect of the dance . . . the traditional ballet (whether of 1890 or 1940) tries for a radically different kind of meaning than that of pantomime description.[3]

Of Tudor's *The Tragedy of Romeo and Juliet* (1943) he writes:

> In a sense, the dance is all recitative, or like a highly figured prose. It is in pantomime style. But so exact is the invention of the gesture, so varied is the timing of motion from figure to figure, as you look, and from one narrative detail to the next, that you have very clearly a sense of rhythmic strength. The rhythm envelops you in a spell.[4]

It is therefore from a pantomime base that rhythmic shape and continuity emerge. Soon, however, there is caution in Denby's evaluation, as he reviews *Undertow* (1945), a ballet that analyses the psychology of a murderer, rejected by his mother at birth: 'One keeps watching the movement all through for the intellectual meaning its pantomime conveys more than for its physical impetus as dancing. Its impetus is often tenuous . . .'[5] By 1948, his reservations about Tudor's ballets are clear. They have 'exceptional virtues . . . their sustained expressive intensity is clearly large-scale . . .',[6] but,

> Their shock value, thrilling at first, does not last; their shaping force is discontinuous; they have a weak and fragmentary dance impetus; they peter out at the end. They can find no repose and no spring because balance is no element of structure in them . . . His ballets are not primarily dance conceptions . . .[7]

So now Denby perceives a blurring of rhythmic shape in Tudor's work. He notes too the problems of spontaneity for performers: 'Tudor's main rhythm is hard to get hold of, it has no beat or lilt. So it is difficult for the dancers to sense where their instinctive changes of pace (their rubato) would be proper.'[8]

Arlene Croce distinguishes issues of narrative movement from those of rhythmic impetus and musicality. Welcoming *The Leaves are Fading* (1975), a plotless suite of dances like an elegy for love, she reviews the decades preceding it as a period of decline in Tudor's work. First, dance movement ideas had become subjugated to pantomime; later, his works became less interesting musically: 'The weakening of dance impetus in respect to story had occurred in Tudor's work long before. The sixties pieces showed also a collapse in respect to music. With that went the keynote of Tudor's style.'[9] But before this decline in musicality,

> When the story interest in a dramatic Tudor ballet dries up, you can usually watch the choreography for the oddity and elegance of its musical line – it can be looked at abstractly so to speak . . . The musical cues in a Tudor work are often diffuse, lapped over with complex harmonies of composers like Schoenberg, Delius, Mahler. One can't predict where the dance impetus will spring from, but that is what makes the dance interesting.[10]

Perhaps this is the root of Judith Judson's remark about the Kirov Ballet performance of *Jardin aux lilas*. Precisely because they lacked the Tudor dramatic style, the dancers, she felt, encouraged focus on the 'beauty' of the abstract structural qualities of the work.[11]

The major importance of structural and musical values to Tudor is demonstrated by the number of his ballets set to existing, uncut symphonic scores or assemblages of complete large-scale movements from multi-movement scores. In other words, he was willing to let musical form shape or negotiate with his narrative conception. This is rarely the case in dance narrative, where the exigencies of story-line encourage choreographers to consider commissions or arrangements.

I am stressing here Tudor's narrative work, because it is for this that he is most celebrated, and especially for the 'psychological' ballets. However, he also created pieces without stories. He has described as abstractions of a kind both *Dark Elegies* (1937), to Mahler's *Kindertotenlieder*, on a general theme of mourning, and *The Leaves are Fading* (to movements chosen from a variety of Dvořák chamber works).[12] But there are other pieces without any through narrative, his setting of the Pachelbel Canon *Continuo* (1971) and the teaching pieces or 'dance arrangements' that he created for young dancers at Jacob's Pillow or the Juilliard School, like *Little Improvisations* (1953) and *A Choreographer Comments* (1960). In this chapter, while concentrating on Tudor's narrative ballets, I will also spend time examining the more abstract works. Compared with Ashton and Balanchine, Tudor's total output was small.

By the time Tudor turned to ballet, he had behind him a solid musical education.[13] He came from a musical family, his father an occasional violinist, his mother a pianist and singer who gave Tudor his first piano lessons. As a boy, he sang in the church choir. Tudor tells us that he went on to study piano with other teachers until the age of eighteen, eventually at one of the London music colleges, and was strong enough technically to make an attempt at Beethoven piano sonatas. For a while, he entertained ambitions of becoming an orchestral conductor. Joining the ballet world only fuelled Tudor's determination to get to know as much about music as possible, attending Promenade concerts at the Queen's Hall in London, chamber music concerts, purchasing records and listening to many more in the booths of record shops. He would also buy second-hand sheet music that he could play through on the piano, which opened up the repertoire considerably given the limited range of recordings available at that time. Accompanying ballet classes at the Rambert studio provided Tudor with a way of getting free classes for himself. Together with the Dalcroze training that Rambert gave her pupils, it undoubtedly developed his sensitivity in relating music to dance movement.[14] On the other hand, Tudor never had Balanchine's professional and theoretical background in music.

Tudor became friendly with Sir Thomas Beecham when choreographing for operas at Covent Garden during the 1930s and later, in America (Tudor's home after 1939), turned to him for advice about the selection of Delius pieces for *Romeo and Juliet*. He also developed a strong collaborative friendship with Elizabeth Sawyer, his pianist at the Juilliard School; she refers to him regularly in her book on dance and music, and pays tribute to him for how much he taught her about musical phrasing.[15] Yet Tudor did not regularly rely on musician colleagues for advice about choice or interpretation of music. As in all things, his style was to be self-sufficient, self-educated. Tudor developed his own ideas of his own accord, and his musical education, which he considered essential to his choreographic career, enabled him to be responsible for his own score assemblages from the start – indeed, for the Frescobaldi arrangement to which he made his very first choreography, *Cross-Garter'd* (1931, based on *Twelfth Night*). At a glance he could tell whether the key sequence between separate pieces would be appropriately smooth, the tempos and mood sufficiently varied. Sometimes, he used complete movements of music. At other times, he had the music cut to suit his needs, more often than not undertaking the cutting himself. Thus, *Gala Performance* (1938) consists of one movement of Prokofiev's Piano Concerto No. 3 (with sections deleted) and then the whole of his Classical Symphony. With a view to its orchestration, Tudor presented John Lanchbery with the shaped Koechlin score for *Shadowplay* (1967). He chose music from *Les Bandar-Log* which had already been recorded, and elected to recapitulate one section from it. Into this music, he inserted two sections from *Le Course du printemps*, which he could not have heard on record, but which he had researched himself from manuscript sources in the Fleischer Collection of the Free Library of Philadelphia.[16]

When working on *Sunflowers* (1971), Tudor made a neat rhythmic outline of the complete score of Janáček's first string quartet, all four parts condensed into one line of score, showing the predominant or leading rhythms. The Labanotator Muriel Topaz recalls seeing an accompanying working book with a rhythmic line representing the dance as an independent component, worked out systematically prior to actual choreography.[17] Most striking are the notes in the Tudor Papers housed in the New York Public Library Dance Collection, showing that, for *Leaves*, not only did he write out the key signature and opening bars of each of the Dvořák pieces that interested him, and make his own analysis of the musical structure, but he also made his own painstaking piano reduction of each of the numbers chosen. The musical hand is not professional, but nonetheless accurate enough for the reductions to have been useful. Again, Tudor brought his musical knowledge to bear on the project. Topaz also notes his brief studies of the system of the Russian pedagogue Joseph Schillinger (1895–1943). Schillinger, who emigrated to America, devised a methodology for relating scientific practice and the arts and a system for applying rational scientific principles to musical composition. The composers Vernon Duke, George Gershwin, Earle Brown and Henry Cowell are all known to have studied the system; many others took advantage of the correspondence course that he devised. I have found no further information relating to Tudor's studies of the system, but Tudor's style was to keep this kind of information very private. Certainly, he had a technical mind; witness his preoccupation with graphic notation (dance notation [Laban] – which he supported with unusual interest for a choreographer –

as well as musical notation), and his analytical diagrams of phrase counts. All this testifies to a disciplined, meticulous mind.

Tudor was a man of wide artistic interests, of curious intellect, and it is important to frame an analysis of his musicality within his broader cultural experience. Although, as his career developed, he tended to play down the influence of other ballet choreographers, there was a kinship with Fokine, another choreographer who emphasised the expression of feeling and personality through use of the whole body. He was also fascinated by the work of Kurt Jooss and the South Asian dancers whom he saw in London during the early years of his career. As a ballet choreographer, he was unusually close to modern dancers and their weightier torso-initiated movement styles. However, quite as much, if not more, Tudor took inspiration from literature and theatre, mostly romantic and early modernist, of the late nineteenth and early twentieth century. Anton Chekov, D.H. Lawrence, James Joyce, Henrik Ibsen, Federico García Lorca, Marcel Proust, Guy de Maupassant – all these writers figure in the Tudor documentation. Stanislavsky's writings might well have provided ideas for improvisational working methods, while Tudor also read avidly within the disciplines of philosophy and psychology. Early on, he developed an interest in film and television. He made eight ballets specially for television during the 1930s, the most acclaimed being the experimental *Fugue for Four Cameras* (1937), which showed Maude Lloyd, sometimes in quadruplicate, dancing each of the four voices of a Bach Fugue in D minor from *The Art of Fugue*. In 1959, he collaborated on *The Eye of Night* with the experimental film-maker Maya Deren. The pedagogical aspect of Tudor's career is very important: the regular teaching of technique class, repertoire (his own and the classics) and creative production classes fed back into his own choreography. It is also significant to his work that, in the 1950s, he became interested in Zen Buddhism: he lived in the Zen Institute monastery in New York from 1962 (becoming its president in 1964) until he died in 1988.

Musical Choices

Tudor has summarised his musical choices in terms of a preference for the romantics: 'I'm nearly always partial to the Romantic period of music, in the late nineteenth century and the early part of this [twentieth century], between 1870 and 1920, I would think, is my range. Contemporary music, outside of the William Schuman [for *Undertow*], I've never used.'[18] Certainly, this reflects what we too might immediately identify with in any skeletal assessment of Tudor's work, based on the ballets that have most often been performed and celebrated. It might also reflect his own evaluation of his work, and his view of dance arrangements or pieces made for students as less important aspects of his repertory. However, Tudor's statement is slightly misleading. On a number of occasions, what he said about his work is contradicted by the work itself. Numerous pieces use scores that were composed after 1920 and have to be called contemporary, written during Tudor's own lifetime. Some of these scores nonetheless look back to nineteenth-century romantic tradition – to give examples, those by Richard Strauss, his *Four Last Songs* (1948) incorporated in *Hail and Farewell* (1959), and Martinů, the *Fantaisies symphoniques* (1955) used in *Echoing of Trumpets* (1963). Others are modernist and forward-looking, such as Copeland's *Music for the Theatre* (1925) used in *Timetable* (1941), Elliott Carter's Third Etude from *Eight Etudes and a Fantasy for Woodwind Quartet* (1950) set in *Dance Studies (Less Orthodox)* (1961) and Werner Egk's *Variations on a Caribbean Theme* (1960), used in *The Divine Horseman* (1969). On the other hand, some of Tudor's musical selections extend further into the past than he tends to suggest. A number of his works use baroque and renaissance music.

The choice of music by the high modernist American composer Carter is especially interesting. *Dance Studies* was created for Juilliard students. In the mid-1960s, Tudor tried his hand with Carter's highly complex concerto for harpsichord, piano and two chamber orchestras (1961), but the project foundered after a few rehearsals.[19] Always one to challenge himself and shift from expected directions, Tudor nevertheless found himself out of tune with advanced developments in twentieth-century music.[20] His single commission was from William Schuman. In a lecture at York University, Canada, he remarked, 'I would really like to commission more music. Unfortunately my career coincided with the period when composers were becoming more intellectual and did not like to put notes on the page.'[21]

There were also financial constraints on commissions. Rambert's Ballet Club could not afford to commission scores. However, in 1936, as an ambitious young choreographer, Tudor had tried to interest Sibelius in collaborating with him on a full-length epic ballet using the Nordic theme *Kalevala*, upon which the composer had already based some music.[22] There were also plans in the late 1940s for Gian Carlo Menotti to write the score for a ballet based on the Proust novel *À la recherche du temps perdu*,[23] the scenario already prepared by Tudor, after he had initially proposed the idea to Britten.[24] Menotti began work on the score. But neither of these projects came to fruition: Sibelius could not commit himself to a collaboration, and, for whatever reason, the material that Menotti came up with did not inspire Tudor to take this project any further. Menotti used his material later in another context. In 1951, Roberto Gerhard notes an interest in collaborating with Tudor, but this too came to nothing.[25]

Tudor did not make any special feature of using contemporary British composers while he lived in Britain, although he used Constant Lambert's music for

Adam and Eve (1932) (the score that Diaghilev had borrowed for a piece with a totally different programme: *Romeo and Juliet*), and Holst for *The Planets* (1934). Lambert also arranged the music for *Atalanta of the East* (1933) and *Paramour* (1934), while Tudor used Britten's arrangement of Rossini pieces for *Soirée musicale* (1938). *Cereus*, a late piece for Juilliard (1971), on a theme of modern American youth, used a contemporary score by a little known British composer, Geoffrey Gray.

Even if he found advanced twentieth-century music unsympathetic, Tudor's choices reveal an enquiring, daring mind: much of the music that he chose was either little known at the time or in no way obvious ballet music with dance rhythms. *Dark Elegies*, for instance, is said to have been the first ballet set to Mahler, who, in 1937, was not the celebrated composer that he is today: his *Kindertotenlieder* (settings of five songs by Rückert) were considered a grim and controversial choice by ballet audiences and critics at the time. Tudor had aspirations to use Mahler's large-scale work *Das Lied von der Erde* only a year later, although he had to wait until 1950 to realise this project in *Shadow of the Wind*.[26] Delius was an interesting choice for *Romeo and Juliet* (a selection of his orchestral works), after Tudor had contemplated using the more obvious scores on this theme by Berlioz, Tchaikovsky and Prokofiev. But, he argued, 'the music of an English landscapist should fit the mood of Shakespeare'.[27] Delius's music also reminded Tudor of Italian melodies and paintings of the period.[28] Some of the Koechlin music for *Shadowplay* was not even on record when Tudor researched it (see p. 270).

The Tudor dancer Maude Lloyd remembers that Tudor 'always wanted to go bigger, to use music that needed big orchestras'.[29] Sometimes, he had the resources that he wanted, for instance, in order to perform *Das Lied von der Erde* in the US. On other occasions, he might aim high and make do with arrangements. It was customary at the Ballet Club for one or two pianos to provide the accompaniment, for the piano to be supplemented by a solo instrumentalist or singer, or for a recording to be used. Holst's *The Planets* was played in a version for two pianos. The fact that there was a piano and voice reduction already available eased the decision to set *Kindertotenlieder*.[30] Lionel Bradley, who meticulously documented the early years of Ballet Rambert, gives a vivid impression of the rather rough record and piano combination for *The Descent of Hebe* (1935, set to Bloch's Concerto Grosso). The gramophone was located behind the stage, the piano in front of it. 'It wasn't bad, but it would have been better if the gramophone had been nearer and one was never aware of the turn over of a record.'[31]

Ballet scores were customarily arranged in the US to suit often meagre orchestral forces. Schuman and Tudor themselves paid for extra string players to supplement the regular orchestra for the first New York performances of

Undertow, after which resources dwindled again for performances on tour.[32] The conductor Antal Dorati himself arranged the Delius pieces for *Romeo and Juliet*, transcribing the orchestration part by part from recordings, the reason being that during war-time the printed orchestral score and parts could not be sent over to New York from Europe.[33] Later productions of the ballet have used a mixture of the original Delius scores and Dorati's transcriptions.

For his ballets, Tudor searched for a kind of music that conjured up mood, or emotional ebb and flow. Late romantic music bears the semiotic signals of continually fluctuating emotions, the more the harmonic dissonance, the more expressionist and anxious the statement, and such feeling Tudor usually grounded and made more specific within a story. Sometimes a story might be prompted by a programme already attached to the music, as in Schoenberg's *Verklärte Nacht*. The poem by Richard Dehmel that inspired the music is the basis of the story of *Pillar of Fire*. Or the story might be prompted by representational elements in the music. Thus, Martinů's *Fantaisies symphoniques* for *Echoing of Trumpets* suggested to Tudor the sound of gunshots (and a soldier does get shot in the piece), and swarming locusts (a metaphor for the dangerous swarm of enemy soldiers troubling a community of women),[34] whilst the rasping trumpets and drums further amplify the horrific war content of the piece. Some members of the audience would also recognise the more subtle programmatic content of the music as it quotes from Dvořák's *Requiem* and borrows the three-note motif from Martinů's *Memorial to Lidice*. On the whole, Tudor's style was not about onomatopoeic or 'Mickey-Mouse' representation of events suggested by the music. It is interesting that he chose not to tell his commissioned composer William Schuman the story of *Undertow*: 'I'd give him pictures. I'd give him geographical and atmospheric things. But I wouldn't tell him what was happening on the stage, because if I had, he might start putting it in his music, and that, I didn't want.'[35] Tudor explained to Schuman:

It is the kind of night in which one feels moisture on the palms of his hands and in which one turns a corner only to pause a minute and look back before proceeding . . . [36]

[The first scene] It should be very calm . . . with occasional, sudden outbursts, which subside right away. These outbursts continue spasmodically for a little while. Then you hear them coming closer together, and finally there's a serenity. That's where your first wonderful melody comes in . . .
[The last 'getaway' section:] Can you write me a four-minute musical essay on fear?[37]

Tudor also subscribed to the theory that music for ballet should not be too strong or complete in itself. He was aware of the power of music to cover up for choreography or to dominate, it and he asked for a more equal relationship between the two media: '

The general audience sitting out in front doesn't realize that it's the music that's sending them most of the time, and not the choreography.[38]

It should be a companionship . . . If the music dictates too much you have to get rid of it.[39]

In ballet the music and the dance are partners, taking in turn the places of junior or senior partners, perhaps not always seeming to get along compatibly, but nevertheless there to complement each other successfully. I do not feel that the composer should have to be burdened with the choreographer as a parasite, living off the blood of the musical creative genius.[40]

Thus he was drawn to *Verklärte Nacht*, of which he remarked, perhaps contentiously to our ears, 'because I felt it was not a completely satisfactory concert piece. It's a work that doesn't really complete itself.'[41] In retrospect, he recognised his mistake in using three Beethoven overtures that he loved for *La Gloire* (1952). The ballet about a great nineteenth-century actress in decline turned into one of his least successful works.[42]

For the similar reasons of not wanting the music to overpower the dance, Tudor avoided using obvious ballet music or music with clear rhythms that suggested movement: 'There is a danger in using music that makes the listener dance with it. In that case the dancers might just as well not be there. Such strongly rhythmed music is useful only to cover up the lack of choreographic ideas.'[43] Significantly, the late romantic music to which Tudor frequently turned is characteristically driven by melodic and harmonic interest, not the rhythmic propulsion and inventiveness of either earlier tonal music or much twentieth-century music. In his musical demands therefore, Tudor is markedly different from Balanchine and Ashton.

Tudor also favoured music without the clear divisions that we associate with traditional music for ballet, preferring a sense of seamlessness and wholeness. The late romantic style of construction is one of continuous flow and free modulation rather than of parts marked by halting cadences. One flowering of energy leads to the next; resolution is constantly delayed. It is fascinating that Tudor had the opportunity to direct Act II of Wagner's *Tristan and Isolde* for television in the late 1930s, a work that epitomises this aesthetic of continuity in structure and emotional expression. The analogy extends further for, just as Wagner removed the divisions between recitative and aria, Tudor removed the gap between mime and dance. It is significant that, although Tudor used a number of separate orchestral pieces by Delius for *Romeo and Juliet*, he stipulated a single-unit stage setting so that the action could continue without pauses for scene changes.

The correspondence with Schuman over *Undertow* highlights how important continuity and seamlessness were to Tudor. There are contradictions, as Tudor argues both for and against giving the listener a sense of the future development of music. Nevertheless, he does stress continuum, sweep and connection, the organic whole, and his points in this respect are crystal clear. In a letter to Schuman (see Ex. 5.1),[44] Tudor emphasises the ideal of structural unity and organic relationship between parts, while he describes a wave-like energy pattern (see Ch. 2, pp. 86–7). His thinking matches late romantic theories of art. The ballet is in three main parts: I Prologue: Birth and Infancy; II The City: Adolescence and manhood; III Epilogue: Guilt.

Airi Hynninen confirms that Tudor was never quite satisfied with the music of *Undertow*,[45] and in one of his lectures, he himself implies an element of compromise: 'The music was fed to me piece-meal. When it arrived it was too late for changes so I had to use it as [it] was.'[46] Parts of it he himself might well have cut from the score: for instance, one cut appears to have been made after the others, another cut passage was reinstated at a later date.[47] He asked for one thirty-bar section to be replaced by a quite different eight-bar alternative, derived from earlier material. He also changed a number of the metronome markings and put forward ideas for filling out a general pause (see Table 5.1).

Undertow remains fragmentary in structure. Music and dance fitting each other neatly and efficiently, 'like a fist in the eye', says Hynninen, the piece moves in fits and starts, a string of small sections of very different character. Tudor did, after all, get his 'piece of furniture'. This structure contributes to a lack of momentum across the work, the momentum that Tudor normally achieved from existing scores and that his 'wave' diagram to Schuman clearly asked for.

Artistic Principles and Working Methods

I have noted Tudor's concern never to let the musical element dominate or be relied upon to give substance to a ballet. He was convinced too that dance should develop along its own lines. In a lecture in New York in 1951, his view is that 'Dance should develop from dance itself, a more conscious knowledge of the use of dance.'[48] His point is about movement development according to its own terms. This seems somewhat extreme considering that he continued to operate in close dialogue with narrative and existing music. Nevertheless, the concept of an independent, self-sufficient dance voice is one that comes up regu-

Now when we get to the second movement, the more I look at it, and the further it goes, the more it looks to me like incidental music. If you turn to your score, you will find that both at the lead into the 5/4 at 11a. and again at the end of this section leading into 11b. you having given your listeners, your audience and me the feeling, or I should say the knowledge, that something new is coming. We should sweep the audience into the new things which are part of the logical and inevitable development of the whole work, without them being aware of it. Here is a drawing of what I mean:

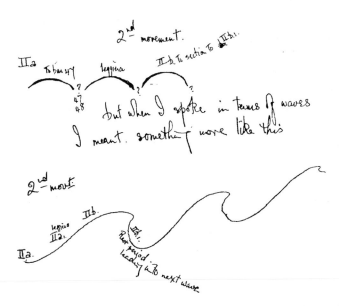

I hope the drawings conveyed something of what I mean to express. Another point that strikes me, is that on going through this part of the music I am not at all able to guess where the composer is likely to be going; (I am trying to have both you and my-self as two different people now with me being an outsider who doesn't know any-thing about the ballet at all but has been privileged to here [sic] the score of the second movement so far). And I do feel with any work of art, music, poetry, even a sculpture, that a glimpse of one part of it should already suggest the impending growth of the whole.

The children music, which was purely incidental always in our conversations has now taken upon itself the importance of a whole unit, which doesn't hold importance to us, an entity that could be taken right out of this symphonic composition and played by itself, whereas it should be so *inter-related with something that comes ten twenty or thirty pages later* that neither it nor those other sections could be extracted without a feeling of dissatisfaction at its incompleteness. You have our earlier notes to refer to, and so have the advantage of me, because it is possible that in the writing each little section did seem as though it could quite staisfactorily [sic] be a little unit, which joined with other similar units could eventually become part of a quite present-able piece of furniture; or its musical equivalent.

Ex. 5.1. Letter from Tudor to William Schuman: extract discussing *Undertow*, 7 January 1945, including facsimile of Tudor's diagram.

Tudor's markings		Markings in the music score
Prologue	ca. 56	ca. 56
Larghissimo at 65	ca. 56	ca. 44
Un poco mosso	60	no metronome mark: 'un poco mosso'
dim. and poco rit through bars 85 to 88 returning to primo tempo		no tempo mark
Section 2a. legato and dolce	ca. 80–84	ca. 84
Leggiero Bar 50	. . 116	ca. 138
piu mosso at bar 80 to	. . 138	no tempo mark
At bar 122	. . 66	ca. 66
. . . . 135 piu mosso	. . 76	ca. 76
. . . . 151 legato, meno mosso	. . 66	ca. 66
. . . . 184 like street corner hymn singing, cantabile	. . 92	ca. 80
. . . . 219	. . 66	no tempo mark
. . . . 260 presto	. . 152	ca. 208
. . . . 341	. . 100	ca. 100
from bar 349 <u>poco</u> piu animato		no tempo mark
at 360 rit. poco a poco to	. . 66	no tempo mark
at 380 marcato	. . 69 to 72	ca. 80
. . 409	. . 116	ca. 100
. . 469	. . 66	ca. 100
accellerando to		
. . 481	. . 114	ca. 120
. . 502 religioso	48	ca. 48
. . 550 poco piu mosso	66	ca. 66
Presto Epilogue	176	ca. 200–208

Nota bene . . . during the second black out at bar 592, instead of the G.P. a roll on the Cymbals?, gong? is sustained until the click of fingers cues in to bar 594 fff.

Table 5.1. *Undertow*, metronome markings: Tudor's note of 21 November 1978 in the Labanotation score, compared with markings in the original music score (right column).

larly in discussion of Tudor's musicality. He tells Topaz in interview, 'My dances are never contrary to or against the music. They could, however, exist without it – they have a rhythmic life of their own.'[49] He continues by illustrating two subtle moments from *Jardin aux lilas* where the dance impulses, a stretching of the torso and a 'diving arabesque', could well be seen to coincide with a high note, a melodic accent (see Ch. 2, p. 78). Dancers are tempted to perform them thus, but in both cases, Tudor wanted the movement to happen just after the musical accent. He began to think about independent rhythmic lines early in his career. It is interesting that, in lecture-demonstrations in London, he would play with approaches that involved working on or presenting dance in silence and show how the dance had a life of its own. Once, he asked the audience for story ideas, chose one of these ideas and some music to set it to, then made movement material in silence before adding the music. At another event, he played the Bloch fugue that accompanies the last scene of *The Descent of Hebe*, showed the dance fugue already made to it in silence, and then put music and dance together.[50] Fernau Hall has clarified that Tudor did not follow the musical fugue form slavishly in any case. He 'followed the form wherever possible, but ignored it where it suited his purpose, and thus he builds up a pattern of his own which forms a kind of counterpoint to the music.'[51]

Tudor's overriding organisational principle was the phrase, the sweep in time analogous to breath, as in a singer's phrase. Beat and metre (and counting) are well in the background of the rhythmic picture. Indeed, Tudor once said:

I simply don't think of the rhythm of dance on a beat-for-beat basis. I think of the phrase and the line and if the music breathes, the dance can breathe with it . . .[52]

I always want the body to sing. Therefore, nearly all my phrases are as though they would be sung. That's why I'm against counting. No one can count if they're singing. Also, a singer has a breath for a certain phrase. Now, we don't actually do this in dancing. But I do create my phrases with that sort of innate thing happening. And so, I devise in phrases of movement, not in a sequence of steps.[53]

Sono Osato recognised that Tudor's musical method made sense in terms of narrative content:

I discovered that if I absorbed the musical phrasing rather than its measures, it would often lead me to the emotional substance of the steps.

I always felt he wanted the body to sing, rapturously, languorously, and longingly in turn.[54]

Tudor often denied the importance of steps in his work, partly perhaps because of his concern to develop new movement, but perhaps too in order to avoid the pronounced articulation of beat and rhythm of conventional ballet steps. Again, we are referring to what Tudor chose to emphasise as principles, which is not necessarily the full truth about his practice. His guidance notes on *Sunflowers* stress the leading role of the torso, much like in some styles of modern dance: 'As in all Tudor pieces, the torso is the most important part of the body, and the legs move in order that the body shall be carried where it needs to go, NOT because the legs are doing something that makes the body go along.'[55] However, as we shall see, emphasis on phrase and breath rather than steps does not mean imprecise correspondence between music and dance.

Tudor's rehearsal methods constantly shifted and developed. They included the well-known exercises in finding character, through reading literature, Stanislavskian exercises, talking through the motivation for movement, responding to imagery and so on, exercises from which material might build without any relationship to music. But he also began new pieces by asking dancers to sit and listen to the music and give him their impressions, sometimes incorporating their suggestions. Intense listening sessions around the record-player were part of the dancers' preparation for the original *Pillar of Fire*.[56] There were also times when he rehearsed musical co-ordination in detail, getting dancers to sing as they moved, to establish precise rhythm with the music: Topaz's 'Notes on the Music and Rehearsal Procedures' in *Jardin* refer to the fact that 'many rehearsals started or ended with Tudor's asking one of the principals to sing or identify on which note a particular movement was executed'.[57] Sometimes he would introduce an orchestral recording into rehearsal so that dancers could respond to instrumental timbre.[58] He understood the powerful contribution of timbre: after hearing the orchestral score of *Undertow*, he altered his original choreography in response.[59] And he welcomed the five orchestral rehearsals scheduled for the Swedish premiere of *Echoing*, generous compared with what he was used to in the US.[60]

Above all, Tudor was concerned with the dynamics and phrasing of movement. Sawyer, his pianist, learnt from him the importance of her supporting dancers in linking their class steps together and finding the shape of a whole phrase. She would do this by playing a single extended strand of music, rather than breaking up the music into a number of strands or phrases. In order to encourage breath phrasing, Tudor would often ask for operatic arias as class accompaniment. He would also draw analogies between dance and piano technique as each, in its own way, support a particular kind of dynamic: economical wrist and finger movements, for instance, achieving the same quality of lightness and speed as *battements dégagés*.[61]

Tudor's class practice involved exercises in rhythmic freedom and flux, shifting phrasing. Martha Hill's imagery is telling as she recalls his interest in seeing how movement material 'would adjust itself to the music . . . like water seeking its own level'.[62] At other times, he might create a phrase and split it with a break in the middle so that it no longer fitted the musical phrasing. Or he might set class steps in one metre and then have them danced to music of another metre.

As the last examples suggest, Tudor enjoyed 'mathematical' choreographic devices. Even in actual choreography, Tudor explored the tension between the musicality that came from narrative drive, emotion and musical breath and one that came from more mathematical devices. The *Sunflowers* rhythmic reduction of the music that he made with a separate rhythmic line planned for the dance is an example of this more objective, pre-plotted approach to relationships between music and dance. We might ask, was this prompted perhaps by his Schillinger experience (see p. 270)? (The posthumously published Schillinger *Encyclopedia of Rhythms*,[63] for instance, documents a mass of different rhythmic patterns.) Topaz recalls other use of techniques to ensure independent rhythmic lines:

like making a phrase one count longer than the musical phrase so that every time you repeated it the accent would fall on a different accent of the music. Instead of coming on the one, the second time it would come on the two and the third time it would come on the three. Or leaving one step out of the sequence so that the first time you did it it was eight [counts], and the second time you did it it was seven.[64]

There is more than one reason why Tudor liked to work with the written musical score. We have seen that he analysed the music from a score, marked up the printed page, even made a piano reduction of his own in preparation for a ballet. Scores undoubtedly also gave him the firm control over the musical element of the piece that he liked to have. After all, his was a controlling artistic personality concerned with the details of lighting design, curtain calls, the arrangement of dancers' names in the programme as well as with choreography and musicality. We recall that he was dubious about commissioning from composers who did not document their work in conventional musical notation.

Hynninen remembers Tudor changing his mind about the relationship between a dance phrase and its music, sometimes wanting to encourage a narrative point to be made clearly, at the expense of relationship to musical detail, sometimes wanting to shape the dance material in more direct response to its accompaniment. In other words, as a piece was revived on different occasions, he might at one time be led by narrative, at another, by the music.[65] Tudor had a very precise view of the musicality of his ballets: even if he changed his mind between revivals, his vision at a particular moment was thought through in meticulous detail.

We know that, for some pieces, he was strongly guided by a particular recording and remained influenced by that recording. For instance, it is likely that he was inspired by the 1928 recording of the *Kindertotenlieder* by Hermann

Rehkemper, only the second Mahler recording ever to have been made.[66] It is possible to relate choreographic ideas to some of the particular inflections in this performance. For instance, in the first song, the soloist performs an accented fall to the ground and rises up again to the impassioned 'Nacht' and 'Schranken' (bars 49, 51); breath suspensions with arms unfolding sideways match Rehkemper holding back during a lilt in the melody line. Tudor used specific recordings in his preparations too for *Jardin* (a 1933 Menuhin recording with the Paris Symphony Orchestra under Georges Enesco, see p. 291) and *Pillar of Fire* (a recording of the Minneapolis Symphony Orchestra under Eugene Ormandy).[67]

While respecting the opinions of his musicians, Tudor did not hold back from offering his own interpretive suggestions, to class pianists, rehearsal pianists and conductors alike. He had ideas of his own, precise ideas, and his choreography placed limits on possible musical interpretation. Many tempo and expression marks have been added to his musical scores, a number of which can be identified as in his own hand (see p. 289). Working notes for *Pillar of Fire* indicate specific details for tempo and dynamics throughout the score.[68] Some of these are supplementary or indeed slightly contradictory to what is already in the score: at bar 41, 'dim.' becomes 'dim & lento', and at bar 69, 'lebhafter' becomes '*poco* lebhafter'. An old American Ballet Theatre piano score bearing the names of the premiere cast contains another set of added markings. Philip Ellis, who conducted performances by the Birmingham Royal Ballet in 1995, has observed that a large part of the score has to be played more slowly for the ballet than for concert performance. In one section, he had particular problems with the slow pace (Part 4 of the ballet, the dance of the Innocents, see p. 318).[69] It is interesting that Tudor stressed not pressing on here, as many musicians might be inclined to do, and, in his working notes, he marks bar 258, in his own German, '*nicht* eilen' ('*not* hasty').

Sawyer remembers how carefully Tudor moulded her phrasing of the Schumann *Kinderscenen* for *Little Improvisations*, asking her to slow the tempo quite radically at certain points: some passages were 'on the verge of disaster'. Yet two members of the Juilliard piano faculty applauded her performance: 'one of the most revealing . . . I have ever heard of that piece'.[70] Neither of them mentioned the alterations in tempo. To them, Tudor's ideas were utterly convincing. Topaz considers that Sawyer's recording of this music is the only one that works for the ballet.[71] Similarly, the score notes for *Jardin* indicate clearly that 'there is no commercial recording of the work which suits Mr Tudor's needs vis-à-vis tempo'.

We turn now to *Jardin* for in-depth analysis. This, Tudor's first extant work, is considered one of the finest pieces that he ever made. By the time of its creation, he had already developed an individual method of working with music.

Jardin aux lilas

In the case of *Jardin aux lilas*, there is no doubt that a story idea first prompted Tudor's interest, after which he had to find suitable music. Originally, Tudor's concept was to base a ballet on a short story by the Finnish author Aino Kallas, which tells of a young peasant couple who are about to marry when the landowner proposes to exercise the *droit de seigneur*.[72] Tudor dropped the idea of *droit de seigneur* in favour of a forced marriage, and the designer Hugh Stevenson's vision of a ballet set in a lilac garden began to take over. The ballet was about character still, but not in any straightforward narrative sense, and Eugene O'Neill's stream-of-consciousness play *Strange Interlude* was an influence.[73] *Jardin* became a ballet about mood, location and memory as much as about story, in Proustian fashion, the lilac imagery conjuring up romantic situation and resonances of warm summer nights. Lilac scent was literally sprayed throughout the Ballet Club at the premiere. Set in Edwardian times, the 'story' given in the 1981 Labanotation score (taken from a programme) is as follows:

Caroline, about to enter upon a marriage of convenience, attends a farewell party to precede the ceremony. Among the guests are the man she really loves and the woman who, unknown to her, has been her fiancé's mistress. Quick meetings and interrupted confidences culminate with Caroline leaving on the arm of her betrothed, never having satisfied the desperate longing for the final kiss.[74]

Originally, the ballet's characters were listed as 'Caroline, the Bride to be; her Lover; the Man she must marry; an Episode in his past; her [Caroline's] Sister; a Sailor; her Young Cousin; a Soldier; a Friend of the Family.'[75] Soon, 'extra' characters to the central four were listed as guests, the number of whom increased to eight when Tudor set the ballet in New York for Ballet Theatre.

Tudor did not find his music easily. For a time, he worked with Fauré's *Ballade for Piano and Orchestra*, but decided that this was unsuitable, perhaps because of the percussiveness of the piano. Then, after considering using Russian music, he eventually found Chausson's *Poème pour violon et orchestre* and found ways for the movements formulated for the Fauré to fit the new music. The early Yehudi Menuhin recording of the *Poème* that initially inspired Tudor (see p. 282) accompanied the premiere of the ballet.[76] Many years later, at the 1967 Bath Festival, Menuhin played live for the ballet. In America, a new arrangement was commissioned for Ballet Theatre performances, by Amadeo Di Fillippi, although the original orchestration has been used subsequently.[77]

Tudor had specific ideas about interpretation at certain points in the score. Sawyer remembers that her piano rehearsal score was covered with points about phrasing,[78] and an old American Ballet Theatre piano score reveals a number of examples of specially 'choreographed' slowings of tempo, for instance, for the first unaccompanied violin solo near the beginning, and during the coda. Those who restage *Jardin* have to work particularly carefully to co-ordinate the solo violinist with the dancers, especially during the cadenzas, ensuring, for instance, that Caroline and the violinist 'breathe together', and that all the notes in the cadenzas are articulated rather than lost in rushed virtuoso display.[79]

For analysis of Tudor's musicality, a number of film versions of *Jardin* exist, many without sound. Together they indicate differences, some of these choreographic, some, I would guess, interpretive (both affecting musical relationships). Tudor was known to make small alterations for new casts and then to move back to earlier versions of his works: sometimes the size of the stage would prompt changes (those in the US, for instance, being much larger than the tiny Mercury Theatre stage in London). A number of scores of *Jardin* exist, in both Benesh and Labanotation, but the three in Labanotation provide good examples of modifications in the choreography over the years. The first was written in 1967 by Muriel Topaz, the second by Airi Hynninen in 1981, when Tudor felt that the earlier score was no longer an accurate representation of his piece, the third based on the Hynninen score but corrected and revised by Topaz in 1992.[80] The most readily available video source is the 1990 PBS broadcast of *Jardin* led by Leslie Browne as Caroline after a staging by Sallie Wilson.[81] It is a problematic recording, the result of many takes and much editing; it masks the spatial aspects of the theatre piece, and it blurs the distinction between stressed and less stressed events and entrances. I have compared this performance with a number of others available, in the New York Public Library Dance Collection,[82] and with a film in the Rambert Dance Company archive of Ballet Rambert performing *Jardin* (c. 1965). This last shows the ballet with the smaller cast as it was originally performed. The number of differences in steps and timing here suggest that the work developed a life of its own within the Rambert tradition, independently of Tudor, or that there might even have been an earlier Rambert 'version' of the ballet (like *Dark Elegies*, see p. 306). During the analysis, I will give examples of the kinds of differences that exist between the American sources. It is interesting, for a start, that the 1990 recording is slower, one minute longer and more lethargic, than the Menuhin recording to which Tudor created the piece. Larger stage spaces in America may have had something to do with this.

Interestingly, the Chausson score already had programmatic beginnings which bear striking links with the Tudor narrative. The music was based on a short story by Turgenev (1818–83) called 'The Song of Triumphant Love' which was originally the subtitle of the score, after the title *Poème symphonique pour violon et orchestre* (1896). Chausson dropped this subtitle and the term

symphonique'. Running through the Turgenev tale is the *idée fixe* of the 'chant
de l'amour', which Chausson may have considered when devising the main recurring theme of his work (Theme 1, first stated by the solo violin). The story,
which takes place in Ferrara in the mid-sixteenth century, tells of two men,
Fabio and Muzzio, in love with the same woman, Valeria. Fabio marries her;
Muzzio travels to the east and, on return, represents a dangerous erotic force
with his playing of a melody (on the violin) that he heard in the East – which
Turgenev calls 'the song of triumphant love'. Here is Turgenev's description of
the occasion when Muzzio first plays this violin song:

> the passionate melody flowed out under the wide sweeps of the bow, flowed
> out, exquisitely twisting and coiling like the snake that covered the violin-top;
> and such fire, such triumphant bliss glowed and burned in this melody that
> Fabio and Valeria felt wrung to the heart and tears came into their eyes: . . .
> while Muzzio, his head bent, and pressed close to the violin, his cheeks pale,
> his eyebrows drawn together into a single straight line, seemed still more con-
> centrated and solemn; and the diamond at the end of the bow flashed sparks
> of light as though it too were kindled by the fire of the divine song.[83]

Triumphant love? Is there not a measure of darkness, ambiguity, even anguish
here? Consider the sinister snake image, the pale cheeks, the feeling of being
wrung to the heart. Indeed, the story is about Muzzio's dangerous effect upon
Valeria and her inner turbulence.

In his book on Chausson, the musicologist Jean Gallois has suggested specific
links between moments in the Turgenev story and this highly perfumed, chromatic, late romantic musical score.[84] More important, and especially convincing, is that Gallois emphasises the obsessive, sinister, spell-like pressures in the
music. His is far from the usual sentimental interpretations of this music or the
musicological treatments that have merely emphasised formal values. Gallois'
account of the music also opens hermeneutic windows for us in our understanding of Tudor's ballet.

I have no way of knowing whether Tudor knew the Turgenev story that
inspired Chausson, but it is intriguing that his ballet too is about a woman,
Caroline, caught between two men (her Lover and the man she has to marry),
and that he uses a violin melody as a symbol of another passionate and socially
prohibited relationship (here between Caroline and her Lover). It is pertinent
that the music can be read semiotically in terms of love in any case. This is by
virtue of the gentleness and intimacy of the solo violin, first heard unaccompanied, and its considered especial emotional expressiveness and closeness to the
human voice in capacity to sing, and later in the ballet, by virtue of highly
passionate musical values. There is a heritage of nineteenth-century pro-

Ex. 5.2a. Chausson, *Poème pour violon et orchestre*, Theme 1.

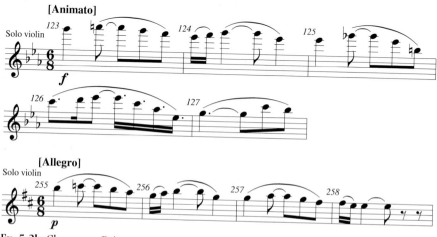

Ex. 5.2b. Chausson, *Poème pour violon et orchestre*, Theme 2 (two versions).

gramme music that presses its symbolisms upon the *Poème*, and Tudor's story confirms these within a narrative.

The solo instrument also has a strangely physical capacity. I am reminded of Roland Barthes' classic 1972 essay 'The Grain of the Voice', in which he proposes an aesthetics of musical pleasure, *jouissance* (with all the erotic connotations of that word).[85] Let us get back to 'the body in the voice' is Barthes' apparent manifesto, and he writes about this possibility as if it is transmitted directly from the body of the musician performer to become an embodied musical feature. He refers to examples of both singing and instrumental playing. Clearly Barthes took such physical music into his own body. There seems to be something particular about the solo voice, whether singer or instrument, that it can insinuate itself into our darkest and most private spaces. As Wayne Koestenbaum has mused upon the opera singer Leontyne Price – 'the singer destroys the division between her body and our own . . . '.[86] Dance can illustrate this intensity visually, as the dancers hear what we hear – and now that solo violin! Furthermore, as is argued later, the issue of timbre, be it of a solo instrument or of an instrumental group, is of particular importance in *Jardin*.

The *Poème* falls roughly into five sections. There is an exposition, Parts 1 and 2 presenting two main themes respectively, the first lento, the second animato (see Exs. 5.2a, 5.2b). Then there is a balancing development, Parts 3 and 4, bringing back the thematic material with variation, including that from the opening, and stepping up the previous animato to allegro. These four sections lead to a fortissimo orchestral climax, after which there is a slow coda. What happens on stage follows the same exposition-development pattern, the focus on individuals standing or moving very slowly and simply (Parts 1 and 3), and then on groups alternating with individual statements. We see the four key figures, Caroline, her Lover, the Man she must marry (or Fiancé), the Episode in his past (or Mistress), and how they relate to one another, and then everything speeds up: the lovers' meetings becoming more fleeting and more desperate, the group presence becoming more oppressive and powerful in preventing moments of privacy, until the major climax, when the whole cast holds still in a tableau. The coda follows as epilogue (after Theme 1 in Part 5). Climaxes on stage correspond with climaxes in the score too; points at which lovers are forced to break apart or where a particularly high level of personal emotion is expressed. *Jardin*, for the most part, proceeds at a hectic pace, constantly swerving from one situation to another. The layout of the music and choreography is shown in Table 5.2. This layout corresponds exactly with the Gallois analysis of the music, except that he includes the first eight bars of Part 3, the Star Gazing, as a bridge passage at the end of Part 2.

Jardin has the equivalent of leitmotifs that link music with drama. The love theme, or Theme 1, is first heard unaccompanied; it introduces the solo violin.

Part 1 3/4 bars 1–96
Opening: Caroline and The Man She Must Marry (Fiancé)
Lover enters
Mistress enters
'White boy' enters
3 Women crossing
Caroline enters
Lover enters
Caroline and Lover Pas de Deux   bar 31 Theme 1 (unaccompanied solo violin)
Mistress enters
Trio Caroline, Lover, Mistress bar 51 Theme 1
Two men enter
Caroline's solo (Cadenza)   bar 65   bar 77 Theme 1
3 Women and 3 Men enter

Part 2 6/8 bars 97–197
Caroline and Lover Pas de Deux
Entrances of four Couples
Four Couples
Caroline crossing
Mistress' entrance
Mistress and Fiancé Pas de Deux   bar 123 Theme 2
Entire Cast
'Sixes'
Caroline and Lover Pas de Deux   bar 180 Theme 2
Two women enter

Part 3 bars 198–239   6/8 bars 198–205   3/4 bars 206–239
Star Gazing
Lover's Solo   bar 206 Theme 1
Caroline enters
Caroline and Lover Pas de Deux   bar 225 Theme 1
Entrances of Fiancé and Mistress

Part 4 6/8 bars 240–300
Mistress' Solo
Chassé Section 2 couples and Caroline and Fiancé   bar 255 Theme 2
Mistress enters
Caroline and Lover Pas de Deux
Two Couples enter   from bar 283, series of 2-bar interpolations of
        Theme 1
Mistress and Fiancé Pas de Deux   bar 285 Theme 2
3rd Couple enters
Caroline and Lover enter

Part 5 3/4 bars 301–47
Caroline swoons[87] bar 301 Theme 1 (CLIMAX)
Quartet bar 317 to the end: Coda
Woman enters
Entire Cast enters
Farewells

Table 5.2. Layout of structure of *Jardin aux lilas*. The division into Parts is mine, but the
dance sections are listed as in the 1981 Labanotation score.

Isolated in this way, it becomes particularly important, and Tudor has it coincide with an equally significant dramatic moment, the first opportunity for Caroline and her Lover to dance together. After this, it is always associated with these two protagonists, like a reminder of their plight, the central dramatic issue.

The first account of the love Theme 1 sets itself apart from the rest of the ballet. It is unusual as solo violin sound, pure melody, without any accompaniment. A preceding drum roll and two beats like heartbeats ask us to attend carefully to it; the exaggerated sustainment of the first note and Tudor's further slowing of the tempo at this point (marked in the piano rehearsal score) also help to make the passage register clearly. What is most striking, however, is how the lovers identify with the violin and its song as if it becomes part of them. Fragile, yet extremely powerfully directed, it breathes with them, a deep melancholic passion (all the more because this is restrained, held within their bodies). Caroline and Lover can be likened to a single musical instrument, moving as one body, either face to face or one pressed tightly behind the other, sometimes literally stepping or gesturing with the notes of the melody. 'You must play the violin with the body,' Sallie Wilson instructs her dancers. Or, given the restrained style, are they played by the violin? Quite appropriately, this short statement has special status in the ballet, but I am inclined to think of it too as having a special resonance, like the violin song did in Turgenev's story. The suspicious, sensual power of music! Caroline and her Lover are for a moment enveloped by that music, moved to another plane of experience. It is a nice point that Caroline enters the stage for the first *pas de deux* to the strings, and on the B-flat that becomes the first note of the solo violin. There is a sudden concentration of focus downwards and inwards to the intimate, both aurally and visually.

The *pas de deux* begins with the Lover approaching Caroline from the wings, and the moment that she feels his hands behind hers, she flexes her wrists sharply, accenting the onset of the unaccented B-flat opening note of Theme 1. Caroline takes his hands up to her shoulders, unfolds her arms upwards and rises on to pointe, slowly and smoothly, following the contour and legato of the violin melody. Close behind, he supports and complements her as if they are one: they are lost in their music, and they are perhaps 'moved' by their music. During the next musical phrase (bars 37–40), Caroline steps away, temporarily anxious about onlookers, and then returns to him. Her steps clearly relate to the melodic rhythm, though not with pedantic precision. The effect is of a gently restraining influence on the movement. Then, his arm folded across her, the pair go on together, again moved, or here perhaps glided, by their music. But the next two phrases (bars 41–3, 44–6) are a striking development, becoming a dance accelerando, now not at all suggested by the musical patterning. The impression is that the pair are still 'with' the overall musical statement, but a sense of urgency develops. They maintain the musical pressure, but now it is as if they are more active, less passive to the violin, in doing so. The first phrase grows into a flurry of *port de bras*; the second turns from a *fouetté* into *balancés* that dissect into triplets the quarter-note progress of the melody – what Hugh Laing called dancing 'between the notes'.[88] The conclusion of the *pas de deux* slows again, back 'in tune' with the musical rhythm, but now, gradually, steps give way seamlessly into 'acting'. Gradually, Caroline and her Lover are no longer lost in their music. The moves are as follows:

1. The Lover kisses Caroline's hand bar 46, beat 1.
2. Reaching away from him, she raises her other hand to her forehead bar 46, beat 3.
3. They walk to upstage centre and the Mistress enters, bars 47 and 48.
4. Surprised by the intruding Mistress, now back in the 'real world', Caroline introduces her to her Lover, bar 49.
5. The Lover abruptly steps forward to kiss the Mistress's hand, bar 50.

Our eye darts in to the kiss, to her hand to forehead, and then we grasp what follows as a series of moves to distinct notes in the melody, separating, breaking our perception of continuity during the final musical crescendo on the solo violin. The *pas de deux* is a wonderfully eventful piece of choreography, shaped to flower from simple beginnings to intricate patterning and then to return to a simplicity hardened by dramatic accents. It is easy to lose its subtlety. Browne muddies motivation in the PBS video; in another video recording,[89] she starts out restlessly and concludes flamboyantly, obliterating the exquisite shaping of Tudor's choreography.

We get just one other brief glimpse of this losing of oneself in sound. It is the only other occasion when Caroline and her Lover dance alone to the Theme, a mere fragment of the Theme (bars 225–30). Here again there is a simple violin line (now accompanied); the relationships between Caroline and Lover (now side by side) and their music are similar. Again, there is a registral shift in the relationship between performer and music, but now much curtailed. But so often, the theme and solo violin (at first so significantly linked) are freed from each other, dissociated from Caroline and her Lover's actual presence on stage. Note that, at other times, the Theme is always orchestrated in such a way as to sound more public, and therefore heard as a memory or threat rather than 'experience'; perhaps some of the characters on stage do not 'hear' it at all, or at least do not understand it for its original meaning (see Ch. 2, p. 71).

The impassioned animato Theme 2 is a type of leitmotif too, particularly associated with the Mistress, although also hinted at during one of the more restless, desperate meetings between Caroline and her Lover. Indeed, both Themes 1 and 2 are associated with love, the struggle and passion of the two main women

protagonists; their increasingly urgent reiteration and combination towards the
end of the piece become a powerful metaphor for the desperate emotional situation in the ballet. It is interesting too that, whenever the Mistress appears, the
music is 'animato' or 'allegro', except during the epilogue when she too realises
that the drama has been played out. Even when she first enters with the other
guests, a succession of descending quaver patterns quickens the pace and hints
at future tension. She is desperate, certainly not resigned. The group of supporting guests nearly always dance to swift music too, so their threatening presence
accelerates the drama to its unhappy conclusion. Some of their music is 'social',
with waltz currents (from bars 164 and 255).

As the drama develops and these two women struggle and compete for their
own needs, their respective fragmented and overlapping Themes follow or anticipate their associated characters. Thus, there are suggestions of off- as well as onstage presences, disjunct voices crossing the action that is in immediate view,
memories, forewarnings, messy reverberations. It is a tease as to what we might
think some of the other characters on stage 'hear' or understand as we might of
these speaking voices, but we, the audience, can absorb them all into a complex
picture of inner turmoil and confusion. We have seen then that, through the
addition of dance narrative, the music develops new voices and presences that
act in dialogue with the dance. It is not just music for dancing but music that
speaks of individuals' minds and emotions.

As already mentioned, Theme 1 becomes more public as the piece progresses.
In the trio that immediately follows the opening *pas de deux*, perhaps only
Caroline and the Lover really recognise the theme, now harmonised and orchestrated, and what it means to them, not the Mistress. Straight after this, in
Caroline's solo to the violin cadenza, the Theme is quite different in spirit, more
tense, disturbed by under-parts that punctuate the notes of the melody. Yet the
possibility of the original thrill of identification is present through much of the
piece, held out though never again fulfilled. When the Theme next appears (at
first orchestrated, somewhat public, though later including wisps of solo violin),
the Lover dances his own soliloquy before three women party guests who comfort him. His initial *plié* in fifth position, *sissonne, chassé* and sequence of small
hops in *arabesque* recall steps from previous statements of Theme 1. Then he
dances alone with Caroline, to a clear rendering on solo violin, the passage that
I have already described. The opening notes of the Theme become a warning
in the bass line as the entire ensemble assembles for the climactic tableau, at
which point it becomes brutally victorious and a frighteningly public statement
of denial on full orchestra (brass blaring out with particular force in the 1933
Menuhin recording to which Tudor originally created the ballet). With the stage
frieze, the sense of identification between body and music is eradicated for good,
disembodied sound; extreme difference is the point. The Theme is entirely

public. So the Theme, after all, has a dark, destructive underside to its magical powers.

Thus, the end of *Jardin* has a significance in the ballet well beyond that of an emotional climax or culmination tidily using the final return of a principal musical theme followed by a quiet coda. It also represents a complete break in time within the piece. The climax does not represent real action or time – Maude Lloyd, the original Caroline, says that, from the start, audiences understood the brief passage when Caroline moves out of the frieze 'feeling and saying goodbye to everybody' to be in her mind.[90] Everyone else on stage remains frozen. Caroline moves as the solo violin links in for the third phrase of the Theme. Time stops, she moves and then, 'as if a film were being run in retrograde',[91] she returns to the frieze. Now too, suddenly, the whole piece up to this point appears like the reliving of memories from a distance, like a dream that breaks when emotions become overwhelming. Then, when all the characters come to life, it is as if Caroline walks from the real present into the future. As Tudor writes in his notes to the Labanotation score:

> The ballet continues a regular course of narrative choreography until the moment of Caroline's swooning into her betrothed's arms. The succeeding sleepwalking episode, which should be handled as though water divination was happening, and the succeeding sequence for the four principals should be looked upon as if the ballet until this moment were being regarded nostalgically from a period still forty years ahead.[92]

In the ballet, the moment of climax is much more extraordinary and exaggerated than in the music alone. Overpowering volume takes over: the photograph stillness comes as a shock, especially as it is marked by such a stark separation of energies, sound from body – maximum power in the music, nothing in the dance. There is also a harmonic jolt, a sudden, unexpected move to E-flat minor, which, though the home key, feels brand new in this particular context. These are the devices that help us to grasp the new concept of time that suddenly emerges. The climax is also a message about transference from private to public, having to relinquish private idealism to the demands of public behaviour, 'dictated' by the public musical forces. In more ways than one, the climax in *Jardin* is a distancing moment in the work, a moment of disjunction or fissure (see Ch. 2, pp. 71–3).

Instrumentation speaks in this work, broadly speaking, solo instruments suggesting what is private, tuttis what is public. The solo violin itself explores a number of different timbres, sweetly singing of intimacy and love – a sinister sweetness (identifying with Caroline and her Lover), later desperate and assertive, at times hysterical, with wild figuration that is virtually drowned out by the

Ill. 6. *Jardin aux lilas*, the departure of Caroline. Original cast on stage at the Mercury Theatre, January 1936, Maude Lloyd (Caroline), and to right Antony Tudor (Fiancé) and Hugh Laing (Lover).

rest of the orchestra surging to climax. We hear the violin more or less according to the power of the accompanying figuration, but we also hear the violin according to how much the choreography helps to bring it to our attention. At times, it clearly becomes the 'voice' of a particular dancer, for instance, the gossiping guest and then the nicer friend who arrive to accompany the Lover in a quiet trio (bars 188, 190). Each woman enters to a violin cadenza, each of these a passage where Wilson stipulates clear violin articulation in order that the dancers appear to run in on the notes. (Yet Menuhin dashes through the notes in his 1933 recording.)

Other instruments also become voices in the piece. The horns from time to time seem to sound a sombre warning. We hear them at the beginning. When the Mistress and another male guest enter (he appears to want to form a relationship with her) (bar 18), the oboe seems to speak with them: the dancers adhere closely to the rhythmic pattern of their melody line, and answering phrases on clarinet and flute are like 'voices off' in the trees. It is significant that, to these 'voices off' phrases, the two dancers make a point of listening for off-stage guests, who actually emerge to cross the stage as these musical voices gather continuity. These guests too can be read as reflecting distinct phrases (flute and clarinet); and then finally Caroline enters (to strings). Thus, at the outset, Tudor signals the importance of sound timbre within the piece.

We have seen then that integration of musical aspects in the analysis of this ballet reveals a new complex picture of inner turmoil and confusion and of public values intruding upon private feeling. Chausson's music adds extra voices in dialogue with the dance, reinforcing onstage voices, adding a dimension of offstage – another place, or another time, as well as contributing, together with movement, to that sense of extreme difference, between embodied sound and the complete separation of sound from body.

Timbral differentiation and climaxes from sheer orchestral force are primary features of late romantic musical style. So is the notion of continuous flow (see pp. 275–6), which Tudor subscribes to not only through his integration of mime and dance, but also through his seamless linking of phrases and episodes. So often in *Jardin*, a scene is overlapped or interrupted by the onset of the next one, without the tidy closure of movement phrasing matched by cadential resolution. So often too, we can observe a rising trajectory towards the end of a scene or episode, literally, in pitch, movement level and crescendo, before it gives way to the next episode. Indeed, rise in energy is emphatic during this emotionally turbulent piece, and energy tends to diminish only to increase again, except at the very end. We see how, for instance, the Mistress ends her main solo with a series of *relevés* that grow in desperation with the musical crescendo and rise in pitch; she holds up on pointe to the bitter end, only releasing the tension to run offstage as the party group usurps her space. The same inhalations and tensions of suspension occur during episodes too: in the first trio, for instance, at the end of the third bar (Theme 1), all three run upstage, 'breathing in' on pointe/demi-pointe as if trying to draw out time. Up in pitch means literally going upstage on many occasions, backs to audience, as if the characters strain to escape. Tudor also achieves a sense of continuous development and flow through the preponderance of asymmetrical phrase structuring during the piece. Rare too are the occasions when dance and music simply repeat together. *Jardin* is about change and growth rather than balance and closure.

Yet Tudor's view of this high romantic music is not straightforward. He stresses that his own ballet is not romantic, but rather dramatic:

The delusions seem to include that of regarding this piece as 'romantic', because there is a romanticism about the scenery with its overwhelming masses of lilacs, and of the predominantly blue lighting . . .

Although the short story based on the idea of the *droit du seigneur* was abandoned, the situation remains a dramatic one, without the former melodrama, and the 'dramatis personae' of the four principals are thrown into relief by the background of the young friends of Caroline with their easy sort-of-romanticism of the adolescents and teenagers.

When Rambert,

tried to get my dancers to 'put more emotion' into it, to 'feel with the emotions', or in other words to 'ham it up' and turn it toward the melodrama that I was so studiously avoiding, then it became necessary to forbid her to attend any further rehearsals of this piece . . .[93]

Tudor adopts a number of devices for checking the sentimentality that has sometimes been interpreted in the music. He adds his own hard edge to the sound experience. Perhaps his most obvious device is the taut public movement style that constantly returns as common denominator. There is the held torso, arms maintained close to its sides, the body taking up little room in space, indicating the repression of strong feelings enforced by social pressure, or one arm shooting dead straight aloft, a gesture of alarm against a fiercely correct body posture. We might look at the pedestrian role of the Fiancé that Tudor created for himself, frighteningly reserved, his walk strict and level with unswinging arms: he partners, gestures and holds on to his power. In *Jardin*, the stiff, public stance is released fleetingly in private, but outbursts of passion and speed are severely contained, most emphatically of all at the moment of major musical climax. The music continues to flow, swell and subside, against Tudor's restraining impulse. Our eye is often drawn to torso, arms and head, the parts that Tudor himself stresses as key to his movement style, but there are many occasions in *Jardin* when arms and torso are held above intricate footwork. This is gentle footwork without pronounced accents, but it nevertheless draws the eye down to the ground, betrays the character's anxiety, and, as steps do so well, it makes us especially aware of rhythmic patterning and relationship to musical rhythm.

Rhythmic devices are a prime means for maintaining emotional tautness. There are occasions when meticulously timed gestures cut insistently across the musical flow. At the opening, for instance, Caroline stands motionless beside her Fiancé, her left hand grasping her right upper arm behind her back. She sharply releases her hand and then slowly moves it, flat and stretched, down to the right wrist; a few moments later, the Lover bursts in to greet her, gestures 'stop, no,' when he grasps the situation and leaves hurriedly. Sharp dance accents cut across musical legato and melodic suspensions, as restless 'moments' that punctuate the musical flow, preventing us from relaxing into this flow and immediately setting the emotional scene for the entire piece.

Tudor also plays against musical rhythm in more developed dance sequences. This has already been demonstrated in the analysis of the first *pas de deux* for

Caroline and her Lover. To an orchestrated account of Theme 1, the trio that immediately follows further demonstrates this kind of independent rhythmic relationship between music and dance. It also shows similar flowering and patterns of accelerando. Refer now to the diagrammatic analysis of the trio's musical-choreographic structure, which indicates differences between the 1967 and 1981/92 Labanotation scores (see Exs. 5.3a, 5.3b). At first, the dancers move closely to the melodic rhythm save for a few 'dotted rhythm' extra steps, their first phrase to the rising melody line ending with a run upstage and 'inhalation' on demi-pointe (see p. 294). Later, the trio respond to changes in musical speed between crotchets and minims, but exaggerate this difference. Restless travelling *petit allegro*, triplets, *sissonnes*, *assemblés*, *jetés*, again dissect the crotchets and contrast with a sculptural configuration and slow-moving *port de bras*: here all three are in a line facing the downstage right corner, the end of a passage downstage to the falling, second melodic phrase. Although there is a clear connection with and sensitivity to musical structuring here, it is as if Tudor wants to convey restlessness and repressed energy through his own differences in pace. Contrast exists both within the dance and between dance and music; the music may be relaxed, but Tudor will not have his dancers let up, for time is short and they have a lot on their minds. I am also reminded here of Croce's appreciation of Tudor's work: 'the oddity and elegance of its musical line – it can be looked at abstractly so to speak . . .' The dynamic ebb and flow and crazy foot rhythms are eventful in themselves. The effect of restlessness and unpredictability is increased by asymmetry: the lack of repetition in the material, the contrasts between unison and two-plus-one arrangements, Caroline and Lover splintering off from the Mistress during Phrase 4 (the trio concludes with the couple completely separated from her).

We also see a restless pulling against musical rhythm by the Coda quartet. The guests process simply into the wings, leaving the two principal couples stepping slowly forwards, Caroline with her husband of the future, the Lover and Mistress brought together as outsiders. Soon they move into lifts, expansive gestures of the legs, and brief forays through space. Significant moments punctuate the episode, two very brief portraits, the dancers facing one direction and then reversed into the other. They form a line from up- to downstage, but each of them is angled differently so that you can see them all and notice that they glance towards each other as well. On repetition, the couple at the back stand in front and vice versa. Then there is the ingenious manipulation of the two couples side by side, partners changing position so that different pairs on the inside can communicate with each other, the Mistress with the Fiancé, and then Caroline with her Lover. A lot happens very quickly in this short quartet, before the real quietening begins. Something of an equivalent occurs in the music, a very long dominant pedal in the bass delaying at the same time as leading us to expect

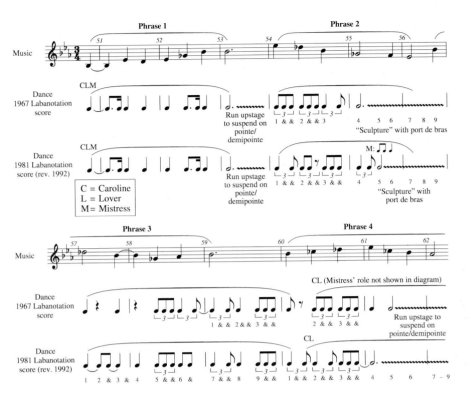

Ex. 5.3a. Tudor, *Jardin aux lilas*, rhythmic diagram of Trio. Caroline, Lover and Mistress, bars 51–62 (first four phrases).

The dance counts occasionally indicated in the score and included here clarify the precise relationship musical pulse, even though Tudor sang rather than counted when rehearsing the ballet himself.

The scores reveal the following differences. Phrase 2 runs on beat later in the 1981/92 score than it does in the 1967 score, travelling slightly further, and with an extra step included at the beginning. The steps in Phrase 3 are identical, but their rhythms are different. The movement material for Phrase 4 differs. It begins, in the 1967 score, with two small *cabrioles*. Instead, in the 1981/92 score, there is an anticipation at faster speed of the small *jetés* and *assemblé* that start the 'Sixes', a later section for six couples in a circle (see p. 300). Tudor, in other words, introduces here a point of cross-reference.

The 1990 PBS broadcast of *Jardin* conforms with the 1981/92 score, although it shows slight timing variations between members of the cast. For example, in Phrase 3, Caroline and her Lover (Leslie Browne and Ricardo Bustamente) finish dancing before the bar-line, rather than after the bar-line as the Mistress (Martine van Hamel) does and which is indicated for all three of them in the score. This is a point where the third dance phrase overlaps the beginning of the (fourth) musical phrase.

The above diagram, showing the relationship between the separate rhythmic lines of music and dance, is probably the kind of diagram that Tudor himself made of *Sunflowers* (see p. 270).

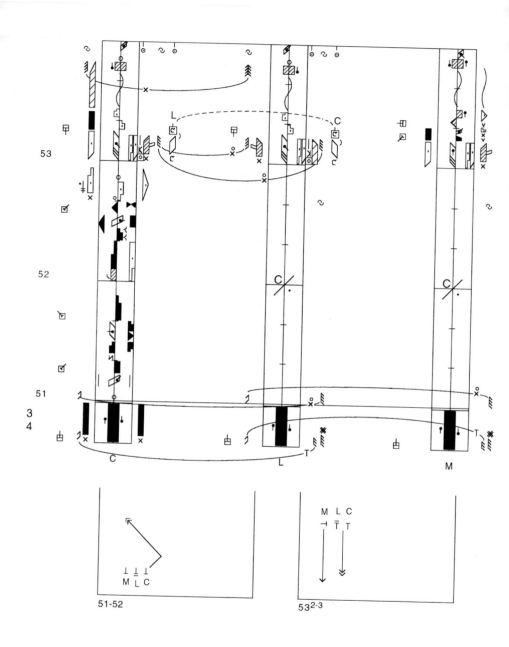

Ex. 5.3b. Tudor, *Jardin aux lilas*, Trio: Caroline, Lover and Mistress.

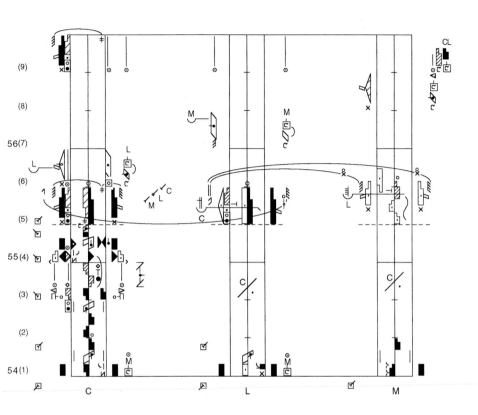

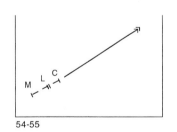

54-55

Ex. 5.3b (contd.)

resolution. But Tudor, as we have seen in the previous examples, expands upon suggestions in the music and exaggerates the effect of musical tension.

When the dancers do let up at the very end of the ballet, the result is like a defeat. There is still further chromaticism and touches of minor tonality before resolution into E-flat major, but soon there is no dance impulse of any kind to meet the music, only hand and arm gestures or simple walking. The Lover rushes to offer a spray of lilacs to Caroline, her Fiancé walks off to get her wrap, and the guests quietly assemble to say goodbye. Gesturing farewell to each guest in turn, Caroline marks out the three beats of the bar on a series of descending trills, an effect of extreme simplicity, minimalism after what has gone before. Then all, except the Lover, calmly walk off stage.

In a couple of instances, Tudor's choreography crosses the metrical organisation of the music. There is the passage called 'Chassé Section' (Part 4: bars 255–8), which exists in two versions in the Labanotation scores, one of which crosses the music. Couples enter one by one, in *chassé pas de bourrée* sequences that are rather like ballroom steps. The crossing version (first shown in the 1967 score) runs in units of 7, 7 and 10 counts, fitting into 4 bars of 6/8 (24 counts in all). The other version (included as one of two alternative versions in the 1981/ 92 score) fits the musical metre throughout with its 6-count units. This is the version used in Wilson's ABT revival (seen in the 1990 broadcast). Tudor changed the choreography to fit the bar-lines – Hynninen believes that he did this in order to cover the large stage of the Metropolitan Opera House – but she persuaded him to change the choreography back to the original version, which is both more subtle and harder for dancers to learn. Hynninen also points out that such treatment is quite typical in Tudor's choreography.[94] Topaz remembers yet another 7, 7, 10 version, beginning on count 2 of the first bar. Tudor eventually gave up trying to get dancers to achieve this level of subtlety and only the two versions remain in the final 'approved' score,[95] both beginning with the musical downbeat.

In another passage called 'Sixes' (Part 2: from bar 164), the dance units stride across the two-bar units of the 6/8 music. For six unison couples in a circle, there are two repeating three-bar units of material: each consists of two little *jetés* with the working legs forwards and then back, a *petit assemblé, glissade* into a *grand jeté*, and finally a *promenade* for the woman, during which she swoops into *plié* and up again. In some versions (the ABT film and, interestingly, the 1965 Rambert film), the three opening jumps also create a 3/4 pattern that cuts across the predominant 6/8 of the music, but which, in fact, matches the pattern of the accompanying bass line. The scores indicate this 3/4 pattern only as the unit begins to repeat for a third time (bar 170) (see Exs. 5.4a, 5.4b).

There is little 'Mickey-Mouse' duplication of strong musical accents in the dance. We recall Tudor's points for Topaz on *Jardin* (see pp. 278–9), and a fine

Ex. 5.4a. Chausson, *Poème pour violon et orchestre*, music for 'Sixes'.

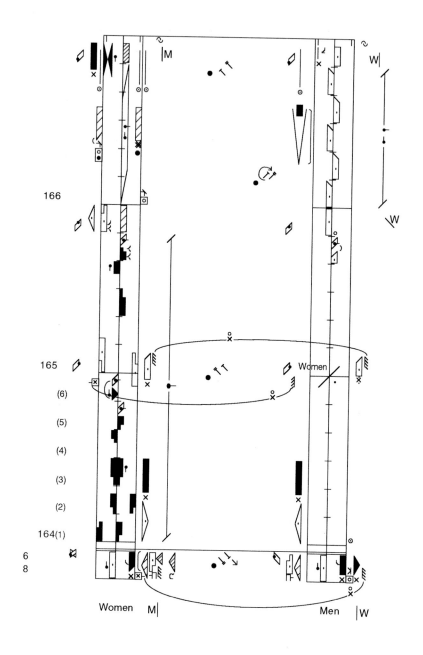

Ex. 5.4b. Tudor, *Jardin aux lilas*, 'Sixes'.

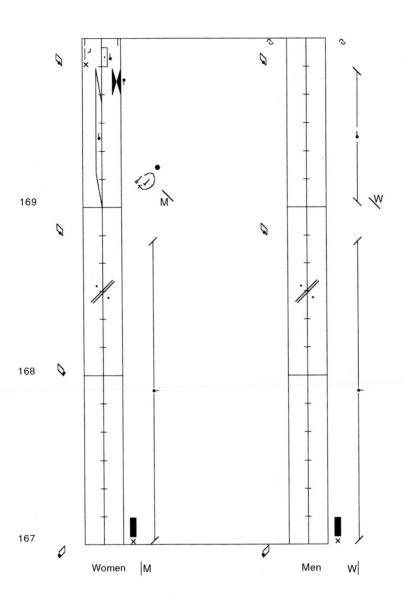

Ex. 5.4b. (contd.)

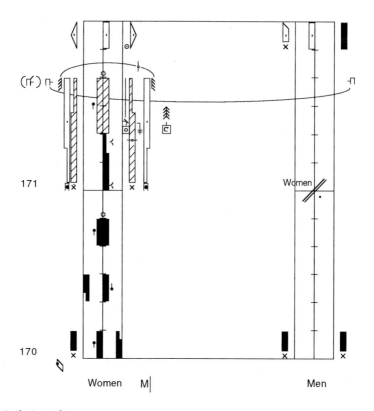

171

170

Women   M|

Men

Ex. 5.4b. (contd.)

example of the subtlety of accent play is the end of the first trio. Here, according to the 1981/92 score, Caroline, her Lover and the Mistress jump upwards with their up-accent on the musical accent (bar 65), while two men run in and jump up immediately afterwards in ricochet effect. In the 1967 score and ABT film, the two men jump first, before the trio: in the score, they jump before the musical accent (with the trio on the accent) and, in the film, just after the accent, and the trio after that. Whichever of these versions is correct in Tudor's terms, and he may well have changed his own mind, it is interesting that none goes for the blatant all-in-unison synchronisation of accents.

According to the Labanotation scores, very few steps in the ballet avoid all relationship to musical pulse: all the examples discussed so far show them relating mathematically, with complete precision, to some kind of pulse in the music, even when nesting within music that moves at a slower rate. Exceptionally, both scores indicate 'five rhythmically even *balancés* to musical retard' at the end of Part 2 (bar 197), when the two women guests who have just danced with Caroline circle the stage. The passage lasts for just over one bar. And there is another passage of *balancés* crossing the musical pulse, during the Mistress's solo (bars 250–1), but this is precisely timed. Topaz recalls the difficulty that this presented the dancer, and, at first, her own difficulties too, as the notator:

> It took some time to discover that what Tudor wanted was a very accurate four in the dance against an unarticulated three in the music, so that the whole phrase existed as cross accents between the dance and the music, although neither dance nor music actually felt accented.

It is significant perhaps in terms of the unaccented look of the movement that Tudor would not count out what he wanted. Topaz continues:

> As Tudor knew better than any of us, there was no point in explaining mathematically to the dancer what he wished, and eventually she learned to 'feel' the rhythm accurately, but the notator had absolutely to understand the phenomenon [mathematically] in order to write it correctly.[96]

This point only confirms the subtlety of Tudor's structuring, both at a broad level, as the choreography connects with the music in ways that are certainly not the most obvious, and at the level of detail. His dance phrases have 'oddity and elegance' of form, but they do not punch out pulse or metre; not, for instance, like those of Balanchine. Rather, *Jardin* introduces the whisper of allegro feet, and breath, always breath – Denby notes how the work became more effective when 'danced here and there with a slight advance before or retard behind the beat'.[97]

*   *   *

Flow and continuity stand out in any assessment of Tudor's characteristic style, often described drawing on sea imagery: dance phrases riding the music 'like waves',[98] or the interweaving of music and dance 'almost tidal in effect'.[99] Tudor's musical style soon made its mark as highly original, if not controversial, and unsurprisingly by the standards of the 1930s, his choreography was often read as inexact or contrary to its music. Bradley spotted his independent musical approach, clearly already established by the time he reviewed *The Descent of Hebe*. He is obviously not comfortable with it: 'It is indeed, a general failing in Tudor's choreography that too often his movements don't match the music with sufficient exactness.'[100] Maude Lloyd remembers in her own early experience with Tudor, that 'he always liked to work against the music and not with it',[101] and 'he fought so against it [the Chausson *Poème*]'.[102]

A lagging rhythmic style, as if, in *Jardin*, 'stepping on grass', is often mentioned by Tudor dancers. Sallie Wilson: 'Don't move until you hear the note start.' June Morris: 'I'm musical to the point that sometimes I anticipate, and

Barbara [Fallis] was the kind that would hear it and do it afterwards . . . He much preferred Barbara's [style] . . . just after the beat in *Pillar* and so that it was through the music.'[103] Hynninen recalls that Tudor preferred the 'untaught, meandering look' at the early rehearsal stage of *Leaves*, 'around' the music and not too 'neat'.[104] However, it is important that this 'lagging' or 'meandering' effect does not necessarily mean a vague relationship to musical note or pulse. Topaz's notes on the 1988 revival of *Jardin* indicate that, however *apparently* distinct the rhythmic lines of music and dance, Tudor required movement to occur at a precise time in relation to the score, with certain steps corresponding to certain notes, 'on' the music in this particular sense.

Conductors had to become accustomed to the idiosyncrasies of Tudor's style. Hugh Laing recalls Leon Barzin's difficulties when Tudor joined New York City Ballet, the conductor having got used to the Balanchine style, which was much more driven by musical beat. Barzin would hold back in *Jardin* to enable the dancers to 'get on the notes', but Laing had to explain that the dance was 'not percussive in the way [Balanchine is]' and he drew a musical analogy: 'I said "It's a fiddle thing, it's not a piano . . . ".'[105] Not surprisingly, the Tudor musical style, like that of Ashton (see Ch. 4, p. 202), was unnatural to the Balanchine dancer. Tanaquil LeClercq describes how Tudor follows the melody: 'It was really the nitty-gritty of getting there on time . . . but he's not musical. You have to run, run, run, and when the orchestra hits the high note, you have to be up, mid-air somewhere.'[106] Contrast her generalisations with Tudor's subtle distinctions between the timings of musical and dance accents in *Jardin* (see pp. 278–9). LeClercq was used to a much more motorically driven musicality.

However, as we have already seen in *Jardin*, there is much variety within the Tudor style: stepping out more or less – and not for long – to the rhythm of the melody line, just tracing its overall continuity and boundaries, relating to an accompanying voice, dancing 'between the notes', or sometimes halting for a moment while the music carries on. And the musical style varies according to the movement style of each piece: Tudor works have their own idiosyncrasies.

Dark Elegies is interesting in that its emotional solo statements project a kind of music visualisation at particular points during the musical phrasing. I am speaking of the American Ballet Theatre version of the piece,[107] as opposed to the different version maintained independently over the years by Ballet Rambert. In the second song *pas de deux* 'Nun seh' ich wohl, warum so dunkle Flammen', these points occur characteristically at the ends of musical phrases, as single or pairs of accents; for each of them the woman strikes an angular, taut picture. The final notes of the musical phrases indicate a slight release or outward breath, on the weak beat of the bar, a relative drop in tension after the preceding accent on the downbeat. However, on each of these final notes, the dancer insists on holding tension within the body and not releasing it until the onset of the

Ex. 5.5. Mahler, *Kindertotenlieder*, II. 'Nun seh' ich wohl, warum so dunkle Flammen'.

next phrase. Thus, at the beginning, Tudor choreographs the dissonance-resolution at the end of the musical motif as a throw of the leg into second position 'resolved' upwards into a high lift, the woman's body narrowed like a pencil, arms tautly by the sides (see Ex. 5.5).

The fact that these dance moments are such clear, accented, staccato pictures in tension seems to divorce them from the preceding fluid running into them. I read this *pas de deux* as a series of abrupt outburst images. Another of these is the high lift, with the woman's face in her hands, after which she pitches forwards into a tight, angular crouch. We see this during the first utterance of song (at [1]), the dance accents occurring at the end of a gentle, legato line (see Ex. 5.6). Soon, to a recurrence of the opening musical motif (two bars before [1a], bars 20–1), the woman lies back across the man's right arm, her body flat like a table, one move, followed by his painfully pathetic gesture of the other arm into an angle over her body, second move (see Exs. 5.7a, 5.7b). At the end of the dance (three bars before [4]), lifted horizontally aloft, she completes the motif by lifting her arms sharply over her head, crossed, supplementing the taut line of her body. This is music visualisation of a kind, the accenting of isolated notes, almost despite the music, and the effect is that the whole musical phrase feels distorted.

The eye seems to lead the ear to perceive the music differently. There are a couple of moments of release of tension, when the couple rock backwards and forwards centre stage, she on her knees, he standing beside her, or when the man kneels behind her lying body and looks right and left to two 'friends' for comfort. Apart from these, the dance undermines all sense of respite and softness in the music.

Ex. 5.6. Mahler, *Kindertotenlieder*, II.

Ex. 5.7a. Mahler, *Kindertotenlieder*, II 'Nun seh' ich wohl, warum so dunkle Flammen'.

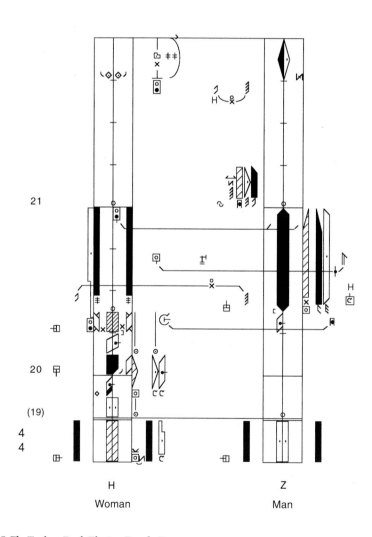

Ex. 5.7b. Tudor, *Dark Elegies*, Pas de Deux.

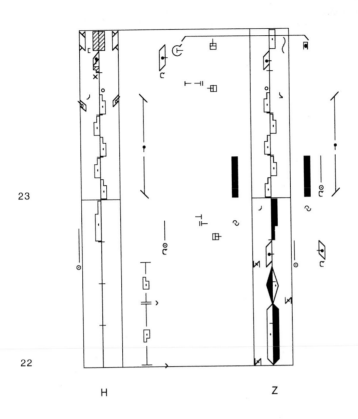

Ex. 5.7b. (contd.)

The Rambert company version of the *pas de deux* is clearly different choreography. Detailed word notes on the choreography written in the 1930s indicate a clear relationship with this version, which is documented both in a silent film and in 1988 rehearsal videos.[108] The notes also testify to the fact that the work changed considerably once it reached America. The Rambert version of *Elegies* has some similar musical tendencies to that of the ABT version, but it is nevertheless very different in general musical style. It seems to respect the shape of the whole musical phrase far more, it allows effects of exhalation as well as inhalation (especially the 1988 version), there are far fewer staccato accents, particularly pairs of accents at the ends of phrases, and it is more overtly emotional. For instance, referring to the image just before [1a], the woman in the Rambert version merely leans lightly against the man's arm (not to make a striking picture and not completed by his other arm). As the new musical phrase begins, she drops further into one fast rocking movement, from which she is pulled back up; then both dancers fall into a run away from and back across each other with a full body drop at the end of the musical statement: 'Doch ahnt' ich nicht.' The timing as well as look of the movement in the ABT version is different; the result is more stilted, much less about giving into weight and anguish (see Ex. 5.7b). We find short passages of stabbing at or printing out the melody line in other parts of *Dark Elegies*, and again they make musical moments sound more choppy than they really are. The Rambert version of the work has a different way of showing emotional turmoil. It is far less inclined to achieve it through discrepancies in impetus and tension between music and dance. In the 1988 performances, the revival during the time of Richard Alston's directorship, the dancers are clearly listening and responding to what they hear, not fighting the musical dynamics. There are choreographic differences between the English and American *Elegies*, but the differences in timing and dynamics are far more extraordinary. Whether they came about because Tudor altered the work in America or because the Rambert version slipped 'naturally' into this more harmonious relationship with the music is an interesting point for speculation. Certainly, the halting, picture-punctuated style is also a feature of *Pillar of Fire*, one of the first ballets that Tudor created in America.

Yet *Dark Elegies* is not just one style. There are also simple repeating bar-length movement patterns in folk-dance style, appropriate to the community statement of the piece, relieving the solo statements of anguish. Their rhythms sometimes match the melody line precisely, with subtle dynamic shading, for instance, the fast heel-and-toe footwork within the line dance of the third song (an idea that apparently stemmed from Tudor's holiday experience of Yugoslav dance).[109]

The *Pillar* style contains greater extremes of held tension within the body than *Elegies*. Freezes and halts are a prominent aspect of Hagar's language, whilst Schoenberg's music, expressionist and more violently anguished than either the Chausson or Mahler, continues to surge around her. There seems also to be a greater freedom from musical pulse than in *Jardin* or *Elegies*, sometimes an almost arbitrary relationship between musical and dance detail: movement motifs recur in different musical contexts, re-rhythmicised, but not necessarily fitting musical rhythmic patterning clearly. Gestures, after all, have to be somewhat restricted in dynamic and timing in order to read with a particular meaning. Whilst the score indicates precision in timing and relation to beat, the performance style acts in tension with this to make more of particular moments of contact and to give the *impression* of fluidity between these moments. The trio in Scene 1 is a good example of this style. Hagar, her flirtatious Younger Sister and the Friend who will become Hagar's husband are dancing. The sister starts alone in a long phrase, with barely any internal repetition of movement, later inviting Hagar to join her in unison. The sister's motifs are a toss of the head, skittering steps from fifth position on pointe out to a parallel second position, a tight crossing of one pointed foot over the other. All these are stated within phrases that clearly bend into the music at moments: like the beginning, where Tudor takes the lilting 6/8 rhythm into a gentle skipping movement, or, later, when a *relevé* in *arabesque* and toss of the head match two wispy curving up-and-over fragments of melody. The musical metre remains a framework but the effect is of musical gusts and eddies supporting particular movements around which other detail appears to establish its own patterns. Perhaps this tricky, apparently 'casual' fluidity of style is a reason why music and dance ended up unsynchronised throughout the 1973 television performance of *Pillar*.[110]

Different interpreters 'staple' different movements to different moments in the music, and some staple more moments than others. Whether or not Tudor would have approved all such stylistic freedoms, I am not sure. Take the phrase of the Young Man from the House Opposite in the seduction *pas de deux* of Scene 1. In the Swedish film of *Pillar*,[111] the man dances freely and urgently within the musical phrase, but, in an earlier film,[112] Hugh Laing weights his lunges precisely with the deep accents in the bass line, giving a brutal, sinister heaviness to his statement. Such dance accenting encourages us to hear the corresponding moments in the music more clearly; conductors might also pick up on what they see and alter their own phrasing and accentuation accordingly.

The ballets described so far illustrate just some characteristics within Tudor's range of musical treatment. Gestural relationships between music and dance become much more of a feature in *Undertow*, while the choreography of *Cereus*, in the temper of contemporary American youth, responds to the pounding pulse of Geoffrey Gray's percussion score. Other pieces use conventional ballet steps and, with them, more conventional ballet rhythms – for parody effect in *Gala Performance*, or for pedagogical reasons, as in some of the dance arrangements for training dancers, like *Little Improvisations* or *Exercise Piece*.

Romeo and Juliet bears the most fragile relationship to its music, indeed it only clarifies Delius's musical structure in the broadest sense of ebb and flow. Many passages of dancing are like a highly styled form of speech, or rather the transparent music suggests thoughts or feelings that, when accompanied by the impulses of movement, develop the impression of spoken articulation. At the opening, Tudor picks out the melodic centre of gravity rather than the downbeat beginning of a phrase, with a simple hand gesture, or a *relevé* that brings Juliet towards the bedroom window. Then, the onset of a musical gesture might be met with stillness or the gentlest bloom of a movement out of nowhere. In the Bedroom *pas de deux*, the sweet opening theme of the *Irmelin* Prelude starts up again on a solo violin, as a musical 'return' (see Ch. 2, p. 86); Juliet simply resolves her devastatingly open backbend, a very slow, quiet return to stability.[113] Often, Tudor visualises one in a pair of musical gestures and leaves the other free to the ear. He does not express any balance within the music. One of the musical phrases ends with a high lift, Romeo carries Juliet literally across the beginning of the next phrase, and then, against the musical phrasing, she switches direction in the lift, dramatically and passionately. A little curling triplet motif takes the pair turning and dropping swiftly to the floor for one last embrace; its other occurrences are left unmarked. Delius' music wanders; it is mesmerising. In the mode of an accompaniment, Tudor's movement gives it edge, variety and tension, through idiosyncrasies of timing, a broad palette of gesture and emotional continuity between these gestures. The rhythmic structure is about as far away as you can get from measured proportions. Delius is one of Tudor's least theatrically incisive musical choices. As Denby suggests, dance continuity from secure contact with musical impetus can easily be lost in such circumstances, although a sensitive conductor such as Beecham could shape his musical interpretation here to support the choreography (see Ch. 2, pp. 99–100).

Compared with Ashton or Balanchine, a strikingly distinctive feature of Tudor's work is its style of phrase or unit construction, and this has important implications for musical-choreographic style. His phrases are often long, their parts flowing seamlessly into the whole, often not repeated, often not balanced by a phrase of similar length in a question–answer or antecedent–consequent format.[114] This is the style of much of the music that Tudor chooses, but, even if he finds easy-on-the-ear symmetries in a score, he goes out of his way to counteract them. He does this just as he sets dance and music in a dialogue of conflicting accents and rhythmic patterns. Relationships between similar units of dance material are often complex: Tudor prefers evolution to straight repetition. Evading our sense of security and expectation so that it is often quite hard to grasp structurally, Tudor's work has a restlessness and anxiety built into it. Thus, the structuring of phrases is a major contributing factor to his expression.

In some of Tudor's late work, the dynamic style is much less pointed than before, yet the asymmetrical disturbances remain apparent. We see this in the short ballet *Continuo*, perhaps the most formal ballet that Tudor ever made. Set to the well-known Pachelbel Canon, which is in fact not a canon at all but a set of variations over a repeating two-bar ostinato, the piece is for three couples. There is minimal content in the conventional sense, a hint or two of courtly dance, a slight move towards individual expression as the couple units break down within groups or into solo statements. I like to think that Tudor was experimenting here with ways of enlivening a repetitive musical structure. One ploy is an unpunctuated flow of steps, no counts, no stepping on the beats, the repeat of a unit material just simply following the end of the last one, with no musical marker – pure continuity. This does not mean rhythmic freedom for the performer – indeed the steps, here too, are timed precisely to the music – but that the unpunctuated flow disguises such connections. *Jardin* responds to pulse much more clearly. Thus the opening phrase of *Continuo*, performed three times around the stage, more or less covers two musical ostinati. As it swells and subsides, but never stops, we sense the shifting internal proportions and organic relationship between its little skips, supported turn and high circling lift in *attitude*. Throughout the piece, Tudor subverts the bald symmetry of the musical ostinato. Dance phrases never express balance: they are constantly in flux and asymmetrical when symmetry might most be expected.

As *Continuo* progresses, a light, lilting pulse develops, responding to musical pulse, but again obliquely, again subverting any sense of balance through straight repetition of rhythmic pattern. If a pattern comes back, it is more likely than not to have a new edge to it. I am reminded of the class games in shifting rhythm that Tudor used to play (see pp. 280–1). Patterns recur in different relationship to musical metre, sometimes because they never fitted it in the first place, sometimes despite the fact that they did fit: a kind of *pas de bourrée* motif followed by *passé* is constantly reinterpreted at different points within the musical bar, and sometimes the *passé* comes straight out of the *pas de bourrée*, or after a short break, or after a longer one. The patterning seems both arbitrary and a tease.

Continuo is such that we can sit back and enjoy its easy quality of movement and totally unemphatic differences, a lulling experience, or we can try to fathom out the details of its construction, and that is a taxing game. It calls for both responses.

If *Continuo* is unusual as one of Tudor's most formal constructions, his other works are very different from each other in their approach to narrative or sequence of events. Plot and situation are more or less developed, statements more or less ambiguous. We are now looking at the large structure of Tudor's work. *Echoing of Trumpets* is one of his most straightforward 'story' works, detailing a series of events: soldiers assaulting women – a particularly graphic episode shows a soldier stamping viciously on a hand holding a scrap of bread; a love duet; the shooting of a woman's lover; a duet between the woman and the body of her lover; the revenge strangling of one of the soldiers; and so on. Martinů's music, the *Fantaisies symphoniques* (Symphony No. 6), constitutes a chain of contrasting sections, some reappearing in different form. This construction suits well a story in which danger lurks constantly and the force of oppression breaks out with alarming regularity. Between these outbreaks are episodes that show the brightness of love, invoke sympathy towards the oppressed women, or demonstrate the growing frustration of a situation that can never be relieved. Episodic music with appropriate programmatic values fits this kind of dance narrative very well, yet it also might be seen as constraining, and it does not release Tudor's most imaginative choreography.

Pillar of Fire is a far more subtle construction, and, like *Jardin*, it does not represent a straightforward time sequence of events. It does not therefore favour a kind of musical organisation where sections of a particular quality and time length occur in a particular order. Here, Tudor is much more interested in encouraging feelings to emerge. He lets us see the events through the eyes of Hagar, but these events are simply a framework around which the emotional ebb and flow of Schoenberg's score can enhance the portrayal of Hagar's emotional situations. The ballet is in two scenes, the first a street showing Hagar's house and the House Opposite and the second a forest. In conventional narrative terms, the seduction of Hagar is the climax in terms of drama, and it happens rather early in the work for a conventional climax, in fact, about one third of the way through the score. Seeing what happens through the eyes of Hagar in itself creates ambiguity, as some episodes could just as well be read as haunting memories rather than actual events. This is especially the case in the second scene which takes place in the forest, the meeting place of the lovers in Dehmel's poem. And why a forest? In the poem, the forest is a site of spirituality, dreams and transfiguration, hardly down-to-earth reality. And when the Friend first reveals his love to Hagar, straightforwardly confronting her, meeting her face close to his, a couple of Lovers in Experience enter to their associated music of evil and disturbance: this seems to signify the return of Hagar's terrible guilt after her seduction far more strongly than a real event.

Tudor divides the music into two halves, breaking his two scenes during the third, central section of the music, but corresponding to the emotional progression suggested by Dehmel's poem, which is also followed by Schoenberg. The Dehmel poem is in five stanzas (or parts), the first introducing the man and woman who walk in the forest; the second being the woman's confession that she is expecting the child of another man; the third recollecting the first; the fourth a monologue by the man who comforts the woman and reassures her that the child will be transfigured as his own; and the fifth indicating that they continue their harmonious walk together and, metaphorically, into the future. Schoenberg never documented his own view of the correspondences between his music and the stanzas of the poem, and there are slight differences of opinion amongst those who have analysed this relationship. Egon Wellesz identifies the correspondences as follows: Part 1 (bars 1–23), Part 2 (bars 24–187), Part 3 (bars 188–228), Part 4 (bars 229–369), Part 5 (bars 370–418).[115] Willi Reich analyses the music a little differently: Part 1 (bars 1–28), Part 2 (bars 29–215), Part 3 (bars 216–35), Part 4 (bars 249–369), and Part 5 (bars 370–418).[116] In Reich's analysis, bars 236–48 are not accounted for in relation to a stanza. Paul Griffiths provides no precise bar references, but brings out an important point about balance:

> The first and third parts (linked in the music as they are in the poem), and the fifth, are brief. The second represents the woman's sorrowful outburst in an intense and passionate development, placed just where it ought to be in a symphonic structure. The balancing fourth section follows the poem in being more calm and rapturous, while also serving the musical form in withdrawing the tension from themes heard in the second part.[117]

Tudor responds to this sense of balance in his choreography, although not in straightforward parallel with the music. There are two, balancing core *pas de deux*: the seduction *pas de deux* in his Scene 1 (Part 2: bars 135–81) and the *pas de deux* with the Friend in Scene 2, which is the point where the Dehmel and Tudor narratives become one (Part 5: bars 370–400). Appreciating that Tudor enhances the musical structure in fitting his narrative around it, the conductor Philip Ellis notes that there is a memorable climactic mirror image towards the end of both these *pas de deux* and to similar musical material: each of the lovers lies back presenting the full stretch of his body to Hagar, holding himself up from the floor on taut arms.[118] Tudor hints at another balance between musical Parts 2 and 4. Part 4 contains another short introductory *pas de deux* (bars 277–94), a foretaste of the extended one yet to come in Part 5. This is interrupted by a final, but nonetheless major burst of desperation and guilt – indeed, this is the 'largest', most violent passage of the entire work – a nightmare for Hagar, who is thrown to the ground, hoisted and overturned above the heads of the seething crowd. Then, vicious contrast, the seducer (the Young Man from the House Opposite) simply walks straight past her with the cruellest absence of recognition. After this, there is steady progression towards happiness through the longer *pas de deux* and coda (both in Part 5).

Music and choreography are both constructed through repeating and developing themes and motifs. Dance motifs are associated with particular characters and situations in the ballet. A connection develops between representations of

Ex. 5.8. Schoenberg, *Verklärte Nacht*.

evil, Hagar's guilt, and the Lovers in Experience from the House Opposite and the two musical motivic strands (A and B) that are introduced at the beginning of the first 'stanza' (see Ex. 5.8).

During this music, Hagar conjures up a vision of the goings-on in the House Opposite (seen dimly behind blinds). Motif B returns at the climax of the seduction *pas de deux*, while motif A accompanies her tortured progression out of the House Opposite and later reminds her of the Lovers in Experience who come from that house (the moment referred to above, see p. 314). Motif A is finally transformed and quietened in the last *pas de deux*. Blended together here with an eased account of the very opening falling melody (see Ex. 5.9a), it is supported by gently fluttering arpeggio figuration (see Ex. 5.9b); voices and memories of a previous horror are now finally calmed.

Through Hagar's fraught presence, there is unrelieved stage tension until the end of the ballet. Heard in concert, the music seems rather less unremitting, though the style, dependent upon the influence of late Wagner, is still one of continuous progression and delayed resolution. Tudor points up further the distinctions between the musical episodes, introducing fragmentary statements that distinguish characters (at the very beginning, for example), as well as dances of uninterrupted momentum; solo statements contrast with flooding crowds or frames of voyeurs, some climaxes given to the single body, others to huge groups erupting and splintering in a manner that carries the eye all over the stage.

Most subtly, Tudor's two scenes introduce different musical-choreographic relationships. Appropriately, in the second scene, there are passages of more harmonious relationship between the choreography and the structure of musical phrases, their repetitions and sequential development. We recall that Denby

Ex. 5.9a. Schoenberg, *Verklärte Nacht*, opening theme.

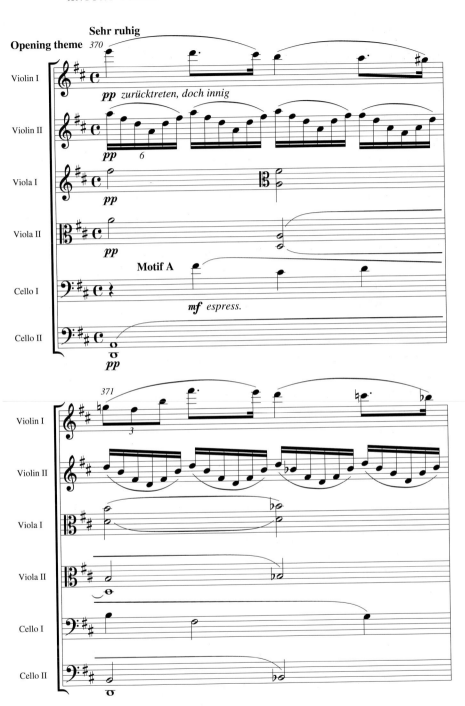

Ex. 5.9b. Schoenberg, *Verklärte Nacht.*

found lacking in Tudor's work a sense of balance in phraseology and the respite that balance brings, but this certainly becomes a feature of the second half of *Pillar.* It spreads from the style of the Lovers in Innocence. This is not symmetry as Balanchine or Ashton would introduce it, but nevertheless enough to make the point (in contrast to the first scene) about the gradual development of a less disturbed emotional world. In the seduction *pas de deux,* for instance, even though there is one big repeat in the music, there is no equivalent in the dance. Indeed, there are no dance repeats at all with the music in this *pas de deux,* except for the man's opening solo motif: Hagar dances on relentlessly, forever trying new ways to rid herself of her guilt and passion. But in both *pas de deux* in Scene 2, we see phrases twice, to the same music. In the first one, the dance repetitions are deflected into different endings, symbolic of incomplete resolution at this point; in the main *pas de deux,* there is a repeated sequence of one *pirouette* leading into another and then on into a turning overhead lift, and then one more *pirouette* and lift, totally at one with the musical structure. Now too, the spatial emphasis is on easy curves and circles. In keeping with this, Tudor makes more of the Innocents in the second scene and of their style of bending harmoniously into musical phrasing and pulse.

The large construction or energy pattern of *Pillar,* up to its nightmare climax in the second scene, relates very closely to the *Undertow* diagram that Tudor drew for the composer Schuman, representing continuous growth and a series of waves increasing in magnitude (see p. 277). This is not the diagram that I would come up with so readily for Schoenberg's music by itself. It is Tudor's choreography that is responsible for this clear design. It is interesting that Ellis too interprets a discrepancy between the centres of emotional weight of score and choreography, an early turbulence in the music that is not expressed in the choreography, a shared degree of violence in the centre of the work, and then a level of unrest in the choreography that rises above that of the music.[119] He discovered that he had to adjust from a concert reading of the score to meet the demands of the ballet's scenario.

Just as in *Echoing of Trumpets,* Schoenberg's music tends to be heard programmatically in this ballet. Usually, it is a voice that complements what we see on stage, more or less closely attached to a person or dance statement. Music can produce a general atmospheric backdrop that supports the swells and lulls in dance energy, or it can seem like speaking. Hagar asks for forgiveness from the community, literally gesturing with the fragmentary musical gestures, first to her Elder Sister, then to the neighbours. Soon, her quiet begging turns to desperate pleading to fortissimo, screaming violin accents. The Elder Sister and her declamatory music (from bar 188) speak anger and disapproval after Hagar's seduction. The Younger Sister dances to a curling violin line for her wheedling insinuations: the violin sound is saccharine. Different lines of musical counterpoint can indicate two different characters and emotional states: for the Man from the House Opposite and Hagar, brutal bass line and screaming panic pizzicato violins respectively; or for the disturbed Hagar, a sorrowful bass motif, whilst, in the background, the Innocents' gentle *bourrées* reflect sighing violin phrases. Tudor's enhancement makes us hear a surprising degree of timbral differentiation from a strings-only ensemble.

Dissonance and consonance broadly refer to emotional tension and release, sometimes to rapid alternations between states. Thus Tudor uses the musical opportunity to delay the resolution and kiss at the end of the final *pas de deux*. The Friend offers himself to Hagar at her feet; she accepts him in a rapturous and sheltering embrace with her leg, and the music reaches the dominant chord that signals cadential resolution to tonic harmony. But then Schoenberg sidesteps the cadence with dissonance, Hagar's anxiety returns briefly, before finally being assuaged with the kiss and corresponding harmonic resolution in the music.

At its most dissonant, music often expresses the powerful emotion of Hagar. If we take the first *pas de deux* with the Man from the House Opposite as an example, the music here seems to represent her inner screams as she leaps into lifts with terrifying tautness through her body. Or it suggests her heart palpitations as her hands whip towards her chest with a pizzicato inner line, or her more legato sobbing with despair. All these movement suggestions can be enlarged and intensified by musical sound, and indeed, in a number of climactic points during *Pillar*, just as in the freeze of *Jardin*, Tudor allows the music to say it all: Hagar is isolated, alone or singled out from the stage texture, and clamped in stillness while the music roars around her. At these points, we are suddenly aware of sound as opposed to visual imagery: the voice of music, as it were, takes over, the voice of pure emotion. The personal becomes magnified, spirit and body divided, audible emotion overpowering the vulnerable, small physical presence. This is very much the Wagnerian kind of stasis. Achieving powerful emotional effect at strategic points through sheer volume of sound is a Tudor hallmark, despite his concern that musical scores should not overpower the dance. His ambition to work with large musical resources (see p. 273), though not often realised, is significant.

Other Tudor pieces, those that tend towards abstraction, present very different issues of large form. *Dark Elegies* is programmatised to a degree by the title of Mahler's score and the content of Rückert's poems, although the choreography omits reference to any specific situation. The ballet expresses different aspects of anguish and sorrow, the folk-dance style group choreography metaphorically calming and sympathising with the communication of individual emotion. *Elegies* is in suite form, clearly five separate dances corresponding with the five separate songs. The last of these is climactic, bringing back as signal of closure a variety of motifs from earlier dances, although to different music.

Sunflowers, a much later piece, is also in many ways formal. It uses the same final closure device of recapitulating motifs seen earlier in the piece. There is a series of solos and *pas de deux*, interspersed with formal group dances that democratise the cast. However, unlike in *Dark Elegies*, these 'dances' do not fit the structure of the musical movements simply and predictably. At the beginning, a leggiero theme repeats and with it a dance theme presented by three of the women in turn. They blend back into the ensemble, and soon changes in musical mood suggest distinctive and more extended solo statements. Musical structure is also the dance premise of the second movement, the recurring musical theme tied closely to a phrase of fast, intricate footwork that evolves with each appearance. At other times, Tudor's phrases fit the music loosely, 'finding their own level' across musical seams.

The movement language in *Sunflowers* is not as forceful a programmatic signal as in *Pillar* or *Echoing of Trumpets*. The piece works within the conventions of a lyrical classical ballet style without stressing idiosyncratic gesture, and, indeed, it is significant to my point that Tudor borrowed from the language of *Sunflowers* for his later plotless work *The Leaves are Fading*. Yet *Sunflowers* does have a kind of story-line progressing through it, energised and considerably darkened by the arrival of two men in the middle of the second movement. The four women are dressed differently, and a rural fence on stage gives a sense of place. Tudor referred to *Sunflowers* as his Chekov piece, and tended to speak of it in programmatic terms:

> The ballet's name directly evokes sunflowers which always keep their heads turned toward the sun, and bloom in the heart of summer. The four ladies of the ballet are friends of long acquaintanceship having known each other for almost as long as they can remember and every summer they seem to have been brought together at this particular bit of countryside . . .
>
> At the opening of the piece, the four are full of 'Ennui,' and are resolutely determined to be happy and carefree together. When the men appear on the scene the true natures of each of the women evidence themselves, and by the time the two men have been able to extricate themselves from this situation, the four women are left with their true natures showing and the piece ends with them alone and separate . . .[120]

Janáček's first string quartet (1923) is in the usual four-movement form but also works within programmatic conventions, its moods increasingly volatile, with passionate and violent outbursts and sudden halts, features used readily by Tudor. The music was inspired by a novella, 'Kreutzer Sonata' by Tolstoy, on the theme of a perilous marriage in which the woman is murdered by her jealous, tyrannical husband, and Janáček seems to want to express a similar emotional torment and drive towards dénouement. Josef Křenek, cellist in the Moravian Quartet who performed the piece in 1924, recalls:

> Janáček asked for complete silence between the movements, with no tuning, approximately of the duration of a slightly extended general pause. He quite simply wanted to prevent the build-up of dramatic tension in the music from being impaired.[121]

And, without altering the notes in any way, Janáček asked the Moravian Quartet to change the dynamics of his quiet ending, to a sudden crescendo up to a fortissimo outburst.[122] Tudor used the loud ending, a final resurgence of musical power over physical presence (typical Tudor style) after a number of other such instances in this piece.

Sunflowers is evolutionary in characteristic Tudor fashion, not only narratively speaking, but in its constant forming and reforming of group formations, and in its variation treatment of dance material. Most intriguing is that its formality evolves too, alongside the development of narrative crisis. In the third movement, one woman takes a man from another woman, and the action is built around two *pas de deux*, each involving the same man. At the end of the movement, the first woman is left stranded, not just against the new couple, but against two symmetrical framing couples (another couple has entered) who re-state a version of the opening *pas de deux* material, to the same musical theme as before. The initial statement of intimacy becomes formalised into a symmetrical picture. In the last movement, the men lift two of the women high, each couple watched from diagonally downstage by another woman, forming two identical trio arrangements side by side. Following some stylised tugging of the men between the two women within each trio, the arrangement is repeated facing the opposite direction, upstage now downstage. But it is now enlarged, the lifted women raising their arms, the others falling to the ground, their chests reaching towards the men in the motif pose from Andrew Wyeth's famous picture 'Christina's World' (1948).[123] An early solo had introduced the Wyeth pose without any object or person in view. The object of wanting is now concrete, and Tudor dramatises the moment by the vertical depth of the physical arrangement. However, sharing the personal statement, doubling it in unison, acts to dissolve its personal force: the crisis is turned ironic again by a formal emphasis on design in space. Following the same principle, the four women conclude *Sunflowers* reaching towards independent corners of the stage, but formalised by their unison. Although not entirely convincing, the ballet is a fascinating exploration of the tension between narrative and abstraction. Perhaps Tudor was prompted in this direction by the tension between narrative and formality in the Janáček score.

If *Leaves* borrowed movement material from *Sunflowers*, it is fundamentally a very different kind of piece. Indeed, *Leaves* stands out from Tudor's entire repertory.

The Leaves are Fading

Set to lesser-known Dvořák chamber music, *Leaves* is in the genre of Jerome Robbins' *Dances at a Gathering* (1969). Tudor had greatly admired this work,[124] a series of short dances to Chopin piano pieces, plotless, lyrical in style, with a heady scent of romance and a smattering of folkisms. He chose Dvořák's music for the last two works that he made: *Leaves* was followed by *Tiller in the Fields*, which used the overture *Amid Nature* and single movements from the second and sixth symphonies.

Tudor preferred to call *Leaves* 'empty' in the Zen sense rather than abstract.[125] His colleague Mary Farkas at the Zen Institute explained: 'it means that the dancers must move in perfect naturalness, human beings with no individual ego sticking out.'[126] Moments here and there read like the most delicate sketch of a story.

Tudor admitted that he had been steeping himself in English romantic poetry when the idea of the ballet came to him, and offered the following clues in a preview interview: 'The beginning, with the verdant green decor, is quite spring-like, and the whole following section is very summery – it moves only gently into the fall . . .' The title makes the point that 'When leaves are fading, they're still on the tree. When they're falling, they're dead.'[127]

At the outset, a woman in a long green dress crosses the stage, pauses and gestures, looking about her pensively – the setting suggests a glade, with a floor dappled by lighting and the branch of a tree overhead – and the place has resonance for her: she is clearly a mature woman 'remembering'. The 'younger' dancers are dressed in pink, fifteen in all, and they appear in large and small ensembles, mostly as groups of couples, and some of them in the series of four *pas de deux* that occur during the course of the ballet. At the end, the woman in green returns back across the stage carrying a red rose; and perhaps the rose, like the lilacs in *Jardin*, is a Proustian device for memory.

Tudor created the main *pas de deux* for Gelsey Kirkland and Jonas Kåge. The dancing of the very small, very light Kirkland entranced Tudor. She says that she 'always shot for the dramatic heart of a moment, even in *The Leaves are Fading*',[128] and yet there is also a simplicity of manner in her performance. Clark Tippet, who was given a solo in the piece (in the Peasant Dance), remembered the pictures that Tudor gave him in rehearsal: 'Weather, clouds, woods . . .';[129] 'He'd say "It's August and you're in a wooded glen in Yugoslavia and you can hear the music. He wanted that kind of, sort of, faun/satyr-like quality that I was emitting at that point in my dancing – real sexual and . . . the same kind of feistiness . . . and a lot of energy.'[130] A couple of stage directions indicate imagery in the Labanotation score (see p. 324). One woman pulls her partner towards her. 'Don't look at them – look at me' (No. 3, bar 23). Kirkland dances mischievously to Kåge: 'C'mon let's play!' (bars 45–7, during his solo, in No. 6).

Leaves nevertheless comes across primarily as a work without plot, Tudor's first major ballet of this kind, indeed with even less of a plot than Dark Elegies. Tudor's main concern is with formality and the relationship of dance ideas to music and, in this respect, the aphoristic Continuo is its logical predecessor. Somewhat like Continuo too, there is no sense of forward progression through changes in mood and action. Leaves is certainly not evolutionary and wave-like in large structure as were so many of Tudor's earlier ballets. It rather makes the point about not really going anywhere, about the moment, nothing fundamentally changing during its course. A number of critics found this a problem, like Deborah Jowitt:

> At some point during the two fine duets that follow the Kåge-Kirkland one, I began to watch the ballet less attentively, to perceive it as long. Later, I thought that perhaps this was because Tudor has given all the dancers similar feelings, similar responses to the music. Except for Kirkland and Kåge.[131]

Or Croce:

> A romantic pastorale, a shade too extended and exquisite for its own good. All adagio in effect.
> [Tudor] misjudged the audience's ability to concentrate on intricacies of partnering and other small differences in so many consecutive or simultaneous pas de deux.

But Croce did note that the piece, by virtue of its unchanging nature, reflected an '"oriental" flow-of-time idea' – again, Zen is not far away. Other, minimalist post-modern choreographers shared this concept of time during the period of Leaves' creation. In this respect, Croce compares Leaves with the piece Field, Chair and Mountain by David Gordon.[132] The Dvořák selection gave a very level impression: 'It never gets very emphatic or very loud, and it exerts almost no independent force.'[133]

In fact, there are a number of moments when the music is both very emphatic and very loud, and the original string quartet scoring has been buttressed by orchestral forces for the ballet. The average tempo tends to moderato rather than adagio. However, the after-effect of the music is muted and slow-moving, just as

1.	Opening ensemble	String Quintet Op. 77, third movement, beginning, Poco andante	C major
2.	Ensemble	Cypresses 7, Andante	E minor
3.	4 women, 2 men	Cypresses 11, Allegro scherzando	A major
4.	Pas de deux 1	Cypresses 6, Andante moderato	E major
5.	Peasant dance	Terzetto Op. 74, Scherzo Vivace	A minor
6.	Kirkland solo	String Quartet Op. 80, third movement, Allegro scherzando	E major
	Kåge solo	String Quartet Op. 80, third movement, Trio	C-sharp minor
7.	Kirkland/Kåge pas de deux	Cypresses 8, Lento	E major
8.	Four couples	Cypresses 4, Poco adagio	E-flat major
9.	Pas de deux 3	Cypresses 5, Andante	A-flat major
10.	Pas de deux 4	Cypresses 2, Allegro, ma non troppo	F minor
11.	Solo couples	Cypresses 3, Andante con moto	G major
12.	Closing	String Quintet Op. 77, third movement, ending, Poco andante	C major

Table 5.3. Structural layout of *The Leaves are Fading.*

she suggests. The endings of each musical movement, for instance, are all gentle and quiet.

We can presume that Tudor was aiming for such an effect. Indeed, he discarded a piece that provided an 'independent force':

At the start, I began by using my very favorite part of the music . . . It just didn't function, and everything started to become boring in the dance. I guess the music was just too strong, too self-sufficient.[134]

Leaves is based on twelve separate musical movements. Most of these are selections from *Cypresses* (1887), twelve short string quartet pieces that had originated as songs (eighteen of them, composed in 1865). Dvořák gave the instrumental work the title *Echoes of Songs*, later *Evening Songs*. He made little attempt to alter the original conception of the songs, although Josef Suk made a number of important alterations when he published ten of the pieces posthumously, reverting to the original song title *Cypresses.*[135] Alterations apart, the string pieces show their song origins clearly in simple ternary or rondo refrain forms with short introductions.

Tudor selected eight of the *Cypresses* for *Leaves* (see Table 5.3). Each is presented complete except for No. 4, from which he cut the central section (24 bars). He framed the work with parts of the slow movement from the String Quintet Op. 77 (1975), its opening (bars 1–38) and, at the end of the ballet, its last 23 bars (bars 108–30); he removed the more lively centre of the movement. From the Terzetto Op. 74 (1887), Tudor took the Scherzo and Trio. The latter was cut after the premiere, not Tudor's choice, but according to the wishes of Lucia Chase, a director of American Ballet Theatre, who was worried that the work seemed too long.[136] The result is a highly repetitious musical structure without the change of tone that the Trio provides, and Hynninen reinserted the Trio when she set the work on the Kirov Ballet in 1992. From the String Quartet Op. 80 (1876), Tudor likewise drew the Allegro Scherzando and its Trio, but he cut one of the repeats in the Trio and omitted the repeat of the Scherzo after the Trio. The inclusion of these Scherzos is important, for the *Cypresses* are generally on the slow side, and even No. 2, which starts Allegro ma non troppo, keeps veering towards meno mosso and andante.

The Labanotation score of *Leaves* was written in 1975 by Hynninen,[137] who has since staged the ballet a number of times. It does not include notes relating to the musicality of the ballet, just an account of the recordings of the music listed in the Schwann catalogue of January 1978 and which Tudor used for his own preparation. In a mere handful of places, counts indicate phrasing divisions beyond those clear from the notation itself or signify a precise attachment to beat. The score is invaluable as a document stemming from the time when *Leaves* was created.

An unusual body of working documentation is available on *Leaves*, and it provides fascinating insights into Tudor's creative processes.[138] It is clear that he took great pains with his musical preparation, the selection and ordering of pieces to form the ballet score, as well as his own analysis of the music. The documentation includes a small music manuscript book that contains fragments from each musical movement, the opening bars to establish identity, the key signature and duration, some descriptive notes on each item, and some notes indicating concern for smooth key continuities between movements. Another notebook contains complete analyses of each piece of music; notes on the dance material for the opening and closing sections of the Op. 77 Quintet slow movement, including a breakdown of the complex crossings of the ensemble; and finally brief summary information on each musical movement with reference back to the earlier analyses. Perhaps most surprising of all is another musical manuscript book containing the complete piano reduction of each piece used in the ballet, in Tudor's own hand.

The documentation suggests that Tudor finalised his musical choices before starting to work out any sequence for them. The order in which he wrote his musical analyses might have been something of an early attempt at an order for the ballet, although this is slightly confused by the fact that two pieces are analysed twice (only minor differences exist between the analyses). Already in place are the opening and closing sections of the Quintet slow movement. This is one of the pieces that is analysed twice during the notes, but each time, the central section has already been cut out, and the first analysis indicates the curtain falling as the music closes. The faster movements are more spread through the analysis notebook than they are in the final score. However, Tudor obviously decided that continuity between movements in terms of key had to take more priority. It seems that he had some difficulty with this: 'Dvořák composed in too many of the wrong keys',[139] he complained jokingly, and the final score shows a very different order of movements. Tudor's piano transcriptions might represent a transitional ordering, a second stage towards the final grouping. No version, interestingly, makes any use of Dvořák's own ordering of the *Cypresses*.

Tudor's musical analyses are a fascinating account of how the choreographer heard his music, its phrasing and its dynamic and expressive content. Most frequently, the analyses indicate Tudor's interest in the idiosyncrasies of the melody line, which does not always fit the bar-line neatly. These are rhythmic analyses of melody. Here is an example from No. 4 in the ballet (*Cypresses* No. 6), indicating his scrupulous concern to understand the musical structure. Tudor picks out the separate melodic fragments lasting 5 counts each (bars 5–8), and then the units of 2 and 3 counts, 1–2, 3–4, 1–3, ending with two rest counts 4 and 5 (which he brackets – they occur in bars 11 and 14). Tudor writes one line of analysis for bars 5–8, then two lines, melody and metrical frame-

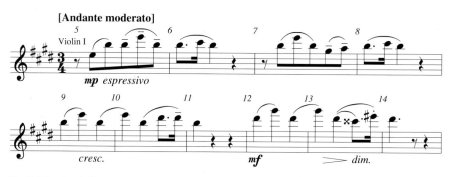

Ex. 5.10a. Dvořák, *Cypresses* No. 6.

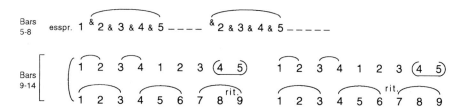

Ex. 5.10b. Tudor's analysis for *The Leaves are Fading* (No. 4, first Pas de Deux).

work, for bars 9–14 (see Exs. 5.10a, 5.10b). Sometimes there are inaccuracies in the analyses, perhaps a bar missing or added. In analysing the first phrase of the Terzetto Scherzo, Tudor is sensitive to the effect of a four-bar extension (bars 9–12), but rather casually writes this as five bars instead of four (see Exs. 5.11a, 5.11b). Expression marks in both the analyses and piano reduction supplement those in Dvořák's score. Perhaps they derive from his listening to the recordings.

The movement style of *Leaves* is lyrical to the extreme, complementing the vocal origins of the music. Arcing leg gestures, sighing falls into a partner's arms, long, yearning, travelling lifts – all these are the dance equivalent to song, and there are any number of occasions when a melodic climax is enhanced by an ecstatically high lift. In the first *pas de deux*, for instance, the woman flies into an overhead lift as the violin peaks, arching back with one arm folded over her body; the vertical excitement increases when, to the melodic descent, she is set down and her partner falls to the floor. But there are also sections in *Leaves* that are foil to the lyricism, drawing the eye down to the feet and steps. Indeed, to make this point, the dancers often carry their arms down by their sides in the opening dances for the large ensemble. The fifth dance to the Terzetto Scherzo is called Peasant Dance because of its folk-step flavouring. Movement too carries memories, for as much as each specific dance number is distinctive, there are cross-references, images recurring and drawing the community together into a harmonious whole. The climactic lift in the first *pas de deux*, for instance, becomes a motif in the one for Kirkland and Kåge; it is also the lift with which they leave the stage at the end of the work. Rachel Richardson sees this image as characteristic of *Leaves* and its particular continuity:

the impression is of continuous movement . . . legs curving around and behind, arms echoing this shape so that the total image is of a 'drifting' or transitory movement, rather than of a clearly defined, 'held' position.[140]

The final ensembles are flooded with movement memories.

If we now look at the large structure of *Leaves*, perhaps the most striking feature is its regular pattern of accumulations, the number of dancers growing as a dance progresses, two to three to four, one couple to four couples, and so on. The first dance is like a wave across the stage: the women drift in and the men enter from the same side, passing between them and carrying them into lifts as they go. But this is not to make a pattern of climaxes, unlike the 'waves' of Tudor's earlier works. The waves just seem to happen and then happen again. They are part of the effect that nothing fundamentally changes. It is significant too that the main *pas de deux* is placed at the centre of the work, not towards the end as major emotional climax, as is more conventional. After it, there are fur-

Ex. 5.11a. Dvořák, Terzetto scherzo.

Terzetto Scherzo

dim

1 2 3 4 5 6 7 8 1 2 3 4 5

Ex. 5.11b. Tudor's analysis for *The Leaves are Fading* (No. 5, Peasant Dance).

ther *pas de deux* (two out of a total of four) and group numbers before the piece closes. While there is no marked anticipation of Kirkland and Kåge, there is a generous amount of time for us to wind away from them afterwards.

The endings of each dance suggest that motion does not stop. Many are made up of circling or winding repeating phrases, all different and often with lifts of some kind, unbroken legato, the flow continuing on into transition material after the music has died away. In rehearsal, as if to exaggerate the point, Kirkland wanted to linger over her ending, after which Tudor told her to 'go through the music'.[141] Even at the end, when the ensemble and woman in green cross back, the effect of closure is lessened by the image of Kirkland in her high 'drifting' lift, taking off to the heavens in a spirit of continuation (like the woman lifted at the end of Balanchine's *Serenade*).

Unsurprisingly, the values of timelessness appear in the characteristic phrasing and musicality of this piece. The approach to musical structure varies rather more than is at first obvious, and many passages lean into the musical pulse. However, it is the freer style of phrasing that carries most in the memory. Dvořák's own song-style with its gently overlapping phrasing and shifting time proportions would seem to suggest this treatment, and Tudor makes his dancers 'sing' in response, even lazily around the music – we recall from his notes how he listened to melody more than beat. Those characteristic winding, circling endings, for instance, do not respond to pulse and are deliciously free from both musical metre and phrase.

Extremes of freedom are otherwise most evident in the *pas de deux*. Here, dance impulses anticipate or follow the music, as a touch of impetuosity, perhaps, or expression of delight in lingering. Flurries of dance excitement lead beyond musical expectations. There is a passage in the first *pas de deux* where material that once fitted pulse (in fact, one of the few counted passages in the score), gets packed into the end of a musical phrase: *coupé fouetté, pas de basque, pas de chat*, then a descent to the knee and up again into *arabesque*, all conventional ballet steps and now necessarily rushed right across the musical beats.

Just as the song melody begins for the third *pas de deux*, a key structural moment after a four-bar introduction, the woman completes her introductory phrase in a gentle, melting descent from a lift into *arabesque fondu*. The resolution, completion of the lift, becomes a new beginning. In a rehearsal film shot at the time of the premiere,[142] Marianna Tcherkassky and Michael Owen make this kind of phrasing the 'theme' of this *pas de deux*. Several lifts are clearly resolved in this way, a touch later than expected over the bar-line, as both ending and beginning, masking the musical seams, making a statement of continuity and wholeness. Resolution gains something special from this particular treatment, a slight *frisson* as the delayed pointed foot meets the floor with special care and tenderness. This phrasing pattern is less clear in the Labanotation score. At one point, bar 25, the last delivery of the main musical theme, the woman is seated across the man's shoulder. She is already up there by the end of the previous musical phrase and is smoothly carried holding this shape across the beginning of the musical theme. It seems as if the music just continues singing without taking a new breath.

As for the 'rhythmic' passages in *Leaves*, some of these even have a motor, percussive quality. In the Peasant Dance, the music plays regularly with a 3/2 across the 3/4 barring, encouraging a clear response to this (see Ex. 5.11), and the dance takes energy from this rhythmic restlessness. The third dance (for four women and two men) is an unusually lively number from *Cypresses*. Small steps, some of them beaten, print out the pulse firmly, with particular brightness when a pair of women side by side perform canon sequences down the diagonal: *cabrioles* and *relevés* into shooting *développés devants*.

There is a memorable moment in the last *pas de deux*, a brief switch from lyricism and attention to melodic contour to rhythmic values. Suddenly, the pair spring towards the audience side by side, with a turning *jeté*, kneel and half-turn to kneel facing the opposite direction. They mark out the rhythm pattern of the melody, their close visualisation making us hear this musical passage with particular clarity (bars 73–4) (see Exs. 5.12a, 5.12b, 5.12c). Rhythm in this context is a bright surprise, introducing a brief burst of extroversion and confidence before the quiet, lyrical ending of the *pas de deux*. The couple are dancing here to the final fragment of the main musical theme, now played for the first time forte, and it is interesting that Tudor now analyses it quite separately from the rest of the theme, indeed gives it stress. He distinguishes it as the beginning of a new section, the Coda. After a six-bar unit, the earlier part of the theme, he hears this fragment as a separate unit opening the Coda.

Both the 1975 and 1976 American Ballet Theatre recordings of the ballet show the dancers getting through this music late, consequently without bringing out this rhythmic relationship. Ballet-master David Richardson has confirmed that there should be a tight fit here, although it seems that dancers and conductor have problems co-ordinating to achieve this effect.[143]

At other places in the work, the dancers' feet whisper a kind of patterning – a few quick steps, like triplet patterns or, in the opening ensembles, a recurring motif of stepping up onto pointe and across into a tight fifth position, the gentlest marking, minimal emphasis. Often, we sense a pattern without fully grasping it; perhaps it never appears like that again. In *Leaves*, some dance material repeats with its music, after a time gap or immediately, but the overriding characteristic is asymmetry (a spatial tendency too), and, typically of Tudor, the choreography is challenging to read. In this context, just as in *Continuo*, the rhythmic and structural challenges do not lead to drama, rather to effects of looseness or free-wheeling. Recall that Tudor loved the 'untaught, meandering'

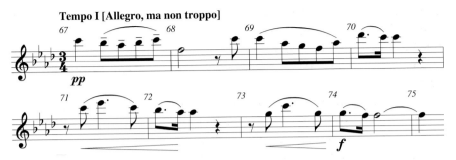

Tempo I [Allegro, ma non troppo]

Ex. **5.12a.** Dvořák, *Cypresses*, No. 2.

Tempo	1°	1	2	3	4	5	6'
Coda	1	2	[. . . . .]				

Ex. **5.12b.** Tudor's analysis for *The Leaves are Fading* (No. 10, fourth Pas de Deux).

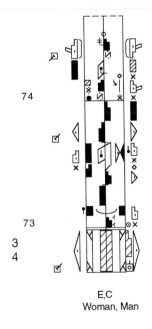

E,C
Woman, Man

Ex. **5.12c.** Tudor, *The Leaves are Fading,* (No. 10, fourth Pas de Deux).

look as he made the piece, and it is significant that he did not want the work timed too neatly and tightly, 'cleaned up'.[144]

The longest *pas de deux* in *Leaves,* for Kirkland and Kåge, is generally considered the loveliest, and it illustrates all the musical-choreographic relationships described. It is also uniquely extended by preparatory allegro solos for her and him, in advance of the slow *pas de deux.* The solos are complex and wayward, like improvisations, with constantly evolving material. A few images recur in new contexts, and there are opportunities in the middle of each solo for a duet moment or two. Tudor simplifies the choreography in the centre of each of the dances: here, some phrases repeat exactly, sometimes following a sequence in the music, other material is just plainer to grasp. The music itself contains considerable repetition, but Tudor responds to this very rarely. Kåge's solo contains a recapitulation of its opening phrase, and the *pas de deux* likewise. These are the only reflections of musical recapitulation in the *pas de deux* and solos, which now provide a good opportunity for seeing how complete dances in *Leaves* develop musically.

Kirkland's solo is set to the Allegro scherzando from Dvořák's String Quartet Op. 80. It is in binary form. Section A is repeated, its fourteen bars divided into phrases of six and eight bars. Section B is built upon the opening material of A. It modulates and culminates in a passage with high sustained notes in the first violin part, over the theme in the viola line; it ends with a kind of recapitulation of the section A material. Characteristic of the melodic material is its movement from 3/4 to 2/4 and back again. The solo is youthful, sensual, and soft in quality, from the moment the woman uncurls her arms shyly over her head. But it is also bold, fast and enthusiastic. Her first phrase takes her out of a turn into a big *grand jeté* towards her partner. She arrives before him in parallel *relevé passé* with the opposition arm gently crossing the body, an image seen during the opening ensemble of *Leaves,* and one of those already familiar from *Sunflowers.* Thereafter, Kirkland's solo work is a combination of tightly knit pointework, *petit allegro* and any number of breathing, lingering, swirling turns. Most often, the movement seems free to play around the musical beat, co-ordinating with the music at the ends of phrases. Kirkland's approach is playful, flighty, passionate, driven, infinitely varied. Sometimes her 'knitting' contacts the pulse; at one point, a series of smooth steps melts into a climbing counter-line (in the first violin part, bars 30–2). The rhythm of these steps is not what is notated. Did Kirkland discover this subtle link and then continue to use it? It is there in both 1975 and 1976 ABT recordings. In the centre of the dance, Kåge joins her and takes her into a series of lifts. These are small at first, reflecting the phrase span. Then there are two high travelling lifts that sing directly with the long, high violin notes, a statement of ecstasy.

In contrast, Kåge's solo, to the Trio of Kirkland's Scherzo, is all about clear

Ex. 5.13a. Dvořák, String Quartet Op. 80, third movement, Trio.

Ex. 5.13b. Tudor's analysis for *The Leaves are Fading* (No. 6, Jonas Kåge's solo).

pulse, particularly the first beat of the bar. This contributes to its showy folk-style. But the movement material is also highly varied in structure and rhythm, picking out not only the pulse but also from time to time the quaver detail in between. Its variety is only articulate through precise, crisp performance. Kåge shows it; often, performers have blurred the rhythmic details.

The music is in the structure AABBC and Coda, although all the sections are based on the same material, and there is a kind of recapitulation of the section A material in the Coda. Tudor cuts out the indicated repeat of section C. The opening material of the Trio is constructed in five-bar phrases (two of these forming section A), each ending with three marked, separated accents (see Exs. 5.13a, 5.13b). Percussive steps and leg gestures reinforce the three accents, each time differently. The big accents become a feature in their own right towards the end of the solo, extended into diminuendo and, in the final bars, further separated by rests. After section C, Kåge takes Kirkland on a journey of lifted jumps that simply stride across the music, ignoring these accents until they draw to a close. Tudor's working notes indicate how he read these bars, and the syncopated passage towards it. They also show that he had already decided to consider the whole passage as a sweep in time rather than as rhythmic detail (see Exs. 5.14a, 5.14b). At the very end of this dance, the accents are question-mark chords demanding cadential resolution, and they are marked choreographically by a series of increasingly intimate holds and lifts.

The *pas de deux* proper provides the resolution, answers the questions. It is

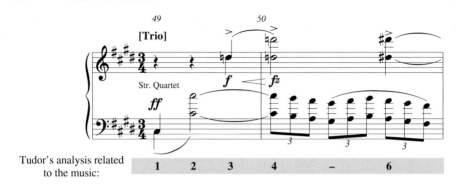

Tudor's analysis related to the music:

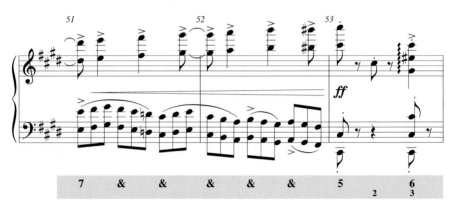

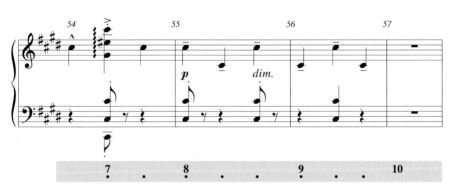

Ex. 5.14a. Dvořák, String Quartet Op. 80, third movement, Trio.

Ex. 5.14b. Tudor's analysis for *The Leaves are Fading* (No. 6, end of Jonas Kåge's solo).

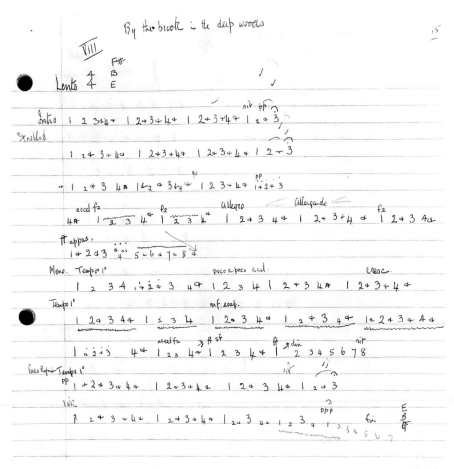

Ex. 5.15. Facsimile of Tudor's analysis of Dvořák's Cypresses No. 8, in preparation for *The Leaves are Fading*.

musing, pensive, a matter of the simplest walking as well as passionate turns and lifts, and Kirkland melts with love. Touches of absorbing detail contrast with larger images. There is the tiny, but neat *pas de bourrée* towards the end of the first phrase, steps between the notes before she stretches into fourth on pointe and falls back into his arms like a sigh. There are the ecstatic lifts that are like a motif for the couple, two of them at the first melodic climax. The ending is extended, as if the couple want to savour this experience for ever (see pp. 328–9), first the recapitulation of the opening dance and musical material, then a phrase of lifts up the diagonal, as she flies from and returns to her kneeling position on his thighs. The couple notice that they are not alone, and then they begin one of Tudor's long, winding departures across the music: she turns, he supports her in another turn, and then he lifts her around him, all clockwise, again and again, and without any breaks between moves.

Ex. 5.16. Dvořák, *Cypresses* No. 8. American Ballet Theatre piano score for Tudor's *The Leaves are Fading*. Pas de Deux for Gelsey Kirkland and Jonas Kåge (No. 7). Phrases 1 and 2, each ending in a 'sigh' or 'fall'.

The music is rhapsodic in structure with some repetition. Tudor's working notes again reveal how he heard the music (see Ex. 5.15). At three points, corresponding with the end of a musical phrase, he has pencilled in phrase marks, indicating the pairs of notes like 'sighs' in the melody line, and the ABT piano score and Labanotation score (see Exs. 5.16, 5.17) clarify that he uses these moments choreographically. The dancer falls back into her partner's arms the first time, at the end of the first phrase, and is then raised up into *arabesque*; the second time, at the end of the second phrase, she falls back and stays there, after a much busier approach to the fall than before, a dance accelerando that the musical sequence does not suggest. The third sigh is the completion of the recapitulation phrase (the phrase from the opening, see Ex. 5.17), but now she sinks onto his thighs, the most intimate of these three moments, bringing the couple very closely face to face (see Ill. 7). The second and third sighs visualise the fall in pitch very clearly, but all of them are about resolution to stability after instability. Two other moments in the *pas de deux* are especially interesting musically. There is the descent from the second ecstatic lift, literally following the melodic descent (Tudor's arrow indicates the melodic direction here). But she ends her full-weight fall into a huge supported backbend in his arms at the *start* of the next musical phrase marked 'Meno. Tempo 1'. Tudor extends the line of his dance phrase to overlap with the music again, to preserve the shape of abandon for a whole bar, as if the image should linger on and on. But I have not yet

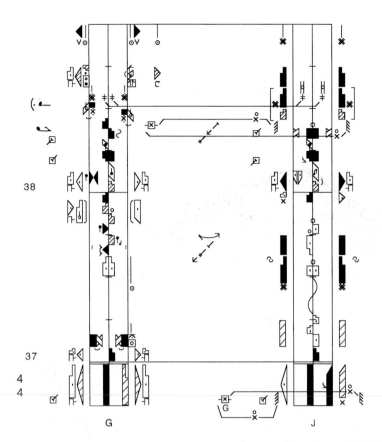

Ex. 5.17. Tudor, *The Leaves are Fading*, No .7, Pas de Deux for Gelsey Kirkland (G) and Jonas Kåge (J). Recapitulation phrase (phrase from opening) ending in third 'sigh'.

seen a performer hold for as long as the score indicates! During a more lively passage in the centre of the *pas de deux*, Tudor echoes a repeating musical rhythm, but not simultaneously. The following three-note pattern (bars 23–4 and 25–6) is absorbed into the choreography:

– but a beat later than in the music, in alternating movements of the arms above the head.

This *pas de deux* and its solos provide an excellent example of how easily the more subtle aspects of musicality can be changed, indeed lost, but also of the power of video records, which, for all we know, show 'mistakes', the idiosyncrasies of a single performance, unintended details. I am referring here to three video performances that are commercially available, one danced by Rose Gad

Ill. 7. Gelsey Kirkland and Charles Ward in Tudor's *The Leaves are Fading*, American Ballet Theatre.

Poulsen and Lloyd Riggins of the Royal Danish Ballet, as young dancers featured in the Erik Bruhn Gala: World Ballet Competition; another by the more mature Altynai Asylmuratova and Konstantin Zaklinsky of the Kirov Ballet (the man's solo omitted); and fragments of the main duet danced by Heidi Ryom and Arne Villumsen in a Swedish documentary film about Tudor's work.[145]

The rehearsal performance by Kirkland and Kåge and the Labanotation score are guides against which to measure the timing of these performances. Kirkland demonstrates the musical phrase structure very precisely, co-ordinating exactly with the musical 'sighs', yet never fully resting at the end of them – her tendency is always to prepare herself quietly for the next material. Thus, she emphasises both musical shape, boundary and continuity, seamlessness. She makes the point particularly clearly with the last sigh, the sinking onto Kåge's knees, which becomes the beginning of a lift: the ending here is literally a beginning, the start of the phrase of lifts up the diagonal.

The following are only examples of the differences between interpretations of the *pas de deux*, the musical differences, or, at least, those that got recorded on video. The least experienced couple, Poulsen and Riggins, diminish the effect of the long, singing lifts during her solo, by hurried timing: the relationship to the violin notes is no longer clear. His solo does not bring out the big musical accents. The performance of both these solos tends to iron out the differences in dynamics and musicality that were originally choreographed into them. When we reach the *pas de deux* proper, the movement to the second and third musical sighs happens late. Indeed, the sinking onto the man's thighs no longer occurs at the end of the musical phrase: it simply starts the next one. Without the subtle phrase overlapping and visualisation of musical pitch that we see in Kirkland's performance, the moment no longer has the effect of a sigh. It would seem from Tudor's own notes as well as from the Labanotation score that musical-choreographic relationship has an important bearing upon the large form of this dance. The sighs, all of which are points of very close relationship, are like structural markers, whilst they also project a clear image of letting go, giving in to weight. Poulsen and Riggins blur these moments. Yet Poulsen does use the repeating rhythm pattern in the violin – in fact, the first time round, rather than giving us the echo effect, she moves her arms right with the music! (In the rehearsal film, a clearly registered 'mistake' in a passage that is not performed full out, Kirkland also waves her arms *on* the musical rhythm at this point).

All three performances were staged by the notator Hynninen. Yet the Kirov is structurally even more different from the notated score than the Danish performance, with extra staccato moments and punctuating flourishes of the arms, an altogether more pointed and dramatic account. It is compelling dancing, but not in a style of easy flow and breath. A harp has been added to the string orchestra in this version. Again, the second and third dance sighs do not coincide with the musical sighs. On the other hand, the fundamental approach is about fitting the music. At the end, for instance, the dancers conform to the musical phrases, even though they are scored to cross them; at other times, they fit detailed steps to particular musical notes. The simple steps between the notes towards the end of the first phrase are meticulously shaped to the musical rhythm (see Ex. 5.18).

Ex. 5.18. Tudor, *The Leaves are Fading*, rhythm of steps, bars 3–4, the Kirkland/Kåge Pas de Deux, in Altynai Asylmuratova's performance. Compare Ex. 5.16, bars 3–4, and Ex. 5.17, bar 37 (bar 3 of recapitulation phrase).

Certainly, the performance is musically very alive – Asylmuratova makes us listen, and she even draws attention to the harp! But I would suggest that this is not the Tudor musical style as he would have rehearsed it. Ryom and Villumsen seem to conform the most closely to the notation score – Hynninen had more direct control over their video performance than over the others. There is also the interesting suggestion that the rehearsal pianist for their performance actively holds back to co-ordinate that second sigh.

In a work such as this, musicality is a major responsibility for dancers, reconstructors and musicians. In any case, what happens to this *pas de deux* in performance is symptomatic of what happens elsewhere in the work, and might well have an important effect on our evaluation of the piece as a whole. My own impression, similar to that of many critics, is that *Leaves* is rather too long for its own good, although nearly all its individual dances are fascinating in themselves. A good sign is that the more I look at them, the more distinctive I find them. However, it is quite possible that clear phrasing, bringing out the many different shades of musicality in the piece, could give performances a crucial lift: rhythmic exactness where the style demands this, different styles of phrasing relationship between music and dance, 'moments' of music visualisation, echo and counter-accent, in all gradations of intensity. I am not advocating one static, rule-bound interpretation, merely interpretations that listen to musical potential.

How much 'difference' across a performance Tudor himself wanted is an important question: Kirkland's performance is precise, but also silky and unforced. Overdoing the point would destroy something of the sense of timelessness. But it is salutary to remember that for Merce Cunningham, also involved in Zen Buddhism, also interested in non-progressive continuities, the dance image is still an impeccably precise image. Subtle distinctions can also be bright distinctions.

Leaves clearly explores the formal relationships between music and dance as a major part of its content. It is atypical of Tudor, but, as we have seen, there are a number of precedents to the work. It also shows great variety in response to music. It demonstrates the liberations from musical metre and freedoms to manoeuvre within the musical phrase that are most characteristic of other late ballets such as *Continuo* and *Sunflowers*. However, whatever Tudor might have said, whether they are stated crisply or merely an undercurrent whisper, the rhythms of ballet steps are also important in this work.

* * *

Denby might well have been cheered by such a work as *Leaves*, unhappy as he was to observe how the dramatic, pantomime impetus took over in Tudor's work, controlling the phrasing and organisation of material and diminishing the qualities of grace and balance that he prized. In other work, Tudor exaggerates the dynamic of continuous development, of Becoming, and the frustrations of delayed resolution; his technique of rhythmic dialogue furthers this expressionist tendency. The expressive result of music and dance 'taking turns in partnership' is often anxious and argumentative.

The latter is not at all Denby's ideal for dance behaviour to music, and we must remember that, over the years, Denby's taste was increasingly driven by the more 'classical', balanced voice of Balanchine (with a nod of recognition to Ashton). But I have tried to show how, within this aesthetic, Tudor introduces a subtle and very compelling musicality. The contact with musical detail is not lost; at times, it is simply quiet, and then, when it reasserts itself, the moment carries with peculiar force. If I am uneasy about the way in which the American *Dark Elegies* pulls Mahler beyond the limits of how I prefer to hear him, or unconvinced by the formal/narrative tensions explored with Janáček in *Sunflowers*, I can only admire how Tudor's tactics shape the scores of Chausson for *Jardin* and Schoenberg for *Pillar*: they seem to enhance the structural and expressive potential within the music. Tudor steers a brave pathway between narrative and musical form. He is not strait-jacketed by narrative: he responds to musical form flexibly and readily, discovers its emotional potential and is enlightening.

Now Denby has one further point to make about Tudor. It is crucial, and it is to do with the difficulties of Tudor's musical style for performers. We recall that dancers had problems getting into the groove of Delius; elsewhere too they need to grasp the opportunities for mutual swell and subsidence of feeling. But some dancers solve Tudor's musical problems very effectively. Denby saw Tudor's style work for him with Markova:

> Now I see that Markova can sense and can show the dance rhythm that underlies his visual phrases. She finds their point of rest. She is easily equal to his dramatic meaning and passion, but she also gives his drama the buoyancy of dancing . . .[146]

> It is the quiet which she moves in, an instinct for the melody of movement as it deploys and subsides in the silence of time, that is the most refined of rhythmic delights. The sense of serenity in animation . . .[147]

Croce suggests that most Tudor dancers work into their roles backwards, 'from dramatic motivation to dance impetus to musical cue'.[148] But do some of them never reach that musical cue? Some dancers today have difficulty understanding the dramatic motivation in his work, let alone digging as deeply as the musical cues.

The Tudor style is indeed fragile, possibly even more so than that of Ashton or Balanchine. However, performed by listening dancers, it belies Denby's remark that 'the more ballet turns to pantomime, the less intimate its relation to the music it becomes'. The discovery of important musical values in *Leaves* comes as no surprise. These values can also be found and celebrated in the most 'pantomimic' of his ballets.

Notes

Introduction

[1] David Raksin quoted by Irwin Bazelon, *Knowing the Score: Notes on Film Music* (New York: Van Nostrand & Reinhold, 1975), p. 246.

[2] Ruth Subotnik, 'Toward a Deconstruction of Structural Listening: A Critique of Schoenberg, Adorno, and Stravinsky', in Eugene Narmour & Ruth A. Solie, eds, *Explorations in Music, the Arts, and Ideas: Essays in Honor of Leonard B. Meyer* (Stuyvesant, NY: Pendragon Press, 1988), p. 83.

[3] Susan McClary, *Feminine Endings: Music, Gender and Sexuality* (Minnesota: University of Minnesota Press, 1991).

[4] Stephanie Jordan, 'Music as a Structural Basis in the Choreography of Doris Humphrey', unpublished PhD dissertation, University of London, Goldsmiths' College, 1986. For further discussion of my analytical method, its application and development, see 'Musical/Choreographic Discourse: Method, Music Theory, and Meaning,' in Gay Morris, ed., *Moving Words: Re-writing Dance* (London and New York: Routledge, 1996), pp. 15–28.

[5] See for instance the following books: Edwin Evans, *Music and the Dance* (London: Herbert Jenkins, n.d.); Roger Fiske, *Ballet Music* (London: George G. Harrap, 1958); Paul Hodgins, *Relationships Between Score and Choreography in Twentieth-Century Dance* (Lewiston, NY: Edwin Mellen Press, 1992); Elizabeth Sawyer, *Dance with the Music* (Cambridge: Cambridge University Press, 1985); Humphrey Searle, *Ballet Music* (1958; 2nd edn., New York: Dover Publications, 1973); Marian Smith, *Ballet and Opera in the Age of Giselle* (Princeton, New Jersey: Princeton University Press, forthcoming); Katherine Teck, *Movement to Music: Musicians in the Dance Stu-* dio (Westport, Conn.: Greenwood Press, 1990) and *Music for the Dance: Reflections on a Collaborative Art* (Westport, Conn.: Greenwood Press, 1989); Roland John Wiley, *Tchaikovsky's Ballets* (Oxford: Clarendon Press, 1985). Many of the other writers referred to here are cited within the course of this book.

[6] Doris Humphrey, *The Art of Making Dances* (New York and Toronto: Rinehart, 1959).

[7] Edwin Denby, *Dance Writings* (London: Dance Books, 1986).

[8] Balanchine, quoted in Antoine Livio, 'Balanchine et Stravinsky 40 ans d'amitié,' *Ballet Danse, l'Avant Scène, Le Sacre du Printemps* (August/October 1980), p. 124.

Chapter 1

[1] Alexandre Benois, 'Khudozhestvennye pis'ma: russkie spektakli v Parizhe', *Rech'*, 25 June–17 July 1909; quoted by Irina Vershinina, 'Diaghilev and the Music of the Saisons Russes', in Ann Kodicek (ed.), *Diaghilev: Creator of the Ballets Russes* (London: Barbican Art Gallery/Lund Humphries, 1996), pp. 80–1. However, as Richard Taruskin points out, there was considerable agreement that the musical component was given poor showing in this first season of the Ballets Russes: *Stravinsky and the Russian Traditions: A Biography of the Works through Mavra* (Oxford: Oxford University Press, 1996), 1, p. 551.

[2] Quoted in 'Balanchine: An Interview by Ivan Nabokov and Elizabeth Carmichael', *Horizon* (January, 1961), p. 47.

[3] Edwin Denby, 'A Note to Composers', (1939) in Denby, *Dance Writings* (London: Dance Books, 1986), p. 63.

[4] Antony Tudor quoted by John Gruen, *The Private World of Ballet* (Harmondsworth, Mid-

dlesex: Penguin Books, 1976), p. 260.

[5] Stephanie Jordan, 'The Role of the Ballet Composer at the Paris Opéra: 1820–1850', *Dance Chronicle*, 4/4 (1981), pp. 374–88; Marian Smith, 'Borrowings and Original Music: A Dilemma for the Ballet-Pantomime Composer', *Dance Research*, 6/2 (Autumn, 1988), pp. 3–29.

[6] The letter to *The Times*, 6 July 1914, is reprinted in Cyril W. Beaumont, *Michel Fokine and his Ballets* (London: C. W. Beaumont, 1935), pp. 144–7.

[7] 'Louis Horst Interviewed by Henry Gilfond', *Dance Observer*, 3/2 (February, 1936), p. 20. A background to Horst's courses is contained in his *Pre-Classic Dance Forms* (1937; reprint Brooklyn: Dance Horizons, 1968) and *Modern Dance Forms* (1961; reprint Brooklyn: Dance Horizons, 1973).

[8] Vershinina, pp. 67–85.

[9] Vittorio Rieti quoted by Joan R. Acocella, 'Vittorio Rieti, An Interview', *Dance Magazine* (January, 1982), p. 77.

[10] Lynn Garafola, *Diaghilev's Ballets Russes* (Oxford: Oxford University Press, 1989), p. 45.

[11] *Correspondence between Richard Strauss and Hugo von Hoffmannsthal* (London: Collins, 1961), p. 150.

[12] Vershinina, pp. 76, 80.

[13] Examples are Antony Tudor's *Jardin aux lilas* (1936) and *Pillar of Fire* (1942).

[14] Garafola, p. 92.

[15] Garafola, pp. 90–5; Constant Lambert, *Music Ho! A Study of Music in Decline* (1934; 3rd edn., London: Faber, 1966), pp. 71–8.

[16] Charles Rickett's letter 'To Thomas Lowinsky', (October, 1917) in *Charles Ricketts: Self-Portrait*, ed. T. Sturge Moore & Cecil Lewis (London: Peter Davies, 1939), p. 283.

[17] Dyneley Hussey, 'Fifty Years of Ballet Music: IV – The Russian Ballet in Exile', *Dancing Times* (May, 1950), p. 472; Andrew Motion, *The Lamberts: George, Constant and Kit* (London: Chatto & Windus, 1986), p. 134.

[18] Edwin Denby, 'On Commissioning New Ballet Scores', (1943) in *Dance Writings*, p. 128.

[19] Horst Koegler, 'Musical Schizophrenia on Our Stages: Reflections on the Current Ways of Handling Music in Ballet and Dance Theatre', *Ballett International* (May, 1990), p. 50.

[20] David Vaughan, *Frederick Ashton and his Ballets* (London: A & C Black, 1977),

pp. 294–5.

[21] Valentine Gross, 'Impressions sur le ballet *Jeux*', *Comoedia Illustré* (June–July, 1913), n.p.; Debussy's letter to André Caplet, 25 August 1912, in François Lesure & Roger Nichols, eds., *Debussy Letters*, trans. Nichols (London: Faber, 1987), p. 262.

[22] Robert Garis, 'Balanchine – Stravinsky: Facts and Problems', *Ballet Review*, 10/3 (Fall, 1982), pp. 9–23.

[23] Igor Stravinsky & Robert Craft, *Themes and Episodes* (New York: Alfred A. Knopf, 1966), p. 24.

[24] Joseph Horowitz, *Understanding Toscanini: How He Became an American Culture-God and Helped Create a New Audience for Old Music* (London: Faber, 1987), p. 202.

[25] E. T. A. Hoffmann quoted by Carl Dahlhaus, *The Idea of Absolute Music*, trans. Robert Lustig (1978; English edn. Chicago: University of Chicago Press, 1989), p. 11.

[26] Dahlhaus, p. 16.

[27] Dahlhaus, p. 28.

[28] Anthony Newcomb, 'Once More "Between Absolute and Program Music:" Schumann's Second Symphony', *Nineteenth Century Music*, 7/3 (April, 1984), pp. 233–50.

[29] Roger Parker, 'On Reading Nineteenth-Century Opera: Verdi through the Looking-Glass', in Arthur Groos & Roger Parker, eds., *Reading Opera* (Princeton, New Jersey: Princeton University Press, 1988), p. 290.

[30] Sibmacher Zynen, *Algemeen Handelsblad*, 1 November 1907; quoted by Lillian Loewenthal, 'Isadora Duncan in the Netherlands', *Dance Chronicle*, 3/3 (1979–80), pp. 249–50.

[31] Donald F. Tovey, *Essays in Musical Analysis: Vol. 1 – Symphonies* (London: Oxford University Press, 1935).

[32] R. Ansell Wells, 'Statics or Dynamics?' *Musical Opinion* (November, 1939), p. 60.

[33] Lydia Goehr, *The Imaginary Museum of Musical Works: An Essay in the Philosophy of Music* (Oxford: Clarendon Press, 1992), p. 247.

[34] Dahlhaus, pp. 117–18.

[35] Rev. H. R. Haweis, *Music and Morals* (1871) quoted by Ruth A. Solie, 'Beethoven as Secular Humanist: Ideology and the Ninth Symphony in Nineteenth-Century Criticism', in Eugene Narmour & Ruth A. Solie, eds., *Explorations in Music, the Arts, and Ideas: Essays in Honor of Leonard B. Meyer* (Stuyvesant, New York: Pendragon Press, 1988), pp. 13–14.

[36] Constant Lambert, 'Music and Action', in Caryl Brahms, ed., *Footnotes to the Ballet* (London: Peter Davies, 1936), pp. 164–5.

[37] John Martin, for instance, was now wholehearted in his praise of Humphrey's *Passacaglia and Fugue in C minor* set to the music of Bach: 'A truly superb masterpiece of choreographic construction', *New York Times*, 19 August 1951.

[38] Alexander Sakharoff, *Reflexions sur la musique et sur la danse* (Buenos Aires: Vian, 1943), pp. 13, 46.

[39] Emile Jaques-Dalcroze, *Rhythm, Music and Education*, trans. Harold F. Rubinstein (London: Chatto & Windus, 1921), p.150.

[40] Victor Seroff, *The Real Isadora* (New York: Avon Books, 1971), p. 134.

[41] Isadora Duncan, *My Life* (1927; reprint New York: Liveright, 1955), p. 224.

[42] Jean D'Udine, *L'Art et le geste* (Paris: 1910), pp. xiii, xvii.

[43] d'Udine, p. 66.

[44] Sakharoff, p. 52.

[45] T. S. Eliot, 'The Metaphysical Poets' (1921) in Eliot, *Selected Essays* (London: Faber, 1953), p. 288.

[46] Roger Copeland, 'Merce Cunningham and the Politics of Perception', (1979) in Copeland & Marshall Cohen, eds, *What is Dance?* (Oxford: Oxford University Press, 1983), p. 320; Copeland, 'Postmodern Dance and the Repudiation of Primitivism', *Partisan Review*, 50/1 (1983), p. 103.

[47] Martha Graham, *The Notebooks of Martha Graham* (New York: Harcourt Brace Jovanovich, 1973), p. 305.

[48] Isadora Duncan, *The Art of the Dance* (1928; reprint New York: Theatre Arts Books, 1969), p. 90.

[49] Joan R. Acocella, 'The Reception of Diaghilev's Ballets Russes by Artists and Intellectuals in Paris and London, 1909–14', unpublished PhD dissertation, Rutgers University, 1984, p. 68.

[50] Garafola, pp. 45–6.

[51] Camille Mauclair, *La Revue*, 1 August 1910, quoted by Deirdre Pridden, *The Art of the Dance in French Literature* (London: A & C Black, 1952), p. 106.

[52] Henri Ghéon, 'Propos divers sur le Ballet Russe', *Nouvelle Revue Française*', (1910) quoted by Jann C. Pasler, 'Debussy, Stravinsky, and the Ballets Russes: The Emergence of a New Musical Logic', unpublished PhD dissertation, University of Chicago, 1981, p. 58.

[53] Pasler, p. 233.

[54] Evans, p. 10.

[55] Arthur Bliss, 'Grace Notes on Ballet', in Peter Noble, ed., *British Ballet* (London: Skelton Robinson, 1949), p. 129.

[56] Bliss, pp. 129–30.

[57] Roger Shattuck, *The Banquet Years* (New York: Alfred A. Knopf, 1955), Chapter 11: The Art of Stillness.

[58] Bertolt Brecht, *Brecht on Theatre: The Development of an Aesthetic*, ed. and trans. John Willett (London: Methuen, 1964), p. 38.

[59] For a discussion of these developments in modern dance, see Stephanie Jordan, 'Music as Structural Basis in the Choreography of Doris Humphrey', unpublished PhD dissertation, University of London, Goldsmiths' College, 1986, pp. 145–61.

[60] John Martin, *America Dancing* (1936; reprint New York: Dance Horizons, 1968), pp. 98, 304.

[61] Copeland, 'Merce Cunningham and the Politics of Perception', p. 320.

[62] Constant Lambert, *Music Ho!*, p. 76.

[63] Ernest Newman, 'A Further Clearing of the Ground', *Sunday Times*, 19 July 1936.

[64] Lincoln Kirstein, *Movement and Metaphor: Four Centuries of Ballet* (New York: Praeger Publishers, 1970), p. 33.

[65] Doris Humphrey, *The Art of Making Dances* (New York and Toronto: Rinehart, 1959), p. 164.

[66] Igor Stravinsky and Robert Craft, *Memories and Commentaries* (New York: Doubleday, London: Faber, 1960), p. 37.

[67] The information about Duncan's works is taken from Diane Pruett, 'A Study of the Relationship of Isadora Duncan to the Musical Composers and Mentors who influenced her Musical Selections for Choreography', unpublished PhD dissertation, University of Wisconsin-Madison, 1978.

[68] Duncan, *My Life*, pp. 75–7.

[69] Gordon Craig quoted in Francis Steegmuller, ed., *Your Isadora: The Love Story of Isadora Duncan and Gordon Craig* (New York: New York Public Library and Macmillan, 1974), p. 175.

[70] Lillian Loewenthal, *The Search for Isadora: The Legend and Legacy of Isadora Duncan* (Pennington, New Jersey: Dance Horizons, 1993), pp. 138–9.

[71] Loewenthal, p. 146.

[72] Ernest Newman, 'Dances of Isadora Duncan', *Living Age*, June, 1921; quoted by

Lillian Loewenthal, 'Isadora Duncan and her Relationship to the Music of Chopin', Proceedings of the Tenth Annual Conference of the Society of Dance History Scholars, University of California, Irvine, 13–15 February 1987, pp. 161–2.

[73] 'Duncan', Nieuwe Rotterdammer Courant, 2 November 1907; quoted by Loewenthal, 'Isadora Duncan in the Netherlands', p. 249.

[74] Zynen quoted by Loewenthal, 'Isadora Duncan in the Netherlands', p. 250.

[75] F[rits] L[apidoth], Het Toonel, 13 (1927), pp. 89–93; quoted by Nancy de Wilde, 'Isadora Duncan's Seventh Symphony in the Netherlands, Reactions to her Choice and Interpretation of the Music', Proceedings of the Tenth Annual Conference of the Society of Dance History Scholars, University of California, Irvine, 13–15 February 1987, p. 172; Lapidoth's opinion is shared by Suzanne Langer, Feeling and Form (London: Routledge & Kegan Paul, 1953), pp. 170–1.

[76] Leo, De Telegraaf, 26 January 1907, quoted by Loewenthal, 'Isadora Duncan in the Netherlands', p. 147.

[77] John Fuller-Maitland, The Times, 7 July 1908.

[78] Jaques-Dalcroze, p. 136.

[79] André Levinson, Ballet Old and New (1918), trans. Susan C. Summer (New York: Dance Horizons, 1982), pp. 31–2.

[80] Henry T. Parker, Boston Evening Transcript, 21 October 1922, in Parker, Motion Arrested, ed. Olive Holmes (Middletown, Conn: Wesleyan University Press, 1982), p. 69.

[81] Ruth St Denis, An Unfinished Life (1939; reprint Brooklyn: Dance Horizons, 1969), p. 215. Duncan's tendency to stand still was also noted by Shawn in The Dome No. 1: Commentary, Phonotape (n.d.) housed in the New York Public Library Dance Collection.

[82] Gordon Craig, 'Isadora Duncan: A BBC Radio Talk', in Your Isadora: The Love Story of Isadora Duncan and Gordon Craig, ed. Frances Steegmuller (New York: Random House and The New York Public Library, 1974), p. 360.

[83] Edwin Denby, 'Carmen Amaya; Isadora Reconsidered . . .' (1942) in Dance Writings, p. 87.

[84] De Wilde, pp. 168–9.

[85] Denby, 'Ballet at Lewisohn: "Les Sylphides" and "Petrouchka",' (1943) in Dance Writings, p. 122.

[86] Selma L. Odom, 'Wigman at Hellerau',

Ballet Review, 14/2 (Summer, 1986), pp. 46–7.

[87] Emile Jaques-Dalcroze (1912), in Rhythm, Music and Education, p. 182.

[88] Jaques-Dalcroze (1918) in Rhythm, Music and Education, p. 228.

[89] Jaques-Dalcroze, (1922) in Eurhythmics, Art and Education, trans. Frederick Rothwell (New York: A.S. Barnes, 1930), p. 37.

[90] Jaques-Dalcroze, (1919) in Eurhythmics, Art and Education, p. 197.

[91] Marie Rambert, Quicksilver: An Autobiography (London: Macmillan, 1972), p. 51.

[92] Lynn Garafola, 'Forgotten Interlude', Dance Research, 13/1 (Summer, 1995), pp. 59–83.

[93] Rambert, Quicksilver, p. 54.

[94] Michel Fokine, Memoirs of a Ballet Master, trans. Vitale Fokine, ed. Anatole Chujoy (London: Constable, 1961), p. 209.

[95] André Levinson, 'La Danse. Pour prendre congé de la rythmique', Comoedia, 12 May 1924, p 4; quoted in Dance Writings from Paris in the Twenties, ed. Joan R. Acocella & Lynn Garafola (Hanover, New Hampshire and London: Wesleyan University Press, 1991), p. 12.

[96] Debussy's letter to Robert Godet, 9 June 1913, Lesure & Nichols, eds., Debussy Letters, p. 272.

[97] Myroslava M. Mudrak, The New Generation and Artistic Modernism in the Ukraine (Ann Arbor, Michigan: UMI Research Press, 1986), p. 144; Garafola, 'Forgotten Interlude', p. 77.

[98] Bronislava Nijinska, Early Memoirs, trans. and ed. by Irina Nijinska & Jean Rawlinson with an introduction by Anna Kisselgoff (London: Faber, 1982), p. 451.

[99] A 1925 letter from Romola Nijinsky to Jacques Rouché; see Garafola, 'Forgotten Interlude', p. 77.

[100] Romain Rolland, Journal des années de guerre, 24 September 1914, quoted by Edward Lockspeiser, Debussy: His Life and Mind, Volume II (1965; reprinted with corrections Cambridge: Cambridge University Press, 1978), p. 183.

[101] Fokine, p. 209.

[102] Beaumont, p. 102.

[103] Levinson, Ballet Old and New, p. 90.

[104] Ernest Newman, 'Symphonies and Ballets Again', Sunday Times, 24 July 1938.

[105] Fernau Hall, 'Symphonic Ballet: A Reply', Dancing Times (August, 1937), p. 556.

[106] Rambert, p. 54.

[107] Fokine, pp. 22, 61–4.

[108] See, for instance, 'Stravinsky on Art and Artists: Comments and Quotations: A Selection by John Taras', *Dance Magazine* (April 1981), pp. 60–2.

[109] Igor Stravinsky, 'Interpretation by Massine', in Minna Lederman, ed., *Stravinsky in the Theatre* (1949; reprint New York: Da Capo Press, 1975), p. 24.

[110] Fokine, pp. 151–2.

[111] Levinson, pp. 88, 90–3.

[112] Levinson, p. 91.

[113] See, for instance, Pyotr Gusev quoted by Yuri Slonimsky in Francis Mason, *I Remember Balanchine* (New York: Doubleday, 1991), p. 38; Balanchine's encouragement to Alexandra Danilova to stage a version to piano in practice clothes, *Chopiniana* (1972); Nijinska, *Early Memoirs*, p. 251.

[114] Michel Fokine, 'Conversations with Edwin Evans' (1923–24) quoted by Joan Lawson, *A History of Ballet and its Makers* (London: Dance Books, 1973), pp. 100–1.

[115] Edwin Denby, 'A Note to Composers' (1939) in *Dance Writings*, p. 62.

[116] Dawn L. Horwitz, *Michel Fokine* (Boston: Twayne Publishers, 1985), p. 156; Elizabeth Sawyer, *Dance with the Music: The World of the Ballet Musician* (Cambridge: Cambridge University Press, 1985), p. 218.

[117] Irina Baronova, lecture-demonstration for Society for Dance Research study day on Fokine, London, 25 March 1995.

[118] Fokine, 'Conversations . . .', quoted by Lawson, p. 102.

[119] Dame Alicia Markova, *Markova Remembers* (London: Hamish Hamilton, 1986), p. 96.

[120] Maria Gorshkova quoted by Lawson, p. 97.

[121] Fokine, *Memoirs of a Ballet Master*, p. 187.

[122] Horwitz, p. 128.

[123] See 'Stravinsky on Art and Artists', p. 62, and Millicent Hodson, 'Nijinsky's Choreographic Method: Visual Sources from Roerich for *Le Sacre du printemps*', *Dance Research Journal*, 18/2 (Winter, 1986–87), p. 12; Claude Debussy, *Le Matin* (15 May 1913), in Richard Langham Smith, ed., *Debussy on Music* (London: Secker & Warburg, 1977), p. 291; interview with Debussy in *La Tribuna* (23 February 1914) quoted by Jean-Michel Nectoux in *Afternoon of a Faun: Mallarmé, Debussy, Nijinsky*, ed. Nectoux (New York: Vendome Press, 1987), pp. 32, 35.

[124] Ann Hutchinson Guest and Claudia Jeschke, *Nijinsky's Faune Restored* (Philadelphia: Gordon & Breach, 1991); Millicent Hodson, *Nijinsky's Crime Against Grace: Reconstruction Score of the Original Choreography for Nijinsky's Le Sacre du printemps* (Stuyvesant, New York: Pendragon Press, 1996).

[125] Nijinska, p. 122.

[126] Nijinska, p. 444.

[127] For a fuller discussion of this work see Stephanie Jordan, 'Debussy and the Dance', in James Briscoe, ed., *Debussy in Performance* (New Haven and London: Yale University Press, 1999).

[128] Quoted by Charles Tenroc, 'Nijinsky va faire dans l'Après-Midi d'un Faune' des essais de chorégraphie cubiste', *Comoedia* (18 April 1912), p. 4.

[129] Rambert, p. 54.

[130] Fokine, p. 209.

[131] Quoted in *The Standard*, 13 February 1913, in Nesta Macdonald, *Diaghilev Observed by Critics in England and the United States 1911–1929* (New York: Dance Horizons, 1975), pp. 79–80.

[132] Richard Buckle, *Nijinsky* (London: Weidenfeld & Nicolson, 1971), p. 241; Buckle, *Diaghilev* (London: Weidenfeld & Nicolson, 1979), p. 185.

[133] Lydia Sokolova, *Dancing for Diaghilev* (London: John Murray, 1960), p. 40.

[134] Interview in *La Tribuna*, quoted by Nectoux, p. 35.

[135] Quoted by Tenroc, p. 4.

[136] For instance, Debussy, letter to Gabriel Pierné, 4 February 1914, quoted by Robert Orledge, *Debussy in the Theatre* (Cambridge: Cambridge University Press, 1982), p. 171; Henri Quittard, *Le Figaro* (17 May 1913), quoted by Buckle, *Nijinsky*, p. 289.

[137] Nijinska, p. 450.

[138] Stravinsky in Igor Stravinsky and Robert Craft, *The Rite of Spring Sketches 1911–1913* (London: Boosey & Hawkes, 1969), Appendix III, p. 36.

[139] Interview with Millicent Hodson, 31 March 1995. I am indebted to Hodson for her discussion with me about the structural details of *Le Sacre*.

[140] Hodson, 'Ritual Design in the New Dance: Nijinsky's Choreographic Method', *Dance Research*, 4/1 (Spring 1986), pp. 71–2.

[141] W. A. Propert, *The Russian Ballet in Western Europe, 1909–1920* (London: Bodley Head, 1921), p. 79.

[142] *The Times*, 16 July 1913, quoted by Macdonald, p. 102.

[143] Stravinsky in Stravinsky & Craft, Appendix III, pp. 38–9.

[144] Hodson, 'Puzzles chorégraphiques: reconstitution du sacre de nijinsky', in *Le Sacre du printemps* (Paris: Cicero, 1990), p. 67.

[145] Jacques Rivière, 'Le Sacre du printemps', in Copeland and Cohen, p. 117.

[146] Evans, p. 162.

[147] *The Times*, 26 July 1913, quoted by Macdonald, p. 102.

[148] *The Times*, 26 July 1913, quoted by Macdonald, p. 103.

[149] For a listing and discussion of Nijinska's choreography, a major source is Nancy Van Norman Baer, *Bronislava Nijinska: A Dancer's Legacy* (San Francisco: Fine Arts Museums of San Francisco, 1986).

[150] Nijinska, 'On Movement and the School of Movement', in Van Norman Baer, pp. 85–88.

[151] Nijinska, 'Reflections about the Production of *Les Biches* and *Hamlet* in Markova-Dolin Ballets', trans. Lydia Lopokova, *Dancing Times* (February, 1937), pp. 617–18.

[152] Nijinska, *Early Memoirs*, p. 113.

[153] Ninette de Valois, 'Modern Choreography: II', *Dancing Times* (February, 1933), p. 550.

[154] David Vaughan, *Frederick Ashton and his Ballets* (London: A. & C. Black, 1977), pp. 28–30.

[155] Van Norman Baer, p. 64.

[156] Nijinska, 'Reflections . . .', p. 618.

[157] Nijinska, 'Reflections . . .', p. 619.

[158] Nijinska, 'Creation of "Les Noces"', trans. and introduced by Jean M. Serafetinides & Irina Nijinska, *Dance Magazine* (December, 1974), p. 61.

[159] Nijinska quoted by Jack Anderson, 'The Fabulous Career of Bronislava Nijinska', *Dance Magazine* (August, 1963), p. 45.

[160] Lisa C. Arkin, 'Bronislava Nijinska and the Polish Ballet, 1937–1938: Missing Chapter of the Legacy', *Dance Research Journal*, 24/2 (Fall, 1992), pp. 6–7.

[161] Solomon Volkov, *Balanchine's Tchaikovsky: Interviews with George Balanchine*, trans. Antonia W. Bois (New York: Simon & Schuster, 1985), pp. 70, 161–3.

[162] Fyodor Lopukhov, *Shestdesiat let v balete* (Moscow: Iskusstvo, 1966), p. 213, quoted by Elizabeth Souritz, *Soviet Choreographers in the 1920s*, trans. Lynn Visson, ed. with addi-

tional translation, Sally Banes (Durham and London: Duke University Press, 1990), p. 256.

[163] Nina Alovert, 'From St Petersburg to Leningrad: Lopukhov's Legacy', *Dance Magazine* (March, 1989), p. 44.

[164] Sections from Lopukhov's *Puti baletmeistera* [*A Choreographer's Paths*] (Berlin: Petropolis, 1925), quoted by Natalia Roslavleva, *Era of the Russian Ballet* (London: Gollancz, 1966), p. 204.

[165] Roslavleva, p. 203.

[166] Roslavleva, p. 206.

[167] Lopukhov, *Puti baletmeistera*, pp. 101–2, quoted by Roslavleva, p. 204.

[168] Translation by Dorinda Offord of Lopukhov's distinctions in *Puti . . .*, p. 61.

[169] This discussion of *Dance Symphony* is summarised from Souritz, pp. 266–77.

[170] Roslavleva, pp. 205–6.

[171] Lopukhov, *Puti baletmeistera*, p. 93.

[172] Souritz, pp. 265–6, 272, drawing too from Lopukhov's *Shestdesiat*, pp. 239–40.

[173] Souritz, 'The Young Balanchine in Russia', *Ballet Review*, 18/2 (Summer, 1990), p. 66.

[174] Souritz, *Soviet Choreographers*, pp. 156–7.

[175] Souritz, p. 267.

[176] Souritz, pp. 95–6.

[177] Jack Westrup, 'A Just Impediment to the Union', *Daily Telegraph*, 18 July 1936.

[178] Quoted by Ernest Newman, 'Some Departures from Strict Logic', *Sunday Times*, 12 July 1936.

[179] Richard Capell, 'Symphonic Ballets: Massine's Little Miscalculation of the Eloquence of Legs', *Daily Telegraph*, 27 June 1936.

[180] Ernest Newman, 'Berlioz and Massine: The "Fantastique" as Ballet', *Sunday Times*, 2 August 1936; 'Symphonies and Ballets Again: If Mendelssohn, Why Not Beethoven?', *Sunday Times*, 24 July 1938.

[181] Anatole Chujoy, *The Symphonic Ballet* (New York: Kamin, 1937); Ernest Newman, *Symphonies and Ballets* (New York: Hurok Attractions, c.1938).

[182] Massine quoted in 'Massine's New Ballets', *Dance* (November, 1940), p. 9.

[183] Baird Hastings, 'Massine's Symphonic Ballets', *Ballet Review*, 23/1 (Spring, 1995), pp. 87–95.

[184] Léonide Massine, *My Life in Ballet*, ed. Phyllis Hartnoll & Robert Rubens (London:

Macmillan, 1968), pp. 11–12, 30–1.

[185] Joseph Horowitz, p. 33.

[186] Denby, 'Massine and the New Monte Carlo', (1938) in *Dance Writings*, p. 52.

[187] Vicente García-Marquez, *The Ballets Russes: Colonel de Basil's Ballets Russes de Monte Carlo 1932–1952* (New York: Alfred A. Knopf, 1990), p. 52.

[188] Alastair Macaulay, 'The Inconstant Muse', *Dance Theatre Journal*, 5/3b (Fall, 1987), p. 12; Jane Pritchard, '"The Nostalgic World of Fantasy": Some Neoromantic Elements in Works by Ashton and Balanchine', *Studies in Dance History*, 3/2 (Fall, 1990), pp. 39–44.

[189] Robert Sabin, 'Gilding the Symphonies', *Dance Observer*, 7/1 (January, 1940), p. 4.

[190] Hermann Kretschmar, 'The Brahms Symphonies: Symphony No. 4 in E minor, op. 98', (1887) in Walter Frisch, ed., *Brahms and His World*, trans. Susan Gillespie (Princeton: Princeton University Press, 1990), pp. 139, 143.

[191] Donald F. Tovey, *Essays in Musical Analysis, Volume I: Symphonies* (London: Oxford University Press, 1935), p. 121.

[192] Adrian Stokes, *Russian Ballets* (London: Faber, 1935), p. 159.

[193] Kretschmar, p. 142.

[194] Constant Lambert, 'Massine Scores New Triumph at Covent Garden', *Sunday Referee*, 2 August 1936.

[195] Léonide Massine, 'On Choreography and a New School of Dancing', *Drama*, 1/3 (1919), p. 70.

[196] Igor Stravinsky and Robert Craft, *Memories and Commentaries* (London: Faber, 1960), p. 42. See also Stravinsky, 'Interpretation by Massine', (1920) in Minna Lederman, ed., *Stravinsky in the Theatre* (New York: Pellegrini & Cudahy, 1949), pp. 24–6.

[197] André Levinson, 'Les deux sacres', (5 June 1922) in *La Danse au théâtre: ésthétique et actualité mêlées* (Paris: Librairie Bloud & Gay, 1924), p. 57.

[198] André Levinson, *Serge Lifar: destin d'un danseur* (Paris: Grasset, 1934), pp. 26–7; quoted in translation from Garafola, *Diaghilev's Ballets Russes*, p. 87.

[199] Serge Lifar, *Ma Vie: From Kiev to Kiev*, trans. James Holman Mason (London: New York: World Publishing, 1970), pp. 17–18.

[200] Lifar, *Le Manifeste du chorégraphe* (Paris: Cooperative Etoile, 1935).

[201] Lifar, 'The Path of Icarus: A Further Manifesto', *Dancing Times* (January, 1938), pp. 511–16.

[202] Lifar, *Le Manifeste . . .* , p. 16.

[203] Erik Satie, letter to Comtesse de Beaumont, 23 March 1922, cited from a copy in the Archives de la Fondation Erik Satie, Paris.

[204] Lifar, *La Musique par la danse* (Paris: Hachette, 1935), pp. 156–9.

[205] Lifar, *Le Manifeste . . .* , pp. 27–8.

[206] A fragment of the music is reprinted in Lifar, 'The Path of Icarus', p. 513.

[207] Cyril W. Beaumont, *Ballets Past and Present* (London: Putnam, 1955), p. 100.

[208] Lifar, *Le Manifeste . . .* , pp. 15–16, quoted in translation by W. G. Hartog in 'The Path of Icarus', p. 514.

[209] Jerome Robbins quoted by George Balanchine & Francis Mason, *Balanchine's Festival of Ballet* (London: W. H. Allen, 1978), p. 370.

[210] Mary Clarke in *The Encyclopedia of Dance and Ballet* (London: Pitman, 1977), p. 189.

[211] Joan R. Acocella, *Mark Morris* (New York: Noonday Press, 1995), p. 201.

Chapter 2

[1] Stanley Fish, *Is there a Text in This Class? The Authority of Interpretive Communities* (Cambridge, Mass: Harvard University Press, 1980), pp. 9, 13.

[2] Fish, p. 14.

[3] Gertrude Stein, 'Plays', (1934) in Stein, ed. Patricia Meyerowitz, *Writings and Lectures 1911–1945* (London: Peter Owen, 1967), p. 63.

[4] Doris Humphrey, *The Art of Making Dances* (New York and Toronto: Rinehart, 1959), p. 161.

[5] James Clifford, 'Introduction: Partial Truths', in Clifford & George E. Marcus, eds, *Writing Culture: The Poetics and Politics of Ethnography* (Berkeley and Los Angeles: University of California Press, 1986), pp. 11–12.

[6] Christian Metz, 'Le Perçu et le nommé', in Metz, *Essais sémiotiques* (Paris: Editions Klincksseck, 1977), pp. 153–9.

[7] Hanns Eisler & Theodor W. Adorno (the latter uncredited), *Composing for the Films* (London: Dennis Dobson, 1947), pp. 59–61 (in the original English edition, Adorno's co-authorship is unacknowledged); Jacques Attali, *Noise: The Political Economy of Music*,

trans. Brian Massumi (Minneapolis: University of Minnesota Press, 1985), p. 6.

[8] Claudia Gorbman, *Unheard Melodies: Narrative Film Music* (Bloomington: Indiana University Press, 1987), p. 64.

[9] Gorbman, 'Narrative Film Music', *Yale French Studies*, 60 (1980), p. 189.

[10] Gorbman, 'Narrative Film Music', pp. 189–90.

[11] Kathryn Kalinak, *Settling the Score: Music and the Classical Hollywood Film* (Madison, Wisconsin: University of Wisconsin Press, 1992), pp. 29–31.

[12] Humphrey, p. 80.

[13] Humphrey, p. 80.

[14] Eduard Hanslick, *The Beautiful in Music: A Contribution to the Revisal of Musical Aesthetics* (1891; reprint New York: Da Capo Press, 1974), p. 36.

[15] Susanne K. Langer, *Philosophy in a New Key* (New York: New American Library, 1948), p. 193.

[16] Stephen Davies, *Musical Meaning and Expression* (Ithaca and London: Cornell University Press, 1994), p. 277.

[17] Igor Stravinsky, *An Autobiography* (1936; reprint London: Calder & Boyars, 1975), pp. 53–4. Richard Taruskin has demonstrated that such sloganeering can give a misleading account of Stravinsky's practice: *Stravinsky and the Russian Traditions*, 2 Vols. (Oxford: Oxford University Press, 1996).

[18] Susan McClary, 'Narrative Agendas in "Absolute" Music: Identity and Difference in Brahms's Third Symphony', in Ruth A. Solie, ed., *Musicology and Difference: Gender and Sexuality in Music Scholarship* (Berkeley and Los Angeles: University of California Press, 1993), p. 330.

[19] Ludwig Tieck quoted by Carl Dahlhaus, *The Idea of Absolute Music*, trans. Robert Lustig (1978; English edn. Chicago and London: University of Chicago Press, 1989), p. 18.

[20] McClary, p. 332.

[21] Edward W. Said, *Musical Elaborations* (New York: Columbia University Press, 1991), pp. 100–5.

[22] McClary, p. 343.

[23] Anthony Newcomb, 'Schumann and Late Eighteenth-Century Narrative Strategies', *Nineteenth-Century Music*, 11/2 (Fall 1987), p. 167.

[24] Jonathan Culler, *Structuralist Poetics* (1975; reprint London: Routledge & Kegan Paul, 1994); Paul Ricoeur, 'Narrative Time',

Critical Enquiry, 7 (1980), pp. 169–90, and *Temps et récit*, 3 Vols. (Paris: Du Seuil, 1983–85).

[25] Newcomb, p. 166.

[26] Stuart Hall, 'The Narrative Construction of Reality', *Southern Review* [Adelaide], 17 (1984), p. 7.

[27] Jean-Jacques Nattiez, *Music and Discourse: Toward a Semiology of Music* (1987), trans. Carolyn Abbate (Princeton: Princeton University Press, 1990), p. 122.

[28] Davies, pp. 42–3.

[29] Roger Sessions, *Questions About Music* (Cambridge, Mass.: Harvard University Press, 1970), p. 45.

[30] Roger Shattuck, 'Stravinsky's Corporal Imagination', in Jann C. Pasler, ed., *Confronting Stravinsky: Man, Musician, and Modernist* (Berkeley and Los Angeles: University of California Press, 1986), pp. 82–8.

[31] Balanchine (1972) quoted by Nancy Goldner, *The Stravinsky Festival of the New York City Ballet* (New York: Eakins Press, 1973), p. 13.

[32] Kalinak, p. xiv.

[33] Marian Smith, ' "Poésie lyrique" and "Chorégraphie" at the Opéra in the July Monarchy', *Cambridge Opera Journal*, 4/1 (1992), pp. 12–13.

[34] Carolyn Abbate, *Unsung Voices: Opera and Musical Narrative in the Nineteenth Century* (Princeton: Princeton University Press, 1991), p. xii.

[35] Abbate, p. xii.

[36] Abbate, p. 13. Two classic essays from which Abbate takes her cue are Roland Barthes' 'The Death of the Author' (1968) and 'The Grain of the Voice' (1972) in Barthes, *Image-Music-Text*, trans. Stephen Heath (London: Fontana, 1977), pp. 142–8, 179–89.

[37] Abbate, pp. 4–9.

[38] Abbate, p. 148.

[39] Abbate, p. 151.

[40] Kevin Korsyn, 'Brahms Research and Aesthetic Ideology', *Music Analysis*, 12/1 (March 1993), pp. 89–103.

[41] George Edwards, 'The Nonsense of an Ending: Closure in Haydn's String Quartets', *Musical Quarterly*, 75/3 (Fall 1991), pp. 227–54.

[42] Richard Taruskin, 'Review: She Do the Ring in Different Voices' [Review of Abbate's *Unsung Voices*], *Cambridge Opera Journal*, 4/2 (1992), p. 190.

[43] Edwin Denby, 'Forms in Motion and in Thought', (1965) in Denby, *Dance Writings* (London: Dance Books, 1986), p. 571.

[44] Francis Sparshott, *A Measured Pace: Toward a Philosophical Understanding of the Arts of Dance* (Toronto: University of Toronto Press, 1995), pp. 215–41.

[45] Ruth St Denis, 'Music Visualization', *The Denishawn Magazine*, 1/3 (Spring 1925), pp. 1–7.

[46] Denby, 'Forms in Motion . . . .', p. 572.

[47] Denby, 'A Note to Composers', (1939) in *Dance Writings*, pp. 62–3.

[48] For a more detailed discussion of some of the rhythmic concepts referred to here, see the analytical methodology (Chapter 3) in Stephanie Jordan, 'Music as Structural Basis in the Choreography of Doris Humphrey', unpublished PhD dissertation, University of London, Goldsmiths' College, 1986, pp. 27–81.

[49] This has been observed and discussed in terms of phrasing patterns, by Vera Maletic, 'Dynamics of Phrasing in Movement and Dance', *Proceedings of The Thirteenth Biennial Conference of ICKL* (1983), p. 110.

[50] Ann Hutchinson, *Labanotation* (1954; 3rd edn., London: Oxford University Press, 1977), p. 491.

[51] The term hypermeasure and, drawn from it, hypermetre, was first used by Edward Cone, *Musical Form and Musical Performance* (New York: W. W. Norton, 1968), pp. 79–80. Both terms have been frequently employed subsequently.

[52] Michel Fokine, *Memoirs of a Ballet Master*, trans. Vitale Fokine, ed. Anatole Chujoy (London: Constable, 1961), p. 101.

[53] Denby, 'Forms in Motion . . . .', p. 571.

[54] Richard Colton quoted in John Mueller & Don McDonagh, 'Making Musical Dance: Robert Irving, Richard Colton, Kate Johnson Karole Armitage', *Ballet Review*, 13/4 (Winter 1986), p. 29.

[55] Kyra Nichols was seen by the author in performance with New York City Ballet, New York, 12 January 1993.

[56] Interview with Elizabeth Sawyer, 25 August 1994; see also Sawyer, *Dance With the Music: The World of the Ballet Musician* (Cambridge: Cambridge University Press, 1995), p. 134.

[57] Raina Katzarova, 'Sur un phénomène concernant le manque de coïncidence entre la figure chorégraphique et la phrase mélod-ique', *International Folk Music Journal*, 12 (1960), p. 69. Others include Felix Hoerburger, 'On Relationships between Music and Movement in Folk Dancing', *International Folk Music Journal*, 12 (1960), p. 70; György Martin, 'Considérations sur l'analyse des relations entre la danse et la musique de danse populaires', *Studia Musicologica* 7/1–4 (1965), pp. 333–4; Ernó Pésovár, 'Three Round Verbunks', *Dance Studies*, 1 (1976), p. 50.

[58] Interview with Elizabeth Cunliffe, 4 June 1993.

[59] Robert Irving in interview with Tobi Tobias, Oral History Project Transcript, New York Public Library Dance Collection, July–December 1976, p. 67.

[60] Anthony Twiner in interview with Howard Friend & Stephanie Jordan, 'The Musician's View; Insights into Music and Musicality at the Royal Ballet', *World Ballet and Dance*, 4, 1992–93, ed. Bent Schønberg (London: Dance Books, 1993), p. 19. Philip Gammon and Barry Wordsworth are also included in this interview.

[61] Interview with Twiner, p. 16.

[62] Interview with Barry Wordsworth, pp. 18–19.

[63] Interview with Twiner, p. 16.

[64] Constant Lambert, 'Music for Ballet', *Dancing Times* (January 1949), p. 193.

[65] Robert Irving, Unpublished autobiography, n.d.

[66] George Balanchine, 'The Dance Element in Stravinsky's Music', (1947) in Minna Lederman, ed., *Stravinsky in the Theatre* (New York: Pellegrini & Cudahy, 1949), p. 75.

[67] Interview with Twiner, p. 15.

[68] Interview with Philip Gammon, p. 27.

[69] Interview with Suzanne Farrell, 21 September 1991.

[70] Barbara Walczak in Francis Mason, *I Remember Balanchine: Recollections of the Ballet Master by Those Who Knew Him* (New York: Doubleday, 1991) pp. 259–60.

[71] James Monahan, *Fonteyn: A Study of the Ballerina in her Setting* (London: A. & C. Black, 1957), p. 25.

[72] Interview with Ashley Page, 6 May 1997, at rehearsal for the lecture-demonstration 'Defining Ballet' at the Royal Opera House, Covent Garden.

[73] Interview with Patricia Neary, 15 November 1991.

[74] Lynn Stanford quoted by Katherine Teck, *Movement to Music: Reflections on a Col-*

laborative Art (Westport, Conn.: Greenwood Press, 1989), p. 179.

[75] Interview with Wordsworth, p. 26.

[76] Interview with Farrell.

[77] Colton quoted in Mueller & McDonagh, 'Making Musical Dance . . .', p. 26.

[78] Langdon Dewey, 'Music and the Ballerina – A Rider in Favour of Margot Fonteyn', *Ballet*, 4/3 (September, 1947), p. 46.

[79] Dewey, p. 45.

[80] Edward Villella quoted (1965) in B. H. Haggin, *Ballet Chronicle* (New York: Horizon Press, 1970), pp. 75, 76.

[81] Violette Verdy quoted by Tobi Tobias, 'Balanchine's Love Songs', *Dance Magazine* (May 1984), p. 40.

[82] Robert Garis, 'The Balanchine Enterprise', *Ballet Review*, 21/1 (Spring 1993), p. 39.

[83] Interview with Violette Verdy, 13 September 1991.

[84] Interview with Twiner, p. 17.

[85] Interview with Gammon, 3 May 1995.

[86] Edwin Denby, 'Beecham at the Ballet', (1944) in *Dance Writings*, p. 212.

[87] Denby, 'Ballet Conducting: Beecham and Bernstein', (1944) in *Dance Writings*, p. 236.

[88] Alicia Markova, *Markova Remembers* (London: Hamish Hamilton, 1986), p. 110.

[89] Irving discusses the timing changes in *Agon* in interview with Tobias, p. 51. The timing changes in *Apollo* are discussed in 'A Stravinsky Portrait', Telecast WNET-TV (1972), producer Rolf Liebermann for Norddeutscher Rundfunk (video housed in the New York Public Library Dance Collection).

[90] Richard Taruskin, 'The Pastness of the Present and the Presence of the Past', in Nicholas Kenyon, ed., *Authenticity and Early Music* (Oxford: Oxford University Press, 1988), pp. 145–6.

[91] Interview with Philip Ellis, 10 September 1995.

Chapter 3

[1] Quoted in 'Balanchine: An Interview by Ivan Nabokov and Elizabeth Carmichael', *Horizon* (January, 1961), p. 47.

[2] George Balanchine, 'Marginal Notes on the Dance', in Walter Sorell, ed., *The Dance Has Many Faces* (1951; 3rd edn., Chicago: a capella Books, 1992), p. 42.

[3] Quoted in Richard Buckle, *George Balan-chine: Ballet Master*, in collaboration with John Taras (London: Hamish Hamilton, 1988), p. 80.

[4] Nathan Milstein, 'My Friend George Balanchine', *Ballet Review*, 18/3 (Fall, 1990), p. 24; See also Maria Tallchief, *Maria Tallchief: America's Prima Ballerina*, with Larry Kaplan (New York: Henry Holt, 1997), pp. 95, 102.

[5] Balanchine preferred not to use the word 'abstract': 'Marginal Notes on the Dance', p. 40.

[6] Petr Gusev quoted by Yuri Slonimsky in Francis Mason, *I Remember Balanchine: Recollections of the Ballet Master by Those Who Knew Him* (New York: Doubleday, 1991), p.38.

[7] Nina Stukolkina in Mason, p. 80.

[8] *Choreography by George Balanchine: A Catalogue of Works* (New York: Viking, 1984), pp. 65–7.

[9] Balanchine, '*Ivesiana*', *Center: A Magazine of the Performing Arts*, 1/5 (August–September 1954), p. 5.

[10] Balanchine & Francis Mason, *Balanchine's Festival of Ballet* (London: W. H. Allen, 1978), p. 779. This subsumed a series of earlier editions stemming from *Complete Stories of the Great Ballets* (1954). In all these books, Mason was the writer acting as Balanchine's scribe.

[11] Arlene Croce, 'Reviews . . . New York City Ballet: In Balanchine and Out', *Ballet Review*, 1/4 (1966), p. 22.

[12] Balanchine, 'The Dance Element in Stravinsky's Music', (1947) in Minna Lederman, ed., *Stravinsky in the Theatre* (New York: Pellegrini & Cudahy, 1949), p. 81.

[13] Igor Stravinsky, *An Autobiography* (1936; reprint London: Calder & Boyars, 1975), p. 100.

[14] Robert Irving in interview with Tobi Tobias, Oral History Project Transcript, New York Public Library Dance Collection, July–December, 1976, p. 92.

[15] Balanchine, 'The Occasion' (1972) in Nancy Goldner, *The Stravinsky Festival of the New York City Ballet* (New York: Eakins Press, 1973), pp. 13–14.

[16] Balanchine, *Playbill* [New York City Ballet programme], June, 1973; quoted by Nancy Reynolds, *Repertory in Review: 40 Years of the New York City Ballet* (New York: Dial Press, 1977), p. 216.

[17] Balanchine quoted in Dale Harris, 'Balanchine: Working with Stravinsky', *Ballet Review*, 10/2 (Summer, 1982), pp. 22, 24.

[18] Balanchine quoted by Jay S. Harrison, 'Balanchine: He Fills Time in Space', *New York Herald Tribune*, 14 June 1959.

[19] Balanchine & Mason, p. 624.

[20] Harrison.

[21] Balanchine quoted in Harris, p. 24.

[22] Jonathan Cott, 'Two Talks with George Balanchine', (1982) in *Portrait of Mr. B* (New York: Viking Press, 1984), p. 134.

[23] 'Balanchine: An Interview . . .', p. 47.

[24] Harrison.

[25] 'Balanchine: An Interview . . .', p. 47.

[26] Morton Baum suggested the *Liebeslieder Walzer*, reported by Betty Cage in Mason, *I Remember Balanchine*, pp. 290–1.

[27] Balanchine & Mason, p. 78.

[28] 'Balanchine: An Interview . . .', p. 47; Harris, p. 24.

[29] 'Balanchine: An Interview . . .', p. 47.

[30] In 1981, for the Tchaikovsky Festival, Balanchine choreographed the Fourth Movement of the Pathétique Symphony No. 6, the first movement of which was omitted, the second choreogaphed by Jerome Robbins and the third played by the orchestra with the curtain down. Balanchine choreographed excerpts from Tchaikovsky's Symphonies 1, 2 and 3 for a television production of *Cinderella* (1949).

[31] Milstein, p. 33.

[32] Balanchine & Mason, p. 125.

[33] Hartmut Regitz, ' "Ich bin wie der Chefkoch eines Restaurants"', *Ballett: Chronik und Bilanz des Balletjahres* (1983), p. 44.

[34] Robert Maiorano & Valerie Brooks, *Balanchine's Mozartiana: The Making of a Masterpiece* (New York: Freundlich Books, 1985), p. 129.

[35] 'Balanchine: An Interview . . .', p. 47.

[36] Balanchine quoted in the *Guardian*, 20 June 1963.

[37] Balanchine, 'Marginal Notes . . .', p. 43.

[38] Balanchine, 'Marginal Notes . . .', p. 42.

[39] Balanchine, quoted in Louis Botto, *Intellectual Digest* (June, 1972), reprinted in Selma Jeanne Cohen, ed., *Dance as a Theatre Art* (New York: Dodd, Mead, 1974), p. 190.

[40] Balanchine, 'The Dance Element . . .' pp. 75–6.

[41] Nicolas Nabokov, 'Stravinsky Now', *Partisan Review*, 11 (1944), p. 332.

[42] Stravinsky & Robert Craft, *Themes and Episodes* (New York: Alfred A. Knopf, 1967), p. 25.

[43] Karin von Aroldingen quoted by Reynolds, p. 310. Reynolds recalls that in 1993

at the New York City State Theatre, Jerome Robbins showed a rehearsal film of *Soupir* with Balanchine 'pounding out the rhythm', clearly hearing it: letter to the author, 12 June 1997.

[44] Merrill Ashley, *Dancing for Balanchine* (New York: E. P. Dutton, 1984), p. 27.

[45] Edwin Denby, 'In the Abstract', (1959–60) in Denby, *Dance Writings* (London: Dance Books, 1986), pp. 465–6.

[46] Denby, 'A Letter on New York City's Ballet', (1952) in Denby, *Dance Writings*, p. 424.

[47] Denby, 'Three Sides of *Agon*', (1959) in Denby, *Dance Writings*, p. 460.

[48] Balanchine quoted in 'Balanchine Celebration', in 'Great Performances' series, directed by Matthew Diamond, produced by Judy Kinberg, Thirteen/WNET, 1993.

[49] José Ortega y Gasset, *The Dehumanization of Art and Other Essays on Art, Culture, and Literature*, trans. Helene Weyl (Princeton: Princeton University Press, 1968), pp. 3–54.

[50] T. S. Eliot, *Selected Prose of T. S. Eliot*, ed. Frank Kermode (London: Faber, 1975), pp. 37–44; 'the emotion of art . . .', p. 44.

[51] Roger Shattuck, *The Banquet Years* (New York: Alfred A. Knopf, 1955), Chapter 11: The Art of Stillness.

[52] Richard Taruskin, *Stravinsky and the Russian Traditions: A Biography of the Works Through Mavra* (Oxford: Oxford University Press, 1996), 2, pp. 1449–55.

[53] Balanchine, 'The Dance Element . . .' p. 81.

[54] Stravinsky, *Poetics of Music in the Form of Six Lessons*, trans. Arthur Knodel & Ingolf Dahl (Cambridge, Mass.: Harvard University Press, 1970), p. 43.

[55] Balanchine, 'The Dance Element . . .' p. 81.

[56] Balanchine, 'Marginal Notes . . .', p. 36.

[57] Stravinsky, *Poetics of Music*, pp. 41–3.

[58] Virgil Thomson, 'Modernism Today', (1947) in Thomson, *Music Reviewed 1940–1954* (New York: Vintage Books, 1967), p. 233.

[59] Boris Asafiev, *A Book About Stravinsky*, trans. Richard F. French (1929; reprint Ann Arbor, Michigan: UMI Research Press, 1982), p. 98.

[60] Shattuck, p. 351.

[61] Richard Thomas in Mason, p. 274.

[62] Interview with Merrill Ashley, 15 September 1991.

[63] Gelsey Kirkland, *Dancing on my Grave*,

with Greg Lawrence (London: Hamish Hamilton, 1986), pp. 68–9.

[64] Richard Taruskin, 'The Pastness of the Present and the Presence of the Past', in Nicholas Kenyon, ed., *Authenticity and Early Music* (Oxford: Oxford University Press, 1988), pp. 169, 166. This essay has also been an important source for my discussion of modernism and musical time.

[65] Elliott Carter, *Flawed Words and Stubborn Sounds; A Conversation with Elliott Carter* (New York: W. W. Norton, 1971), p. 56.

[66] Denby, *Dance Writings*, pp. 177, 201, 322.

[67] Interview with John Taras, 30 August 1994.

[68] Taras and Marie-Jeanne were recording the rehearsals of *Concerto Barocco* for the George Balanchine Foundation archival project, in New York, 16 and 17 June 1996.

[69] Kirkland, p. 84.

[70] Milstein, p. 33.

[71] Interview with Hugo Fiorato, 16 February 1994.

[72] 'An Interview with Gordon Boelzner', *Ballet Review*, 3/4 (1970), p. 54; Boelzner refrained from offering an interview to the present author.

[73] Interview with Fiorato.

[74] Interview with Victoria Simon, 19 October 1991.

[75] James Lyons, 'Can a Conductor be too Good?' *Dance Magazine* (November, 1958), p. 25.

[76] Irving in interview with Tobias, p. 51.

[77] Interview with Taras.

[78] Irving in interview with Tobias, p. 51.

[79] Interview with Fiorato, who quotes Balanchine here.

[80] Lincoln Kirstein, 'Rationale of a Repertory', in Reynolds, p. 10.

[81] Interview with Suki Schorer, 17 September 1991.

[82] Balanchine quoted by Harrison.

[83] Balanchine & Mason, p. 125.

[84] Stravinsky & Craft, *Memories and Commentaries* (London: Faber, 1960), p. 37.

[85] Stravinsky quoted by Cott, p. 143.

[86] Letter from Stravinsky to Kirstein, 9 September 1953, in Robert Craft, ed., *Stravinsky: Selected Correspondence* (New York: Alfred A. Knopf, 1982), Vol. 1, p. 287.

[87] Balanchine quoted in the *Cincinatti Enquirer*, 18 June 1972; see Goldner, p. 35.

[88] Programme note for the original production of *The Four Temperaments*, Ballet Society, 20 November 1946.

[89] Farrell quoted in Robert Tracy, *Balanchine's Ballerinas* (New York: Linden Press/ Simon & Schuster, 1983), p. 158. The first version of the work (1966) presented the music three times, elucidated by three different choreographic treatments.

[90] Tanaquil Le Clercq in Barbara Newman, *Striking a Balance: Dancers Talk About Dancing* (London: Elm Tree Books, 1982), p. 163.

[91] Toumanova in Mason, p. 104; Balanchine, 'Ballet on Record', *Listen* (February, 1941), p. 6.

[92] For instance, Fred Danieli in Mason, p. 211.

[93] Balanchine, 'Ballet on Record', p. 7.

[94] Leon Goldstein (violinist in the orchestra of New York City Ballet) in interview with Beth Genné, 1978, phonotape, New York Public Library Dance Collection.

[95] Philip Gammon referred to this during Stephanie Jordan's 'In Focus' lecture-demonstration with the Royal Ballet at Covent Garden, 11 November 1993; see also Jordan, 'Ballet Imperial', *Dance Now*, 2/4 (Winter, 1993/ 94), pp. 28–37. My analysis of Balanchine's cuts stems from the 1993 revival by the Royal Ballet.

[96] Buckle, p. 220.

[97] Interview with Jane Pritchard, 22 March 1995.

[98] Interview with Fiorato.

[99] Interview with Violette Verdy, 13 September 1991; Harrison.

[100] Balanchine quoted in Cott, p. 136, 101. Arthur Mitchell in Mason, p. 395.

[102] Maria Tallchief quoted by Marian Horosko, 'See the Music, Hear the Dance', *Dance Magazine* (July, 1983), p. 96.

[103] Farrell in interview with David Daniel during the seminar 'Balanchine the Musician' at the New York Public Library for the Performing Arts, 13 January 1993.

[104] Maiorano & Brooks, pp. 49–50. Solo instrumentalists often attended ballet studio rehearsals alongside pianists.

[105] Philip Gammon in interview with Howard Friend & Stephanie Jordan, 'The Musician's View: Insights into Music and Musicality at the Royal Ballet', in Bent Schønberg, ed., *World Ballet and Dance*, 4, 1992–93 (London: Dance Books, 1993), p. 23.

[106] Interview with Fiorato.

[107] Jonathan Mcphee quoted by Katherine Teck, *Music for the Dance: Reflections on a Collaborative Art* (Westport, Conn.: Greenwood Press, 1989), p. 139.

[108] Interview with Merrill Brockway, 16 September 1991.

[109] *The Four Temperaments*, Labanotation score by Mary Corey (New York: Dance Notation Bureau, 1985).

[110] *The Four Temperaments* (recorded live, 1961, Symphonieorchester des Bayerischen Rundfunks conducted by Hindemith), Orfeo M 197 891 B, 1989.

[111] *Episodes* (section to Webern's Symphony, first and second movements), Labanotation score by Muriel Topaz, Lucy Venable and Ann Hutchinson (New York: Dance Notation Bureau, 1959).

[112] An interview with Gordon Boelzner, p. 59; interview with Fiorato, June 22nd, 1994.

[113] Solomon Volkov, *Balanchine's Tchaikovsky: Interviews with George Balanchine* (New York: Simon & Schuster), pp. 128–9.

[114] André Levinson, *Ballet Old and New* (1918), trans. Susan C. Summer (New York: Dance Horizons, 1982), pp. 92-93.

[115] Claudia Roth Pierpont, 'Balanchine's Romanticism', *Ballet Review*, 12/2 (Summer 1984), p. 16.

[116] For a summary of the changes, see *Choreography by George Balanchine*, p. 118.

[117] The gradual process of restoring cuts was recalled by Simon in interview.

[118] Interview with Barbara Weisberger, 8 January 1994.

[119] Interview with Weisberger.

[120] Jack Anderson, *The One and Only: The Ballet Russe de Monte Carlo* (London: Dance Books, 1981), p. 43.

[121] Denby, 'A Letter on New York City's Ballet', (1952) in Denby, *Dance Writings*, p. 423.

[122] Pierpont, p. 7.

[123] In interview, Fiorato recalls that the insertion had certainly been made by the time he first knew *Serenade* in the 1940s.

[124] Alastair Macaulay, 'The Ambiguities of *Serenade* (1934) – George Balanchine', in *Choreography: Principles and Practice – Report of the Fourth Study of Dance Conference* (Guildford, Surrey: National Resource Centre for Dance, 1986), p. 192.

[125] This early score of *Serenade* by Ann Hutchinson is housed in the Language of Dance Centre, London. Another later score is by Virginia Doris (New York: Dance Notation Bureau, 1984). The early film of *Serenade* was shown in the 'L'heure du concert' series, Canadian Broadcasting Corporation, 1957.

[126] Balanchine & Mason, p. 532.

[127] David Brown, *Tchaikovsky: The Years of Fame 1878–1893* (London: Gollancz, 1992), 3, p. 122.

[128] Don Daniels, 'Academy: The New World of *Serenade*', *Ballet Review*, 5/1 (1975–76), p. 10. The formal device with 'expressive means shifting' recurs in later works such as *Duo Concertante* and the final version of the *Divertimento from Le Baiser de la fée*.

[129] *Serenade*, in 'Balanchine in America', produced and directed by Judy Kinberg and Thomas Grimm, co-production Thirteen/WNET and Danmarks Radio, 1990. A third film, made in 1973, is directed by Hugo Niebeling, RM Productions, screened BBC, 25 October 1975.

[130] Macaulay, p. 196.

[131] Macaulay, p. 200.

[132] Pierpont points to this visual symmetry, p. 16.

[133] *Choreography by George Balanchine*, p. 179.

[134] Tallchief quoted by Reynolds, p. 82.

[135] Robert Sabin, *Musical America* (March, 1950); quoted by Reynolds, p. 82.

[136] *The Times* (London) critic (1950); quoted by Reynolds, p. 83.

[137] Pat McBride quoted by Joel Lobenthal, '*Symphonie Concertante* Revived', *Ballet Review*, 11/2 (Summer, 1983), p. 14.

[138] 'An Interview with Gordon Boelzner', p. 57.

[139] Stravinsky & Craft, *Themes and Episodes*, pp. 24–5.

[140] Interview with Richard Moredock, 19 September 1991.

[141] Denby, 'A Letter about Ulanova and the Royal Danish Ballet', (1951) in Denby, *Dance Writings*, p. 378.

[142] The step terms referred to here both come from the 1963 score of *Concerto Barocco* by Ann Hutchinson and Jacqueline Challet-Haas (London: Language of Dance Centre, 1963).

[143] *Symphony in C*, Labanotation score by Ann Hutchinson (New York: Dance Notation Bureau, 1948).

[144] For a summary of the changes, see *Choreography by George Balanchine*, p. 178.

[145] Balanchine & Mason, p. 265.

[146] Beaumont quoted by Anatole Chujoy, *The New York City Ballet: The First Twenty Years* (1953; reprint New York: Da Capo Press, 1982), p. 261.

[147] For a slightly more detailed discussion of this point, see Jordan, 'Musical/Choreographic Discourse: Method, Music Theory, and Meaning', in Gay Morris, ed., *Moving Words: Rewriting Dance* (London and New York: Routledge, 1996), pp. 24–6.

[148] Stravinsky quoted by Goldner, p. 170.

[149] Key sources on the creation of *Agon* are Irene Alm, 'Stravinsky, Balanchine, and *Agon*: An Analysis Based on the Collaborative Process', *Journal of Musicology*, 7/2 (Spring, 1989), pp. 254–69 (also the larger work from which it is drawn, 'Stravinsky, Balanchine and *Agon*: The Collaborative Process', unpublished MA dissertation, UCLA, 1985); correspondence between Stravinsky and Kirstein in Craft, ed., *Stravinsky: Selected Correspondence*; Charles M. Joseph, 'The Making of *Agon*', in Lynn Garafola & Eric Foner, eds., *Dance for a City: Fifty Years of the New York City Ballet* (New York: Columbia University Press, 1999), pp. 99–117.

[150] Alm, 'Stravinsky, Balanchine, and *Agon*', pp. 261–2.

[151] Reynolds, p. 185.

[152] The six video recordings are in 'L'heure du concert' series, Canadian Broadcasting Corporation, 1960; 'USA Dance: New York City Ballet', produced by Jac Venza, directed by Charles S. Dubin, NET, 1966 (excerpts); the Zweiter Deutsche Fernsehen broadcast, directed by Klaus Lindeman, co-produced by Continental Film Berlin, RM Productions Munich and Unitel, 1973; New York City Ballet company video, 1982; 'Balanchine Celebrates Stravinsky' in the 'Great Performances/Dance in America' series, produced by Judy Kinberg, directed by Emile Ardolino, Public Broadcasting Station, 1983; and 'Balanchine Celebration' in the 'Great Performances' series, produced by Judy Kinberg, directed by Matthew Diamond, Thirteen/WNET, 1993. The 1957 Labanotation score was written by a team from the Dance Notation Bureau. Ann Hutchinson Guest led the team and was assisted by Muriel Topaz, Billie Mahoney, Margaret Abbie, Myrna Shedlin, and Allan Miles. The 1987 score was written by Virginia Doris, as taught by New York City Ballet dancer Sara Leland to Les Grands Ballets Canadiens in 1985. The *Agon* analysis here develops from

Jordan, '*Agon*: A Musical/Choreographic Analysis', *Dance Research Journal*, 25/2 (Fall, 1993), pp. 1–12. For an excellent, detailed discussion of changes in *Agon* over the years, see Leigh Witchel, 'Four Decades of *Agon*', *Ballet Review*, 25/3 (Fall, 1997), pp. 53–78.

[153] Robynn J. Stilwell, 'Stravinsky and Balanchine: A Musico-Choreographic Analysis of *Agon*', unpublished PhD dissertation, University of Michigan, 1994, p. 286.

[154] Balanchine quoted by Vera Stravinsky & Craft, *Stravinsky in Pictures and Documents* (New York: Simon & Schuster, 1978), pp. 429–30.

[155] The New York City Ballet Programme for the premiere of *Agon*.

[156] Stilwell, p. 288.

[157] Stilwell, pp. 30, 42–3.

[158] Denby, 'Three Sides of *Agon*', (1959) in Denby, *Dance Writings*, p. 461.

[159] Balanchine, *Stravinsky and the Dance: a Survey of Ballet Productions 1910–1962* (New York: Dance Collection of the New York Public Library, 1962), p. 58.

[160] Denby, 'Three Sides of *Agon*', p. 462.

[161] Stravinsky noted jazz elements in the music too, 'traces of blues and boogie-woogie' in the Bransles de Poitou and Simple; see Stravinsky & Craft, *Dialogues and a Diary* (London: Faber, 1968), p. 54.

[162] Stilwell, pp. 89–90.

[163] Reynolds, p. 183.

[164] Mitchell quoted by Reynolds, p. 183.

[165] Mitchell quoted by Reynolds, p. 183. Denby, too, noted the 'breath' of 'crescendo and decrescendo within the thrust of a move' in 'Three Sides of *Agon*', p. 462.

[166] Ann Hutchinson Guest recalls that Balanchine would experiment with manouevres here to see where they would lead, unbounded by musical structure in these circumstances, while he still established points of connection between music and dance as the Pas de Deux evolved (in interview with the author, 29 May 1992).

[167] Denby, 'Three Sides of *Agon*', p. 463.

[168] Evidence is from the two Labanotation scores consulted and from a 1979 Benesh score (notated by Peter Boyes as staged by Brigitte Thom for the Dutch National Ballet); also from the author's interviews (15 November and 16 August 1991, respectively) with dancers Patricia Neary and Victoria Simon, who now stage *Agon*.

[169] Robert Craft, 'Ein Ballett für zwölf

Tänzer', *Melas*, 24/10 (October, 1957), pp. 284–8. Also Craft's notes accompanying the recording of *Agon*, CBS 72438, 1966.

[170] Denby, 'Three Sides of *Agon*', p. 462.

[171] Olga Maynard, 'Balanchine and Stravinsky: The Glorious Undertaking', *Dance Magazine* (June, 1972), p. 45; Balanchine quoted in Harris, p. 22.

[172] Croce, 'Other Verdi Variations', (1979) in Croce, *Going to the Dance* (New York: Alfred A. Knopf, 1982), p. 153.

[173] Darcey Bussell of the Royal Ballet moves her back similarly in the New York City Ballet performance broadcast in 1993.

[174] Hodson reports that the contrapuntal procedures in *Cotillon* were considered 'perfectly normal' by all the dancers who helped her with their memories of the work; in interview, 3 March 1995.

[175] Interview with Marie-Jeanne, 16 June 1996.

[176] Interview with Farrell, 21 September 1991.

[177] For further discussion and examples of metrical and hypermetical incongruity between music and dance, see Jordan, 'Music Puts a Time Corset on the Dance', *Dance Chronicle*, 16/3 (1993), pp. 295–321.

[178] *The Four Temperaments*, in 'Choreography by Balanchine: Part 1', in the series 'Dance in America', produced by Emile Ardolino, directed by Merrill Brockway, WNET/13, New York, 1977.

[179] Robert Irving, quoted in 'Celebrating *The Four Temperaments* – 1', *Ballet Review*, 14/4 (Winter, 1987), p. 30.

[180] Croce, 'Two by Balanchine', (1976) in Croce, *Afterimages* (New York: Vintage Books, 1979), pp. 205–6; see also Reynolds, p. 331.

[181] Balanchine, 'The Dance Element . . .', p. 75.

[182] Maiorano & Brooks, p. 31.

[183] Denby, quoted by William Mackay in Denby, *Dance Writings*, p. 22.

[184] Denby, 'Balanchine's *Mozartiana*', (1945) in Denby, *Dance Writings*, p. 295.

[185] Maiorano & Brooks, p. 115.

[186] Paul Parish, 'The Preghiera of Balanchine's *Mozartiana*', *Ballet Review*, 19/3 (Fall, 1991), p. 36.

[187] Farrell, *Holding on to the Air: An Autobiography*, with Toni Bentley (New York: Summit Books, 1990), pp. 252, 255.

[188] Croce, 'Bounty', (1981) in Croce, *Going to the Dance*, pp. 404–5.

[189] Maiorano & Brooks, p. 117.

[190] Maiorano & Brooks, p. xix.

[191] Croce, p. 406.

[192] Croce, p. 406.

[193] Denby, 'A Letter on New York City's Ballet', p. 417.

[194] Maiorano & Brooks, p. 40.

[195] *Mozartiana*, in 'A New York City Ballet Tribute to George Balanchine', produced by John Goberman, directed by Emile Ardolino, WNET/13, New York, 1983. This film was shot over two nights of performance.

[196] Farrell in interview with Daniel.

[197] Video of New York City Ballet rehearsal at Saratoga, 21 July 1981, housed in the New York Public Library Dance Collection.

[198] Record performance of *Mozartiana*, filmed 11 February 1983, housed in the New York Public Library Dance Collection.

[199] Parish, p. 43.

[200] Croce, p. 406.

[201] Farrell, *Holding on to the Air*, pp. 162–3.

[202] Farrell, *Holding on to the Air*, p. 253.

[203] Croce, p. 405; Macaulay, 'Balanchine's World', *Ballet Review*, 12/1 (Spring 1984), pp. 91–2.

[204] Balanchine quoted in Antoine Livio, 'Balanchine et Stravinsky 40 ans d'amitié', *Ballet Danse, L'Avant Scène, Le Sacre du printemps* (August/October, 1980), p. 124.

Chapter 4

[1] Frederick Ashton, 'Notes on Choreography' (1951) in Walter Sorell, ed., *The Dance Has Many Faces* (1951; 3rd edn., Chicago: A Cappella books, 1992), p. 33. This is the published version of an essay 'The Principles of Choreography' written in 1948, now in the Ashton archive, Royal Opera House, Covent Garden.

[2] Ashton in interview, 'Frederick Ashton – 75 This Week: A Real Choreographer', produced by John S. Gilbert, BBC, 20 September 1979.

[3] Zoë Dominic & John Selwyn Gilbert, *Frederick Ashton: A Choreographer and His Ballets* (London: Harrap, 1971), p. 77.

[4] Dame Ninette de Valois in interview with Geraldine Morris, 6 February 1992.

[5] David Vaughan, *Frederick Ashton and his Ballets* (London: A. & C. Black, 1977), p. 51.

[6] Marie Rambert, 'Ashton's Early Days', in 'Homage to Ashton' section, *Ballet Annual*, 15 (1961), p. 45.

[7] Unpublished letter from Lincoln Kirstein to Richard Buckle, quoted by Julie Kavanagh, *Secret Muses: The Life of Frederick Ashton* (London: Faber, 1996), p. 399. This book together with Vaughan's book on Ashton (note 5) are the major source books on Ashton's work used for this chapter.

[8] Rudolf Nureyev quoted by Kavanagh, p. 480.

[9] Kavanagh, p. 350.

[10] Ashton, 'Notes on Choreography', p. 91.

[11] Ashton, 'The Subject Matter of Ballet' (1959), in Vaughan, p. 409.

[12] John Lanchbery quoted in Kenneth La-Fave, 'Music Man', *Ballet News*, 3/6 (December, 1981), p. 31.

[13] Interviews with Lanchbery, 30 September and 4 October 1994.

[14] De Valois quoted by Richard Shead, *Constant Lambert* (London: Simon Publications, 1973), p. 9.

[15] Kirstein quoted by Richard Buckle, *The Adventures of A Ballet Critic* (London: Cresset Press, 1953), pp. 170, 57.

[16] Constant Lambert, 'Music for Ballet', *Dancing Times* (January, 1949), pp. 192–3.

[17] Constant Lambert, *Music Ho! A Study of Music in Decline* (1934; 3rd edn., London: Faber, 1966), p. 162.

[18] Shead, pp. 104–5.

[19] Angus Morrison quoted by Shead, p. 62.

[20] A reconstruction of the revised full score of *Tiresias* was broadcast on BBC Radio, 1995.

[21] Vaughan, p. 133.

[22] Kavanagh, p. 393.

[23] Kavanagh, p. 189.

[24] Robert Irving quoted by Mark Steinbrink, 'Footnotes', *Ballet News*, 3/2 (August, 1981), p.8.

[25] Philip Gammon in interview with Howard Friend & Stephanie Jordan, 'The Musician's View; Insights into Music and Musicality at the Royal Ballet', *World Ballet and Dance*, 4, 1992–93, ed. Bent Schønberg (London: Dance Books, 1993), p. 20.

[26] Kavanagh, pp. 513–14, 546–7, 574.

[27] Interview with Alexander Grant, 21 July 1995.

[28] Alexander Bland, 'Birth of a Ballet', *Observer*, 10 March 1963.

[29] Ashton also approached Walton to write a score for *Macbeth*, a ballet that was never realised, also as first choice composer for *Ondine*: Vaughan, pp. 291–2, 434–8.

[30] Vaughan, pp. 196–7.

[31] Ashton quoted by Don McDonagh, 'Au Revoir?', *Ballet Review*, 3/4 (1970), p. 15.

[32] The score is now in the Rambert archive; see Jane Pritchard, 'Two Letters', in Stephanie Jordan & Andrée Grau, eds., *Following Sir Fred's Steps: Ashton's Legacy* (London: Dance Books, 1996), p. 107.

[33] Richard Alston, 'Appropriate Steps', *Dance Theatre Journal*, 2/3 (Autumn, 1984), p. 8.

[34] Alastair Macaulay, 'Ashton's Classicism and *Les Rendezvous*', *Studies in Dance History*, 3/2 (Fall, 1992), p. 10.

[35] Noël Goodwin, 'Ashton and the Music of Dance', *Dance and Dancers* (November/December, 1988), p. 18.

[36] *The Times*, 25 April and 5 June 1940.

[37] Ashton quoted in Hans-Theodor Wohlfahrt, 'Ashton's Last Interview', *Dance Now*, 5/1 (Spring, 1996), p. 30.

[38] Rambert, p. 46.

[39] Intrview with Grant.

[40] Kavanagh, p. 535.

[41] Robert Irving in interview with Tobi Tobias, Oral History Project transcript, New York Public Library Dance Collection, July–December, 1976, p. 59.

[42] Ashton, 'The Production of a Ballet', unpublished essay (1948), copy in the Ashton archive, Royal Opera House, Covent Garden.

[43] Vaughan, p. 205.

[44] Vaughan, p. 374.

[45] Vaughan, pp. 142, 206.

[46] Vaughan, p. 279.

[47] I am grateful to Lars Payne, orchestral librarian of the English National Ballet, for assisting me in reading this score.

[48] Lambert, 'Music for Ballet' p. 193.

[49] Vaughan, p. 394.

[50] Kavanagh, pp. 173–4.

[51] Sacheverell Sitwell, *Liszt* (1967; rev. edn., New York: Dover Publications, 1967), p. 375.

[52] See also Alastair Macaulay, 'The Inconstant Muse', *Dance Theatre Journal*, 5/3b (Fall, 1987), pp. 12–14.

[53] Jane Pritchard, 'The "Nostalgic World of Fantasy": Some Neoromantic Elements in Works by Ashton and Balanchine', *Studies in Dance History*, 3/2 (Fall, 1992), pp. 39–44.

[54] Charles Harrison, 'Critical Theories and

the Practice of Art', in Susan Compton ed., *British Art in the Twentieth Century: The Modern Movement* (London and Munich: Royal Academy of Arts and Prestel-Verlag, 1986), p. 57. Harrison borrows Eric Newton's term from his 'The Centre Party in Contemporary Painting', *The Listener,* 29 May 1934.

55 John Piper in Richard Ingrams & Piper, *Piper's Places: John Piper in England & Wales* (London: Chatto & Windus, Hogarth Press, 1983), p. 22; Andrew Causey, 'The Spirit of the Landscape', in Compton, p. 260.

56 Jane Alison & John Hoole, Foreword to David Mellor, ed. *A Paradise Lost: The Neo-Romantic Imagination in Britain 1935–55* (London: Lund Humphries, 1987).

57 William Chappell, *Studies in Ballet* (London: John Lehmann, 1948), p. 55.

58 Vaughan, pp. 133, 239; Kavanagh, p. 240.

59 Letter from Ashton to Dick Beard, quoted by Kavanagh, p. 356.

60 Letter from Hans Werner Henze to Ashton, quoted by Kavanagh, p. 425.

61 Bryan Robertson in interview, 'Kaleidoscope', BBC Radio 4, 7 October 1988, transcript, p. 11.

62 Ashton, 'The Subject Matter of Ballet, p. 409.

63 Barbara Newman, *Antoinette Sibley: Reflections of a Ballerina* (London: Hutchinson, 1986), p. 161.

64 Edwin Denby, 'In the Abstract', (1959–60) in Denby, *Dance Writings* (London: Dance Books, 1986), pp. 465–7.

65 Henning Kronstam quoted in Alexandra Tomalonis, 'Dancing for Ashton', *Dance Now*, 3/1 (Autumn, 1994), p. 40.

66 Margot Fonteyn, 'A Choreographer of Genius', in 'Homage to Ashton', p. 50.

67 Ashton quoted in Wohlfahrt, p. 28.

68 Ashton's descriptive term in interview [before rehearsing *Meditation*], Review: Ashton in Camera, produced by Dennis Marks, directed by John S. Gilbert, BBC, 10 March 1972.

69 Interview with Antoinette Sibley, 22 February 1993.

70 Interview with Faith Worth, 6 October 1992.

71 Interview with Cynthia Harvey, 27 September 1996.

72 Vaughan, p. 240.

73 Ashton in interview with Clement Crisp, *Covent Garden Book*, 15 (1964) reprinted in Selma J. Cohen, ed., *Dance as a Theatre Art* (New York: Dodd, Mead & Co., 1974), p. 170.

74 Angus Morrison in interview with Beth Genné, 7 April 1985.

75 Vaughan, p. 203.

76 Ashton quoted by Dominic & Gilbert, p. 77.

77 Pamela May quoted in 'The Royal Ballet Ashton Programme: Panel Discussion', in Jordan & Grau, p. 161.

78 Philip Hope-Wallace, *Time and Tide*, 4 May 1946.

79 *Manchester Guardian*, 26 April 1946.

80 Vaughan, p. 204.

81 Ashton quoted in Richard Buckle, ' "Abstract" Ballet', *Ballet*, 4/5 (November, 1947), pp. 22–3.

82 Beth Genné, 'My Dearest Friend, My Greatest Collaborator', in Jordan & Grau, p. 64.

83 Alastair Macaulay, 'Spring', *New Yorker* (25 May 1992), p. 81.

84 A.V. Coton, 'Three Classics of Ballet', *Ballet Today*, 1/7 (September/October, 1947), p. 21.

85 Macaulay, p. 81.

86 May quoted in 'The Royal Ballet Ashton Programme . . .', p. 162; Vaughan, p. 206.

87 Geraldine Morris, 'Ashton and Abstraction: A New Approach to Three Ballets of Frederick Ashton', unpublished M.A. dissertation, University of Surrey, 1991, p. 79.

88 Video sources include broadcasts of the ballet: in the 'Parade' series, Granada Television, produced by Peter Potter, directed by David Giles, 1973 (Sibley and Dowell leading the cast); 'The Queen's Jubilee Gala', produced by John Vernon, BBC, 30 May 1977 (Merle Park and David Wall); the opening of the ballet in 'Ballet', documentary on American Ballet Theatre by Frederick Wiseman, BBC, 25 December 1996 (Cynthia Harvey and Charles Askegard). Video sources also include company videos in the archives of the Royal Ballet and Birmingham Royal Ballet, the earliest of these being of a rehearsal, with Fonteyn and Somes leading the cast (n.d.).

89 Macaulay, p. 81.

90 The version of the phrase as performed by Dowell and Somes in sources listed in note 88.

91 Interview with Harvey.

92 Ashton quoted by Macaulay in a letter to the editor, *Dancing Times* (October, 1996), p. 17.

[93] Genné points out that, originally, Somes, like Fonteyn, was differentiated as the centre man, wearing a top with two full sleeves, unlike the other two men in single-sleeve tops, p. 67.

[94] Interview with May, 4 May 1995.

[95] Interview with Morrison.

[96] Kavanagh, p. 310.

[97] Interview with Harvey.

[98] Somes in TV documentary 'Ballet'.

[99] Cormac Rigby, 'A Ballet of Perfect Englishness', Dance Now, 1/4 (Winter, 1992/93), p. 22.

[100] Interview with Morrison.

[101] Letter (n.d.) from Philip Hope-Wallace to Ashton, in the Ashton archive, Royal Opera House, Covent Garden.

[102] Anthony Twiner in interview with Friend & Jordan, 'The Musician's View . . .' p. 17.

[103] For further discussion of the musicality of this piece and others by Ashton, see the author's 'Ashton's Musicality: Some Preliminary Observations', Dance Theatre Journal, 11/1 (Winter, 1993–94), pp. 16–19.

[104] Lambert, Music Ho!, p. 119.

[105] Arlene Croce, 'How to Be Very, Very Popular', (1974) in After-images (New York: Vintage Books, 1979), p. 84.

[106] See the author's 'Ashton and The Sleeping Beauty', Dance Now, 2/2 (Summer, 1993), pp. 43–9.

[107] Vaughan, pp. 248, 330. The reference to the Alain Resnais film is mentioned in Peter Brook's article on Marguerite and Armand, The Observer, 17 March 1963.

[108] Ashton in interview with Walter Terry, 18 October 1953, phonotape, New York Public Library Dance Collection.

[109] Kavanagh, p. 388.

[110] Ashton in interview, 'Kaleidoscope', 7 October 1988, transcript, p. 12.

[111] 'Following Sir Fred's Steps: A Conference Celebrating Ashton's Work', Roehampton Institute London, 13 November 1994.

[112] 'Sir Frederick Ashton in Conversation with Alastair Macaulay', Dance Theatre Journal, 2/3 (Autumn, 1984), p. 6.

[113] Interview with Harvey.

[114] Michael Somes, 'Working with Frederick Ashton', in 'Homage to Ashton', p. 53.

[115] Interview with Anthony Dowell, 8 June 1993.

[116] Dowell in 'Dance Masterclass: The Dream', produced by Colin Nears [exec. producer] and Bob Lockyer [producer], BBC, 9 April 1988; the point was also emphasised in a lecture-demonstration led by Dowell and Sibley at the 1994 Ashton conference, 12 November 1994.

[117] Interview with Sibley.

[118] Ashton in 'Dance Masterclass.'

[119] The film is housed in the Rambert Dance Company archive. Both the 1962 and 1979 BBC films of Les Rendezvous demonstrate this rhythmic pattern: The Royal Ballet: Les Rendezvous, produced and directed by Margaret Dale, BBC, 22 April 1962; An Evening with Frederick Ashton, produced by John S. Gilbert, Colin Nears and Brian Large, BBC, 15 September 1979.

[120] Macaulay, 'Spring', p. 83. Macaulay remembers Georgina Parkinson saying this at the Dance Critics Association Conference on The Sleeping Beauty in New York, June 1987.

[121] Interview with Harvey.

[122] Croce, p. 84.

[123] Macaulay, 'Dancing on Dry Ice', Dancing Times (February, 1997), p. 413.

[124] Interview with Bruce Sansom, 6 April 1993.

[125] Adrian Grater, 'Following the Fred Step', in Jordan & Grau, pp. 92–100.

[126] The Royal Ballet: La Fille mal gardée, produced by John Vernon, BBC, 4 May 1981 (Lesley Collier as Lise); The Royal Ballet: La Fille mal gardée, produced/directed by Margaret Dale, BBC, 27 December 1962 (Nadia Nerina as Lise).

[127] Denby, 'Ashton's "Cinderella"', (1949) in Dance Writings, p. 360.

[128] Christopher Carr at a Ballet in Focus discussion evening at the Royal Opera House, Covent Garden, 11 April 1996.

[129] Interview with Faith Worth, 6 October 1992.

[130] See note 119. I am indebted to Tania Inman, librarian at the Benesh Institute, for her assistance in analysing this passage from Faith Worth's 1964 score, also to Geraldine Morris for showing me yet another version of the timings for examples a and b.

[131] Igor Stravinsky and Robert Craft, Dialogues and a Diary (London: Faber, 1968), p. 50.

[132] Lawrence Morton, 'Incongruity and Faith', in Edwin Corle, ed., Igor Stravinsky (New York: Duell, Sloane & Pearce, 1949), pp. 194–5.

[133] Stravinsky & Craft, p. 50.

[134] Vaughan, p. 222.

[135] Ashton, 'The Production of a Ballet'.

[136] Sibley in a lecture-demonstration at the 1994 Ashton conference, 12 November 1994. A video recording of this presentation, which showed her coaching Fiona Chadwick in this solo, is the source used in this analysis. There are minor rhythmic variations between different performances of this solo.

[137] John Lanchbery & Ivor Guest','The Scores of La Fille mal gardée: 1. The Original Music; 2. Hérold's Score; 3. The Royal Ballet's Score', Theatre Research, 3/1,2,3 (1961). The third of these articles was reprinted in Clement Crisp & Mary Clarke, Making A Ballet (New York: Macmillan, 1974), pp. 139–151.

[138] However, in 1837, Donizetti's opera L'Elisir d'amore was not known in Paris, where Elssler danced in La Fille mal gardée.

[139] Interview with Lanchbery. Other key sources on the Ashton-Lanchbery collaboration are Lanchbery's interviews with David Vaughan, 9 October 1973, and with John Gruen, broadcast WNCN-FM, New York, 20 May 1979, both phonotapes in the New York Public Library Dance Collection.

[140] Lanchbery & Guest in Crisp & Clarke, p. 139.

[141] Ashton, 'My Conception of "La Fille mal gardée"', in Guest, ed., Famous Ballets I/ La Fille mal gardée (London: Dancing Times, 1960), p. 10.

[142] Author's interview with Lanchbery.

[143] Noël Goodwin, programme note, the Royal Ballet, January 1978.

[144] Irving in interview with Tobias, p. 52.

[145] The Times, 3 April 1964.

[146] Irving, unpublished autobiographical material, n.d.

[147] Twiner (quoting Ashton) in interview with Friend & Jordan, 'The Musician's View . . .' p. 20.

[148] Croce, 'The Royal Line', (1976) in After-images, p. 222. The author's analysis of Month develops from two articles, 'A Month in the Country: The Organization of a Score', Dance Research Journal, 11/1&2 (1978–79), pp. 20–4; 'A Month in the Country: Multi-Layered Musicality and Meanings', in Jordan & Grau, pp. 47–54.

[149] Description from the programme.

[150] Ashton quoted by Oleg Kerensky, 'Frederick Ashton Meets Ivan Turgenev', New York Times, 25 April 1976. My description of the creative process also draws heavily from Vaughan, pp. 393–403.

[151] Claudio Arrau with the London Philharmonic Orchestra conducted by Eliahu Inbal, Philips: SAL 6500 422, 1972. A recording of the ballet is available in Britain on HMV Greensleave, featuring the orchestra of the Royal Opera House, Covent Garden conducted by John Lanchbery with Philip Gammon playing the piano solo; ESD 7037, EMI (Australia) Ltd, 1977.

[152] Interview with Lanchbery.

[153] Kavanagh opens up this discussion, pp. 547–8.

[154] Kavanagh, pp. 548–9.

[155] Lynn Seymour in interview with John Gruen, 'The Sound of Dance', WNCN-FM, New York City, 26 April 1976.

[156] Interview with Julia Trevelyan Oman, 14 July 1994.

[157] Croce, p. 221.

[158] Kierkegaard, Søren, Either/Or, trans. David F. Swenson & Lillian Marvin Swenson, with revisions and foreword by Howard A. Johnson (1943; English edn., Princeton: Princeton University Press, 1959), p. 95. See also Sarah Kofman & Jean-Yves Masson, Don Juan ou le refus de la dette (Editions Galilée, 1991); J. W. Smeed, Don Juan: Variations on a Theme (London: Routledge, 1990).

[159] These two possibilities were suggested by Penelope Doob, interviewing Karen Kain at the Society of Dance History Scholars conference in Toronto, 13 May 1995.

[160] Kerensky.

[161] Letter from Ashton to Edwin Evans (n.d.), New York Public Library Dance Collection.

[162] Ashton in interview with Robin Ray, 'Dance Month: The Dream: A Month in the Country', produced by John Vernon & Colin Nears, BBC, 7 May 1978.

[163] In later programme notes, the phrase 'and the original scoring . . . at times sketchy' was omitted.

[164] Vaughan, p. 444.

[165] Perhaps significance is attached to it because it is one of the few selections of music in the minor key in the entire ballet.

[166] Liszt quoted by William S. Newman, The Sonata Since Beethoven (New York: W. W. Norton, 1972), p. 87.

[167] Roland Barthes, 'Day by Day with Roland Barthes', in Marshall Blonsky, ed., On Signs (Oxford: Blackwell, 1985), p. 115. See also Edward A. Lippman, 'Theory and Prac-

tice in Schumann's Aesthetics', *Journal of the American Musicological Society*, 17 (1964), pp. 310–45.

[168] Lanchbery & Guest in Crisp & Clarke, pp. 141, 149.

[169] See Carolyn Abbate's interpretation of Salome 'gazing' at Jochanaan in the Richard Strauss opera: 'Opera; Or the Envoicing of Women', in Ruth A. Solie, ed., *Musicology and Difference: Gender and Sexuality in Music Scholarship* (Berkeley, Los Angeles, London: University of California Press, 1993), pp. 225–58.

[170] Interview with Lanchbery.

[171] Interview with Dowell.

[172] Interview with Sansom.

[173] Interview with Sansom.

[174] Interview with Lanchbery.

[175] Anita Young was seen teaching the variation in repertory class at the London Studio Centre, 2 May 1995.

[176] The Royal Ballet: *Cinderella*, directed by John Vernon, Covent Garden Pioneer, 1964.

[177] *Cinderella*, Producer's Showcase, NBC-TV, 29 April 1957.

[178] Interview with Jean Bedells, 17 May 1997.

Chapter 5

[1] Edwin Denby, 'Forms in Motion and in Thought', (1965) in Denby, *Dance Writings* (London: Dance Books, 1986), p. 571.

[2] Denby, 'Fokine's "Russian Soldier"; Tudor's "Pillar of Fire"; Balanchine's Elephant Ballet', (1942) in *Dance Writings*, p. 94.

[3] Denby, 'Tudor and Pantomime', (1943) in *Dance Writings*, pp. 130–1.

[4] Denby, '"Dim Lustre" and "Romeo and Juliet"', (1943) in *Dance Writings*, p. 159.

[5] Denby, 'Tudor's "Undertow"', (1945) in *Dance Writings*, p. 306.

[6] Denby, 'A Briefing in American Ballet', (1948) in *Dance Writings*, p. 524.

[7] Denby, p. 524.

[8] Denby, 'A Fault in Ballet Theatre's Dancing', (1944) in *Dance Writings*, p. 260.

[9] Arlene Croce, 'Sweet Love Remembered', (1975) in Croce, *Afterimages* (New York: Vintage Books, 1979), p. 174.

[10] Croce, p. 173.

[11] Judith Judson speaking from the floor at 'Border Crossings', Dance History Scholars Conference, Ryerson Polytechnic University, Toronto, 14 May 1995; letter from Judson to the author, 14 July 1997.

[12] Marilyn Hunt, 'Antony Tudor: Master Provocateur', *Dance Magazine* (May 1987), p. 39.

[13] Biographical information has been taken primarily from three sources: Judith Chazin-Bennahum, *The Ballets of Antony Tudor: Studies in Psyche and Satire* (New York: Oxford University Press, 1994); two interviews with Tudor by Marilyn Hunt, both available in transcript: for the Oral History Project of the New York Public Library Dance Collection, 20 June 1985, and for the Kennedy Center Honor Oral History Program, 11 November 1986. The Chazin-Bennahum book is a major source on Tudor, together with two issues of *Dance Perspectives*: John Percival, 'Antony Tudor: Part One, The Years in England', 17 (1963); Selma J. Cohen, 'Antony Tudor: Part Two, The Years in America and After', 18 (1963).

[14] There is a photograph showing Tudor at the piano in the Juilliard School, in Elizabeth Sawyer, *Dance with the Music: The World of the Ballet Musician* (Cambridge: Cambridge University Press, 1985), p. 85.

[15] See note 14.

[16] Selma J. Cohen, 'Tudor and the Royal Ballet', *Saturday Review of Literature*, 13 May 1967, p. 75.

[17] Interview with Muriel Topaz, 23 August 1994. There is a copy of Tudor's rhythmic reduction of the music in the Dance Notation Bureau library, New York, but without any accompanying dance line. Topaz also discussed Tudor's interest in the Joseph Schillinger method in this interview.

[18] Tudor in interview with Hunt (1986), p. 48.

[19] Interview with the American Ballet Theatre pianist Howard Barr, 4 April 1996.

[20] Interview with Topaz.

[21] Notes of Tudor's tenth lecture at York University, Toronto, 23 November 1971, in the Tudor Papers, New York Public Library Dance Collection.

[22] Chazin-Bennahum, pp. 59–60.

[23] Gian Carlo Menotti in interview with Walter Terry, June 1980, phonotape, New York Public Library Dance Collection.

[24] Donna Perlmutter, *Shadowplay: The Life of Antony Tudor* (New York: Viking Penguin, 1991), p. 193.

[25] Roberto Gerhard, 'On Music in Ballet: II', *Ballet*, 11/4 (May, 1951), p. 29.

[26] Leo Kersley, 'Choreographers of Today',

Ballet Today (June, 1960), p. 14.

[27] Tudor quoted by Alfred Frankenstein, *San Francisco Chronicle*, n.d.; see Chazin-Bennahum, pp. 122–3.

[28] Tudor quoted in John Gruen, *The Private World of Ballet* (Harmondsworth, Middlesex: Penguin, 1976), p. 261.

[29] Maude Lloyd quoted in Marilyn Hunt, 'A Conversation with Maude Lloyd', *Ballet Review*, 11/3 (Fall, 1983), p. 21.

[30] Tudor in interview with Hunt (1986), p. 25.

[31] Transcript of the journals of Lionel Bradley (by Jane Pritchard), Rambert Dance Company Archive, London, entry of 6 December 1936.

[32] William Schuman in interview with John Gruen, 3 July 1975, Oral History Project transcript, New York Public Library Dance Collection, p. 14.

[33] Sono Osato, *Distant Dances* (New York: Alfred A. Knopf, 1980), p. 434.

[34] Jack Anderson, 'Antony Tudor Talks about His New Ballets', (1966) in Selma J. Cohen, ed., *Dance as a Theatre Art: Source Readings in Dance History from 1581 to the Present* (New York: Dodd, Mead, 1974), p. 175.

[35] Tudor quoted in Gruen, p. 262.

[36] William Schuman quoted in Selma J. Cohen, 'Antony Tudor: Part Two . . .', p. 85

[37] William Schuman quoted in 'Toasting Tudor: The Capezio Awards', *Ballet Review*, 14/3 (Fall, 1986), p. 36.

[38] Tudor quoted in Gruen, p. 260.

[39] Zita Allen, 'The Heart of the Matter', *The Soho Weekly News*, 3 May 1979.

[40] Letter from Tudor to Sawyer, 8 April 1975, quoted by Sawyer, p. 43.

[41] Tudor quoted in Gruen, p. 261.

[42] Tudor quoted in Gruen, p. 261.

[43] Tudor quoted by Frankenstein, *San Francisco Chronicle*, 1947; see Chazin-Bennahum, p. 9.

[44] Letter from Tudor to William Schuman, 7 January 1945, Tudor Papers, New York Public Library Dance Collection.

[45] Interview with Airi Hynninen, 26 August 1994. Hynninen said that she could tell from the style of Schuman's music that it was a commission.

[46] Notes of Tudor's lecture at York University, Toronto, 23 November 1971.

[47] The edited music score of *Undertow* is housed in the Dance Notation Bureau, New York.

[48] Tudor quoted by Jennie Schulman, 'Antony Tudor: Henry Street Playhouse, April 8th, 1951', *Dance Observer*, 18/6 (June/July, 1951), p. 93.

[49] Notes from Topaz' interview with Tudor, 22 May 1981, Tudor Project, Dance Notation Bureau.

[50] Chazin-Bennahum, p. 79.

[51] Fernau Hall, 'Symphonic Ballet: A Reply', *Dancing Times* (August, 1937), p. 556.

[52] Tudor quoted by Frankenstein, 1947; see Chazin-Bennahum, p. 9.

[53] Tudor quoted in Gruen, p. 266. On rare occasions, however, Tudor did use counts.

[54] Osato, p. 194.

[55] Letter from Tudor to Isabel Mirrow, 12 November 1985, quoted in Chazin-Bennahum, p. 220.

[56] Perlmutter, p. 132.

[57] Topaz' 'Notes on the Music and Rehearsal Procedures' for the 1988 revival of *Jardin aux lilas*, Tudor Project, Dance Notation Bureau.

[58] Tudor in interview with Hunt (1986), p. 18.

[59] Schuman in interview with Gruen (1975), p. 15.

[60] Chazin-Bennahum, p. 200.

[61] Interview with Sawyer, 25 August 1994.

[62] Martha Hill in interview with Leslie Rotman, 3 May 1990, Tudor Project transcript, Dance Notation Bureau, p. 7.

[63] Joseph Schillinger, *Encyclopedia of Rhythms* (New York: C. Colin, c.1966).

[64] Topaz in interview with Leslie Rotman, 14 February 1990, Tudor Project transcript, Dance Notation Bureau, p.7.

[65] Interview with Hynninen.

[66] George Dorris gave this information to Chazin-Bennahum, p. 68.

[67] Interviews with Sallie Wilson, 24 August 1994 and with Howard Barr. Wilson refers to the 1933 recording by Menuhin, HMV DB 1961/62 (reissued on Biddulph Recordings LAB 058, 1992). The *Pillar of Fire* recording is HMV DB 2439/442, c. 1935. Barr's evidence was corroborated by Leo Kersley in a conversation with Mary Pritchard, and by information provided by Thomas Blagg.

[68] Tudor Papers.

[69] Interview with Philip Ellis, 10 September 1995.

[70] Interview with Sawyer.

[71] Note from Topaz to the author, 15

March 1997.

[72] Cyril W. Beaumont, *Complete Book of Ballets* (London: Putnam, 1937), p.1013.

[73] Chazin-Bennahum, p. 61.

[74] *Jardin aux lilas*, Labanotation score by Airi Hynninen (1981) corrected and revised by Muriel Topaz (New York: Dance Notation Bureau, 1992), p. i.

[75] Programme of 30 January 1936.

[76] Arnold L. Haskell, 'Ballet Club's New Production: Charming Period Piece', *Daily Telegraph*, 27 January 1936.

[77] Interview with Howard Barr.

[78] Interview with Sawyer.

[79] Interview with Sallie Wilson; note from Topaz to the author, 15 March 1997.

[80] Topaz's revisions conform to the final 'approved' version of the ballet as set forth by Sally Brayley Bliss, sole trustee of the Antony Tudor Ballet Trust. It was Tudor's wish to have an approved version of each of his ballets rather than to offer alternative versions, even if he was the source of these alternative versions.

[81] American Ballet Theatre in *Jardin* led by Leslie Browne, staged by Sallie Wilson, in 'A Tudor Evening with American Ballet Theatre', produced and directed by Judy Kinberg and Thomas Grimm, WNET/Thirteen and Danmarks Radio, 1990.

[82] For instance, silent excerpts of *Jardin* performances in the 1950s with Nora Kaye as Caroline; rehearsal footage of Juilliard students in the work, filmed by Dwight Godwin, production and filming supervision by Martha Hill, 1967; a TV film, staging by Sallie Wilson, directed by Viola Aberle and Gerd Andersson, produced by Måns Reuterswärd, a Gava production in association with NOS Television, The Netherlands and SVT 2, Sveriges Television, 1985.

[83] Ivan S. Turgenev, *Selected Stories*, trans. Constance Garnett (London: Heinemann, 1974), p. 223.

[84] Jean Gallois, *Ernest Chausson* (Librairie Arthème, 1994), pp. 440–6.

[85] Roland Barthes, 'The Grain of the Voice' (1972) in Barthes, *Image-Music-Text*, trans. Stephen Heath (London: Fontana/Collins, 1977), pp. 179–89.

[86] Wayne Koestenbaum, *The Queen's Throat: Opera, Homosexuality, and the Mystery of Desire* (New York: Poseidon Press, 1993), p.43.

[87] In earlier versions of *Jardin*, Caroline stays upright rather than swooning; see, for instance, the moment captured in Roger Wood's 1950 photograph of New York City Ballet, in Lincoln Kirstein, *Movement and Metaphor: Four Centuries of Ballet* (New York: Praeger Publishers, 1970), p. 233. The moment is performed similarly in the 1965 Ballet Rambert film of *Jardin*, housed in the Rambert Dance Company archive, London, and in the 1953 National Ballet of Canada film by Carol Lynn housed in the New York Public Library Dance Collection.

[88] Hugh Laing quoted in Cohen, 'Antony Tudor . . .', p. 84.

[89] *Jardin aux lilas*, American Ballet Theatre, in 'American Ballet Theatre in San Francisco', A National Video Corporation production, directed by Brian Large, produced by Robin Scott, 1985.

[90] Maude Lloyd, 'Some Recollections of the English Ballet', *Dance Research*, 3/1 (Autumn 1994), p. 46.

[91] Sally Banes, *Dancing Women: Female Bodies on Stage* (London and New York: Routledge, 1998), p.176.

[92] Tudor's notes for the 1981 *Jardin* Labanotation score, p. iv.

[93] Tudor's notes for the 1981 *Jardin* Labanotation score, pp. iii-iv.

[94] Interview with Hynninen.

[95] Interview with Topaz.

[96] Topaz, 'Notating and Reconstructing for Antony Tudor', *Dance Notation Journal*, 4/1 (Spring 1986), p. 14.

[97] Denby, 'A Letter on New York City's Ballet', (1952) in *Dance Writings*, p. 423.

[98] Anabelle Lyon quoted in Cohen, p. 83.

[99] Agnes de Mille quoted in 'The Dance Magazine Awards', *Dance Magazine* (May 1974), p. 42.

[100] Transcript of the journals of Lionel Bradley, entry of 16 May 1937.

[101] Lloyd quoted by Percival, p. 24; and in interview with John Gruen, 13 July 1975, Oral History Project transcript, New York Public Library Dance Collection, p. 14.

[102] Interview with Wilson.

[103] June Morris in interview with Marilyn Hunt, 18 November 1976, Oral History Project transcript, New York Public Library Dance Collection, pp. 7-8.

[104] Interview with Hynninen.

[105] Hugh Laing in interview with Marilyn Hunt, 9 May 1986, Oral History Project transcript, New York Public Library Dance Collec-

tion, p. 39.

[106] Tanaquil LeClercq in Barbara Newman, *Striking a Balance: Dancers Talking About Dancing* (London: Elm Tree Books, 1982), p. 156.

[107] American Ballet Theatre's *Dark Elegies* is included with *Jardin* on the WNET/Thirteen and Danmarks Radio broadcast, see note 84.

[108] These notes are housed in the Rambert Dance Company archive, together with a number of company video recordings of *Dark Elegies*.

[109] Peggy Van Praagh, 'Working with Antony Tudor', *Dance Research*, 2/2 (1984), p. 57.

[110] *Pillar of Fire*, staged by Sallie Wilson, in 'A Close-up in Time', directed by Jerome Schnur, produced by Jac Venza, WNET/Thirteen, 1973. This was reported by Wilson in interview.

[111] *Pillar of Fire*, produced by Kjell Forsting for Swedish Television, 1971.

[112] This excerpt is included in 'Modern Ballet', no. 7 in 'A Time to Dance' series, produced by Jac Venza, WGBH-TV Boston, for National Educational Television, 1958.

[113] This duet is included in 'Modern Ballet'.

[114] Topaz notes this in 'Specifics of Style in the Works of Balanchine and Tudor', *Choreography and Dance (The Notation Issue*, ed. Topaz), 1 (1988), pp. 14, 26. Some Tudor work using more conventional ballet steps and sequences has a more traditional phrase structure.

[115] Egon Wellesz, *Arnold Schoenberg*, trans. W. H. Kerridge (1925; reprint Westport, Conn: Greenwood Press, 1970), pp. 66–73.

[116] Willi Reich, *Schoenberg: A Critical Biography*, trans. Leo Black (1971; reprint New York: Da Capo Press, 1981), p. 8.

[117] Paul Griffiths, programme note, Birmingham Royal Ballet, 1995.

[118] Interview with Philip Ellis, 10 September 1995.

[119] Ellis, lecture given at Roehampton Institute London, 13 May 1996.

[120] Letter from Tudor to Isabel Mirrow, 12 November 1985, quoted in Chazin-Bennahum, pp. 219–20.

[121] Milan Skampa, preface in Leoš Janáček, *String Quartet No. 1* (Vienna, London: Universal Edition, 1923), p. vi.

[122] Skampa, critical report in Janáček, pp. viii–ix.

[123] Identified by Chazin-Bennahum, p. 220.

[124] Tudor in interview with Hunt (1986), p. 46.

[125] Gruen, 'Tudor Returns with a New Ballet', *New York Times*, 13 July 1975.

[126] Mary Farkas, 'Antony Tudor: The First Zen Institute', *Choreography and Dance (Antony Tudor: The American Years*, ed. Topaz), 1/2 (1989), p. 66.

[127] Tudor quoted by Alan M. Kriegsman, 'Tudor's "Fading Leaves"', *Washington Post*, 30 September 1975.

[128] Gelsey Kirkland, with Greg Lawrence, *Dancing on My Grave* (London: Hamish Hamilton, 1987), p. 163.

[129] Clark Tippet quoted in 'Creative Process: Personal and Creative Growth', no. 258 in 'Eye on Dance' series, Arc Video dance, produced by Celia Ipiotis and Jeff Bush, WNYC-TV New York, 1988.

[130] Tippet in interview with Lesley Farlow, 15 April 1991, Oral History Project transcript, New York Public Library Dance Collection, p. 22.

[131] Deborah Jowitt, *Village Voice*, 11 August 1975, p. 84.

[132] Croce, 'Enigma Variations', (1979) in Croce, *Going to the Dance* (New York: Alfred A. Knopf, 1982), p. 179; 'Opus Posthumous', (1985) in Croce, *Sight Lines* (New York: Alfred A. Knopf, 1987), p. 279.

[133] Croce, 'Sweet Love Remembered', p. 172.

[134] Kriegsman.

[135] John Clapham, *Antonin Dvořák: Musician and Craftsman* (London: Faber 1966), p. 226.

[136] Interview with Hynninen.

[137] *The Leaves are Fading*, Labanotation score by Airi Hynninen (New York: Dance Notation Bureau, 1975).

[138] See the Tudor Papers, New York Public Library Dance Collection.

[139] Tudor quoted by Gruen, 'Tudor Returns with a New Ballet.'

[140] Rachel S. Richardson, 'Conflict and Harmony: Some Issues in the Construction of Meaning Through Dance-Music Relationships in Antony Tudor's *The Leaves are Fading*', Proceedings of the Nineteenth Annual Conference of the Society of Dance History Scholars Conference, University of Minnesota, Minneapolis, 13–16 June 1996, p. 6.

[141] Interview with Howard Barr.

[142] *The Leaves are Fading* rehearsal, American Ballet Theatre, filmed for the Jerome Robbins Archive by Gardner Compton, New York Public Library Dance Collection, 1975. There is also a 1976 ABT performance video of *Leaves* in the Dance Collection.

[143] Interview with David Richardson, 6 April 1996.

[144] Interview with Hynninen.

[145] 'The Erik Bruhn Gala: World Ballet competitions', Primedia Productions, directed by Norman Campbell, 1988; 'Essential Ballet: Stars of Russian Ballet', Philips Classics Productions, directed by John Michael Philips, 1993; 'Antony Tudor', directed by Viola Aberle and Gerd Andersson, Dance Horizons, 1992.

[146] Denby, 'Markova's Dance Rhythm; Tudor's 'Romeo and Juliet', (1943) in *Dance Writings*, p. 107.

[147] Denby, 'Markova at Ballet Theatre', (1945) in *Dance Writings*, p. 304.

[148] Croce, 'Sweet Love Remembered', p. 173.

Select Bibliography

Abbate, Carolyn, *Unsung Voices: Opera and Musical Narrative in the Nineteenth Century* (Princeton: Princeton University Press, 1991)

Balanchine, George, *Stravinsky and the Dance: a Survey of Ballet Productions 1910–1962* (New York: Dance Collection of the New York Public Library, 1962)

Balanchine, George, and Mason, Francis, *Balanchine's Festival of Ballet* (London: W. H. Allen, 1978)

Chazin-Bennahum, Judith, *The Ballets of Antony Tudor: Studies in Psyche and Satire* (New York: Oxford University Press, 1994)

Davies, Stephen, *Musical Meaning and Expression* (Ithaca, London: Cornell University Press, 1994)

Denby, Edwin, *Dance Writings* (London: Dance Books, 1986)

Evans, Edwin, *Music and the Dance* (London: Herbert Jenkins, n.d.)

Farkas, Mary, 'Antony Tudor: The First Zen Institute', *Choreography and Dance* (*Antony Tudor: The American Years*, ed. Muriel Topaz), 1/2 (1989)

Fiske, Roger, *Ballet Music* (London: George G. Harrap, 1958)

Friend, Howard, and Jordan, Stephanie, 'The Musician's View; Insights into Music and Musicality at the Royal Ballet', *World Ballet and Dance*, 4, 1992–93, ed. Bent Schönberg (London: Dance Books, 1993)

Garafola, Lynn, *Diaghilev's Ballets Russes* (Oxford: Oxford University Press, 1989)

Goldner, Nancy, *The Stravinsky Festival of the New York City Ballet* (New York: Eakins Press, 1973)

Hodgins, Paul, *Relationships Between Score and Choreography in Twentieth-Century Dance* (Lewiston, NY: Edwin Mellen Press, 1992)

Humphrey, Doris, *The Art of Making Dances* (New York, Toronto: Rinehart, 1959).

Jordan, Stephanie, 'Music as a Structural Basis in the Choreography of Doris Humphrey', unpublished PhD dissertation, University of London, Goldsmiths' College, 1986.

Jordan, Stephanie, and Grau, Andrée (eds.), *Following Sir Fred's Steps: Ashton's Legacy* (London: Dance Books, 1996)

Kalinak, Kathryn, *Settling the Score: Music and the Classical Hollywood Film* (Madison, Wisconsin: University of Wisconsin Press, 1992)

Kavanagh, Julie, *Secret Muses: The Life of Frederick Ashton* (London: Faber, 1996)

Lambert, Constant, *Music Ho! A Study of Music in Decline* (1934; 3rd edn., London: Faber, 1966)

Lederman, Minna (ed.), *Stravinsky in the Theatre* (1949; reprint New York: Da Capo Press, 1975)

Levinson, André, *Ballet Old and New* (1918), trans. Susan C. Summer (New York: Dance Horizons, 1982)

Nattiez, Jean-Jacques, *Music and Discourse: Toward a Semiology of Music* (1987), trans. Carolyn Abbate (Princeton: Princeton University Press, 1990)

Reynolds, Nancy, *Repertory in Review: 40 Years of the New York City Ballet* (New York: Dial Press, 1977)

Sawyer, Elizabeth, *Dance with the Music* (Cambridge: Cambridge University Press, 1985)

Searle, Humphrey, *Ballet Music* (1958; 2nd

edn., New York: Dover Publications, 1973)

Smith, Marian, *Ballet and Opera in the Age of Giselle* (Princeton, New Jersey: Princeton University Press, forthcoming)

Taper, Bernard, *Balanchine* (London: Collins, 1964)

Taruskin, Richard, *Text and Act: Essays on Music and Performance* (New York, Oxford: Oxfrod University Press, 1995)

Taruskin, Richard, *Stravinsky and the Russian Traditions*, 2 Vols. (Oxford: Oxford University Press, 1996).

Teck, Katherine, *Movement to Music: Musicians in the Dance Studio* (Westport, Conn.: Greenwood Press, 1990)

Teck, Katherine, *Music for the Dance: Reflections on a Collaborative Art* (Westport, Conn.: Greenwood Press, 1989)

Vaughan, David, *Frederick Ashton and his Ballets* (1977; 2nd edn., London: Dance Books 1999)

Wiley, Roland John, *Tchaikovsky's Ballets* (Oxford: Clarendon Press, 1985)

Index